Some people at work asked me how I became a confident feminist. I told them my mother trained me to be that way. I wish I got the message 20 years ago!

♡ All Mother's Day 1995

Harriot Stanton Blatch

ELLEN CAROL DuBOIS

Harriot Stanton Blatch and the Winning of Woman Suffrage

Yale University Press
New Haven and London

Published with assistance from the Louis Stern Memorial Fund.

Set in Sabon type by Best-set Typesetter Ltd., Hong Kong.

Printed in the United States of America by Thomson-Shore, Dexter, Michigan.

Library of Congress Cataloging–in–Publication Data
DuBois, Ellen Carol, 1947–
    Harriot Stanton Blatch and the winning of woman suffrage / Ellen Carol DuBois.
        p.   cm.
    Includes bibliographical references and index.
    ISBN 0-300-06562-0   (cloth: alk. paper)
    1. Blatch, Harriot Stanton, 1856–1940. 2. Suffragists—United States—Biography. 3. Feminists—United States—Biography.
    4. Women—Suffrage—United States–History. I. Title.
HQ1413.B545D83   1997
324.6'23'092–dc21
[B]   97-7293
                                                                        CIP

A catalog record for this book is available from the British Library.

The paper in this book meets the guidelines for permanence and durability of the Committee on Production Guidelines for Book Longevity of the Council on Library Resources.

10 9 8 7 6 5 4 3 2 1

Give a rounded-out picture of the suffragists, showing their ideals and their courage, their fears and their weaknesses, the youth and old age inner contest . . . , the ordering and the obeying, and as far as possible the content of the propaganda. . . . Unless you do set down your own relation to the public life of your time, dear Mrs. Blatch . . . young men and women to come will have no way of understanding these times or your place in them. . . . One who writes history has to have data he can put his hands on, you see.

Mary Beard to Harriot Blatch, September 22, 1935

Contents

Acknowledgments

Other biographers will surely agree with me that writing about a life seems to take almost as long as actually living it. While working on this book, I have accumulated many debts. My first and greatest thanks go to Rhoda Barney Jenkins, whose curiosity about her grandmother equaled my own. She has been the perfect family liaison, providing me with rich resources and unlimited hospitality and interfering in the process of writing this book not in the slightest. I particularly want to thank her for the many wonderful family pictures. Harriot's other grandchildren, Harriet de Forest and John Barney, were also very helpful and gracious. Also thanks to Colleen Jenkins-Sahlin, who represents the next generation in this extraordinary matrilineage. Arthur and Alice Milinowski and Caroline Babcock Furlow, children of Harriot's closest friends, shared with me their childhood memories of her. Through all of them I felt I came closer to knowing the woman at the center of this book.

A special thanks to Ann D. Gordon, whose stewardship of the Stanton-Anthony Papers project and whose friendship has undergirded much of my work on the Stanton-Blatch women. Also thanks to her coeditor, Patricia Holland, and to Gail Malmgreen, who did all the archival work I did not need to do on Elizabeth Stanton's years in England.

Some good friends read all or most of this manuscript and have helped me identify major errors and more serious infelicities. For this I thank: Lois Banner, Nancy Cott, Lynn Dumenil, Linda Gordon, Anne Firor Scott, and Alice Wexler. Joyce Appleby, Dan Czitrom, Alice Echols, Willie Forbath,

Chana Kai Lee, Steve Leiken, Karen Orren, and Robert Wiebe gave me the benefit of their astute criticisms on particular chapters. A special thanks to my biography writing group—Nina Gelbart, Robert Rosenstone, Debby Silverman, Alice Wexler, and Steve Zipperstein—for teaching me how to write such a book.

I have profited from the work of other scholars of the period and of the history of feminism. I particularly mention Guy Alchon, Polly Beals, Margaret Finnegan, Sherna Gluck, Jim Hijiya, June Hopkins, Helen Horowitz, David McDonald, and Sandy Moats. Robert Brown of Basingstoke, Hants, may never see this book, but on a trying day, he found and gave me a picture of Harriot's house, the Mount, which he had taken before it was demolished. I had many helpful research assistants on this project, among them Carol Cini, Tadd Ferguson, Kymm Gauderman, Kira Hilden-Minton, Shawn Johansen, and Anastasia Simmons. Neil Basen, Mari Jo Buhle, David Doughan, Nancy Schrom Dye, Sherna Gluck, and Molly Shanley provided help of various idiosyncratic and indispensable sorts. For anyone else whose name has fallen out of my memory and into one of the many dusty files I have accumulated over these fifteen years, my apologies. I truly appreciate all the help I have received.

Financial support came from the National Endowment for the Humanities, from a University of California Presidential Fellowship, from the UCLA Faculty Senate, and from the UCLA Center for Politics and Public Policy.

As I was preparing this manuscript for publication, my father was in the final stages of a terminal illness and I was helping my mother care for him. My final thanks are to my parents, who taught me about life, family, and death, and therefore laid the basis for this book.

Introduction

In January 1936, American newspaper headlines were full of growing international anxiety and tentative domestic optimism. It could safely be said that most Americans' attention was focused on the future but that that future looked anything but safe. Meanwhile, a small group of New York women were thinking about a past few others remembered: the history of the woman suffrage movement. The campaign to enfranchise the women of the United States might have been a century rather than two decades in the past for all the attention it commanded in popular memory. Indeed, the entire issue of women's rights, which had permeated political rhetoric and preoccupied legislative debates not so long before, and which had drawn tens of thousands to the streets to advocate or to challenge, was now only a minor theme of public discussion; and the eager speculation on the future of womanhood, which had once been the mark of modernism, was now regarded as out of date. But to this group of women "feminism" was a term of pride and a live concern for the future.

These stubborn feminists were meeting to plan a public celebration in honor of the eightieth birthday of Harriot Stanton Blatch. To them the significance of her long life was self-evident and the importance of honoring her compelling. Harriot Stanton Blatch was the chief strategist of the woman suffrage movement in the largest and most important state in the Union, New York. She was also the senior stateswoman in the campaign that produced the Nineteenth Amendment to the U.S. Constitution and one of the nation's foremost female progressives both before and after World War I. Above all, Harriot Blatch was the representative of America's most venerable feminist matrilineage, a living embodiment of the historical depth and the intergenerational breadth of the women's rights tradition. Her life's work grew out of and elaborated the achievements of her mother, the great nineteenth-century reformer and intellectual Elizabeth Cady Stanton. Harriot had been raised not only to pursue the goal of woman suffrage with life-long ardency, but to regard it as a crucial part of a larger vision of social democracy, economic equality, and political justice. Harriot was proud to be both a feminist and a progressive, even now when both labels seemed historical artifacts.

Being Elizabeth Cady Stanton's daughter was a source of intense pride to Harriot Stanton Blatch, but it had also complicated her life. She had lived with a dilemma that almost no other feminist had yet faced: the struggle for women's rights was her heritage, her past as well as her future. Men had long been wrestling with the achievements of the men who had come before; coming into their own could set them against their fathers. In coming into power, Harriot faced a complex anxiety of influence that was a relatively new experience for women. Her life suggested that women's ascent into history required them not only to come together but to differentiate themselves from each other as well. As her mother's daughter, she was more inclined to break away from other women than to bring them together. A consistent innovator, she was at the head of the march at the beginning of American suffragism's modernization, though less so in its final stages. Nonetheless, the enfranchisement of American women is unimaginable without her contribution.

Despite the uncongenial times, the small planning committee assumed the tasks of organizing Harriot Stanton Blatch's birthday celebration with skill and gusto. Indeed, there was a kind of pleasurable familiarity in undertaking the different elements of the job: they had to raise money, interest the press, attract participants, and make a clear public statement of purpose. These were precisely the kinds of activities they had done countless times in the past, when as young suffragists they had served their political apprenticeships under her direction. Perhaps the biggest difference was that now Harriot Blatch was not planning strategy and devising tactics, not the "big boss" to whom all others answered. Being the object of the event rather than its director was an uncommon experience for Harriot and an uncomfortable one as well. Raised according to an ethic of female self-sovereignty, she was generally unwilling to rely on anyone other than herself, but age and infirmity were increasingly forcing her to face her inescapable dependence. So this event was both a celebration of her power and an acknowledgment of its diminution.

The press release that the committee issued to announce the birthday celebration provided a brief biography of Harriot Stanton Blatch's life and career.[1] The woman suffrage movement was conceived by her mother in 1848, and eight years later Harriot followed, its devoted younger sister. No mention of her father, once a great and famous abolitionist, was made; it was as if she were solely of woman born. "A childhood spent in sympathetic companionship with her mother" began her preparation for a life of large purpose. After graduating from Vassar College, she traveled in Europe, married an Englishman, William Henry Blatch, and raised a daughter. But while her young adulthood was spent abroad working in the British socialist movement, she remained aware of the unfinished work of women's enfranchisement. On her mother's death in 1902 she returned to the United States for good: in the words of the press release, she "looked over the field" of her ancestral reform and began to assess how victory might be won before another generation passed from the scene.

In inheriting her mother's unfinished task, Harriot knew well that the woman suffrage movement had already missed several opportunities for advancement; either it must make one last sure push for victory, or it would fade into insignificance, a reform that history had passed by. She believed that the key to winning suffrage in the twentieth century lay with the masses of women wage-earners, who were transforming what it meant to be a woman in the modern age. Working women were so important because of their numbers, because of their forthright public presence, and because they made it clear that autonomy for women was fundamentally an economic matter. Harriot's leadership of the American suffrage movement was based on this conviction, but a winning suffrage movement also required the unity of all women. So she recruited women from the other end of the economic ladder as well, "bringing the rich and privileged women to an understanding of their responsibility to the cause." Her awareness of class differences was more acute than that of any other major suffragist, and from this perspective, she can be credited with making the final decade of American suffragism as comprehensive—and complex—as any women's movement in U.S. history.

Harriot's other great contribution to winning woman suffrage was her political skill. The irony of the twentieth-century American suffrage movement was that so many women were determined to win the vote and yet were more disdainful of political matters than virtually any other arena of male prerogative. But for Harriot Blatch this was not the case. She was modern suffragism's first great politician, and her leadership during the crucial 1915 New York suffrage referendum prepared the way for the subsequent battle at the national level. She insisted that votes for women could not be gained by education, moral improvement, civic uplift, or any of women's other traditional methods of social action. Rather, political equality must be won politically; to secure it, women would have to learn how to wield legislative, partisan, and electoral tools. She had unbounded energy for dealing with those who seemed disfranchised women's natural enemy, male politicians. Everything that made her who she was—her maternal heritage, her years in England—fed into this distinctively confident political sensibility.

Despite an unparalleled effort, the great New York referendum of 1915 that Harriot led was defeated. Along with most other suffrage radicals, Harriot moved on to the national field. As the suffrage ranks divided into "militant" and "moderate" camps for the final great push for a federal constitutional amendment, she sought a third way. While Alice Paul and the militants pulled in the direction of civil disobedience, and Carrie Chapman Catt and the moderates stuck to the path of congressional lobbying, Harriot tried to combine both approaches into a militant but explicitly political challenge. The essence of her vision, the creation of a dedicated voting bloc made up of women who were now enfranchised by action at the state level, became the basis of the Woman's Party (later the National Woman's Party), which she helped to form in 1916. This strategic deployment of women's voting power anticipated the political future women would face once their struggle for suffrage was successfully concluded.

Many former suffragists came to honor Harriot at her eightieth birthday celebration. They came from both sides of the acrimonious split that was fracturing American feminism in the aftermath of the Nineteenth Amendment. At the anniversary celebration were suffrage veterans who advocated legislative "protection" and others who insisted on constitutional "equality" as women's greatest need. Among the most prominent defenders of sex-based protective labor legislation was Rose Schneiderman, the dynamic trade unionist who had just finished a stint as the only woman member of the labor advisory board of the National Recovery Administration. She and Harriot had known each other for almost thirty years, during which time their relations had gone from sororal to antagonistic and back again. From the other side of the postsuffrage women's movement came Alice Paul, leader of the National Woman's Party, mother of the Equal Rights Amendment, and Harriot's successor as the most famous militant suffragist in America. One notable suffragist name was absent: Carrie Chapman Catt, former president of the National American Woman Suffrage Association, leader of its successor organization, the League of Women Voters, and recipient of numerous awards for her suffrage leadership. Catt had been asked to participate but had declined.[2] No surprise here: ever since the years of the New York suffrage movement, when Carrie Catt and Harriot Blatch had been the state's two foremost suffrage leaders, they had been bound in an intense rivalry.

The invitations sent out for Harriot's birthday anniversary went to activists and intellectuals running the full range of American progressive politics, indicating the many political and intellectual circles in which she moved. She was no single-issue feminist but rather a "many idead woman," which is how she liked to describe her mother. The theme chosen for the evening was "Democracy and the Future." Inez Haines Irwin, journalist and historian, was the toastmistress and Roger Baldwin, from the American Civil Liberties Union, was the master of ceremonies. John Dewey, Margaret Sanger, Charles Beard, Pearl Buck, and 250 other guests came to honor her. From England, aging Fabians sent in their admiring memories. Sylvia Pankhurst wrote ominously: "We are faced with a new reaction which . . . has snatched from the Women's Movement all which it has gained . . . Fascism is a real menace to humanity, and above all to women and all that the Women's Movement stands for."[3]

Finally it was Harriot's turn on the dais. She was always elegantly turned out, and this evening was no exception. Beautifully dressed in a blue silk made especially for the occasion, she began to speak, "her white head bending over her notes" according to the modest article the event rated in the *New York Times*.[4] In her heyday, Harriot Stanton Blatch had made front-page headlines. She had been a public speaker of unmatchable skill, but she was already beginning the decline that would lead to her death a few years later. Her remarks rambled a bit, and guests who had not seen her in some time may have whispered among themselves in embarrassment. But to those who knew her well and remembered her in her prime, the essential Harriot Stanton Blatch was still present: her broad vision, her historical sensibility, her political insight, her unrelenting commitment to political action.

Her remarks turned to a defense of woman suffrage. With demagoguery in full force in Europe, the monstrous product of popular enfranchisement and unscrupulous leaders willing to manipulate mass emotion, democracy was falling into disfavor, and with it, the achievement of enfranchising the female half of humanity. Harriot Stanton Blatch would have none of this. She had always believed that politics of all sorts had an unavoidably emotional dimension, that "human beings move because they feel, not because they think." Suffragists' understanding of that principle, the joy and fervor they had introduced into their movement, had been a fundamental element in their success. Harriot's insistence that political action of all sorts was necessarily emotional, for men as much as for women, was a product of her lifelong effort to break apart the exclusive association of politics with men and of men with reason, a view that exiled women and sentiment to the margins of public life. In an age of dictatorial threats and antidemocratic reaction, she was determined to retain her faith in mass political movements, remembering them as the sweetest fruit of a democratic franchise. "This I can proclaim, I am still as firm a believer in democracy, as when my ideals had no set-backs."

"I am here to represent the feminist side in this discussion of the future of Democracy," she declared. What difference did it make that women were now enfranchised? "Women doubled the electorate. And this is progress, even if it does not mean greater wisdom and efficiency. To represent more points of view, tends to keep life calmer, more satisfied by peace, better fitted in time to sit in council." Moreover women, though militant in defense of their rights, had won their victory with minimal violence. Men's democracy "grew by riots, revolutions, wars. Women conquered in peace and quiet." This, too, was an important lesson to remember in considering democracy's grim future. Finally, extending the vote to half of humanity, although a political reform long past due, had happened just in time. Now women could join with men in "taking part in the great changes which are revolutionizing the governments and social and economic systems."

"I hear that Mrs. Catt is 'disappointed in women' and Mrs. [Beatrice] Webb in Russia," Harriot wrote to her friend and follower Caroline Lexow Babcock some months later, in a hand increasingly shaky with age. "Why should either have expected other outcomes. Did they not believe in education? Neither women nor the people of Russia had any education, why should they be expected to act as if they had profited by long and adequate training?" As always, her greatest resource was her long perspective, a historic sensibility that reached before her own time and after as well. "My mother used to say," she went on, "we will not know the capabilities of women until 'they have enjoyed freedom for at least two hundred years.'" Even as global prospects were failing and feminist understandings were disappearing, even as her own capacities were slipping, she was hopeful: "The failures of a decade cannot shake my faith in democracy and liberty. Feed your belief daily, keep on working, and win out!"[5]

I

Daughter

Harriot Stanton was literally born into the role of defender of her sex, exemplar of her mother's faith in women's limitless capacities, living proof of women's equality with men. She was raised and educated to be self-confident of her obligation to act in and affect the larger world. In the panorama of her life, she certainly seems to have fulfilled her destiny, and to have brought her mother's greatest legacy—the demand for political equality for women—to fruition. And yet such an overview needs to be amplified with an appreciation for the substantial self-creation that went into making Elizabeth Stanton's daughter into Harriot Stanton Blatch.

From a political perspective, this approach means paying attention to how the daughter elaborated on and modernized the ideas of the mother, how women's rights and political equality changed in the twentieth century and what subsequent notions of women's emancipation emerged from its realization. From a personal and psychological viewpoint, this overview means appreciating what a long, complex, and unresolved process it was for Harriot to separate from her mother and become her own person. A difficult process under any circumstance, individuation for her was complicated by the contradiction between her mother's message of female self-realization and the overwhelming power of Elizabeth Stanton's personality and precedent. Other Victorian girls followed their mothers into lives predicated on self-sacrifice and family service; Harriot followed her mother into self-assertion and individual achievement, and there were more difficulties attendant on this path than the glittering promise of powerful mothers might lead us to imagine. Harriot had to undertake a substantial sojourn away from the Stanton influence and her women's rights destiny in order to return and fulfill it. It took exposure to external influences for her to make herself into what she was born to be: America's first second-generation feminist leader.

"Not as another baby, then, was I welcome, but as a girl their hearts rejoiced over me." Beginning her memoirs at age eighty, this is how Harriot Stanton Blatch described her birth as the second daughter and sixth child of Elizabeth Cady Stanton and Henry Brewster Stanton. Feminism was her birthright. "I was born on January 20, 1856 to that great woman, born in the very cradle of the feminist movement, for it was in my native village of Seneca Falls, New York, that the first Woman's Rights Convention of the world met in 1848."[1]

Through four sons and twelve years of marriage, Elizabeth was frustrated in her desire for a daughter, a child that could bring together her prolific maternity and her grandest reform ambitions. "Your maternal heart seemed as though it could not be satisfied without a daughter," wrote Angelina Grimké Weld, who shared a similar aspiration.[2] Finally, in 1852, Elizabeth's first girl-child, Margaret Livingston Stanton, was born. This was a conse-crated birth. "I am at length the happy mother of a daughter," Elizabeth wrote to Lucretia Mott. "Rejoice with me all womankind, for lo! a champion of thy Cause is born. I have dedicated her to this work from the beginning. I never felt such sacredness in carrying a child as I have this one, feeling all the time strongly impressed with the belief that I was cherishing the embryo of a mighty female martyr. Glorious hope! May she wear the crown of martyrdom bravely & patiently, and leave her impress on the world for goodness & truth."[3] Quite a welcome to a newborn!

By contrast, the birth of her second daughter, four years later, was appar-ently unplanned and ambivalently received.[4] There were financial pressures: five other children and an abolitionist husband who did not bring in a large or steady income. Elizabeth thought that her decision to have a large family was considered an "extravagance" and unseemly in her abstemious aboli-tionist circles.[5] Also, she seems to have been afraid of the birth, "that one agonizing pain . . . that dreaded never-to-be-forgotten ordeal." This fear was uncharacteristic, as she had widely advertised her amazonlike capacity to give birth without interruption to her regular daily routine. Her account of

Margaret's birth—a twelve-pound baby born after fifteen minutes of labor and delivered without a doctor attending, mother up and about in less than a day—was intended as a source of great pride and an augur of her daughter's glorious destiny. Fortunately, Elizabeth's fears about this next birth were not realized, and the child was delivered just as quickly as her older sister, with only two labor pains.[6]

But the deepest problem posed by Harriot's birth was Elizabeth Stanton's growing desire to launch her public career as a reformer, which the birth was bound to frustrate for several years more. Elizabeth and her women's rights partner, Susan B. Anthony, had just initiated a full-fledged women's rights movement in New York State. Anthony, the only remaining unmarried woman in the women's rights inner circle, was busy traveling about the state, circulating the petition that they had written for submission to the legislature, demanding the greatest of women's rights, equal suffrage. Elizabeth planned strategy and wrote political tracts right up to Harriot's birth, inviting coworkers to come to see her when she was too pregnant to leave home, anxious to get as much done as possible in the "month [of] grace still."[7] After the birth, as she wrote to Anthony, it was some consolation that "the result is another daughter." Six months later she was still writing, "I pace up and down these two chambers of mine like a caged lioness, longing to bring to a close nursing and housekeeping cares."[8]

If looking back on this scenario in later years gave Harriot any pain, she dealt with it, as she did so much else, by subsuming the personal dimension in the political and joining in protest against her mother's involuntary domestic isolation, identifying with her mother's position more than her own. When editing her mother's letters for publication many years later, she collapsed several letters to Susan B. Anthony together, so that in Elizabeth's announcement of Harriot's birth, Harriot the editor allowed her mother to complain openly: "I feel disappointed and sad at this grievous interruption of my plans. I might have born an orator before spring, you acting as midwife."[9]

After Harriot's birth, Elizabeth's conflicts only intensified. First of all, the pace and direction of political events in the late 1850s, the accelerating conflict over slavery and expanding political options for protesting it, made her domestic confinement all the more unbearable. "If I were a man and not pinned here," Elizabeth wrote to Anthony in 1857, "how I would hie to New York . . . and become one of the Tribune's corps of regular writers!"[10]

To make matters worse, her husband was constantly away from Seneca Falls in Albany or Washington. Immediately before and during the Civil

War, Henry Stanton was so politically preoccupied that he played a minor part in his family's life. A crucial figure in the shift of American abolitionism from moral suasion to political methods, he was desperately searching for a place for himself in the latter (which he never found). After participating in the Free Soil preliminaries to the Democratic party in New York, he shifted to the new and more promising Republican party, in which he was involved at the time of Harriot's birth. Elizabeth Stanton resented the fact that her husband had all his time and energy for public life, while she, for whom politics was her life's blood, was overwhelmed with the care of their children and home. "How rebellious it makes me feel when I see Henry going about where and how he pleases," she wrote to Anthony, when Harriot was still a baby and mother and child were trapped at home alone together. "I . . . contrast his freedom with my bondage, and feel that, because of the false position of women, I have been compelled to hold all my noblest aspirations in abeyance."[11]

Here is the place for a word, though not too much more is possible, about the role of Henry Brewster Stanton in Harriot's life. Years later, when she had become a popular and accomplished public speaker, she proudly claimed that her parents had been renowned orators and that her abilities in this area came from both of them. She identified almost exclusively with her father when it came to her insightful political judgments, which were such a distinct element in her mature woman suffrage leadership. Yet as a genuine presence in her life, particularly in these early years, her father was mostly absent. He came and went frequently, both to be where the political action was and to earn money as a journalist for the family. His letters from Washington or Albany to Elizabeth were full of the political detail that she craved, with only an occasional message of "love to the chicks." The few specific injunctions were directed to the older children, all boys, to do their chores and so on. In the extant letters, only once did he ask about either of his daughters— whether Margaret (age five) had started dancing school yet.[12] Margaret remembered him as a good playmate and "the man bountiful who brought us presents from the metropolis."[13] In Harriot's autobiography, he is virtually nonexistent. Her growing up seems to have been parthenogenetic; she was so thoroughly born of her mother that a father was superfluous. Decades later, Harriot's grandchildren remembered hearing not a word about Henry Brewster Stanton, although Elizabeth Stanton was a vital living memory.[14]

Although Elizabeth promised Susan Anthony that Harriot would be "my last baby," by the summer of 1858 she was pregnant again, the result of what Anthony bitterly characterized as "a moment's pleasure to herself or her husband."[15] In March 1859, when Harriot was just three, her brother Robert, Elizabeth Stanton's seventh and last child, was born. Elizabeth's labor was "long and very very severe," and it took her much longer to recover from than any of her other births.[16] Within six months, however, her situation had begun to improve. In October 1859, her father, Daniel Cady, died, and although she deeply grieved his death, it also freed her from the conflicts she had with him about her independent ways. After his death, she was more able to call on her mother's help with her children. In 1858, she had sent Harriot and Margaret to Johnstown, New York, for their first extended visit. After Judge Cady's death, she regularly sent her daughters there for the summer. This arrangement solved the worst of Elizabeth's domestic pressures. When Robert was a little baby, she was able to accomplish much more outside the household than she had when Harriot was an infant. In May 1860, she addressed the New York legislature, attended the women's rights and antislavery conventions in New York City, and undertook a major struggle on behalf of divorce law reform. From this point on, Elizabeth Stanton's political career accelerated and the energy she devoted to politics steadily increased.

In other words, the first years of Harriot's life coincided with her mother's most intense discontent with the duties of woman's sphere. At one level, the experience must have been painful for Harriot. Especially close to her mother because of her sex, Harriot had little to shield her from her mother's growing resentment with the domestic limits of her life. In the relationship of mother and daughter currents of intimacy and anger ran together to create a strong river of feeling. Yet in all of Harriot's writings and speeches, there is a curious silence about her childhood with Elizabeth Stanton, a maddening lack of detail about what it was like to be her daughter. One of the few exceptions is an unusually intense description in her memoirs of an early separation from her mother at age three. When Elizabeth returned after two weeks away, "my sister gave her an enthusiastic embrace," Harriot wrote, "while I shyly edged toward her, slipped into her lap, buried my face in her bosom, and wept as if my heart would break."[17] Over the years, she had much to say about her mother but almost all of it served to make a political point or to shore up her own authority in the suffrage movement. This preference for propaganda over personal detail was undoubtedly reinforced by obeisance to one of her mother's most basic precepts, the importance of respecting "what is most sacred in the solitude of individual life," of protecting the privacy of one's deepest feelings, but it also indicates her habit of recuperating through political meaning what was difficult to grapple with through emotion.[18]

But there is another side: although Elizabeth's resentments over her maternal responsibilities were stronger when she was raising Harriot than with any of her other children, it was Harriot who identified most with the women's rights faith of her mother. While Margaret grew up to be, in her own words, a "lukewarm suffrage saint," Harriot spent her life vindicating, enhancing, and transforming the base her mother had laid down for American suffragism.[19] Perhaps embracing her mother's beliefs as an adult was one way Harriot solved the emotional dilemma these convictions caused her as a child.

From her other children and from her own description, we know that Elizabeth Stanton was a highly nurturing mother who did not believe in restraining or disciplining children, but instead in allowing them full expression of their natural childish exuberance. Margaret characterized her as "a sunny, cheerful, indulgent mother, whose great effort was to save us from all the fears that shadow the lives of most children," and this is consistent with Elizabeth's own description of her mothering.[20] Harriot's memory was that no one could read to children with "more gusto"; though an unrelenting "mentor," she was always playful and inventive, so that her children were eager for her lessons.[21] To be sure, Elizabeth Stanton was a particularly intelligent and loving mother. Nonetheless, the precepts by which she raised her children were consistent with a belief that was growing in middle-class society that the young were better governed by love and "suasion," that is by women, than by fear and punishment, that is by men.

Elizabeth also taught her daughters about the worth and capacity of women, a lesson not so common in the culture. She claimed to have begun her motherhood with a prejudice in favor of her own sex, which she did not give up until she had raised several boys.[22] Later, as a traveling lecturer, her most popular speech was "Our Girls," in which she called for girls to "grow up hearty and romping, free and unrestrain[e]d, developing alike the physical, the mental and the moral powers."[23] According to a young, unreconstructed male (Henry's nephew), these lessons in the equality of the sexes were learned too well by the Stanton girls. In his opinion, Maggie's and Hattie's self-confidence was positively repulsive; while he characterized the four older boys as "healthy, hearty kids who had little restraint put upon them," he remembered bitterly that "Aunt Lib taught her daughters that they were the chosen few . . . and so must regulate the affairs of the universe."[24]

Elizabeth Stanton's deliberate feminist mothering provided an upbringing for her daughters, very different from what the average young women of their sort faced in the 1850s. She was determined to prepare them to go out into the world, not only to make their individual marks on it, but to embody her convictions about women's capacity. In addition to being a matter of formal education, this approach was, at a more fundamental level, an effort to shape their personalities and their characters. One mark of her success is that both daughters came of age, finished college, searched for and found a vocation, and struggled to balance families and public life without suffering the kind of physical and mental collapse that dogged so many female rebels of this generation.

Despite her loving manner and unlimited hopes for her children, Elizabeth's motherhood could be a harsh discipline. She taught her daughters a horror of weakness and dependence in women. (For example, when unable to meet a speaking engagement because of morning sickness during her final pregnancy, she lied about the reason, lest she "should illustrate in my own person" the notion that motherhood and public life were incompatible for women.[25]) Of the two girls, Harriot learned this lesson best, perhaps too well. Even as a child, she prided herself in her fierce independence of spirit. "I had self reliance, backed up with courage sufficient to carry through an operation to the end," she wrote in her memoirs.[26] Harriot learned her mother's lesson to act only on the basis of what one personally knew to be true, to avoid the danger of allowing what was derisively called "loyalty" to any other person or idea to supersede this obligation to make independent and informed judgments.[27]

Thinking for herself was thus not only desirable, but an obligation of the highest order, ironically an act of deference and respect to her beloved mother. These contradictions can be detected in one of the few extended anecdotes Harriot told about her mother in her autobiography. While away from home, Harriot had fallen, and the nursemaid, afraid of being reprimanded, made the child promise not to tell anyone what happened. Over the next year, Harriot developed a chronic backache and a persistent nightmare (of a suffering woman "whose spine was frozen because she ate too much ice cream"). The point of the story as Harriot recalled it in her memoirs was her mother's incisive, scientific mind, which allowed her to deduce what had happened and get Harriot the right treatment. "Probably if Freudianism had been in full swing . . . there would have been hosts of people who would have urged my mother to take her dreaming daughter to a psycho-analyst," Harriot wrote (in the 1930s) but having such a mother made this superfluous. Maybe, though, the historically inserted "psycho-analyst" would have observed that the nightmares were not only about the material pain in her back, but about the guilt in her heart, which was relieved only when she severed her loyalty to the nursemaid and told her mother the truth.[28]

Despite Elizabeth Stanton's notorious prejudice in favor of her own sex, the family environment subtly favored boys over girls. First of all, there were four boys to set the tone before any girls were born. When Harriot was a toddler, her brothers ranged from Neil, a teenager, to Theodore, who was nine. Elizabeth treasured their rambunctiousness even as she complained of the demands it put on her.[29] Her autobiography is full of stories of the boys climbing trees, nearly drowning in the Erie Canal, and experimenting with profanity in front of dinner guests. It was just this sort of unlimited vitality and freedom of expression that she wanted for girls; she loved girls as they might become, not as they were raised to be. "Our young fry are all quite enthusiastic over the new game of archery," she wrote to her cousin when Harriot was fourteen. "Maggie and Hattie coquettishly play on the edges as girls are wont to do!!"[30] Though she did her best to bring her daughters up without conventional restraints, she was not raising them in a vacuum and many other forces interfered, so that even the Stanton girls were held to standards of decorum, restraint, and modesty that were not applied to their brothers.

Harriot shared this prejudice. She adored her brothers, and like Elizabeth, chose stories centering around them to illustrate the atmosphere of her family in Seneca Falls when she was a little girl. The story she told most frequently, including at her eightieth birthday celebration where it was meant to illustrate the early and strong roots of her feminism, had to do with the invigorating tonic of having to meet the standard of robust play her brothers set.

> An early memory of Seneca Falls is of our garden which covered some ten acres. The cherry trees stand out clearly in my mind, especially two huge trees near the house at the back—a white oxheart and a black. My big brothers, Neil and Kit and Gat, used to climb them, and bring down to their small worshippers baskets of the luscious fruit. In time I took to climbing, and with my skill was connected a most emphatic feminist retort. I was high in a heavenward journey in a big chestnut tree . . . when my father happened to see me and called out in some agitation: "My daughter come down, you will fall." Poised calmly on the branch, instantly I argued, "Why don't you tell Bob to come down, he's three years younger and one branch higher?"[31]

She harbored no resentments at inequality in her family, contending all her life that she was raised in an atmosphere of perfect equality, where sex discrimination was unknown.[32]

Then there was Margaret, four years older. The two girls were thrown together constantly, along with their youngest brother Robert. From the first, Margaret seems to have adored her little sister, reportedly leaping with joy when she was told of her birth.[33] When she compared herself to Hattie, she thought that her sister had been favored with the more spectacular virtues. "I have no remarkable genius in any direction but I have some practical talent in the ordinary affairs of life," she wrote in a sketch of her family in 1885. My sister . . . may be said to have a good deal of genius; she is an eloquent speaker, a fine writer, talks well, and recites with great effect, and added to all this she has rare physical beauty."[34] In later years, she was always ready when called on to help Harriot, and seems to have been proud of her sister's accomplishments, preserving numerous clippings about them.[35]

Harriot did not return her sister's generosity. In her memoirs, she granted Margaret the lower female virtues. She was "mild and gentle," "an example of patient and good spirits and an even temper," "always equable" and "by nature a caretaker." She was not, however, independent-minded, but instead was beset by the loyalty to the opinions of others that Harriot rejected as so dangerous to individual autonomy. "I learned by demonstration in my sister the danger of not thinking for one's self."[36] To this fatal flaw was apparently added Margaret's inability to rise to the standard of female fortitude which Elizabeth Stanton had set. Later in life, Margaret was hit by a streetcar and was left with a permanent limp, which Harriot, according to her granddaughter, regarded with suspicion, as if it were a voluntary weakness that she should have worked to overcome.[37]

In 1881, traveling in Europe and away from her sister, Harriot wrote in her diary that "I have never yet known of sisters among whom . . . there did not exist an admiration of one."[38] Presuming that her own family not only was included but was the source of her observation, we might also be led to guess that Harriot considered herself the favored daughter. By general consensus, she was both the brighter and the more beautiful. But this might well be an oversimplified version of how Harriot herself saw her family constellation. Margaret was universally regarded as the warmer and more nurturing of the two; even Harriot's grandchildren sometimes preferred her company.[39] Elizabeth appreciated this aspect of Margaret's character, too. She wanted many things from her daughters—not only vindication for her theories of women's equality, but also care and concern in her old age, and this she got from Margaret.

The sections of Harriot's autobiography having to do with the earliest years of her childhood are set not in Seneca Falls, but in her grandmother's household, in Johnstown, New York, fifty miles away. Although she only spent a few weeks every summer here, she loved the rivers and hills of the Mohawk and Hudson river valleys, and these were the scenes in which her dreams were set.[40] Undoubtedly, a child's summers "away" leave sharper memories than daily life at home during the year, but her choice to focus on Johnstown suggests other aspects of how she remembered her childhood. Johnstown was where Elizabeth Cady had grown up. By situating her child-hood memories there, Harriot was able to portray herself as following in her mother's footsteps, and at the same time to treasure her independence. She described how "thrilled" she was to learn to read from the same Johnstown woman who had taught her mother forty years before. She also dwelled on the "dolorous" Presbyterian atmosphere that figured so vividly in her mother's autobiographical account of Johnstown.[41]

Choosing a Johnstown setting also allowed Harriot to keep Elizabeth at a distance, at least on a literary level—to render her a shadowy though adored figure who swept into town during a crisis or when her daughters needed her, but was frequently elsewhere. Perhaps Harriot could begin to know herself better away from her mother than under her wing. The time away from her powerful and opinionated mother, a mother whom she adored, may have been a kind of relief to the young Harriot, a chance for her to develop her own beliefs and personal power, to nurture the individual character that her mother believed was women's greatest necessity. In the Johnstown portions of her autobiography, Harriot described her mother only twice, and then briefly. For the most part, Harriot and Margaret were left to the care of others.

The Cady household in Johnstown as Harriot remembered it was all female. Of all Elizabeth's children, only she and Margaret went. Her older brothers were left to their own devices in Seneca Falls during the summer and Elizabeth kept the baby Robert with her as well. After Grandfather Cady died in 1859, neither Harriot's father nor her uncles visited much. If Seneca Falls was shaped by the masculine element, women ruled at Johnstown. "The Johnstown household in summer consisted of my grandmother, my aunts, Tryphena Bayard and Harriet Eaton, my sister Margaret and myself," Harriot remembered.[42] The Johnstown reminiscences capture an important truth for Harriot: all the strong figures there, both positive and negative, were female. Under the care of these women, Harriot's personality and sense of self flowered, especially her fierce individualism. One of the greatest differences between her childhood and that of her mother was that no father ruled her life in the way her mother's had been. Women shaped her will, both by encouragement and by opposition.

The most important figure for Harriot in Johnstown was the matriarch of the household, her grandmother, Margaret Livingston Cady. Elizabeth barely mentioned her mother in her description of the Cady household in her own autobiography. Although "queenly" and "self reliant," she was "weary with the cares of a large family"; Elizabeth's portrait of her family's dynamics is dominated instead by the figure of her father.[43] By contrast, Harriot's account of the Cady household pictured Margaret Cady as a woman of liberal convictions—"a Garrisonian extremist"—with "rare courage," political savvy, and an imposing physical presence.[44] By the time Harriot came to the Cady household to spend her summers, her grandmother was a widow, untrammeled by her husband's authority or her children's needs; but even taking these changes into account, Harriot attributed to her a much more powerful personality and greater influence than Elizabeth Stanton had. A biographer at the time thought that it was from her mother that Elizabeth had "imbibed that dauntless independence of thought and speech . . . the courage of one's convictions."[45] Elizabeth's elder daughter, named after her grandmother, also thought her mother had inherited "her brains, beauty and fight" as much from Margaret Cady as from Judge Cady.[46] But Elizabeth never acknowledged the debt, because like Harriot, she, too, may have sometimes found her powerful mother too much for her. Grandmothers were extremely important in this family, often taking over childrearing from their busy, feminist daughters, frequently more warmly remembered than the powerful mothers themselves.

Harriot's memories of her grandmother were sweet and sensuous: "When I had slipped into her room very early, I loved to stand and watch her smooth and smooth her black silk stockings, as she sat swaying in the little white bamboo and reed rocking chair." But her grandmother exemplified the more virile virtues as well. In her memoirs, Harriot gave her the highest praise: "She was a born politician." From Margaret Cady, her granddaughter claimed to have learned "how to mold people and circumstances." In Elizabeth's autobiography, she told a story about her father's law books and the sufferings of his female clients to explain her own discovery of the importance of politics and the law. Harriot's autobiography featured a parallel story in which her grandmother was the central figure. In an important church election, Margaret Cady realized that she and the other women were about to be cheated out of their votes. The situation called for "secrecy, manipulation, leadership," all supreme virtues in Harriot's eyes; Grandmother Cady rose—"her full height, five feet eleven inches"—to the occasion. Thrusting her arm into the voting urn, she made it impossible for the women's votes to be skimmed off the top and thus disregarded. Harriot was thrilled by her grandmother's heroism, and the incident functions as an early political epiphany.[47]

Elizabeth's two older sisters, Tryphena Bayard and Harriet Eaton, were almost as important in Harriot's childhood as Margaret Cady, but as negative rather than positive figures. Harriot imagined that her grandmother was "much freer and finer . . . alone with her grandchildren, without the aunts weaving nets of convention about her."[48] Perhaps she meant to say the same about her relationship with them: Tryphena and Harriet were undoubtedly two of the major forces countering the women's rights upbringing Elizabeth was trying to give her daughters. If Maggie and Hattie were taken for their summer trip to Johnstown by one of their older brothers, they could sit at the window of the stagecoach and drink in all the thrill of a fifty-mile journey away from home; if "chaperoned" by one of their aunts, they were told that "little girls must ride inside," and the ride was more like "torture."[49] If Elizabeth wanted to educate her girls at home or to send them to boys' schools, the aunts made sure that they saw the inside of more conventional female educational institutions, so that they might know what was expected of a normal young girl of their station.

Harriot was especially critical of Aunt Tryphena Bayard, the oldest of the Stanton sisters and ten years Elizabeth's senior. Aunty By, "tall, handsome and severe," was a "trial," especially to youthful spirits, "a severe disciplinarian," and a champion of propriety. She was also much more conservative than either Margaret Cady or Elizabeth Stanton. Everyone in the household, from Harriot to her grandmother, lived in fear of her disapproval. Harriot conceded, however, that "she had plenty of brains, a real flair for finance, and looked out for the money interests of more than one member of the family."[50] She used these skills, and whatever money lay behind them, to control family members, including Harriot herself. Harriot may have devised a unique form of retribution. Late in her life, she told Alma Lutz, Elizabeth Stanton's first biographer, the story that Edward Bayard, "Aunty By's" husband, had been in love with Elizabeth and asked her to run off with him.[51]

Harriot's memories of Aunt Harriet Eaton were less harsh, even though she had many of the same faults of conventionality and conservatism. Among other things, "Aunty Had" was beautiful, and for Harriot (who was herself very handsome as a girl) beauty was definitely important; it was both a virtue of its own and a reflection of desirable inner qualities. This was the aunt after whom she was named, but when still quite young she attenuated the connection and announced that she was changing the spelling, following the more antiquated form that had been given to one of her grandmother's children who had not survived infancy. Aunty Had apparently thought that her little namesake was not being adequately educated (by her mother, at home) and sent her off to an old-fashioned dame school in Johnstown.[52] "The aunts" were the object of many of Harriot's remembered resentments, and she blamed them exclusively for decisions about her upbringing to which she objected, especially about her schooling. By fastening sole responsibility on her aunts, Harriot avoided anger at her mother.

A similar observation might be made about yet another female member of the Stanton family constellation during Harriot's youth, Susan B. Anthony. Stanton and Anthony had met in 1851, and by the time of Harriot's birth, they were deeply involved in their friendship and their women's rights collaboration. Anthony came down from Rochester to Seneca Falls frequently, helped with the children, and together she and Elizabeth discussed, plotted, and wrote on behalf of equal rights. Not only was she involved with tending the children, but she was allowed to discipline them. According to Harriot, "Bob to his dying day used to say that Susan was the only woman except his mother, who had ever spanked him."[53] Anthony was in and out of the Stanton house constantly when Harriot was a child. Nonetheless, Harriot's childhood attitude toward Anthony remains difficult to discern. There is no direct evidence left from those years, no letters between them, for instance, and everything Harriot wrote in later periods which refers to Anthony reflects the political motives of the moment. While Elizabeth was still alive and even later, when Harriot was leading the New York suffrage movement, she paid considerable homage to her mother's friendship with Anthony, which had become a suffrage icon for the solidarity of women on behalf of political equality.[54]

Then, near the end of her own life, Harriot developed a tremendous resentment toward Anthony, almost as if she held her personally responsible for the lack of attention being paid to Elizabeth Cady Stanton by those seeking to preserve the history of the woman suffrage movement, and for Anthony's elevation to the status of suffrage saint. This attitude is reflected in what Harriot had to say in her memoirs about Anthony, which was neither flattering nor loving. As Harriot portrayed her, Anthony had all the vices Elizabeth lacked and none of her virtues. She was severe, physically intimidating, and intellectually dependent on the more brilliant Elizabeth. "Susan's smile was never on the edge of laughter, but always had an apologetic touch," Harriot wrote. "The general impression she gave of severity was heightened by an eye defect she suffered throughout her life. [She was wall-eyed.] . . . This gave the Stanton boys the notion that Susan could see round corners and unearth their mischief."[55] Even Harriot's habit of referring to her mother's friend as Susan rather than Miss Anthony (all the children did the same) had the effect of diminishing her, bringing her down to their level (Anthony was all the while referring to Elizabeth as Mrs. Stanton) even as it expressed their intimacy.

It was almost as if Susan Anthony, not the absent Henry Stanton, played the role for Harriot of bad parent, a perfect contrast for her portrait of her all-loving mother. To describe her mother as perfectly maternal and without flaw, Harriot concentrated many of her criticisms, especially with respect to political matters, on Anthony. While Elizabeth "drew you to her service by her abounding love," Susan ruled "more by compulsion than by attraction."[56] Harriot particularly blamed Anthony for the loss of her mother to political activism. "Her advent was not a matter for rejoicing," Harriot wrote candidly, "for it meant that [our] resourceful mother was to retire as mentor and be entirely engrossed in writing a speech for Miss Anthony to deliver at some meeting, while she kept the children out of sight and out of mind."[57] Harriot had already begun to share her mother's fascination with reform and politics. Even so, she resented sharing her mother with a growing repertoire of extrafamilial concerns.

In 1862, the Stanton family moved from Seneca Falls to New York City so that Henry could accept a political appointment in the New York Customs House.[58] Elizabeth had her own reasons for moving; she was eager to be closer to the center of the reform activities in which she was increasingly absorbed. Elizabeth found a "nice four story house . . . 'high up' "—that is, farther north—to rent, so that she and the children could take advantage of Central Park. In the fall and spring they walked and ran; in the winter they skated. The younger children began to attend public schools, albeit sporadically, after being educated at home by their mother in Seneca Falls. For Harriot, these years were most important as a time during which she regained her mother, but under more expansive terms. She began to know her not simply as a warm bosom and clever playmate, but as a reformer and a public figure. Sharing in her mother's "causes" in these early stages was a way of both allowing her to go out into the larger world in which she so evidently thrived and having her mother to herself.

These years in New York City also coincided with the Civil War and Reconstruction, and reflected all the social chaos and high political emotion of that era. At this stage in her life, Harriot's world was simultaneously as large as the world historic events she was witnessing and as small as the close family relations through which they were mediated. Her brother Gerrit enlisted in the Union Army and at least one of her cousins was killed in the war.[59] Her father was driven from office by a war-related scandal, which smacked of collusion with the enemy.[60] She met "the famous old Negress, Sojourner Truth," who was a guest in their house.[61] The closest the war came to her family was when Elizabeth and her older sons were caught in the murderous New York City draft riots of the summer of 1863. Twenty-one-year-old Neil narrowly missed being roughed up or worse as "one of those three Hundred dollar fellows" (he had refused to enlist). The four-story house proved a blessing: Elizabeth secured the children and servants in the top of the house, and then "prepared a speech if necessary to go down and open the door and make a grand appeal to them as Americans and citizens of a republic."[62] Margaret and Harriot, away as usual for the summer in Johnstown, only heard about the danger when Elizabeth appeared with her sons on Margaret Cady's doorstep, fleeing the chaos.[63]

Harriot especially remembered the reform activities she was finally able to share with her mother. During these years, Elizabeth was at home and close to her children, but also intensely involved in reform politics, including the 1864 Fremont presidential campaign and the 1863 National Loyal Women's League petition drive for an amendment to abolish slavery. Harriot lovingly recalled in her autobiography, "It is as clear as if it were yesterday's experience, sitting in the dining room of our house in New York, just after we had moved from Seneca Falls . . . scraping lint for the wounded in the hospitals. My mother and Maggie sat opposite us at the table cutting the old linen into small squares which Susan and I then ravelled into lint."[64]

Like other children in the 1860s, Harriot was profoundly affected by the political drama of the Civil War and abolition. "The events of the Civil war remained in my memory because they were woven together with poignant personal happenings," she remembered.[65] For Florence Kelley, born in 1857, the memory of Abraham Lincoln's death was her "earliest dated mental picture."[66] So too for Jane Addams, who was four years younger than Harriot. "I suppose all the children who were born about the time of the Civil War have recollections quite unlike those of the children who are living now," Addams wrote.[67] For girls whose parents encouraged them to care about these greater political realities, the impact of the Civil War was especially important in enlarging their horizons; for Harriot, this early and powerful introduction to the world outside domestic life coincided with the special bond she was beginning to forge with her mother, their shared political passions. Between these twin forces—one intimate, the other historical in the largest sense—she was developing a political sensibility that was unusual for a woman and that would be hard to satisfy in the institutions and interests available to her sex in that period.

In 1868, Elizabeth Stanton moved her family away from New York City to Tenafly, New Jersey. The Tenafly house, which was larger and more luxurious than any in which the Stantons had lived, was purchased with Elizabeth's inheritance from her father and was her home far more than her husband's, who spent most of his time across the river in New York City.[68] Politically, Elizabeth Stanton and Susan Anthony were breaking away from former male allies and giving voice to a much more radical and militant suffragism than they had ever declared before. During these years, Elizabeth railed against men, including her family and friends, with a new kind of fervor. "When I think of all the wrongs that have been heaped upon womankind," she wrote to Martha Wright in 1871, "I am ashamed that I am not forever in a condition of chronic wrath, stark mad, skin and bone, my eyes a fountain of tears, my lips overflowing with curses, and my hand against every man and brother! Ah, how I do repent me of the male faces I have washed."[69] For these same reasons, she may have begun to draw closer to her daughters, who were growing up, able to share more with their mother and depend on her a bit less. In these years Harriot starts to appear in Elizabeth's letters, voicing opinions of her own on matters pertaining to women's rights. Anthony reported that Harriot advised her mother to "tell all" she knew about the adulterous triangle known as the "Beecher-Tilton scandal."[70]

In 1869, Elizabeth also began her decade-long career as a traveling lyceum lecturer, which took her away from home as much as eight months of the year. Although traveling was hard, and she claimed she did it only to earn the money to send her children to college, she loved the adventure and the notoriety of being on the lyceum circuit, as well as the freedom from domestic concerns.[71] While she was away, the Stanton household was under the supervision of long-time housekeeper Amelia Willard, who exercised minimal authority over the younger children. Harriot was left to her own devices much of the time. She and Margaret continued to be thrown together, but she was probably closer to her younger brother Bob.[72] In almost classic teenage girl fashion, her passion in these years was for riding horses because it gave her "a sense of control," the "satisfaction of a complete sense of command as nothing else."[73] There is no evidence that she as yet had any important friendships outside her family.

Away from New York City, Harriot's education was again becoming a problem. She was initially enrolled at a day school in Tenafly, but when the schoolmaster punished the boys for playing with the girls, she walked out, knowing that her mother would support her.[74] An all-girl boarding school, Rockland County Female Academy, was located fifteen miles away, and at first Harriot was eager to go, especially after her mother agreed to let her take her horse with her. But by the second night she was back (she rode the horse home), complaining that she could not sleep.[75] Her mother found the episode amusing. Eventually a place was found for her at the Englewood Academy, a small, private, all-girls school only two miles from her home, where the schoolmaster "understood human nature" and the school's two teachers were to Harriot's liking.[76]

Harriot was proud of what she called her educational "migration" during these years.[77] Her family did not criticize or reprimand her—on the contrary, the entire odyssey became part of family lore and was one of the few details of her childhood that Harriot passed on to her daughter and granddaughters.[78] Behind her proud boast that she was too independent to tolerate school lay an attachment to her family and especially to her mother that was so strong it was hard for her to be satisfied anywhere else. And Elizabeth, despite her desire to be off and involved with her own interests, indulged her daughter's unwillingness to replace home with school. Added to this dynamic was the problem that all of these schools were woefully inadequate for a girl as intellectually curious and self-confident as Harriot. In particular, none could prepare her to pass a college entrance examination. Florence Kelley, who was the same age as Harriot, found that even in a city as large as Philadelphia, there was not a single school where a girl could receive adequate preparation to enter college.[79]

Elizabeth resented the fact that history had deprived her of the opportunity to go to college, and she was determined that her daughters would be college graduates. Maybe even more than political equality, higher education seemed to her the fundamental antidote to women's degradation.[80] Institutions of higher education were opening to women at a rapid rate, and by 1870 the number of women enrolled in full-fledged collegiate courses of study had reached about three thousand. Still, this number was less than 1 percent of women between the ages of eighteen and twenty-one.[81] Nor were the choices satisfactory. In the early 1870s, there were only about a half-dozen schools where women could get a full-fledged college education.[82] They could attend Oberlin or Swarthmore, colleges with significant numbers of women but small and without many intellectual resources. They could be pathbreakers at universities, such as Cornell, Boston University, or the University of Michigan, which provided a more comprehensive and liberal education but where most students were male. Or, beginning in 1865, they could enroll at Vassar, the first all-female college, which was still characterized by many of the intellectual and social limitations that afflicted lesser female educational institutions. As M. Carey Thomas, who entered college at about the same time as Harriot, wrote, "The educational problem [for women] is a terrible one—girls' colleges are inferior and it seems impossible to get the most illustrious men to fill their chairs, and on the other hand it is a fiery ordeal to educate a lady by coeducation."[83]

From her own unhappy experience with all-female education, Elizabeth was especially committed to coeducation, which she believed the best environment for equality of the sexes. As she wrote in the early 1870s, coeducation was the firmest and wisest basis for American higher education both because there were differences of sex "in the moral and spiritual world as well as in the vegetable and animal kingdoms" and because this "difference in the sexes is too subtle and, as yet, too little understood, to attempt to shape all the conditions of life with reference to it."[84] In 1870 she began her search for the right college for her daughters by visiting Swarthmore, and reported to her cousin and confidante, Elizabeth Smith Miller, that it was "a quiet Quaker institution, in a healthy, warm situation, thorough in its teachings, where boys also go. You know I am a firm believer in the benefits of coeducation of the sexes, which is peculiar to our country, and which we should never abandon."[85] Swarthmore had the support of Lucretia Mott, as well as a precollegiate program, which both Margaret and Harriot needed before they could qualify for a regular college education. But Swarthmore educated its male and female students differently, and even its dedicated president acknowledged that it was still "little more than a boarding school."[86]

Elizabeth was more excited about the possibility of sending her daughters to Cornell. In the 1850s, she and Susan B. Anthony had been actively involved in a movement to establish a secular, nonracist, and coeducational "People's College," which resulted in the founding of Cornell.[87] There were many things to recommend Cornell. Harriot's older brother Theodore had been a member of the first class there, and Andrew D. White, the university's president, was a strong supporter of coeducation. A transfer student from Vassar, Emma Eastman, was about to become the first woman to graduate. Since there was as yet no college residence for women, Elizabeth wrote directly to Ezra Cornell to inquire about building a house in Ithaca and moving there "for the coming ten years" so that her children could live "under my constant care and supervision." A more difficult issue was meeting Cornell's entrance requirements, since there was no preparatory department to help undereducated women bring themselves up to standard.[88]

Harriot was eager to go to Cornell.[89] Its educational philosophy was relatively liberal, and she could study subjects in which she was becoming interested, such as economics and history. In addition, because it was essentially a male institution, students were allowed much personal freedom, and this also appealed to her. M. Carey Thomas and Florence Kelley, two of Harriot's contemporaries who also went on to become leaders of the women's movement, chose Cornell for similar reasons and loved their years there. "Oh Anna it is worth everything to be here," Thomas wrote to a friend her first term there. She was happy despite the loneliness, because she so much liked being responsible for herself and being treated like an adult.[90]

Harriot was not so fortunate and, despite her strong preferences to the contrary, ended up at Vassar. In 1871, when Maggie was nineteen and Harriot fifteen, they were enrolled in Vassar's precollegiate program and went on to graduate in 1875 and 1878, respectively.[91] The deciding factor in favor of Vassar seems to have been the opinions and money of "the aunts," whose conservatism extended to women's education and to an insistence on supervision over the activities and behaviors of young girls, especially those so advanced as to attend college.[92] Two aspects of the situation are worth noting. One is that Elizabeth Stanton did not control something as crucial to her as her daughters' education; the other is that she was restrained in her choices not by the patriarchal father about whom she complained so profusely but by dominating older sisters. Even so, Harriot's anger was reserved entirely for her aunts, and she did not protest that her mother had failed to stand up for her daughters or for her own principles.[93]

Vassar College had been endowed by Poughkeepsie brewer and banker Matthew Vassar to provide women with uncontested access to higher education. Otherwise it represented a relatively conservative idea of how women should be schooled. The curriculum was "orthodox," stressing fine arts, ancient languages, natural science, and mathematics.[94] The faculty consisted of twenty-one women teachers with only a seminary education, and seven professors, all but two male.[95] For president, Vassar selected John H. Raymond, who was considered even by his supporters to be cautious and conservative in "his attitude towards the questions of the day and the sphere of women."[96] Raymond ruled over Vassar with a heavy, paternalistic hand, sermonizing to the women twice weekly and insisting on daily chapel.[97] In general, Vassar students' lives were closely supervised. Following the practice of female seminaries, a "lady principal" was appointed, detailed rules were posted, and women instructors were required to oversee the student residence halls.[98] It is not difficult to imagine how poorly this level of social restraint sat with the independent-minded Harriot.

From the start, Harriot disliked Vassar. Resorting to the tricks she had employed so successfully in New York and Tenafly, she tried to drop or transfer out several times, only to find herself back in Poughkeepsie, "check-mated" by family authority in all her attempts to escape. In her autobiography she judges Vassar harshly, describing it as "a slough of despond." She characterized the place as "sequestered" and wrote with disgust of "the Vassar world of immature women." She objected to the absence of any courses in modern history or economics, and especially protested the students' ignorance about politics and the larger world outside the college.[99] So negative was her portrait of Vassar, particularly in light of the fact that it was Vassar that many years later sponsored the preparation and publication of her memoirs, that her coauthor, Alma Lutz, consulted with others about toning down these sections, which may have been even more unrelenting in earlier versions.[100]

At the core of Harriot's unhappy memories of Vassar was the fact that it was an all-female institution, "composed entirely of a disfranchised class." Harriot recognized that the student body "was definitely discouraged by the authorities from taking any interest whatsoever in its own political freedom," but she also blamed the women students themselves for Vassar's limitations. She set herself above the other students, socializing with the faculty, arranging with the president for a special course of study, and exaggerating the uniqueness of her interests. She was particularly critical of the religious revivals that swept through the college. She also missed the presence of men as "social creatures."[101]

One gets the sense that Harriot found most of these women disappointing. Her mother had raised her with high standards for womanhood, and Harriot did not find that many of the other students at Vassar met them.[102] Compared to her "home atmosphere," college was conservative and constraining, and compared to her mother, other women were timid and conventional.[103] The notion of women's equality as Harriot understood it at this early point was quite different from the women's rights faith of her mother. Although she believed that she was by birth and training the equal of any man, she had not yet had any experience that she could recognize as discrimination, no painful thwarting of her aspirations because she was a woman.[104] Missing from her sense of herself as an advanced woman was any feeling of identification with or responsibility for other women. She was profoundly linked to her mother, of course, but in her mind, the two of them were unique, superior creatures. She had little patience for the world of women as it was; Elizabeth had been the same as a young woman. Eventually Harriot would acquire a more generous identification with other women, along with her own sobering experiences of discrimination, disappointment, and prejudice. But always at her core remained this equation of womanhood with strength and behind it a tendency to split women's humanity into mutually exclusive classes of powerful and powerless, the former having the ability and obligation to care for the latter.[105]

In 1874, Harriot began the regular collegiate course, along with sixty-five other young women. Her first year, she took Latin, modern language (she chose German), mathematics, and literature. During her sophomore year, her grades started to improve, and she began to develop an interest in science, beginning with physiology and zoology. The turning point in her education came her junior year when she enrolled in Maria Mitchell's astronomy course, like so many other Vassar students, and came out with straight A's.[106] Mitchell was a great teacher and "an inspiring personality," the ideal role model for Harriot at this point.[107] She was an educator, committed less to the collectivity of women than to each student as an individual, determined to encourage their aspirations rather than (to borrow a phrase from Lucy Stone) to "cultivate their discontent." She was a genuine female first (as a member of the American Academy of Arts and Sciences), and Harriot's time with her clarified the young woman's expectation that she too would break through the barriers of antiquated convention, living a life of equality with men.[108] According to Susan B. Anthony, "Maria Mitchell said of [Harriot] that she was the finest scholar in her classes."[109]

Of lasting importance for Harriot's life, Maria Mitchell was a scientist, one of the few and certainly the foremost woman in that small class of (mostly) men, who held out science's glittering promise of knowledge, power, and authority for Harriot's generation. The language of scientific method spoke directly to Harriot, and the opportunity to study with Mitchell was undoubtedly Vassar's greatest gift to her. Science offered the opportunity to cultivate a disciplined, educated mind, to train oneself to observe and record, to analyze and deduce, to make of one's intelligence an instrument of incomparable power, to learn the laws of the universe and illuminate the hidden order of experience. Harriot left Mitchell's laboratory committed to the scientific method and to further study, presumably in the physical or natural sciences. She graduated as one of the top students in her class. She also left with a lifelong avocation for astronomy and, especially in her later life, would travel around the world in search of eclipses, a wonderful, eccentric obsession in honor of her teacher.[110]

Harriot's second great discovery during her Vassar years was that she had a passion for politics. As she wrote of this period, "politics were the breath of my nostrils." She had been raised with a strong-minded awareness of reform causes, but during her years at Vassar she discovered politics in the more formal and male sense, the politics of party. Just about the time her last efforts to escape Vassar for Cornell were thwarted, she became absorbed in the tumultuous 1876 presidential campaign. Her father, now a journalist with the *New York Sun*, was "heart and soul" in favor of the party's candidate, Governor Samuel J. Tilden of New York. All summer long, Harriot read the newspapers avidly and "night after night we talked of Tilden's career." In the process she drew closer to her father than ever before. In her autobiography, her detailed and affectionate description of her relationship with him in this period stands out because she had so little to say about him elsewhere. Her willingness to be tutored in politics may have finally drawn her to his attention, and like a good Gilded Age son, she eagerly took up her father's partisan affiliation, thereafter describing herself as having been born and raised a loyal Democrat.[111]

Much later, Harriot told her biographer that she "got political training from her father, [a] journalist, who covered all the big conventions for the Sun and talked over issues and public affairs with his family."[112] This was a distortion. Even in the election of 1876, Elizabeth was thoroughly aware of what was at stake in the presidential contest and wrote regularly to her daughter about her political opinions.[113] During that summer, however, Elizabeth was traveling back and forth to Philadelphia, to protest the exclusion of women from the Centennial Exposition. Meanwhile, Harriot stayed in New York City sharing the partisan pleasures of the election with her father. In Harriot's mind, her mother's passion was women's rights and her father's was politics, and she was more interested in the latter. Eventually, Harriot's greatest accomplishment would be to unite these two: to take the feminism that she learned from her mother and the attention to party politics she learned from her father and weld them together to make woman suffrage an issue that political parties must confront.

Back at Vassar for her junior year, Harriot became a missionary for the salutary impact of partisan politics on women's collegiate education. She organized a mock election among the students. In their graduation yearbook, her classmates recalled the intensity of her support for the "cute and robust" Samuel J. Tilden, who nonetheless lost the mock election 256 to 71.[114] The outcome of the general election was more hotly contested and it took many months and much chicanery for the Republicans to secure the presidency. Given her father's belief that Tilden's candidacy represented true reform principles, Harriot was disillusioned—"my first big political disappointment"—when Tilden accepted without protest the backroom deal that gave Hayes the presidency. Hayes's victory meant that the Reconstruction era had drawn to a close, and with it the political verities of her parents' generation. Tilden "showed lack of grit and none of the courage my father had led me to believe our candidate had." Both Tilden and her father lost their heroic stature in her eyes, but her sense of herself as a political woman was firmly established.[115]

Harriot went on to found the Vassar Political Club because so many Vassar students "were not well informed on the topics of interest of the day." Her classmates appreciated her initiative and responded enthusiastically. They elected Harriot president not only of the Political Club but also of their senior class. One graduate of the class of 1878 remembered with particular fondness the club's requirement that members read the newspaper every day, which became a lifelong habit. The Vassar administration, in contrast, thought that student-run discussions of currency and finance were a bit unseemly and attempted to rein in the experiment. "The Constitution, readily adopted by the Club, disappeared in the deep recesses of the President's office," reported the class of 1878 yearbook, and the group reemerged with a more academic gloss as the Club of Political Science.[116]

Vassar provided one other discovery. There, Harriot finally broke out of her exclusive attachment to her family and became involved in her first major friendship, with the daughter of a Buffalo patent medicine manufacturer. Portentously enough, the girl had the same name and even came to use the same archaic spelling. Harriot Ransom may have been Harriet when she arrived at Vassar, and throughout her college years that is how her name was spelled in the school newspaper, which she edited. But by the time of graduation, she was spelling her name like her new friend, a profound token of their attachment, and Harriot Blatch refers to her with great affection in her memoirs as "she with the *o* in her name."[117] Harriot Ransom was more interested in things literary and aesthetic, Harriot Stanton in politics, economics, and history, but they learned from each other. When Harriot Stanton resigned as editor of the student paper, Harriot Ransom took her place; and when Harriot Ransom's literary club produced a dramatization of George Eliot's "The Spanish Gypsy," Harriot Stanton took the male lead (to excellent reviews).[118]

There is no evidence that this was a passionate involvement, which Harriot Stanton's distaste for girlish frivolity would have probably led her to regard as quite beneath her. This special friendship was focused instead on serious matters, the very stuff of college education: discussions about what made for great literature and art, how to arrive at genuine independence of thought, how to distinguish between scientific truth and mere opinion, what was the meaning of life, how should young women live it.[119] This profound and intense attachment lasted the rest of their lives, and getting to know Harriot Ransom was a revelation to Harriot Stanton.[120] She was beginning to understand that so long as her world was bounded by her family, no matter how exceptional it was, she would remain limited. "In my life so far," she wrote, "I have met but one broad mind, and that is Harriot [Ransom]'s."[121]

At this point in Harriot's life, when her interests and attachments outside her family were beginning to expand, it becomes possible to see more of the character of her relationship with her mother. Harriot's separation from her mother, despite its delays and hesitancies, combined with Elizabeth's increasingly empty nest to produce an anguished reaching out, a powerful, even manipulative attempt to hold on that must have been difficult for Harriot to resist. Elizabeth's letters to Harriot at college interlaced maternal claims with ingratiating apologies into a powerful mix. Harriot did not write home enough: "Did naughty mother scold her dear little one when she was tired and busy and ask her to write letters?"[122] Harriot's well-being was important to her mother because she was counting on it to sustain her in her own coming infirmity and dependence. "Take care of yourself for my sake," Elizabeth chided, "that in my old age you may be to me a comfort and support instead of an added load for me to carry."[123] "I have made up my mind to stick to you henceforth like a burr," her mother wrote. And in a cri de coeur that is striking for both its fierceness and its abstraction, "I must have something in human shape to love."[124] In the summer of 1878, Margaret, who had lived at home after graduation, announced her intention to marry Frank Lawrence of Omaha, and Elizabeth's protestations of love to Harriot became desperate. "There has awakened in my soul an unspeakable tenderness for you," she wrote soon after Margaret left, in one of her most passionate letters. "It is a blessed thing to love somebody, and I know no other being more worthy of love than you, my precious child. You are altogether lovely to me."[125]

Harriot graduated from Vassar in June 1878. By the end of her years there, she was willing to acknowledge that although America's venerable universities "with their accumulation of wealth and tradition" were still barred to women, Vassar had been a "good institution" that had made it possible for her to get a fine higher education.[126] According to Margaret, President Raymond was extravagant in his praise for Harriot, telling her mother that he had "rarely ever come in contact with such a clear, thinking, active, brilliant mind."[127] Her classmates acknowledged her superiority with a more ironic edge. Their yearbook predicted that "our most worthy president, Miss Stanton . . . in 1880 [would be] nominated to the Presidency by the Great Independent Party" and would forthwith be elected first woman president of the United States, handily overcoming "all prejudice in regard to sex." She would be known as "the Friend of the Laboring Man" and renowned for her other liberal principles, among which, however, women's rights was not mentioned. In a dramatic twist of fate, the prediction went on, President Stanton would turn over her office to Samuel Tilden, because she was so selfless as well as so smitten with him. She would end her days in a position fitting to her imperial bearing, as queen of the Sandwich Islands, where she would pursue her studies with quiet dignity.[128]

Harriot was not quite as sure as her classmates where her path lay. The problem that now faced her, as it did all first-generation college women, was what to do with her education. Together she and her mother devised a plan. She would continue the training in public speaking she had begun at college, and then join her mother on the lyceum circuit "to permit us to enjoy the infinite pleasure of traveling together the remainder of my days."[129] This plan met Elizabeth's needs far better than it did Harriot's. A future of mother and daughter traveling and speaking together reversed the psychological direction that Harriot had started to travel away from Elizabeth. A career as a lyceum lecturer might permit Harriot to establish her economic autonomy, but it was hardly likely to strengthen her psychological independence. Both her parents were famous for their oratorical abilities, and it did not escape notice that Harriot was about to follow them into the family business.[130]

In the fall of 1878, Harriot enrolled in the Boston School of Oratory. There she learned skills—how to "throw" her voice across a large hall, for instance—that later made her such an effective public speaker.[131] Elizabeth became closely involved in her daughter's preparation for her career. She wrote letters to old Boston friends, some of whom she had not been in contact with since the 1869 split in the suffrage movement, asking them to help her daughter.[132] She confused her daughter's prospects and her own, experiencing uncharacteristic bouts of insecurity about her own limitations as a public speaker. "I want you to be thoroughly prepared before making your debut so that you may feel satisfied with your own work," she wrote to Harriot. "I suffer the miserable feeling all the time of condemnation of my own efforts."[133] She was torn between having Harriot out on the lecture circuit with her and making sure that Harriot was perfectly trained for her new career. If Harriot decided to take a second year of study in Boston, Elizabeth intended to spend the winter with her there.[134] At last, in July 1879, reform newspapers carried an announcement that "Miss Harriet [sic] Eaton Stanton, daughter of Elizabeth Cady Stanton, will make her debut on the lyceum platform the coming season."[135]

These initial efforts to launch a career as a professional orator were short-lived.[136] Harriot prepared only one lecture, on Edmund Burke's political thought. This was an odd choice for the much-anticipated daughter of American reformers. By choosing to speak on the great originating voice of British conservatism, Harriot dramatically indicated her intention to go her own intellectual and political route. Ever so gently, the notices in one Iowa town suggested that Miss Stanton's selection of a topic was, "under the circumstances, a mistake."[137] In addition, unlike her mother, who had always been drawn to the romance of pioneer life, Harriot did not like traveling under the grueling conditions forced on a western lyceum lecturer.[138] Perhaps most unpleasantly, comparisons between mother and daughter were inevitable, and did not favor Harriot. Newspaper reports complimented her formal oratorical manner, her ability to speak without notes, and her "sweet and musical" voice and dramatic hand gestures, but were primarily charmed by the idea of a famous mother and debuting daughter on the same stage.[139] Harriot would be a great speaker—someday—but the audience's affection was for the present focused on Elizabeth. Many years later, Harriot thought that audiences preferred Elizabeth because she was older and because unlike her mother, who spoke on "women's issues," she chose to speak on "political topics."[140]

Harriot's first season as a lyceum speaker was her last. Elizabeth ended the 1879–80 season exhausted and ill, and, no longer buoyed by the prospect of her daughter traveling with her, also retired from the circuit.[141] There is no record of what Elizabeth's feelings were about this disappointment, but we do know that Susan B. Anthony put almost as much transcendent hope as her friend into Harriot's apprenticeship as a public speaker. "I did so wish dear Hattie were with us, that we might have seen & felt that we had a new force consecrated to our movement, grander & greater than any who have ever yet planted themselves on our platform," Anthony wrote dejectedly to Margaret. Women's rights was "the greatest reform of all time," Anthony declared, "and your mother's grand-children and great grand children, if not her own children, will thus regard it."[142]

In her recollections of her postgraduate years, Harriot made short shrift of her failed oratorical career. She explained the crisis of vocation she faced and the way she sought to resolve it with an anecdote which illuminates quite well that, at least at this point, the overwhelming example and overbearing expectation of her mother were her problem, not her solution. "Puzzled about the future," Harriot had decided to "call on two old friends of my parents with the object of extracting wise counsel from them." She visited Wendell Phillips, "one of the successful voyagers on the world's tempestuous seas." Phillips's response to her request "for hints as to a possible course" was the obvious one: "Why come to me? No one is better fitted to guide and direct than your mother." He meant, of course, not that he feared interfering with maternal privilege, but that Elizabeth Stanton had given a lifetime's thought to independence and autonomy for women. But Harriot needed an alternative to her mother's authority, not to be remanded to it. She felt put off, comparing herself to an eager pet dog kicked away as a pest. By contrast, William Lloyd Garrison gave her just the reception she wanted. He was warm, kind, and paternal. "Seize the first bit of work that offers," he suggested, "if it is honest and honorable. It will lead to something better."[143] This advice, flimsy as it might be, was just the counterauthority Harriot needed to strike off on her own.

As if on cue, Harriot was offered the chance to go to Germany as the paid companion and tutor for two wealthy American girls, friends of her family.[144] Theodore was about to return to France, where he had been living since graduation from Cornell, and she could sail with him. She quickly decided to go, and in May 1880 the two sailed for Europe.[145] Elizabeth wrote to Amelia Bloomer that she expected Harriot to "remain abroad two or three years to travel, read and study for her profession," which nonetheless remained to be identified, "unless," she worried, "caught in the trap of matrimony, from which Good Lord deliver her."[146] She sent Harriot off with a more positive charge. "I do want you to love and work for humanity, to go on with my work when I am done, to make life easier in any direction for those who come after you."[147] Harriot would spend the next two decades of her life in Europe, and when she returned, it would be on these terms but also on her own.

2

Vocation

In 1880, at the age of twenty-four, Harriot Stanton had before her the tasks of other "advanced" young women of her generation and class. As a dissenter from the conventional meanings of womanhood, she had to arrive at her own sense of being in the world; she had to solve the problem of vocation. This dilemma as it presented itself to women of her class was not so much a matter of economics as of occupation, belief, and lifestyle. What would be her life's work, her social contribution? In what values would she find transcendence and purpose? And what would she do about marriage and motherhood, sexuality and intimacy? Taken together, her answers would constitute her "self," and establish her relation to the more conventional members of her sex, her way of being a woman. Like others of her generation, these problems occupied the years immediately after college, and she had to leave home, leave America, to pursue them. Her decision to go to Europe was a way of beginning her more personal journey through unknown territory.

The highly individual choices she made had their equivalents in numerous other "new women's" lives. Jane Addams has given us an indelible portrait of the young college graduate gone abroad to find clues to a way of life that did not yet really exist for her sex. Each such story is deeply subjective and profoundly internal, and yet many have similar outlines. Jane Addams,

Florence Kelley, M. Carey Thomas, Mary Church, and Harriot Stanton all went to Europe in the early 1880s, after an initial unsuccessful attempt at finding a postgraduate vocation at home. They began their journeys traveling with relatives, and they each made attempts at continuing their education by participating in formal, postgraduate programs. Eventually, each woman returned to the United States, her own personal journey remade into a larger vision of women's possibilities.[1]

But Harriot confronted the dilemmas of her generation with a difference— her mother. She was one of the first second-generation feminists. As the daughter of an "advanced" woman, solving the problems of women's vocation did not mean turning away from her mother's heritage. On the contrary, her mother's charge to her was to rebel against and remake the common understandings of womanhood. At one level, this heritage undoubtedly gave her special resources with which to pursue the postcollege search for self. Because she was raised with great pride and confidence in her judgment and abilities, and encouraged to expect that she would make a mark on the world, forging an unconventional path for herself as a woman did not incur great psychological stress and was not accompanied by intense emotional conflict and periodic collapse. If anything, she was overprepared by her upbringing to challenge the norms of womanhood. There was no overt crisis in her young adulthood, as there was, for instance, in Addams's. Her mother's distinctive "aversion to weakness" in women, her insistence that both she and her daughters be always strong of mind and spirit, can be understood as a determination to guard against the dangers of collapse that dogged other female rebels of her generation.

Yet following in her mother's footsteps also presented Harriot with its own kind of obstacles in the search for self. Even in the most advanced arenas, confronting the most modern ideas, in pursuit of the most progressive goals, she always seemed to be reinforcing her mother's authority at the expense of her own. Her mother had placed on her a weighty charge to follow in her footsteps and become a social reformer and a fighter for women. As the final vindication of her own activist commitments, Elizabeth Stanton needed her daughter to share in them. This was a heavy claim, and it took Harriot a long time to find a way to meet it on her own terms.

Everything Harriot had done in preparation for sailing for Europe in May 1880 had an aspect of leaving her mother behind. In her brief stint as a professional lecturer, she had spoken on men and "politics," avoiding anything that smacked of "women's" topics. (Theodore had not needed to do this; he was already writing on the topic of women's rights.[2]) As "a young person in a fog" as to what to do with her life, she had sought out men for advice and could not understand when one of them suggested that "no one is better fitted to guide and direct than your mother."[3] And now she was leaving America, her motherland, behind. Young, self-confident, and sure she had never experienced discrimination by sex, a century later she would have been called a postfeminist, exhibiting in equal measure arrogance and naïveté about the condition of her sex. She thought she had all the world's options opened to her, but inclined strongly toward choices associated with men, to prove—to "society" and to herself—that she was truly an emancipated woman.

If anyone had a crisis on Harriot's departure, it was Elizabeth. Maggie had married two years before, and now Elizabeth's fifth and sixth children were leaving her as well. She wrote to Theodore and Harriot frequently, and her letters were seductive compendiums of political gossip, homey details, and effusive professions of maternal love. She urged her children to write lots of letters. "Letters at last!!!" she exclaimed in June, when she finally heard from them.[4] It was as if, now that her children had left, she felt more attached to them than she had all the years that she had had them in her home and was eager to be off on her own. She regretted "how much more I might have done for the perfect development of my children . . . [which] depressed me."[5] She spent her sixty-fifth birthday packing a trunk for Harriot and fantasizing that she could "jump in myself, and remain snugly ensconced in a little corner."[6]

Meanwhile, freshly arrived with her brother in Berlin, Harriot was enjoying herself thoroughly. She was a strikingly beautiful young woman, medium in height and slim in build; her lips were full, her eyebrows delicate and black, and her eyes a deep violet. In her autobiography, she wrote breezily of her social life in these years.[7] Like her mother's reminiscences of her own years between school and marriage, she recalled a busy and active social life full of mixed-sex entertainments, dancing, and flirting.

In June, her college friend, Harriot Ransom, joined her in Germany.[8] Their social life was organized around the American embassy in Berlin, which was headed by the newly appointed ambassador, Andrew D. White, former president of Cornell. (At this point, Theodore, a graduate of Cornell, was engaged to White's daughter Clara; within a few months however, they had concluded "that they did not love each other and parted in the most friendly relations."[9]) The two Harriots socialized with White's son, Fred, and they all partied and dined at the embassy and at the American Hotel in Berlin.[10] Along with the two young girls for whom she had responsibility, Harriot

Stanton remembered herself as the member of "a happy quartette just hovering round our very early twenties."[11]

In her post–World War I reminiscences, Harriot gave an antimilitary cast to many of her memories of Germany in the early 1880s, observing "how the fuss and feathers of national defense . . . sucked the lifeblood of the people." At the time, however, world wars and the deadly consequences of aggressive nationalism were still in the future. In 1880 she seemed to have been quite attracted by young, uniformed officers. Her friend Harriot Ransom eventually "fell in love with [and married] a Prussian officer." They particularly enjoyed turning the tables on potential beaus, pitting their cleverness and strength against the young men's foolishness and gullibility. Since "it was *verboten* of course for an officer, when in uniform to carry anything in public," the American girls devised "a game . . . to embarrass the poor slave" by flirtatiously asking an officer to hold their packages for extended periods. During these years, "Berlin [was] at its height. . . . [it] shone" and Harriot kept her affection for it for the rest of her life.[12]

The playful, social young woman presented in the memoirs contrasts with a more private and serious self that can be found in the diaries Harriot kept in these years. These diaries, among the few truly private documents that she preserved in her personal papers, make it possible to see something of her internal struggles to define her own perspective on the world and imagine her place in it.[13] She had already learned to keep her inner life far from the view of others. From her mother, she had absorbed the importance of distinguishing between "personal life" and its upheavals and public life and its standards.[14] Elizabeth Stanton's insistence on the privacy of emotions was reinforced by her condemnation of weakness and dependence, vulnerability and need, especially in women. Harriot learned both these lessons well. Her tendency to stand back from (or above) others was deeply ingrained. There was a kind of aloneness that surrounded her and acted as a barrier to others, and time has done nothing to erode it.

The diaries reveal Harriot as a reserved person, difficult to get to know and sometimes even to like. She was aware that others thought she was "affected" rather than "amiable."[15] She maintained an emotional distance between herself and other people; very few personal encounters and relationships make their way into the diary. Sure that she "should never have any use for such an endearing style," she never bothered to learn the informal, *du* German verb form. She criticized herself for this reserve but accepted it as her "nature," and nature, she believed, always followed its own laws.[16] Though harsh toward others, she was not a particularly severe critic of herself, and her reform ambitions were rarely turned inward, as they might have been if she had been a member of either an earlier, more religious, or a later, more psychological generation.

For these reasons of character, Harriot was well suited to undertake the disciplined, objective, unsentimental work of scientific observation and analysis that presented itself to the intellectually ambitious of her generation. In the diaries, we see her as an eager, young social scientist, approaching everything around her as a potential "fact," a tiny window onto the laws that ordered human life. Science promised her that the meaning of everything, no matter how unfamiliar, could be discerned, ordered, and brought under control. "A truly deep mind, when presented with a view of a strange custom or system, seizes upon it and seeks to understand it," she wrote of the standard to which she held herself. "Such a mind condemns nothing strange to it, whether that something be ancient or modern."[17] She approached everything she saw in Berlin—a visit to a giant locomotive factory, the wards and museum of the Charité lock-hospital, a drive through the city on Easter Sunday—with the same attitude: observe carefully, make distinctions, record all details, and use the information to draw conclusions about the larger structures and laws of society. "Think if there was some International Bureau of statistics," she wrote enthusiastically, "which made a point of collecting and arranging the rich treasures thus scattered through the world!"[18]

Harriot's scientific education had begun in Maria Mitchell's Vassar observatory. There she had been taught that all experience was coherent and orderly, organized around "inexorable law." It was the modern age's privilege and glory to discover these laws, to uncover and comprehend the order of the universe by the disciplined application of scientific method. At first, she aspired to be a scientist of the natural world. She adored Mitchell and retained a serious interest in astronomy all her life.[19] In her European diaries, she was repeatedly drawn to contemplation of the natural world, which spoke to her more profoundly than the human dramas around her. She especially appreciated nature's inexorable development, independent of intent or action, requiring neither intervention nor reform. At a private garden at Lucerne, she marveled at a natural geological formation which had been beautifully sculpted by centuries of erosion. "These stones, for better or worse, have fulfilled their destiny!" she wrote. "They have ground [down] because the law of their nature prescribed it, they did not measure truth by what it would lead to."[20] There is a wistfulness in this comment and an impatience with her inherited obligation to be a reformer, to intrude on what is to make it what ought to be.

Among the aspects of her mother's charge against which she especially struggled in these years was the problem of spiritual meaning. Harriot had been taught that a combination of scientific rationality and reform activism could and should take the place of religion as an uplifting faith, that it was only "sacred humanity" she should revere. Elizabeth had urged her children to join her in a "religion of good works in this life [rather] than a sentimental worship of some far away ideal."[21] However forward-looking this "religion of humanity" was for the mother, it was an inherited faith for the daughter. Elizabeth Stanton had forged her perspective in a struggle against the patriarchal authorities of her early life—her father and God the father. But to Harriot, the call to "worship mankind" represented the voice of parental authority. In part for this reason, her mother's faith offered Harriot few of the clues to meaning that she craved. Although the "religion of good works" was intended to resolve the conflict between the head and the heart, it did not fill the need for spiritual transcendence. While utopian visions of human perfection might be inspiring, they did not provide much balm for the soul in the contemplation of brutal social reality. "Work is worship!" Harriot wrote in one burst of hopeful resolution, but didn't that also imply that worship was work?[22] She longed for a more positive faith, something that she could maintain as an inspiration despite her powerful analytic and sociological impulses to master and control.

Wandering through Europe, the appreciation of and reverence for natural beauty provided Harriot with her moments of greatest peace and even the occasional experience of forgetting self. She "feasted her soul" on the dramatic mountains and lakes of northern Italy and Switzerland. "B[ellagio] is the most exquisite place I have yet seen," she wrote in her diary. "The sky was inky black, lighted now and then by sharp flashes of lightening [sic] and thunder rolled mighty peals from peak to peak."[23] But because this aesthetic reverence for nature was such a freely chosen and personal faith, not a conviction learned from and shared with a larger community, it was fragile. What Harriot called "the ideal" was always in danger of collapsing into the "real," at which point transcendence turned into disappointment. Mont Blanc, so sparklingly white at a distance, turned out to be gray and dirty under her feet.[24] The impulse to analyze always threatened to intrude. "When something pleases me deeply I do not want on paper to analyze it minutely," she admonished herself.[25] Yet even the experience of transcendence was grist for her scientific mill. Glorying in the "soul impression" produced in her by the sun flickering through trees on a drive outside of Paris, she felt compelled to "analyze the feeling."[26] This pull toward the transcendent was a spiritual longing that remained strong throughout her life.[27]

Elizabeth Stanton's "religion of humanity" worshiped the free and realized individual. Harriot modified it to focus on the progressive and orderly society. Without benefit of formal training, she was essentially making herself into a member of the first generation of social scientists. The shift from individual to society was an epistemological move made by her entire generation.[28] Influenced by the natural sciences, Harriot's late nineteenth-century cohort understood human society by analogy to a biological organism, complex yet coherent. In this model, the framework for human good was no longer simply the rights that accrued to individuals, but the orderly and harmonious functioning of the entire social organism. Social progress displaced individual perfection as a goal. Harriot's vision of a healthy, forward-looking humanity moving in conjunction with social law rather than against it emphasized productive industry, regular and orderly change, and accumulated wealth. Violence, revolution, disease, superstition—to Harriot these were all indications of social error.

Throughout her diary, Harriot's carefully cultivated powers of social observation were concentrated on differences of national character. After winter and spring in Berlin, she began to travel more widely. She observed and commented on German industry, Italian agriculture, Swiss village life, French religion, and American and English tourists. She not only differentiated peoples but ranked them in terms of those values which she believed to be absolute measures of human happiness and social progress. "That country is truly great which is industrious, intelligent, truthful, rich in science and literature, and will eventually be respected."[29] (Whether her own country met these standards had not fully been determined, and what she wrote or thought about Americans frequently had a defensive character to it.) As she moved farther south, she saw more dirt, poverty, and disease, which indicated social disorder and earned her disapproval rather than her sympathy. "I thought I had seen poverty and deformity in Berlin," she wrote when she visited Italy, "but Verona far surpasses it. I never saw so many dwarfs and other forms of terrible monstrosities."[30]

It does not take too much to see the fundamentally conservative quality of much of this way of thinking, and furthermore to imagine that it was in part a kind of rebellion against her mother's insistent radicalism. At this point in her life, there was little that was unconventional in Harriot's social judgments or in her comparisons between nationalities. The northern Protestant countries were superior to the southern Catholic ones. Middle-class people were superior to the poor. Strikes were bad; unrelenting industriousness was good. And inasmuch as social science encouraged such detailed attention to the varieties and differences of human beings, it was a fairly abstract move to proclaim the equality of such patently incomparable individuals. "Equivalence" was a better standard for social organization than "equality of power" because the proper goal was "a harmonious, organic society in which each man made his own particular contribution to the social good." Eventually this habit of making invidious national distinctions was tempered by more openly democratic convictions, but she always retained the traces of what was essentially a racialized way of thinking. In her European travels, she was especially contemptuous of Catholics and Jews.[31]

The one arena with respect to which Harriot's early thinking about social organization was not conventional and conservative, but critical and disruptive, concerned that other great physical and cultural division of humanity, sex. The difference of sex was a central preoccupation of social science, a category that, like that of nation, was both rooted in the biological and inclined to the political. Evidence of the essential quality of the male/female distinction was everywhere.[32] Like most of her generation, Harriot took the "fact" of sexual difference for granted. "Madame de Barrau and I had a long discussion today on sex, woman's position, etc.," Harriot wrote of a meeting with the French women's rights advocate who would eventually become Theodore's mother-in-law. "We utterly disagree. She believes sex is but an accidental physical phenomenon. That the minds of men and women are exactly identical."[33]

Harriot's view that the difference of sex was not "accidental" followed her mother's current way of thinking. Elizabeth Stanton had once been one of the great proponents of the similarity of the sexes in all that mattered, but she had come to believe that the difference of sex was a fundamental principle, a characteristic of soul and spirit and not merely of the body's outer shell.[34] Many of the sociological observations that Harriot recorded in her diaries focused on the difference that sex made. Although she rejected "theories" of womanhood, preferring observations and evidence, she seems to have been looking for difference. She recorded what men and women looked like, what work each did in every country she visited, how physical disease manifested itself differently in male and female bodies. "Dr. Gnauch told me that . . . they had more men than women patients in the Insane Department, and that the men were more violent," she wrote after her tour of the lock-hospital in Berlin. "That the men were more interesting for they would express they [sic] ideas more readily, and that their delusions were far more plastic."[35] Differences of race were inflected by and sometimes overwhelmed by distinctions of sex: Jewish women "have not the characteristic features of their race" while "the men are universally ill favored. This appears an argument for the theory that characteristics run in the lines of sex."[36] While

Harriot believed that the distinction of sex was universal, she did not assume that the content of that distinction was constant. Women's role and women's work, she observed as she traveled about Europe, varied by local custom and economic condition.[37]

Already at this early stage, Harriot was grappling with a crucial dilemma in thinking about sex: how to resist the tendency of social science to reason from the omnipresence of sex difference to a "social law" of women's subordination. On the one hand, she accepted many of the basic premises of social science about sex difference. She believed that women showed less variation from the human average than men; that the more developed a society, the greater distinction it showed between male and female; that evolutionary processes worked by sexual selection, which affected men and women differently; and that a highly elaborate division of labor, including sexual division, correlated with productivity and wealth. She was a thoroughgoing social evolutionist. On the other hand, as we have seen, she had completed her college education with confident and expansive notions of women's capacity. In her diary, she noted Percy Bysshe Shelley's rhetorical challenge: "Can man be free if woman be a slave?"[38] Her mother, a student and admirer of the pioneering scientists of society, had already questioned the "narrow" teachings of social science on women's status.[39] Harriot would eventually arrive at the same conclusion and make herself part of a revisionist effort to demonstrate that both biological evolution and social progress favored women's achievement and an enlargement of their social role.[40]

For the moment, she noted in her diaries the contradictory scientific evidence on women's and men's relative status. From an article in the September 1881 issue of the *Revue scientifique anthropologie*, she took pages of notes on the innumerable physical indications that allegedly demonstrated female inferiority: "Women eat like children . . . breathing is more intense in man   the organs are more normally developed in males . . . woman has larger left shoulder blade than right, as all inferior races. . . . Woman has the foot flatter—sign of inferiority."[41] Presumably she found many of these claims ludicrous and preferred another set of contrasts, also recorded in her diary, that "in point of Evolution, women are more differentiated, more developed than men," though the evidence for this side was equally absurd: "One instance, less hair on body."[42]

Nowhere was the task of reconciling social science thinking about the fundamental importance of sex difference with the inclusion of women in humanity's future progress and social development more challenging than with respect to sexual passion. Questions about the origins and consequences of sexual desire reintroduced concerns about the individual to challenge her generation's single-minded focus on society. Late nineteenth-century notions of sexual difference did not usually allow much room for female sexual passion. On the contrary, women's elevation above sexuality, and men's irresistible sexual drive, were among the more venerable bases of building systems of sexual distinction. By upbringing, observation, and personal experience, Harriot subscribed to the belief that sexual passion was a fact of nature, a good and true thing with its own laws, and that this applied to women as well as to men. Reinforcing this view was scientific thinking which elevated the status of human sexuality, once dismissed as the lower, less godly, and more animalistic part of the human condition, into a healthy and natural passion, the foundation of biological evolution and social progress. In her diaries, Harriot recorded several incidents related to her by scientific experts that "proved" that the "innate instincts of passion in mankind" were equally powerful for women and for men.[43]

And yet she knew well enough that women's experience with strong sexual love could easily lead them into the limited, traditional fate of their sex, confined to domesticity and maternity. This was a road of which she was already wary. She knew that youthful passion did not last a lifetime, but that bad marriages did, and that they were particularly destructive to women. Her mother, forever the romantic, believed that a young person about to marry should revere to the point of worship his or her intended. Apparently, Elizabeth no longer felt this way about her own husband and mourned the absence of a "son of Adam" in her own life she could worship.[44] In fact, she had much less confidence that her daughters would enjoy the transcendence of true conjugal love than that her sons would. She especially worried that Harriot, the daughter she thought had skill and ambition enough to undertake a successful professional life, would become "caught in the trap of matrimony, from which Good Lord deliver her."[45]

As a result, Harriot noted in the first pages of her diary that she had "felt for some time that I should rather ought to promise myself not to marry. That marriage would destroy my usefulness." She had "seen and heard to [sic] much of life, to be blind to the fact that our young ideas, dreams of love cannot last. That is those dreams of earthly bliss, of everlasting beauty, those mere physical attractions, which do indeed make up the thoughts and beliefs of most youth."[46] But this stern resolution was being tried by the romantic encounters she was beginning to have, now that she was away from the supervision of parents and teachers. She began her diary with thoughts on a serious affair of the heart. "I am beginning to know another human-soul, and a man's soul. And now I am beginning to see myself in truer lights." She went on to speculate about physical passion. "Reason can tell you you ought to feel enthusiasm," she wrote, "your body can make you feel it."[47] How was she to negotiate between her growing appreciation for and experiences of the naturalness of female sexuality and her well-grounded fear of the conjugal slavery to which it could lead in women's lives?

Given the romantic individualism with which she had been raised, she first turned to the writings of Ralph Waldo Emerson for some wisdom on the subject. She liked what he had to say in his "Essay on Love": from the genuine admiration of character, a truly lasting union could be formed. "Somewhere for me there is . . . a counterpart," she wrote, "and . . . in time we shall meet." When she found her "elect soul," she trusted that her feelings would be not only strong but enduring, an ideal and everlasting thing that she could worship safely, like the natural beauty she found so soul-stirring in her travels. She paraphrased Emerson's "Essay on Love": "When character begins to be admired, then the true palace of beauty is approached."[48]

Like so many other venerable thinkers to whom she turned, however, Emerson seemed to her to be thinking only of men. Women were not part of the dilemmas he sought to resolve or the solutions he had to offer. "To him *soul* is sexless," Harriot noted. "He deems all our experiences here a training for 'Love that knows not sex.' This seems an infinity from the truth." In a philosophical system in which love was so disembodied, she sensed that women could easily be left behind, relegated to the mundane world of intercourse, pregnancy, and childbirth, while men found uplifting, spiritual connection with each other. As far as Harriot was concerned, Emerson read women out of the possibilities of lasting love, relegating them to the realm of ephemeral physical experience. As an alternative, she turned to William F. Channing, the rogue, second-generation transcendentalist who was a favorite of her mother's, and recorded what he had to say about human sexual love: it was "a capacity infinitely beautiful and varied growing out of the bisecting of humanity, which we call sex." Thus the difference between women and men formed the basis for sexual passion, for the human aspiration for transcendent love, and ultimately for religion itself.[49]

A "soul union," a perfect unity of the magnetic opposites of masculine and feminine, provided the ideal soil for creative genius: this was the belief of pioneering social scientists such as Auguste Comte, the founder of positivism, who made of his distant, unrequited love object the wellspring of his social vision and of "the religion of humanity" he predicted social science could eventually become. Similarly John Stuart Mill credited Harriet Taylor with the inspiration for his best ideas.[50] Harriot also believed in the intellectual inspiration of a true union. "Is it not the union of two minds which brings distinction? Every great man, when his inner life is revealed, proved to have been inspired by a woman. Success is the fruit of intellectual sex union," she observed. Yet once again, she faced the problem of masculine bias, of inequality in a system that otherwise promised such beautiful sexual symmetry. "Why have not more women been distinguished?" she asked herself. Because women were limited to being the wives of great creators, rather than being creators themselves. "To women as a whole such inspiration is denied. Society scoffs [at] the man who is absorbed by a feminine intellect. Society is so constituted that every man feels a hesitation if not aversion to inspiring a woman . . . to work in intellectual life." She railed against such a fate. She had no intention of becoming some man's muse. George Eliot "had this male inspirer"; so would she![51] So she waited and hoped that she would meet her "elect soul," and that he would be someone who could allow her to love, to be loved, to marry, and yet to continue on the path of "larger usefulness" for which she was destined and for which she was preparing herself.

Harriot spent the beginning of her second year in Europe traveling south and west of Berlin, finally arriving in Paris, where her brother was now living. After breaking off his engagement with Clara White in the winter of 1881, Theodore had left Berlin for Paris. Two things drew him there: a plan for a book on the varieties of modern French radicalism and a romance with Marguerite Berry, daughter of a freethinking French Protestant family. The book eventually appeared as the first English-language study of the women's rights movement in Europe. In May 1881 Theodore and Marguerite were married.[52]

Harriot came from Berlin for the wedding, where she met Marguerite's unique family. This included not only Gabriel Berry, a French civil servant, his wife and children, but the de Barrau family, with whom the Berrys had been living for many years. This nineteenth-century version of a blended family was built around the friendship of Mesdames Berry and de Barrau and their joint commitment to giving their children the most advanced education possible. Mesdames Berry and de Barrau were, in Harriot's words, "close friends and wonderfully well-suited counterparts for years, the former managing the domestic menage, and the latter promulgating the theories and plans of education." They lived together in what Harriot described as a "charming, spacious villa buried in a large garden" in Paris. Here she found much that was wonderfully familiar: a female-led (though not male-absent) household, the close, almost conjugal relationship between the two women, and the expectation that every family member, children included, would voice and defend "an individual point of view." "The family atmosphere carried me back to my own home."[53]

Harriot was particularly drawn to Caroline de Barrau, whom she described as "an exceptional daughter of France of the aristocratic, protestant element."[54] Madame de Barrau was the virtual head of the household and the first person important enough to Harriot to become a distinctive figure in her European diaries. From a wealthy, landed Protestant family, de Barrau was both strongly prorepublican and elitist, a perfect role model for Harriot in these years, a more conservative variant on her own mother. When Harriot came back to Paris in the summer, the Berrys had gone south and she spent her time with Madame de Barrau. They went sight-seeing in and around Paris together, and had numerous discussions about women's rights, women's education, and the future of republicanism.

Madame de Barrau was particularly concerned with the higher education of women. Working on the theory that the prohibition of women in French public universities was more customary than codified, she and other French women's rights activists pushed for the integration of higher education by simply moving to enroll adequately prepared women for university study. Her daughter, Emilie, along with other young women "intellectually prepared for work of university grade, appeared at the proper time and place for enrollment" and succeeded in being admitted to the study of medicine at the University of Paris.

As she rode about Paris with Madame de Barrau, Harriot listened to the Frenchwoman's proposal that she do the same in her own field of social science. "It was during this visit in Paris that Madame de Barrau broached the idea that . . . I should return for the winter to study economics at the famous School of Political Economy" in Paris.[55] The Ecole Libre des Sciences Politiques had been established a decade before and seemed the perfect institution for Harriot to carry out what she had come to Europe to accomplish: to train herself for her future vocation. The school was self-consciously liberal and antirevolutionary, dedicated to the "scientific" study of social affairs, focused on history and political economy, and committed to the preparation of a politically independent, educated elite able to administer a modern state.[56] Harriot had been in Europe for more than a year without undertaking any truly systematic study; Madame de Barrau's proposal came as a blessed solution to her vocational dilemma.

Harriot agreed to the plan, though not without some final internal struggle between her spiritual and her scientific impulses. She went off to the de Barrau estate in southern France for a late summer holiday to think about her future. A second volume of her diary, begun at this time, records some of this conflict. On the one hand, she believed that the human mind represented a "vast power," one that could control Nature. "Mind is eternal," she wrote, "all powerful enough to make itself immortal." On the other hand, it seemed to her that she was happier, more at peace, without the compulsion to bring everything under her personal control, in the contemplation of the natural world. "I think the more I study mystery I notice it," she wrote. "I bend my knee at the shrine of Beauty, Love, Emotion, Intuition," she wrote in the next entry.[57] Even so, she knew that her future lay with the knowable, not the unknown, that to cede power over human affairs to a greater force, to live her life in contemplation of complexity rather than in energetic, activist interventions to improve human affairs, was too great a break with her heritage. She scratched out the sentences worshiping mystery and left only those praising mind.

There was more than a little irony here: the path she was choosing was the forward-looking way of freedom, and yet she was deeply constrained by her own past in choosing it. Perhaps this is why she ended this section of her diary with an energetic, almost angry condemnation of her upbringing for its intellectual and moral limits. "A mind cultivated in the widest regions, educated in a liberal, radical household, exceedingly free upon the questions of the day," she wrote in what stands as an indictment of her own childhood, "such a mind, according to my view, may be lamentably narrow." From now on, she was determined to become a truly broad-minded person, unencumbered by past or place. Her home would be nothing less than the whole world. "Such a mind is cosmopolitan, is impartial, it has no country, it suffers from no prejudices."[58]

If the decision to apply to the Ecole Libre des Sciences Politiques was a conflicted one for Harriot, how much more painful it must have been when she came back to Paris in the fall, only to learn that she had been denied admission.[59] The school, which was a private institution and therefore not amenable to the strategies used to integrate public universities, rejected her application. (Not until the 1930s did it admit women.[60]) This was a turning point for Harriot's own women's rights convictions. Until this time, she had claimed that she had never experienced discrimination, had been raised equally with her brothers, and had received an education as good as any man's. "It is not until lately that I have felt the crime of my womanhood," she told a women's rights meeting in America a year later.[61]

The blow was intensified by a call from America to return home to take care of her ailing mother.[62] Harriot's various accounts suggest her conflicting responses to this summons back to her mother's side at a time when her independent future was particularly unclear. On the one hand, the obligation to return home allowed her at least a temporary escape from her defeat in France. She attributed the rejection of her application to the shallow traditions of liberty and republicanism in France, and found refuge from the assaults against her sex in her revived identification as an American. Describing her trip home for a American woman suffrage audience soon after, she turned it from a humiliating retreat into a triumphant return. "And now this ship, baffling the February storm, was sweeping nearer the land where the people reign," she wrote melodramatically. "My heart beat high as I thought it was in my native country where women were free, more honored than in any nation in the world. As I stood on the deck, the strong sea-wind blowing wildly about me, and the ocean bearing on its heart-wave mountains, visions of the grandeur of the nation lying off beyond the western horizon, rose before me. And it was a proud heart that cried—'My Country!' "[63]

On the other hand, the call to return home was what Jane Addams, rebelling against a similar threat to her independence, called "the family claim."[64] The language Harriot used to describe this episode in her autobiography suggests that she was being deprived of control of her own life and that she resented it. "A summons came to return to America," she wrote. "It was quite definitely stated that I would be expected by February, 1882." It was, she noted, a "disappointment."[65]

Clearly, it was time to make a life for herself that could compete with the pull of her mother. On board ship, she met an attractive, thirty-year-old Englishman, William Henry Blatch, Jr., "Harry" to his friends. He was going to the United States on business for his father, who managed a brewery on the outskirts of London. As it turned out, he was not much of a businessman, or even a reformer. Whether or not Harry was the "elect soul" she had longed for, the physical attraction between them was immediate and strong. In her memoirs, she described her first sight of Harry Blatch, a beautiful and passive object emerging into her gaze: "A Scotch plaid, rolled like a huge chrysalis, had rested day by day on one of the settees in the companion-way off the forward deck. Suddenly one evening the chrysalis split open and out stepped a tall, dark Englishman."[66] The only record we have of Harry's reaction to the meeting is from Harriot. Brought to her side by a game of whist, he was "determined to stay where fate had placed him, at my right hand. Later when we met in the South of France, he told me he was not thinking of the game of whist at all, but of the game of life."[67]

On arrival in New York, Harriot stopped to visit with her aunts and then proceeded on to Tenafly, where she found her mother exhausted and sick.

For some time, Elizabeth Stanton and Susan Anthony had been working on their monumental compendium, *History of Woman Suffrage*. Under the pressure of this task, Elizabeth's usually stalwart constitution had given way. In 1880 she had had pneumonia, but had rallied to continue her work. After the first volume of the *History* was published in May, she had become so ill that Theodore had posted a notice in the women's rights press to discourage additional demands on her.[68] Now Harriot found her saddled with the major responsibility of the second volume, because Anthony, impatient with the desk-bound life of the historian, was away from Tenafly attending the conventions and meetings she loved.[69]

Added to this burden were problems with the content of the *History*. Volume 2 covered the late 1860s, during which time the woman suffrage movement had split into two opposing factions—Stanton and Anthony's National Woman Suffrage Association, and the American Woman Suffrage Association, headed by Lucy Stone and Henry Blackwell. How were dispassionate chroniclers, which is how the editors of the *History* advertised themselves, to portray the political and historical claims of their rivals for leadership of the suffrage movement? The dozen years since the split had only ripened the hostility between Anthony and Stone. Anthony did not want to legitimate the American Association by including it in her *History*, and Stone did not want to legitimate the *History* by allowing her organization to be included. In an effort to bypass the antagonism between Anthony and Stone, Stanton asked Julia Ward Howe, one of the leading figures in the American Association, if she would write an account of its history, but Howe declined. This not only reignited Anthony's fury but enraged Stanton, who now joined fully in her partner's resentment.[70]

When Harriot got to her mother's house in New Jersey in early March, her assigned task was to read proof as it came back from the printer. Instead, she proposed that she concentrate on writing an account of the American Association. She pointed out that the editors had advertised that "the book was to be a history of the suffrage movement and not merely of the National Woman Suffrage Association." "I contended that since the two associations were and had been in an internecine war," she recalled, "it would certainly do credit to the authors if they rose above the roar of battle and gave space for a record of the work of their antagonists." Elizabeth basically supported this proposal, while "Miss Anthony was more flatfooted," as Harriot remembered it.[71] According to Anthony's biographer, Susan paid Harriot a one hundred–dollar fee only because Elizabeth insisted; she "did not want to do it" because she thought Harriot had "'leaned over backward' in her desire to be fair."[72]

In her long, retrospective account of her work on the *History*, Harriot complained that compiling the chapter was "a dog's life," and that since she was not listed as the author but only, in a footnote, as the "compiler," the task was "thankless" to boot. But the project served her in several ways. Instead of just reading proof, she had her own creative work. Moreover it was a way to help and protect her mother—by "ward[ing] off criticism" of the *History*—yet doing so on her own terms. Finally, it may have helped her in her search for independence to act as the spokeswoman for the people she had been raised to regard as "the enemy." She emphasized the effort it took to lift herself above her inherited biases, to give a fair and friendly account of the "association which was violently in opposition to the body into which I had been born and bred." She was on her own in this project. "My mother, though under the same roof as me . . . was to be consulted 'at no point.'" The chapter was "my responsibility, and mine alone."[73]

The finished essay, sixty thousand words and nearly 120 pages, was included as the final chapter in volume 2 of the *History of Woman Suffrage*. Harriot worked from journals published by the American Association to give the society's own account of its history. Her presence in the chapter was minimized not only by her method but by the way that the chapter was typeset, so as to obscure the distinction between the editor's words and those of the sources she extracted. Harriot made her selections carefully, to stress the founding and first years of the American Association and early efforts to unite the two organizations. She may have found more to appreciate in the American Association than she anticipated. Several of the American stalwarts—Antoinette Brown Blackwell, Thomas Wentworth Higginson, Phoebe Hanaford, and Julia Ward Howe—were early exponents of the kind of organic, social science arguments that she herself found so compelling.[74]

Nonetheless, the entire episode of completing the second volume of the *History* became a battle between Anthony and Stanton's children for their mother's loyalty during her remaining years. Harriot blamed Anthony for her mother's exhaustion. Years later, she told her mother's biographer that it was during those weeks of working on the *History* that she had first begun to have her doubts about Anthony's reputation for great executive ability and total devotion to the cause.[75] Anthony was defensive about the Stanton children's charge that work on the *History* was making their mother sick. On the contrary, she insisted, Elizabeth "suffered more from her fear that she should never finish the History than from the thought of parting with all her friends."[76] In the end, though, Elizabeth decided her own fate. More than anything she was tired of Anthony's increasingly limited focus on woman suffrage.[77] Her energetic mind was outrunning her large and lumbering body. She wanted to think about religion, sexuality, and the origins of women's subordination, and to this end her daughter's company and interests suited her much better. She was determined to live her last years with her family, not, as Anthony had chosen, in the service of her cause.

On May 27, 1882, Elizabeth and Harriot sailed for Bordeaux. Anthony arranged for "a large number of the friends" to give her partner an elaborate farewell, perhaps sensing that this marked the end of an era in their collaboration.[78] Elizabeth also seemed to regard the voyage with foreboding. She spent the first night at sea "thinking over everything that was painful in my whole life, and imagining all the different calamities that might befall my family in my absence."[79] Harriot alone was genuinely happy with the arrangement. In her memoirs, she wrote about "the joy of eloping with my mother."[80] This curious turn of phrase suggests her eager anticipation of a prolonged intimacy with her mother, the beginning of a new relationship in which her mother was joining her in her life rather than vice versa. The phrase also suggests some association between marriage and the mother-daughter bond in Harriot's mind, a sense that they were either linked or counterposed, or both.

If the steamer back to Europe was an elopement, the next few months were a honeymoon. Harriot and Elizabeth were to summer in the south of France, near the Berry estate. Elizabeth was to relax, recuperate, and spend time with her first grandchild, Theodore's daughter, Lizette. Harriot arranged to study French and mathematics at the University of Toulouse. They took rooms together at the Convent de la Sagesse, near the university. For centuries, the convent had housed renegade women of the elite. Elizabeth wrote that the convent's garden, "with its big trees, clean gravel paths, and cool shade, was the most delightful spot."[81] "We have large pleasant rooms in the second story of the main building of the convent, with two spacious French windows in each," she wrote. "After dinner, we walk in the garden, where the birds sing and the fountains play, or we sit in our room, I mending stockings while Hattie reads Emerson aloud."[82]

Harriot was Elizabeth's major companion in their first weeks at La Sagesse. By contrast, a group of young nuns figures much more prominently in Harriot's diary than her mother does, serving as a temporary antidote to her mother's presence and power, a kind of secret rebelling against her maternal legacy. Harriot was drawn to the sisters by their peaceful bearing and their girlish camaraderie. "The very garb of the sisters was suggestive of peace and unity," Harriot recalled. "When gathered in a circle in the shade of one of the many huge trees, busy with their sewing and reading, they reminded me of soft-colored, white-hooded moths that had alighted for rest in some peaceful nook."[83] The nuns took her with them as they went through their devotions, and despite her well-developed prejudice against Catholicism, she allowed them to draw her into the mystery of unquestioning belief which was at the core of their lives. Her diary entries suggest that this temporary sojourn through the peaceful, female-centered world of the sisters of La Sagesse was a brief and partial vacation from the intellectually vigorous life she had been raised to lead.

Eventually, however, she ended her flirtation with Catholicism. The very contentment that Catholicism produced made her suspicious of it. Catholicism "makes you light-hearted and light headed," Harriot wrote, "but it also makes you fickle and negligent." Above all, Catholicism "makes you incapable of feeling your moral degradation," which was the feeling that she counted on to fuel her chosen vocation.[84] Harriot might fantasize about the peaceful routine of the nuns, but she was destined to think, act, and change the world, not to sew, chat, and pray.[85] In her memoirs, Harriot recalled the presence in Toulouse of several men who "prevented my running any risk of being swept into the spinsterhood of the nuns or the Catholicism of the convent." "Besides," she added coyly, "I was awaiting the visit of a young Englishman, who was to change the immediate current of my life."[86] From the time that Harry Blatch came to visit her in Toulouse in September 1882, events moved quickly toward marriage. In her memoirs, holding back from any acknowledgment of choice, passion, or agency, she wrote only of "the natural ebb and flow of life's tides" that moved her from France to England and, as if without any will, toward marriage.[87] The diaries cease here.

In October 1882, mother and daughter arrived in England and plunged into preparations for Harriot's marriage to Harry Blatch. Both Harriot and Elizabeth wanted the ceremony to be performed by an American.[88] Unlike Theodore, whose citizenship was unaffected by becoming the husband of a French citizen, Harriot was going to lose her status as an American citizen by becoming the wife of an Englishman, the consequences of which would haunt her for most of her life.[89] Not allowing herself to be married within the Church of England was the first of many ways during the twenty-six years of her marriage that she tried to resist this fate and to retain her identity as an American. Elizabeth wanted to have the ceremony performed jointly by two American clerics residing in London, her dear old friend and confidante, William Henry Channing, and Moncure Conway, a radical Unitarian whose criticisms of Christianity were much like her own. But Channing refused to cooperate with Conway, whom he considered too "latitudinarian" and dismissive of the sacramental elements of marriage.[90]

With the resolution of this crisis pending and the wedding date only two weeks away, Elizabeth took a few days out to attend a women's rights convention in Glasgow.[91] Harriot seized the opportunity to assume charge of her own wedding. She wrote to Moncure Conway that Channing's refusal to cooperate with him "shows me that Dr. Channing is more orthodox than I had supposed." She, too, considered marriage a "holy sacrament," but to her that sacredness came not from divine blessing but from "the real aspirations of living men and women." Therefore, her preference was for Conway to perform the ceremony. "On my wedding day of all days, I feel I must be wholly true, and would I be that if I had invoked the blessings of a Being in whom I have no belief?" She was fighting not only against a Christian belief that she did not share, but against her mother's authority. "What my Mother's sentiments would be, I do not know, [or] if her convictions differ from mine," she wrote to Conway, "but in this matter, my veracity not my Mother's is in question."[92]

Away from Harriot, Elizabeth was also thinking about marriage. The last time she had been in Great Britain had been forty years before, at the beginning of her own conjugal life, with its mixed pleasures and disappointments. She shared with a friend her concerns about losing her daughter. "I do feel for you," the friend wrote back, "and yet rejoice when I remember what you told me of your son-in-law—that he is worthy to be your daughter's husband and your son."[93] Elizabeth's misgivings were less about Harry Blatch than about marriage itself and what it would do to her relationship with her daughter. When Theodore married, Elizabeth had been unambivalent in her delight. To Marguerite Berry, she had written that her own two daughters had left home, "so I am counting on all the pretty girls my boys will bring to fill their places."[94] By contrast, she feared that Harriot's marriage would deprive her of a daughter and her closest companion rather than bring her a son. For Elizabeth the wedding was an ending, rather than a beginning, and her account of it is awash with backward looks and morbid associations.[95]

On her return to London, Elizabeth made one last futile effort to reconcile Conway and Channing, which delayed the wedding two days.[96] Finally, on November 15, Harriot and Henry were married in the Portland Street Chapel, with Elizabeth's choice of clergy, William Henry Channing, officiating.[97] Harry's large family was there, as were many of Elizabeth's friends and associates. Harriot's closest friend, Harriot Ransom, who had recently married a Prussian officer named Arthur Milinowski, was pregnant and unable to attend. But she reported to her brother how Harriot Stanton felt about her impending marriage. "I only want to tell you, the only one to whom I should care to speak of it in a letter," she wrote carefully, conveying something of the confidence with which Harriot Stanton must have written about her feelings, "that to day is Harriot Stanton's wedding day in all probability and that her letters betoken great happiness."[98] Otherwise, there is no record of Harriot's experience of the wedding.

Maybe, like Elizabeth, Harriot was concerned about reconciling her marriage with her daughterhood. There is one final detail that suggests this. In Harriot's own memoirs, in the edition of her mother's letters and diaries which she prepared for publication, and in her mother's biography, which she supervised, Harriot got the date of her own marriage wrong. "On November 12, 1882," Harriot proudly recalled, "Reverend William Henry Channing pronounced William Henry Blatch and Harriot Eaton Stanton husband and wife on the anniversary of Elizabeth Cady Stanton's birth."[99] Like Harriot's remembrance of her return to France in her mother's company as an elopement, the suggestion of a psychological association between the two relationships is too powerful to miss. Whether the mistake about the date of her wedding retrospectively reflects Harriot's confusion, excitement, guilt, or regret, it does suggest that in marrying she had not fully left her mother behind.

After so many doubts about "whether I ought to marry," who was the man Harriot had chosen, and what kind of life would she be establishing with him? Unlike her mother, she had not married an older man with an established reputation who would pave the way for her in public life and against whom she would have to struggle for public influence. On the contrary, Harry Blatch was not highly educated, not particularly intellectual, and uninterested in politics and reform concerns. Harriot, not Harry, was the one who already had well-developed public preoccupations, whose associations and interests reached out beyond the family circle, who cared more about the world than the home. For the years they were in England, Harry had managerial responsibilities in the May Brewery of which his father was co-owner, but he was encouraged to live the life of a gentleman, as a way to counter the family's embarrassing origins in "trade."[100] He loved nature, his children, and his family. Susan B. Anthony, who had come at Elizabeth's invitation for an extended visit in England, observed that "darling Hattie Stanton . . . seems happy in the man and the lot she has chosen." "Hattie's Harry," she observed, "seems a very kind hearted, loving and intelligent man, deferring in everything to her—if it will only last!!"[101] In Harry,

Harriot had gotten the devoted, adoring husband she had decided would be necessary for her to carry on with her public work despite marriage and motherhood.

Harry provided Harriot with a domestic existence of pleasure and luxury, a counterpoint to the sober, serious life of high purpose to which she had consecrated herself. The wedding breakfast itself was a harbinger of things to come, a rich, six-course repast, including everything from lobster and oysters to pheasant and veal.[102] The most extended anecdote about Harry in Harriot's memoirs also concerns food, and captures the sumptuous aspect of their marriage. The Blatches were hosting a lunch for the famous Fabian couple Sidney and Beatrice Webb, who had come to investigate Harriot and assess her politics. The asceticism of the Webbs provides a counterpoint to and foil for the Blatches' luxurious "French" style of life, for which Harry is given the credit. While the Webbs preferred plain food consumed as efficiently as possible, Harry subscribed to the continental "custom of cessation of all labor at midday, a leisurely meal, and the aesthetic value of food and wine." Harriot described how the Webbs were forced to wait as he lingered over each course, "pouring olive oil into a salad spoon, dripping it over the leaves as he moved them to and fro." She thoroughly enjoyed their discomfort.

At the same time, she also wrote that she admired the "gentle leadership" that the "open, sensitive" Sidney provided for his wife, whose "abrupt manner" and insistence on her own superiority (at least to other women) may have struck too close to home for Harriot. When Sidney "gently reprimanded" Beatrice for smoking too many cigarettes at lunch, Harriot approved. "I felt anyone would have stopped anything in face of such a gentle appeal to one's judgment." Perhaps she enjoyed a similar kind of quiet husbandly authority in her own marriage. Still Harry had his limits. At the end of the lunch, he stepped out of his sphere and began to answer the Webbs' questions about Harriot's political opinions. Harriot described this unlikely move with condescending humor: "Perhaps pepper and mustard had gotten into his nose, and set his mind vibrating violently."[103]

Observations of friends and family suggest that in the first years of their marriage, Harriot and Harry ("the two H's," Elizabeth called them) actively enjoyed each other's company.[104] They partied, created a well-ordered, luxurious home, and shared sensual pleasures—nature's beauty, good food, and sex. Eventually Harriot seemed to have tired of this bourgeois "good life" and after her years in England, she preferred a much more spartan existence in rented rooms, with little furniture. Perhaps in reaction against the material preoccupations of the years of her married life, she later foreswore any interest in or skill for shopping, and was critical of the consumerism that was becoming increasingly important in women's lives. The one indulgence she continued to allow herself was expensive and well-cut clothes.[105] But for now, she enjoyed the wealth and luxury of her life with Harry.

Harriot also liked Harry's large, close-knit family. From the start, she was "struck by the resemblance, physical and mental, of my relatives in New York State."[106] Harry's father, William Henry, Sr., had risen to wealth and power through partnership in an important Hampshire brewery. The entire family lived in Basingstoke, once an ancient market in Roman Britain and now a minor industrial town an hour's train ride from London. The Blatches, though still saddled with the stigma of being "in manufacturing," were firmly planted in the town's small elite. The acknowledged patriarch, William Henry, Sr., kept close control over his five adult children.[107] He had three daughters and two sons, of whom William Henry, Jr., was the second child and the oldest male. This was the first really male-dominated family Harriot had ever known intimately. In religion William Henry, Sr., was a Congregationalist, in politics a Tory, but he seems to have been tolerant, perhaps even fond, of his strong-minded daughter-in-law.[108]

Four of the senior Blatch's children were married and had children, forming a small army of fourteen cousins who grew up and were educated together. The one unmarried Blatch was Harry's sister Alice, who seemed doomed to the dreary life of the home-bound spinster. Harriot felt especially close to Alice. "Discontent? Of course she was," she recalled. Taking on the problem, Harriot selected an appropriate vocation for her, that of kindergarten teacher. Alice Blatch went on to become one of the many public-spirited Englishwomen to be elected to office in local government, but what pleased Harriot even more, at least in the retelling, was her sister-in-law's later romantic fate. After the war, when Alice was in her late fifties, she married a much younger man, George Edwards, secretary of Scotland Yard, rewarded with a late life love after so many years of civic devotion.[109]

While William Henry, Sr., lived next to his place of business, Harry and Harriot moved into their own home in Basingstoke, up the hill from the family brewery. This two-story brick home, named the Mount, had a library, parlor, dining room, kitchen, and four bedrooms. It also had indoor plumbing, a walled garden, and a small entry portico that made it look like an American house.[110] Harriot furnished and appointed it with beautiful things, and took great pride in the tastefulness of every detail. She was constantly involved in finding and retaining the numerous domestic workers who came and went and ran the place. One woman, however, stayed on: Elizabeth Bransom served as nanny to her children and later to their children, too.[111] Describing the early years of her own marriage, Elizabeth Stanton had written of her great pleasure on "reigning supreme" in her own home, of seeing that everything in it was orderly and artistic, and Harriot, with fewer demands on her and more material resources, seems to have felt something similar.[112] "Hattie takes great pride & pleasure in her house & her personal appearance, all of which I heartily approve," Elizabeth wrote proudly of her daughter.[113]

In the context of sleepy Basingstoke, Harriot Blatch must have seemed a modern woman indeed. She was an "American," a creature new to the neighborhood. (Family story has it that the servants were surprised when they met her since "up to that time they had only seen Americans portrayed in country theatricals as black minstrels."[114]) Neither she nor Harry went to church, and when a woman in a nearby village was criticized for organizing concerts on Sunday, she came to the Mount for consolation and support. Sexual scandal disrupted the household. Flora Stark, the wife of one of Harry's brothers-in-law and an artist, had an affair with an American gentleman while visiting the Blatches. Under Harriot's roof a romance blossomed, Flora got pregnant, and a love-child was born. This pushed Harriot's tolerance past the breaking point, and she insisted that the child be passed off as the husband's. "Premature! Ridiculous! Nail perfect, nine months to the day," the working-class housemaid announced of this elaborate bourgeois fiction. Harry wanted to register the baby's birth, as the law required, but Harriot "set upon" him not to do so, and he yielded, though under protest.[115]

There was even a whiff of scandal about Harriot's first pregnancy. "Did you know that Hattie Stanton expected to be sick in August, a bare nine months?" one of her mother's friends wrote suspiciously to another.[116] Elizabeth remained in England after the wedding, and Harriot prepared to become a mother under her own mother's watchful and demanding eye. Elizabeth Stanton did not particularly care about short-term babies, but the good health with which a woman conducted her pregnancy was a matter of great feminist pride with her. Elizabeth regarded "sick women with such disgust" that she made those who had difficult pregnancies feel guilty for their weakness.[117] So long as Harriot could live up to them, her mother's stern standards set the terms for her own conduct. Luckily, she had inherited the sturdy Cady constitution and experienced no serious discomfort during this pregnancy. In her ninth month, she was organizing a political meeting of women interested in establishing a cooperative store in Basingstoke.[118] Elizabeth remained in England for the birth, secured a Quaker woman doctor to attend, and wrote to Anthony that "now we stand with arms akimbo waiting for the young man or woman as the case may be."[119]

Nora Stanton Blatch took her time and was born a month later, on September 30. Elizabeth proudly reported that "the first bugle blast of the event was at dinner and in six hours all was over."[120] The baby, dedicated to women's emancipation from the moment of her birth, was named after the heroine of Henrik Ibsen's scandalous new play, just translated into English. (There was no "h" at the end of Nora, it was made clear, lest anyone think that the baby had a touch of Irish blood in her.[121]) A week later, Elizabeth recorded her happiness "that the three generations of us are together."[122] The Reverend Channing came down to Basingstoke to bless and name the baby, though Harriot insisted that he not undertake a formal baptism, but provide instead a "little talk to the parents about their duties."[123]

A month after Nora's birth, Elizabeth finally left Harriot and sailed back to America. A year and a half had passed since she and Harriot had "eloped" to France. This time it was Elizabeth whose description of their relationship drew on romantic if tragic emotions. "When Hattie and I parted, we stood mute, without a tear, hand in hand, gazing into each other's eyes. My legs trembled so that I could scarcely walk to the carriage. The blessed baby was sleeping, one little arm over her head."[124] Over the next few years, she returned to Basingstoke for two more visits. Being an active grandmother was a great pleasure to her, and Nora, who grew into a self-assured, strong-minded little girl, was the apple of her eye. "She is large & strong, as straight as an Indian," Elizabeth wrote of Nora when she was nine. "She rides like the wind (astride!) she has no fear."[125] In correspondence, Elizabeth called Nora "the Blessed Babe."[126] Nora in turn revered Elizabeth, both for her grandmotherly indulgence and her great authority, and the name she chose for her, Queenmother, was the name that the whole family adopted for Elizabeth in her final years.[127]

By contrast, Harriot left no explicit record of her feelings about Nora's childhood. Her reticence about things private threw a nearly total pall over the subject. In her autobiography there is no mention of her child's birth. The few existing descriptions of mother and daughter come from the pen of Elizabeth and include all three generations. "This morning while I was dressing, Hattie sat on my bed & read all the American letters," Elizabeth wrote in 1890 to her other daughter, Margaret. "Nora brought them up laughing & calling out a big American mail this morning."[128] Even the pictures of Harriot and Nora invariably included Elizabeth, and are positioned so that both Harriot and Nora seem her daughters. All of this suggests that for both mother and daughter, their relationship was set in the context of Elizabeth's overarching presence and Harriot's continuing sense of her own daughterhood.

3

England

Now that she had risked marrying, Harriot's new dilemma was to combine work and domesticity, to take down the barriers between women's and men's spheres so as to conjoin public activity and private relations in a complex, modern, "new woman's" life. During her years in England she finally chose a public direction for herself, which was both like and unlike that of her mother. After years of resisting the pull of her mother's reputation, Harriot conceded the inevitable and accepted the enfranchisement of women as her life's work. But there was as much originality as imitation in the leadership she offered woman suffrage, in the way that she understood women's emancipation and linked it up to political equality. Her experiences in England, where the principle of coverture still shaped the legal status of women, helped her to see that the problem she was struggling with in her own life, how to combine private life and public labor, was the key to the future of women's freedom. Even more fundamentally, England gave her a way to take the dilemma of the married working woman out of the moralistic framework in which it had so long been considered and to recast it in a modern, scientific mode.

The social scientific perspective that Harriot finally chose and which did so much to advance her women's rights convictions was evolutionary socialism. As one of the first influential women in the British Fabian Society, Harriot rethought the tasks of suffragism with a new level of attention to the realities of class. She came to see the relationship of working-class and middle-class women differently from how she had been taught to regard it, which was that wealthy women were responsible for uplifting the poor. She began to understand that elite, leisured women had at least as much to learn from as to teach women of the working classes, especially when it came to facing the conflicts of public and private life. These two new elements of Harriot's perspective on women's emancipation—recognizing that women were going to live public and private lives simultaneously, and that working-class women could provide leadership in rebuilding a vision of the emancipation of their sex around this reality—prepared her to become one of the first figures in the modern American suffrage movement.

In 1880 British Liberals swept the Tories out of power and, after two decades of relative inactivity, prospects for women's rights in England began to improve. The state regulation of prostitution, which had long been the object of organized protest by women, was dismantled. In 1882, the most notorious contribution of English law to women's subjugation, the rule of coverture (by which women lost all legal rights upon marriage) also began to be undone, as British wives were granted limited rights to their own property.

In connection with the Liberals' decision to sponsor a new reform bill to enfranchise England's millions of agricultural workers, the woman suffrage movement also revived.[1] In the spring of 1884 British suffragists organized protest meetings around the country to generate support for the inclusion of women's votes in the upcoming Reform bill. Harriot arranged for a public meeting in Basingstoke, featuring a nationally known speaker, Florence Fenwick Miller. Basingstokers were more used to temperance revivals and football matches than to political protest meetings, and how they regarded this unusual event, we cannot know, but for Harriot it was quite important. Not only was it "the first time she had ever addressed an audience in England," but it was the first time she had ever spoken at length on behalf of woman suffrage, for until now she had left the subject to her mother. One impressed observer characterized her as a "girlish and lovely young wife . . . her voice . . . at once pathetic and sympathetic, her look far-away as of one dreaming dreams of a far-away future . . . her manner childlike in simplicity" and credited her training to "her eloquent mother."[2]

Despite the ascendancy of the Liberals and the close association of most suffragist leaders with the Liberal party, the prospects were bleak for women's votes in connection with the upcoming Reform bill. Prime Minister

William Gladstone was clearly determined to keep the Liberal party clear of the taint of woman suffrage. Eager to exploit the breach, Conservatives took up the issue. Some advocated votes for women taxpayers as an antidote to the enfranchisement of agricultural workers, a reassertion of suffrage as the "right of property"; others simply hoped to prevent any expansion of the franchise by saddling it with votes for women.[3] William Henry Blatch, Sr., a dyed-in-the-wool Tory, chaired Harriot's Basingstoke meeting and declared that he would rather give votes to propertied women than to "300,000 Irishmen who were continuously shooting their landlords from behind hedges and walls." While thanking old Mr. Blatch for his support, Florence Fenwick Miller separated herself from his contempt for the enfranchisement of lowly male agricultural laborers. Harriot did not.[4]

The situation probably reminded her of the political upheavals through which her own mother had passed in the 1860s—and on which Harriot had been politically nurtured. Then, Republicans had opposed woman suffrage, and opportunistic Democrats had moved to exploit the conflict. Now it was Liberals who were betraying women's rights, and Conservatives who were offering support. Then, rejected by the champions of the ex-slaves, some women leaders, including Elizabeth Stanton, took comfort in an elitist sense of their own superiority over their would-be allies. Now, Harriot took similar offense that Liberals preferred lowly agricultural workers who had not even organized for their own enfranchisement to educated, leisured women like herself who had long been demanding the vote.

Harriot rose to explain these important historical precedents to her audience. "When franchise was about to be conferred on the ignorant, unenlightened negroes of America," she explained to a crowd whose total exposure to "blacks" was limited to traveling minstrel shows, "the women of America"—she meant the women of her class and race—"were unmindful of the opportunity which was presented to them." They put themselves politically at the mercy of "Sambo," she explained. Now the educated women of England were about to make the same mistake. "The intelligence, the political capacity of the women of England was surely equal to that of the farm labourer upon whom the vote was now to be conferred," Harriot insisted, and the tax-paying, educated women of England ought not to permit the "rights of property to be explained away" by consenting to their own disfranchisement.[5]

The explicit elitism of Harriot's argument, the appeal to race transformed into the appeal to class, is striking. The lessons she had drawn from her mother's failure to link woman suffrage to black suffrage seemed to be that other democratic movements interfered with rather than supported the expansion of women's rights. Nor was she alone in drawing undemocratic conclusions for woman suffrage from the American experiment in franchise reform. Moncure Conway, the man she had wanted to preside over her marriage and an American who also identified with abolitionism, praised her Basingstoke speech in an article in the *Pall Mall Gazette* and agreed with her conclusions. Applying the lessons of American Reconstruction to contemporary British politics, he insisted that the British trade union movement was unshakable in its opposition to women's equality and that "the cause of women is the cause of the cultivated."[6]

Meanwhile, from the margins of the British suffrage movement, the contradiction of appealing to the rights of property to expand the franchise in this late day and age began to generate a different kind of argument. Edith Simcox, a British socialist and pioneering organizer of trade unions for women, complimented Conway for his timely defense of woman suffrage but criticized his class assumptions. Working-class men, she argued, believed that women in the wage-labor force deserved "a fair day's wages for their work," and admitted women as voting delegates to their trade union congresses. "If the enfranchisement of women had depended upon the representatives of the trade unions in congress assembled," she claimed, "it would have been carried years ago." This was an overly rosy portrait of support by working-class men for women's equality, as Miss Simcox would soon learn, but it did reflect the emergence of a new kind of suffragist argument, based in socialist ideology and working-class experience, which Harriot would take up within the decade.[7]

For the time being, however, Harriot's perspective on democracy remained conservative and rooted in the developments (and defeats) of the past and in the United States. The Reform bill passed in 1884, granting the parliamentary suffrage to male householders but withholding it entirely from women, including the relatively small number who were independent property holders. Elizabeth wrote to Harriot, who was "depressed over the situation," to indulge herself in the domestic retreat that Harry's income permitted. "If the friction outside your home is more than you can stand, shut your door and rejoice that you have one to shut."[8] But Harriot was eager to launch her career as a political reformer and impatient with delay.

In the years after 1884, new political prospects began to appear for women eager for an expanded public role. In 1883, when party workers were barred from being paid, the two major political parties began to court women to serve as volunteer local activists. In 1884, Tory women, who were the first to rush to the hustings, founded the Primrose Dames, and three years later the Women's Liberal Federation was formed. Harriot attended its inaugural meeting with great hopes, but as in 1884, male Liberals still held that the time was not yet ripe to make women's enfranchisement a party issue. Visiting in England at the time, Elizabeth reported that Harriot "blushed for her sex, that women could be so dead to all self respect as to complacently listen to such insults and worse still, echo them in their own speeches."[9] Nonetheless, suffragists stayed within the Women's Liberal Federation and hammered away at the issue of party support for votes for women. Harriot was a frequent and popular speaker at local Liberal clubs.[10] At the Plymouth Workingmen's Liberal Association, she spoke on "why working men should support women's suffrage." Women were already in politics, she argued. "Keeping them from the ballot box" would only serve to render their political involvement irresponsible.[11]

Liberal men's resistance to woman suffrage notwithstanding, Harriot found the opening up of politics to women—regular, men's, parliamentary politics—very much to her taste. As far back as college, she had been drawn to party politics, but thought of this as her father's, rather than her mother's, legacy. Now she found herself in a context in which the contradiction between being a woman and being interested in conventional party politics was disappearing. "Interested as I was in politics," she wrote in her memoirs, "those twenty years [in England] were absorbing."[12] In a report on the British suffrage movement in the American suffrage journal the *Woman's Tribune*, Harriot observed that the British suffragists all paid close attention to parliamentary developments and legislative possibilities. She urged American women to imitate the British, establish "standing committees near the halls of legislation," and do "what men do" when they want a bill passed: lobby the legislators.[13] Years later, she insisted that this long tradition of partisan political activity among British women was the reason that they, rather than the Americans, were the first to attempt modern and militant methods on behalf of votes for women.

Women in England were beginning to be a force in local politics and even to hold municipal office in growing numbers. As Harriot later explained, local government was established in England in the second half of the nineteenth century, at which time a woman suffrage movement was in existence and attentive to the possibilities for political rights at a sub-parliamentary level. While American women were making gains in education and employment, "the English movement [ran] almost exclusively to political lines." Unmarried women won the right to vote for and sit on local poor law boards in 1865 and school boards in 1870. By the end of the decade, women's votes had helped to elect eighty women as poor law guardians and over one hundred to school boards. Those elected included Annie Besant,

Florence Fenwick Miller, Emmeline Pankhurst, Lydia Becker, Elizabeth Garrett, Jane Cobden and other well-known figures in the British women's movement.[14]

Harriot was particularly enthusiastic about women's involvement in local government. She was an active member of the Women's Local Government Society, formed by her friend Jane Brownlow in 1886. In her memoirs, she emphasized the emergence of "the machinery necessary for local self-government which went on under my eyes" during her years in England.[15] She approved of local activism for women of the leisured class who were lacking in socially useful work because it would require the same skills of them as of men in public service: "exact technical knowledge, business habits," and responsibility to a "larger and watchful constituency."[16] As her reputation grew, she was frequently approached to run for office herself. But she always declined, lest it compromise her insistence that she remained an American citizen despite her marriage. Although there was no "law that gave me any choice in the matter . . . it satisfied my self respect . . . to refuse to take a definite step indicating that I considered myself a subject of Queen Victoria."[17]

Harriot's feelings about her status as an American citizen were closely entwined with her attachment to her mother and her sense of personal entitlement. There was something symbolic in the fact that love and marriage threatened to deprive her of her legal identity, wrenching her from her political matrilineage as an American. The injustice she felt about having British citizenship forced on her was as personal and painful as any consequence she ever suffered from being a woman. "My birthright as an American citizen has been stolen from me," she insisted. "Could there be a more glaring injustice than this? Within a few months of each other, one of my brothers and I married foreigners. He remains what he was born and bred. I lose my American citizenship."[18] In reality, it was not until 1907 that U.S. courts formally ruled that marrying foreign nationals would cost American women their citizenship. She repeatedly protested the situation until the laws concerning married women's nationality were changed in the postsuffrage period.[19]

Harriot's loss of citizenship was part and parcel of the loss of individuality that marriage still signaled for women in England. Despite the partial extension of property rights to married women in 1882, the convention of married women's civil death continued, far more than it did in the United States, to shape British women's economic, political, and social lives. From one perspective, coverture was a legal atavism, but from another it was the formal tip of the iceberg of women's fundamental subordination within marriage that had yet to be tackled. In the late 1880s, the British women's rights movement began to face these issues.[20] The debate on women's role in marriage which took place in England in these years emerged from a consideration of the continuing impact of coverture and the economic dependence women suffered in marriage.[21] Writers commonly observed that the economic dependence of wives on husbands not only underlay what Olive Schreiner characterized as the "sex parasitism" of women, but also formed one of the pillars of the bourgeois way of life. Thus, not only activists proceeding from a women's rights point of view but also socialists criticized women's position in marriage. In 1885, Eleanor Marx and Edward Aveling wrote about the prostitution of conjugal love in bourgeois society. In the *Westminster Review*, Mona Caird exposed the sexual discontent of women within marriage.[22]

Harriot made her own contribution to this debate. In 1885 she wrote an article for the *Englishwoman's Review* attacking the socially condoned uselessness of married women of the leisured classes. Excused by their wealth from the actual labor of running a household, the domestic lives of elite women had been drained of productive meaning, but still they held firm to their cloister. Hidden deep in "a Castle of Indolence," Harriot argued, leisured women needed to recognize their obligations to the larger society, their capacity for socially constructive labor, and the special role they might play as "the entering wedge of education" in the social welfare work of local government. Unlike her later writings, she argued here only for work with purpose, not for paid labor. Harriot seemed to include herself in these generalizations about unwanted elite leisure, and yet her writings on the subject fueled a blossoming career as a political essayist. While condemning sex parasitism, she did not seem particularly afflicted by it. Her tone conveyed a sense of herself as strong, capable, and unconfined by the conventional expectations of her era and her class.[23]

Harriot also wrote about the conflict between individual development and family responsibility in modern married women's lives for an American audience in 1891. The paper, an important and complex discussion of the challenges facing women's rights in the modern era, was titled "Voluntary Motherhood" and was read for Harriot in her absence at the first annual meeting of the National Council of Women of the United States. From one perspective, Harriot was intervening in the long debate between English Malthusians and socialists about appropriate population levels by asserting a third, feminist position: that women, on whom the responsibility for the bearing and raising of children rested, must insist that children be wanted before they are conceived. This is how historians of the 1970s, for whom the sexual and reproductive dimensions of women's rights are fundamental, read Harriot's 1891 essay when they rediscovered it.[24]

At another level, closer to Harriot's own nineteenth-century concerns, "Voluntary Motherhood" responded to the disturbing claim frequently made in these years that women's individuality was necessarily compromised by their obligation to the biological fate of collective humanity, known as "the race." Harriot recast motherhood as the source of, rather than the limit to, women's rights. She acknowledged that under current conditions there was a conflict between women's "race obligations" and their individual desires. Given the powerlessness and dependency of modern mothers, she argued, "more and more the best women turn from the work of motherhood and join the ranks of competitive labor, or seek in society and politics a field for the free play of their ambitions." But the solution, she insisted, lay not "in depriving women of public freedom; rather in according them absolute domestic liberty," including full control over conception and childrearing, a broad education, and above all financial independence. Under conditions of greater freedom, as "in the time of the matriarchate" in the long ago past, women could be both breadwinners and mothers. Even now, when such double obligations drained and depleted women, she still believed that "if the choice lies between this and financial dependence of one woman upon one man, then every well-wisher of the race must say, let the woman be self-supporting."[25]

Like many advanced, scientific-minded women of her generation, Harriot revered motherhood as an idea; she considered women's unique contribution to "race improvement" far more important than men's penchant for individualism and material progress. "Through countless ages mother-love has been evolved and been working out its mission," she wrote in her "Voluntary Motherhood" paper.[26] Although profoundly pronatal, this ideology stressed the social contribution of motherhood rather than the personal relationship. It is possible that the actual interaction that women like Harriot had with small children may have seemed especially confining because of the grand ideology, the global aims, they made of motherhood. Perhaps it was the very intimacy of the mother-child bond that held her back, for there is some evidence that in her relationships with other women's children she was affectionate and playful, more so than with her own.[27]

Ironically, Harriot did not deliver her "Voluntary Motherhood" speech herself because she was pregnant again, and moreover having a hard time of it. This pregnancy, a full eight years after the birth of her first child, was planned and deliberate; Harriot had waited until Nora was older and her own career as a reformer was well launched before having a second child.

(Perhaps she did not want to visit on her children her own experience of having her birth frustrate her mother's desire for a public life.) But this second pregnancy was more difficult than the first. Elizabeth, in England on what would prove to be her last visit abroad, wrote to put off her return to the United States because "Hattie has been so ill I could not leave her."[28] In June, Harriot gave birth to a second daughter, Helen. After Elizabeth left, Maggie took her place and attended to her sister. As with so many of the details of Harriot's personal life, our only record of the event comes from someone else, in this case Nora, who was not happy about the new baby. Helen's birth meant her own displacement. "No sooner was mother up and around than talk started about my going away to school."[29]

Nora's educational needs were proving difficult to meet. Harriot, who considered herself an expert on education, inclined toward advanced educational ideas such as coeducation and admired the "American" system of publicly funded education. Harry, backed by his family, wanted Nora to get a conventional, upper-class education to help remedy the family's class burden of having risen up "from trade." Initially he prevailed, and Nora, just nine, was sent to board at the Roedean School in Bristol. She hated everything about it: the rote learning, the British boarding school culture of "crushes" and devotion to older students, and the abrupt removal from her family. Her response was to follow in a grand Stanton family tradition: she had been raised on stories of how her own mother had repeatedly run away from school and so she did the same thing. Harriot had taken a horse; Nora took a train. "A deep laid plot started to germinate in my mind. I counted my pennies. . . . And so it transpired that after a six weeks absence I arrived as an uninvited guest back at Basingstoke," only to find baby Helen in her bedroom.[30] After a second try at Roedean, she ran away again, and was allowed to remain at home with a governess to educate her.

As with other aspects of their domestic lives, Harriot and Harry reversed standard parenting roles. She was the authority, he was the nurturer. Nora remembered her father as the beloved playmate and gentle teacher of her youth. He was always answering her curious questions. They rode around the countryside together, "I on my pony and he on his bicycle." While Helen was an infant and Nora was feeling displaced, he took her on an adventurous bicycle trip to Wales. Everyone could see that Nora adored her father, from the time she was a little girl until he died in 1915.[31]

Harriot by contrast was not especially comfortable with children. In this she was quite different from her mother. Even Harriot's grandchildren, surely the most likely people in the world to appreciate her maternal qualities, found her too concerned with shaping and instructing to be sufficiently nurturing. Nonetheless, she was a deeply involved, constantly present mother. Like her own mother, she saw her primary responsibility as seeing to it that her daughters met the highest standards of achievement and self-esteem as women. Nora was discouraged from being coy, timid, or deferential, from anything conventionally feminine. She was not even allowed to play with dolls of the traditional sort.[32] Under this regime, Nora grew into an unusual child. "She was a superior being," Katherine Stetson, daughter of Charlotte Perkins Gilman, recalled, after meeting Nora when she was thirteen. She was "brilliant, forceful, commanding, fond of having things her own way."[33] Sylvia Pankhurst, who was about the same age as Nora, also found her memorable. She was "a slim little maid of remarkable daring and swiftness, with hair cut short like a boy's."[34]

The complex issues of women's independence within marriage and the residual impact of coverture as a legal doctrine moved to the center of the British woman suffrage movement in these years. Since the 1870s, a conservative faction of suffragists had confined the demand for votes to unmarried women. So long as property holding was still a qualification for men to vote, and marriage generally barred women from holding property, there was some logic to the arguments of these "orthodox" suffragists, who demanded the vote for the only women who could hold property, widows and spinsters. However, in the 1880s, once wives could hold property and property qualifications for men's voting were weakened, a significant gap opened up between male householders who could vote and married women who owned property but could not vote. In response, a group of more radical suffragists, led by Ursula Bright and Elizabeth Wolstoneholme-Elmy, mounted an offensive against "the marriage bar" within the suffrage movement. Harriot and her mother supported votes for women regardless of marital status.

In 1889, Bright and Wolstoneholme-Elmy organized an explicitly anti-coverture suffrage society, the Women's Franchise League.[35] The league agitated for the removal of the disabilities of marital status as well as sex from all franchises, local and parliamentary, and from the right to run for elective office. By linking the demand for woman suffrage to the attack on coverture, the Women's Franchise League functioned as a bridge between natural rights ideas, which had originally inspired the woman suffrage movement, and sexual and economic issues on which it was going to turn in the future. In its brief history, the league drew on all the new and important currents in the British women's rights movement: engagement with party politics, involvement in local government, focus on the disabilities of marriage, and the rise of Fabian socialism. As Harriot put it later, "There rose from its ashes the militant work of the Women's Social and Political Union in England, and the work of the Women's Political Union in America."[36]

For Harriot, the Women's Franchise League marked the beginning of her transformation under the political and intellectual influences of British politics. Up to this time, she had stayed closed to developments in England: "Deep in my heart I remained an American."[37] Now, England offered something that America lacked, a forward-looking suffrage movement, the prospect of uniting her mother's and father's political legacies, and a context in which she could develop her skills as a reform activist and political leader. Three years before, on her first trip back to the United States after her marriage, she was still anxious to move back. "When we went out to work or drive," Harriot Ransom's brother Paul reported of Harriot Blatch's visit to Buffalo, "she would often see a snug little house that would please her and . . . say, There, Harry! wouldn't that be a nice place for us to have. She seemed very anxious to come to America."[38]

By the time Harriot returned to the United States for a second visit in 1889, a few months after the founding of the Women's Franchise League, she was eager to return to England and remained in the United States only a few months.[39] Right before she left, with her mother in tow, she spoke at the 1890 "unity convention" which brought back together the two factions of the American woman suffrage movement. There, Harriot declared that "on the great socialistic questions of the day—capital and labor, woman suffrage, race prejudice—England was liberal and the United States conservative."[40] This statement signaled a reversal of Harriot's commitments—until now, she had repeatedly declared that democratic America was superior to aristocratic England. The young woman who had always believed that the refined and educated classes were leaders in all social improvements was now speaking approvingly of "socialistic" ideas.

On her return to England, Harriot immersed herself in the work of the Women's Franchise League. She rose to become one of the league's most important members and through the process developed a sure sense of her own strategic leadership. She was a member of the Executive Committee and shared the position of honorary secretary with Ursula Bright, an indication that her suffrage apprenticeship was coming to an end. By late 1892, Harriot's name was included in a list of thirty British women notable for their work "toward women's freedom or freedom generally."[41] Membership in the Women's Franchise League also introduced Harriot to Emmeline Pankhurst, who later led the radical reinvigoration of the British suffrage movement. At the time, both were young matrons, struggling with the overshadowing reputation of a venerable intimate—for Emmeline her hus-band, Richard Pankhurst, for Harriot, her mother.[42] They were also both mothers of young girls and formed a friendship on this basis. In her memoirs, Sylvia Pankhurst recalled several visits she and her sister Christabel made to Basingstoke, and the impact that Harriot made on her. "Not one of all the ladies who came to the house, distinguished as I thought them, could com-pare with her."[43]

The Women's Franchise League won married women's suffrage at the municipal level, where unmarried women had been voting for some time.[44] Harriot argued that this achievement provided the key to the far more serious problem of the marital distinctions in the parliamentary franchise, because once voting rights for women without regard to marital status were secured at the lower level, parliamentary suffrage could be claimed on the same basis. Ursula Bright wanted to focus on parliamentary suffrage and insist on a clause explicitly repudiating the distinctions of coverture in local voting, but Harriot's approach prevailed.[45] In 1894 the Local Govern-ment bill passed without reference to women's marital status. Of this achievement, Sylvia Pankhurst later wrote, "The last blow at Coverture had been struck!" for which she credited Harriot Blatch's "great courage and powerful advocacy."[46] Having put the problem of coverture at center stage, the Women's Franchise League had succeeded in keeping it from ever again interfering with political rights. Campaigns for parliamentary suffrage for women were no longer hampered by divisions over the married women's vote.

The Women's Franchise League marked a transition within the British women's rights movement in another way. Although the league rooted itself in the natural rights discourse of a former era, the class issues of the emerging politics of British socialism are apparent throughout its brief history. Once the league succeeded in eliminating concerns about coverture from suffrage politics, British women faced the prospect of enfranchisement with the same limitations as men, chief of which were those of class. In addition, the league's focus on coverture drew attention to the economic dimensions of working-class women's lives, and therefore to the growing presence of wage-earning mothers in the working class. And finally, British suffragists were beginning to look to the rising power of the working class to resolve what was starting to look like permanent opposition from the Liberal party. Sylvia Pankhurst recalled how Ursula Bright "wistfully" hoped to enlist the aid of "the toiling masses" but was too weary from her long battle against coverture and too uncomprehending of working-class politics to do this effectively.[47] It was left to a new generation of suffrage leaders, among them

Harriot Blatch and Emmeline Pankhurst, to reorient their efforts around these new socialistic possibilities.[48]

A brief trip back to the United States at this point and a public conflict with her mother underlined the importance of the challenge British socialism was posing to women's rights and the way Harriot was changing to meet it. Harriot had not seen her mother, who could no longer tolerate an ocean voyage, for almost three years. Nora, now eleven, came with her and loved America on first sight. But baby Helen, who had never met her grandmother, was sick with a lingering cough and stayed in England with Elizabeth Bransom, the nursemaid.[49] In 1894 New York was in the midst of its first genuine woman suffrage upsurge in decades, a statewide round of meetings, rallies, and petition campaigns to force the upcoming constitutional convention to support women's political rights. Elite women, members of New York City's political, economic, and cultural ruling class, were newly involved in suffrage agitation. In response to "antis" of their class, they charged that votes for women were crucial to allow them to maintain leadership of their sex. These wealthy suffragists were Elizabeth Stanton's crowd and Harriot frequently spoke with or instead of her mother at their meetings.[50]

Harriot had once identified with such elite women, but now she was beginning to see social relations and political questions from the other side of the class divide. She did her best to explain her new perspective to her wealthy audiences. At parlor meetings in their elegant homes, she incongruously talked about "the industrial side of the question," the growing number of wage-earning women and the link between their public labors and their need of the vote. She dismissed the charge that woman suffrage was unwise because government needed quality rather than quantity in its voters as one of those "little anti Republican innuendoes I hear so often here in America." In her opinion, "the danger is not in the ignorance of the poor, but in the apathy of the educated and the rich."[51] When her mother made a little pun having to do with the genteel leisured lives of her audience, Harriot did not even get the joke. "My mind is so full of the industrial aspect of the question," she apologized.[52]

Elizabeth had gone off in the opposite direction. She accepted the argument that woman suffrage threatened to add to "the ignorant vote," and joined the chorus calling for literacy restrictions on the ballot. Harriot disagreed in a strongly worded public letter to her mother, which was prominently featured in the major American women's rights journal. Working people needed political power even more than the rich, she insisted, precisely because "the conditions of the poor are so much harder than yours or mine." On issues that affected the poor, Harriot argued, "the proletariat, whether able to read or not, can give a more valuable opinion than any other class." "Every workingman needs the suffrage more than I do," Harriot wrote, "but there is another who needs it more than he does, just because [her] conditions are more galling, and that is the working woman."[53]

Harriot's public dissent from her mother over educated suffrage was an extraordinary act. On the personal level, it constituted a bold and unmistakable statement of separation between mother and daughter, an indication of new maturity for Harriot. The words Harriot used to describe her feelings on learning of her mother's position—"humiliation," "chagrin," "painful"—suggest the emotional meaning that this open disagreement had for her. But the exchange of letters was also a deliberate, public act (one in which Elizabeth may have colluded) and Harriot most likely calculated on the dramatic effect that a daughter's challenge to her mother would have. The late nineteenth-century women's movement cultivated a deferential manner toward what little female authority had been established. Harriot, the most famous suffrage daughter in the United States, was challenging her mother's political eminence and asserting her own.

Harriot's public opposition to educated suffrage was a declaration that she was leaving behind her former genteel elitism in favor of a more democratic and socialistic, yet equally women's rights politics. She was rethinking and reorganizing her women's rights heritage around a new set of premises, especially the centrality of the wage-earning woman to the future of women's emancipation. The elitism previously so prominent in her approach to women's rights was giving way to a new faith in democracy. She emerged from this period a spokeswoman for a new syncretic politics that drew from both women's rights and socialism to argue on behalf of women in a way that was different from either. Her mother's opinions on these matters, especially her late-life turn to socialism, may well have reflected and followed her daughter's convictions.[54]

Just as the originality of Harriot's leadership can be obscured by the assumption that her role was simply derivative of her mother's, the larger significance of the creative confrontation between women's rights and socialism in the late 1880s and 1890s is easy to miss. Sylvia Pankhurst, an astute chronicler of the period, observed that before this period, her parents, who had always felt drawn to socialism, had stayed away because of the organized movement's dreadful hostility to women's emancipation. From the 1890s on, such choices were no longer necessary and it became increasingly possible to stand both for women's rights and for a challenge to the individualistic logic of the capitalist system.[55]

Harriot's shifting attitudes to democracy, class, and women's rights reflected the impact of the Fabian Society, the newest and most promising
development in British socialism. Fabian socialism was not working class
and it was not revolutionary, but it was also not all male and not, at least at
first, economistic. The women in the society, numbering about one-quarter
of the membership, were not there because they were wives and daughters of
Fabian men but because they were women interested in socialism in their
own right. The Fabians' fluid approach to socialism recalled the expansive
meaning that "the social question" had had before Marx. By contrast, the
Marxist Social Democratic Federation, the dominant voice in British socialism at the time, addressed only wage earning, which it believed was best left
to men, and assumed the permanence and desirability of women's economic
dependence in the family.

Harriot joined the Fabians in 1890 or 1891. How she came to the Fabians'
notice or they to hers is not clear. Through the Women's Franchise League
and from her mother, she knew Annie Besant, the most notorious woman
member of the society, who was in the process of shifting her attention from
socialism to the spiritual philosophy of Theosophy. Harriot thought that
Besant was "making a [theosophical] drive at Mrs. Pankhurst and me," and
went to hear Besant's farewell speech to the Fabians. Instead of Theosophy,
however, Harriot was recruited to Fabianism.[56] Her membership was sponsored by Edward Pease, one of the Fabian Society's original founders, and by
his wife. By 1894, after Helen's birth, she became more involved with the
Fabians.

Women Fabians were of two camps with respect to issues having to do
with women. One group avoided such concerns as a mark of secondary
status, an obstacle to these women's aspirations to function as equals with
men in the world of reform. Beatrice Webb, who became Harriot's chief
opponent within the Fabian Society, was of this sort. So was Emma Brooke,
a writer, who did her best to challenge male authority in private but in public
objected to any special status for women. Harriot found Brook exasper-
atingly "ladylike" in her methods and Webb controlling and hostile to
women's rights.[57] Harriot was part of a second group of Fabian women, who
identified openly with women's rights and wanted the society to debate and
support issues of sexual equality. With the exception of Harriot, the members of this group were not prominent; Mrs. Fagan (no record of her first
name), for instance, was also an activist in the Women's Franchise League
and may have helped bring Harriot into the society. By 1893, the major
achievement of this women's rights group had been to secure the appointment of a committee to compose a Fabian tract "advocating the claims of
women to all political and civil rights enjoyed by men."[58]

The women's rights Fabians were determined advocates of woman suffrage. They protested when trade union and socialist men advocated a nonpropertied suffrage for men but remained silent about the parliamentary franchise for women. Beatrice Webb had gone further and made herself notorious by signing an antisuffrage petition. When Harriot joined the Fabians, the Webbs made a special trip to Basingstoke to interrogate her on what they regarded as "that fanaticism, woman suffrage."[59] But voting was not the primary issue around which these factions battled over an approach to "the woman question" in the 1890s. Rather the central issue was how socialists would approach the growing numbers and changing character of women in the labor force.

At issue were two ways of regarding wage-earning women. The classic trade union position, reinforced by newer social science presumptions, opposed women (and children) in the labor force as a by-product of wage-slavery. This position, updated to cleanse it of overt hostility to working women, was supported by many male Fabians and some women, and championed by the Webbs. The other tradition was that of women's rights, whose advocates had been urging since midcentury the opening up of trades and professions to women who wanted to support themselves. Harriot and the rest of the women's rights faction were much closer to this position, but understood that it had to be reconciled with socialist criticisms of the wage relationship. They had to incorporate into their defense of women in the labor force a critique of the wage-labor system. To do so, they broke with the older women's rights approach by calling for state regulation of the wage relation to insure that working-class women could earn enough to aspire to economic independence.

How to regard women's wage labor—as a promise or a curse—turned back on the issue of woman suffrage in a variety of ways. The demand for woman suffrage had long stood as the symbolic center of an ideology of women's self-determination, and support for it paralleled the spread of economic individuality among women. In the late eighteenth and early nineteenth centuries, the demand for woman suffrage sunk its roots in the soil of property rights, but its full flower as a mass movement took place in the atmosphere of women's wage labor. Woman suffrage could never become a mass movement until it built a constituency among working-class women and grappled with what wage earning meant to women's lives. As a tool of political power as well as a symbol of women's independence, woman suffrage was also linked to issues surrounding women workers. The Fabians were in the lead in calling for government action to regulate and remedy the conditions of modern labor. What would this emerging body of labor and social welfare law have to say about the fate of wage-earning women? And

what would be the impact of the enfranchisement of women, their empow-
erment as political actors, on the shape of these laws? As the achievement of
woman suffrage grew nearer, the debate among women themselves about the
place of women in the labor force and the impact of labor laws on them
accelerated and diversified. State policy toward working women, it seemed,
would be one of the most important areas in which enfranchised women
would shape their continuing emancipation.

British law had addressed the conditions of industrial workers ever since
the 1840s, but for a long time women in the labor force were too few and the
conditions of all wage workers too terrible for legislation to differentiate
extensively between men and women. Moreover, early women's rights advocates were vigilant lest the law be used to keep women out of paid employment. By the 1880s, the situation had begun to change. So numerous and
impoverished had grown the female wing of the wage-labor force that in
1893 "Lady Factory Inspectors" were appointed to make a special survey of
their conditions and report on their findings to the Royal Commission on
Labour. On the basis of their report, the home secretary announced his
intention to bring a new Factory Act before Parliament, many of the provisions of which especially affected working women. The new act placed severe
restrictions on home workshops, brought home laundries under the act and
thus restricted the hours permissible to work in them, and—of greatest
potential significance—allowed the prohibition of work designated as dangerous to subclasses of workers, notably women.[60]

The proposed extension of the Factory Acts and the unequal impact they
would have on women and men drew response from all sides. The classic
women's rights position was articulated by Jessie Boucherett, aging spokeswoman for women's rights liberalism. Boucherett deplored the attempt to
drive out home work as a new attack on married women's right to work, as
well as an unacceptable government intervention into the wage relation.[61]
She still subscribed to the classic liberal notion that "the rough arm of the
law" threatened the development of that "friendly feeling" between em-
ployer and worker which must always be encouraged. Meanwhile other
women who believed in the emancipation of women began to support
factory legislation directed specifically at women.[62] This was a first for the
British women's movement. Under the leadership of Lady Dilke, the
Women's Trade Union League, which had fought against separate labor
legislation for women since its founding in the 1870s, now took the opposite
position and supported the proposed Factory Act.[63]

To support its reversal of position, the Women's Trade Union League
drew on the authority of the influential social scientist Karl Pearson. In an

important article in the *Fortnightly Review*, Pearson acknowledged that "par excellence the woman's problem of the future" was how "to reconcile maternal activity with the possibilities of self-development open to women." Nonetheless, he dismissed the basic principles of women's rights—equality and independence—as outdated and "individualistic," and contemptuously stereotyped the women who believed in them as those "who abstain from marriage and have not the sex-impulses strongly developed." Inasmuch as women's maternity relegated them to a state of permanent dependency, Pearson argued, the special provisions for women in the proposed Factory Act appropriately provided "legislative protection and state support for those who are temporarily or permanently disabled from protecting or supporting themselves." Unregulated capitalism, he contended, placed a premium on childlessness; to counteract this, society must reward those who elected maternity, by combining restraints on women's labor with a system of "national insurance on motherhood."[64]

Harriot was as eager as Karl Pearson to demonstrate that "women's emancipation is only possible during a socialistic as distinguished from an individualistic stage of society" and she also deplored the fact that, as presently constituted, the women's movement was incapable of drawing in the women of the working classes. Like him, she regarded maternity as the highest and most honorable of social functions and believed it must be accommodated in public policy. But she did not regard maternity as a disability, dependency among women as socially functional, or individuality as an outmoded value, inasmuch as it had never been fully secured for her sex. Nor did she share Pearson's conviction that it was time to throw "John Stuart Mill's *Subjection of Women* overboard."[65] To reconcile women's rights principles with socialist understandings, she realized that nothing was more important than to weigh in on the raging debate about women's wage labor, and to remake women's rights ideas into a means of acknowledging, addressing, and remedying the suffering of the masses of working women.

Like Pearson, Harriot could see that the mounting conflict between maternity and paid employment was "the very pivot of the whole economic question for women." But the solution, she believed, could not be found in driving married women out of the labor force. While paid employment was "fraught with difficulties for married women," there was no going backward. "Female labor in industrial production is a great fact and a fact that has come to stay," she insisted. Married women workers would not voluntarily return to economic dependency on their husbands.[66] At her first public speech before the Fabian Society in February 1894, Harriot aggressively criticized the Factory Act as a solution to the needs of women workers.

Speaking as part of a series entitled "The Implications of Collectivism," she declared, "Some people regard as the problem of industrial life how to keep married women out of the factory. Collectivism will solve the problem [of] how to keep them in."[67]

In the wake of her public debut as a Fabian, Harriot was elected to the Executive Committee of the society, an honor as yet paid to only a few women.[68] She was also invited to join the committee that had been authorized the year before to draw up a tract on women's rights. Harriot was a major find for the committee. She was one of the few women with the range of skills—oratorical, analytical, literary—to write and defend the women's rights tract that the committee had been charged to prepare, and virtually the only such women's rights veteran who could rise to the socialist challenge. The plan was for her to draft a tract and revise it in response to criticism, and for the society to publish it under her name. For Harriot, to author the Fabian Society's first official statement on women's rights and women's labor was a precious opportunity to influence the debate.[69]

In the fall, Harriot took rooms in London, so that she could work on the project while Nora tried yet another school in the city. Starting from principles with which all Fabians must agree—the positive contribution of state action to social welfare, economic efficiency as a standard for social reform, concern for the welfare and elevation of "the race"—she worked to demonstrate that the women's rights principles of equality and independence for women were compatible with a focus on working-class women and with socialism.[70] As much as the daughter of wealth, she argued, "the woman of the people has the right to be regarded as an individual" and to receive a broad and liberal education in preparation for her place in the world. "It may be perverse in lowly wage-earners to show individuality as if they were rich," Harriot wrote acidly, "but apparently we shall have to accept as fact that all women do not prefer domestic work to all other kinds."[71]

Harriot's insistence that individuality remain the core goal of women's emancipation even within a socialist framework formed the core of her case against any form of labor legislation that discriminated between men and women. Sex-based labor legislation was particularly pernicious for women in the skilled trades, she argued, for it burdened them with restrictions—for instance against night work—that men did not have to meet and thus constituted yet another barrier to equal opportunities for skill, security, and achievement with men. While other social scientists dismissed skilled women workers as an insignificant minority in a large sea of sweated labor, to Harriot they were the vanguard of women's emancipation. "What reason is there to doubt that women would have made rapid strides in every skilled pursuit had they been under the same law as men?" she challenged. Women needed to undertake work for a lifetime, not merely until marriage, and to develop ever greater skill and be paid well for it.[72] As skilled workers, women deserved to be rewarded just like men, "not in so called protection, but in the currency of the state."[73]

Harriot's long-standing emphasis on women's strength rather than their weakness nicely reinforced this focus on working-class women. She dismissed the notion of women's categorical weakness as a sex and believed that what she called the "invalid theory of women's emancipation" (pun intended) originated among women of leisure, who projected it onto the masses "as a handy excuse for their own inefficiency." The great majority, the working-class mass, of the female population, she contended, led lives that required strength and endurance. "[Woman] not tough?" she challenged. "Why half her indiscretions would kill off a whole generation of men!"[74] And if women were not inherently "weak," neither were men inherently strong. Men needed the protection of the state "as much as women." Undoubtedly, her insistence on male workers' weakness was as disturbing to accepted socialist wisdom as was her assertion of women's strength.[75]

A crucial part of Harriot's case, distinguishing it from the prior women's rights criticism of sex-based labor legislation, was the care she took to clarify that she believed wholeheartedly in the principle of state regulation of the conditions of labor. Her objections were not to state protection of labor, only to laws that were drawn up with respect to sex rather than sector. She argued just as strongly for laws to protect unskilled workers, male as well as female, as she did against burdening skilled women workers with special prohibitions. It was impossible, Harriot argued, to "protect" workers in any effective way by concentrating on women without men. In any given industry, if women's hours only were regulated, employers could elude inspectors by arguing that their night work or overtime was being performed by men. And as for trades considered dangerous for women, how could they not be dangerous for men as well? "A process which injures any class of workers a great deal, must be lamentably injurious to every class," she insisted.

She particularly emphasized the importance of regulating labor by age rather than by sex. One of the most powerful defenses of special labor legislation for women, indeed in favor of efforts to remove women from the labor force altogether, was the assertion that paid labor undercut maternity and that women workers could not be good mothers. Harriot accepted the general principle that the state was responsible for ensuring the health and well-being of future generations but argued that this principle led away from the regulation of women's labor and toward the prohibition of child labor instead. As she read the Lady Commissioners' Report, which had investigated the charge that women's labor force participation produced higher rates of infant mortality, she saw evidence instead that high infant mortality rates were correlated with the labor of children, not their mothers.[76] She was sure that the prohibition of child labor was made more difficult because the state regulated the labor force by sex rather than by age. "It is difficult to believe that English legislators are moved solely by considerations for the well being of the race," she argued, "when they forbid night work for a woman and allow her boy of fourteen to slave ten hours every night . . . and permit her girl of thirteen to be imprisoned . . . as many hours as a woman of forty."[77]

For the women's rights tradition to be opened up to women of the working class, the position of middle-class women and their relations with working-class women also needed to be reconsidered. Why was it, Harriot asked, that the "marked improvement in the condition of the well to do or educated woman" had so far been accompanied by "little or no progress in the condition of the woman of the people?"[78] Part of the answer must be that bourgeois women relied on the underpaid labor of working-class women to free them from domestic obligation. Until "the professional woman . . . [has] recognized that it is her cooperation with other women which has given her freedom to specialize . . . the movement for the emancipation of women [will remain] a well-dressed movement." Harriot did not call for women of wealth to forswear paid domestic service; nor did she linger, as had her mother long before, on utopian fantasies of collective homemaking.[79] A good social engineer, she urged greater specialization and professionalization among women, so that one day the housemaid, cook, or nursemaid would be as skilled and well paid as the writer, actress, or social reformer whose household work she performed. Despite its limits, Harriot's inquiry into the economic interdependence of women of different classes laid the theoretical basis for a different political vision of class relations among women, which acknowledged the dependence of wealthy women on the labor of the poor and the obligation to make the message of independence and individuality for women meaningful not just to the few but to the many.

Over the next six months, Harriot drafted and redrafted her tract. She had support from most other women on the Women's Tract Committee.[80] Her major opposition came from outside the committee and particularly from Beatrice Webb, who was establishing herself as an authority on the living and working conditions of poor women, and from her husband, Sidney. Both Webbs were vocal opponents of the political traditions of women's rights and vigorous defenders of special labor legislation for women workers. (Sidney had written that women's lower wages were justified in light of their lesser efficiency as workers.) Although neither Webb was on the Women's Tract Committee, George Bernard Shaw, Sidney's closest political ally, was and he brought their opinions into its deliberations.[81]

During these years Harriot disliked both the Webbs and Shaw,[82] although after World War I, she and Beatrice came to agree on many points. As with many of the men whose powerful reputations she wished to diminish, she ridiculed Shaw physically. "He looked as if a good wind would uproot him and his argument," she recalled. "His skin was colorless, his hair and beard, an indefinite sandy hue and very sparse." Although she found Beatrice Webb quite beautiful—she had "dark and piercing eyes, [a] tall, graceful figure"— she seemed to Harriot one of those thwarted women whose boundaries of action were too narrow for their ambitions and power. She was manipulative, overbearing, excessively opinionated, and snoopy: when the Webbs made their first visit to Basingstoke, Beatrice (who was childless) was on the lookout for evidence of maternal neglect.[83]

As the months passed, opposition within the Fabian Society to Harriot's ideas grew. She submitted three different versions of her tract, each one generating more objections and disagreements than the last. Ten months after having been invited to join the committee, she had had enough and formally declined to make any further changes.[84] At this point, the lead in the debate over women's labor passed from the Tract Committee, with its women's rights analysis, to the Executive Committee, with its conventional socialist critique of women's wage labor. When the Executive Committee organized a series of lectures to cultivate support for the Factory Act, Harriot and other members of the Women's Tract Committee vigorously objected.[85] They organized a special meeting of Fabian women to insist that it was possible to oppose specific laws which discriminated against women and yet retain support of the principle of factory legislation. At the annual meeting of the Women's Liberal Federation, Harriot led a group that secured a resolution to combine support for "the general provisions" of the Factory Act with "apprehension [over] those clauses which propose certain restrictions on women workers which are not extended to men." But the socialist press, Harriot protested, misrepresented all these efforts, obscuring the distinction between the Fabian women's position and that of those who would oppose all labor legislation from a laissez-faire point of view.[86]

In mid-1895, Parliament passed the Factory Act, including special limitations on night work for women. Acting without proper notice to the general membership, the Executive Committee published Beatrice Webb's appreciation of the new legislation, instead of the women's rights pamphlet that had been commissioned.[87] Despite the distinctions Harriot had worked so hard to make, Webb wrote that "there lurks behind the objection of inequality an inveterate skepticism as to the positive advantages of Factory legislation."[88] Harriot objected and Shaw wrote privately to Sidney Webb that "Mrs. Stanton Blatch pours forth vials of vitriol on me and insists that Mrs. W is wrong about the Factory Acts. . . . She accuses me of conspiring with the Webbs to rush [Beatrice's article] through without letting even the lady members of the executive see it."[89] Her protests had no effect, and Beatrice Webb's defense of labor law which discriminated by sex, rather than Harriot Blatch's insistence on the importance of protecting male as well as female labor, became the Fabians' first statement of how the society regarded women's work.[90]

In the midst of these defeats, after months of highly charged debate over the consequences of working mothers' labor on society and family, Harriot's own children became seriously ill. In October 1894 Nora and Helen both came down with whooping cough, still a serious and mysterious childhood disease. "I don't know what they do nowadays, but in 1894 no one could do anything," Nora remembered much later. "Elizabeth [the nanny] was worried sick and we both whooped and whooped and tore our little bodies asunder." Harriot postponed a lecture in which she had planned to lay out her ideas for the women's rights tract. Instead, she arranged for nurses and consulted doctors, who had little to tell her and less to make her children better. Eleven-year-old Nora recovered but the two-year-old baby, Helen, remained weak. "The whooping cough stopped," Nora remembered, "but she could not assimilate her food." Harriot attended meetings sporadically and continued to work on the tract, but anxiety and fear, it seems fair to presume, took their toll.[91]

Meanwhile, Helen kept getting sicker. In late 1895, Harriot canceled her plans to go to New York for the grand celebration Susan B. Anthony had arranged for her mother's eightieth birthday. Elizabeth, who had made her last visit to England in 1891, had never seen Harriot's second child. "That I must forego the pleasure and satisfaction of being present at the celebration you are contemplating is the deepest disappointment of my life," Harriot wrote to Anthony.[92] Privately, Harriot wrote to a friend that "my little Helen is still very frail. I have a trained nurse constantly with us now."[93] According to Nora, her mother was "frantically consulting doctors in London, Paris, everywhere," but "no one could save [Helen]." Still, no one thought the child was in imminent danger, and Harriot expected her to recover up until the day of her death. "It was not till Thursday morning about 6:30 that we saw a change in her," Harriot wrote. "In an hour the little spirit had slipped away." On June 11, 1896, just short of her fourth birthday, Helen Blatch died.[94]

Helen's death was the first that Harriot (forty years old at the time) had witnessed. "I had never seen any one die before, and in her case there was nothing but a sweet gliding away." She had an autopsy performed to learn more about the cause of death. She may also have been dealing with family charges that she had neglected the baby. Although the results were inconclusive, she did note that there was evidence of "slight, very slight chronic inflammation of the bowels, the result of cold she caught in the bowels when I left her . . . to come home and get Nora ready for school." Harriot organized the small family funeral in the greenhouse and drawing room of the Mount. Her brother, who came over from Paris for the funeral, reported that she worked "like a Trojan" on the details. A Unitarian minister from London spoke, Esther Bright (Ursula's niece) played the violin, and the rooms were flooded with sun and spring flowers. The coffin was placed in the baby's perambulator, which was taken out into the garden, and family, friends, and the many Blatch cousins solemnly followed it. Helen was cremated. "I am having made a silver vase for the ashes," Harriot wrote to her mother, "and when I die I want dear little Helen's dust mingled with mine & buried."[95]

Elizabeth could not be there, so Harriot and Theodore wrote her letters describing the funeral. From both accounts, it seems that Harriot responded to Helen's death with great restraint, an emotional posture approved by her class, encouraged by her upbringing, and necessitated by her personality. "Hatty broke down for a moment on meeting me," wrote Theodore, "but she does not look so worn out as I feared would be the case." In recreating the moment of her daughter's death for her mother, Harriot rendered it peaceful rather than wrenching. "There was not a struggle," she wrote, "she breathed more and more slowly and gently, and had a sweet smile on her face." Lingering over its beautiful details likewise helped her to tame her feelings about the death: "In the midst of the greenhouse, which had been bright all the spring with flowers stood the carriage with its precious burden. . . . Round the coffin were great branches of white tabernium and on the top were lovely copper-coloured roses and quantities of maidenhair fern." Theodore, writing under similar emotional strictures to bring overwhelming feeling under conscious control, wrote, "One is almost tempted to say that such a funeral is pleasant." "I am not broken down by my loss," Harriot assured her mother, but Helen's death was nonetheless everywhere.

"I love to be in the rooms where she was, and touch and handle the things she liked. She seems to be there."[96]

How Elizabeth responded at the time is not recorded. But Susan B. Anthony's letter to Harriot about Helen's death has been preserved, and it is as intense in feeling as Harriot and Theodore's letters are reserved. "My heart sympathies go out to you each all, and your dear mother. How her mother's heart is aching for the first great sorrow of her darling Hattie," she wrote after receiving the simple engraved announcement of Helen Stanton Blatch's death. "Darling, I only wanted to tell you I am grieving with you."[97]

Harriot never wrote or said anything publicly about Helen's death. She seems to have done her best to erase Helen's existence from the public record. The child is not mentioned in her memoirs, nor is there anything in Harriot's will about a silver urn or her daughter's ashes. Only Nora, who wrote about her sister's death many years later, preserved her memory.[98]

Was the intrinsic sadness of Helen Blatch's death affected by the additional meanings of its coincidence with public events? Infant mortality rates were politically contested propaganda in the debate over women's labor. Harriot had boldly asserted that women who worked outside the home did not neglect their maternal responsibilities or contribute to the ill health of their children, and in the midst of this debate, her own child had died. There are intimations that other members of the family, the more conservative Blatches, attributed some of the blame to Harriot, with her modern ways and constant comings and goings.[99] Did the public meanings that Helen's death might have had amid the acrimonious debate over working mothers give Harriot one more reason—if any more were needed—to keep her feelings to herself? Was her understanding of social relations and public policy uninformed by her private tragedies? Many years later, when she was speaking on street corners for woman suffrage and a heckler charged that suffragettes neglected their families and were not good mothers, she was ready with a "quick retort," which she retained for her memoirs: "My dear young man, I am a grandmother. All my progeny, although I was graduated from college, are bouncing and lusty."[100]

Helen's death was the beginning of the end of Harriot's life in England. Within three months, she was back in the United States, in the bosom of what was left of her natal family.[101] For the next eight years she traveled back and forth between New York and Basingstoke. In a spacious apartment in the upper reaches of Manhattan, she lived with her mother, Nora, Maggie, and her brother Robert. Harriot spent her time studying, writing, and broadening her political contacts. "I am 'behind the times' in America," she wrote to Vassar historian Lucy Maynard Salmon.[102]

From their West Ninety-fourth Street apartment, Nora, now fourteen, took the trolley to Horace Mann School, the experimental institution connected with Columbia University. This was the kind of progressive, mixed-sex schooling that Harriot had long been seeking. Helen's death had been very hard on Nora; together with her many unsatisfactory schools, it left her "feeling terribly old as I entered my teens." Coming to the United States was a genuine liberation for her.[103] For the next five years, Harriot and Nora spent the seven months of the school year in New York, returning to the Mount for the summer to be with Harry, who was as yet unable to leave Basingstoke. Even though Nora missed her beloved father, she hated returning to England and longed to get back to New York. There she had her school, which she loved, and her Queenmother, who although immobilized by age and weight, "was my guide and philosopher." Elizabeth taught her granddaughter "the facts of life," prominent among which was "the history of women and of her long subjection." Another feminist generation was in the making.[104]

In 1901, Nora was admitted to Cornell, the university that Harriot had wanted to attend. After a third of a century as a nominally coeducational institution, Cornell was still hostile to female students. "I had never in my life up to the time that I went to Cornell met with any sex prejudice," Nora claimed, echoing her own mother. She felt that the prejudice against women had not lessened appreciably from the days of M. Carey Thomas and Florence Kelley, and she and other members of her class took it on themselves to change the situation. By her sophomore year, Nora had become the first woman ever to be admitted into Cornell's civil engineering course. Because it was the "greatest tribute I could give to my dear Queenmother," she and a group of friends organized Cornell's first woman suffrage society, which remained in existence for the next fifteen years.[105]

In the summer of 1902, after Nora's first year at college, the household in Basingstoke was finally broken up and Harry moved to the United States. He probably had no choice: old Mr. Blatch had died and the fact that Harry's wife and daughter had left England cost him his position at the brewery. "Our income went down by one-half and a home in England and one in America became impossible," Nora recalled. Harry took up residence in a cottage on Long Island, spending his time gardening and engaged in "chemical experiments." According to family lore, he never really adjusted or was happy in the United States.[106] Harriot lived sometimes with him, sometimes with Nora in Ithaca, and sometimes in rooms she kept in New York City.

After Basingstoke, she never again had her own home. That part of her life was over, done in by Nora's growing independence, Helen's death, the waning of conjugal passion, and serious political defeats.

By the time Harriot made the final move to the United States, her mother was visibly declining. "I am so glad to be with Mother again," she wrote to Susan B. Anthony after she closed her home in England. "She has failed sadly since last spring and needs Maggy or me to be near her constantly. I wish you could be in New York at the time of the 87th birthday as I'm sure there won't be another."[107] Even on her death bed, Elizabeth was still envisioning Harriot's rise to woman suffrage leadership. Her last surviving letter to Anthony was a request that she see to it that New York suffrage leaders, whom Elizabeth suspected of jealousy toward her daughter, issue Harriot "an official invitation to the state convention in Buffalo and to all other important conventions in this state."[108]

Elizabeth Stanton died on October 26, 1902, as her family loved to recall, sitting up in her chair and still working. Harriot was in the next room, along with Maggie and all but one of her brothers.[109] As she had done for Helen, Harriot arranged the funeral, which was a small, private affair. In a letter written to her mother's friend Helen Gardener, she described Elizabeth's death with the same determined peacefulness she had summoned to write about Helen's death, six years before: "Could any death be more ideally beautiful—more what she would have wished? I can see her now standing there in her last hours, with that delicate halo of soft white curls around her death-touched face, pleading once again the cause of the mothers of the race."[110] Less benign, more uncontrolled emotions surfaced a few weeks later in connection with a controversy over the disposition of her mother's brain. This same Helen Gardener publicly claimed that Stanton had donated her brain to science to help resolve the debate about whether women's brains were inferior to men's. The issue was moot since Elizabeth had been buried for some time and, as Susan Anthony observed, "was already beginning to return to mother nature."[111] But Harriot was furious, wrote letters to the newspapers, and publicly ridiculed Gardener's claims. "My mother never did anything to pain those nearest to her and whom she loved, and I am quite sure she would never have done this."[112] This bizarre incident raised an issue that would eventually become crucial to the meaning of Harriot's life: who possessed Elizabeth Stanton, now that she no longer belonged to her self?

Again, Susan B. Anthony's reaction to death stands in contrast to Harriot's. She could barely contain her devastation at her partner's demise; her world seemed literally to collapse. "It seems impossible that the voice is hushed that I have longed to hear for 50 years, longed to get her opinions of things before I knew exactly where I stood," she wrote. "It is all at sea. . . . What a world it is—it goes right on and on—no matter who lives and who dies!!"[113] Blessedly, the great woman had left a daughter, and Anthony was counting on Harriot to be her mother's successor. "Harriot Stanton Blatch is a splendid woman and she will say and do a great many good things," Anthony observed in the wake of Elizabeth Stanton's death. "I am waiting and watching to see what she will accomplish in an organized way."[114] Just two years later, however, she was noting her disappointment that Harriot's political inclinations made her seem "more like her father than her mother."[115]

Harriot did not return to England again until 1915. Reflecting then, when she was at the height of her influence in the American women's movement, on the importance of her years in England, she wrote, "I realized what an opportunity the sojourn there of twenty years had been. . . . I became convinced . . . of the greater importance of achieving economic changes than of tearing away political ornaments."[116] The reform campaigns and perspectives available to women in England in the 1880s and 1890s—the final attack on coverture and the emerging feminist critique of marital dependence, the rise of Fabian socialism and the intensifying debate on women workers—had altered her understanding of the challenges facing women in modern society. The fierce individualism on which her mother's understanding of women's rights had rested was not so much replaced as transformed by her own social and historical understanding that whatever emancipation women would achieve must take place in the context of women's wage labor.

Yet women's political equality—the "tearing away of political ornaments"—still had to be secured. After a decade and a half of modern politics in England, Harriot devoted the next two decades to winning votes for women in the United States. From one perspective, this was the completion of her mother's agenda, and yet so much about her suffragism was different because of what she had seen and done in England. Women would gain political equality, Harriot now believed, because of the impact of "the women of the industrial class, the wage-earners, reckoned by the hundreds of thousands . . . the women whose work has been submitted to a money test, who have been the means of bringing about the altered attitude of public opinion toward women's work in every sphere of life."[117] To the reorganization of her mother's movement around this understanding and these women she now turned.

4

Class

The America to which Harriot returned was vastly different from the one she had left in the early 1880s. Politically, economically, culturally, technologically, her motherland was undergoing fundamental change at a rapid rate. When she returned in the late 1890s, this epochal transformation was reaching a peak. As Nora, now a teenager, put it, moving from London to New York made her feel "as though a dynamo was driving me."[1] By 1900, the science and technology that Harriot so revered, aided by the massive expansion of the wage-labor force that was revolutionizing labor (especially that of women), had made the United States the most productive nation in the world.

Yet these tremendous accelerations in productivity and wealth were running headlong into venerable political beliefs and social practices that could not accommodate such changes. Most notably, deep-seated convictions about the necessary compatibility of free-market capitalism and a national identity built around democracy were challenged by a great and growing gulf between rich and poor. The Great Depression of 1893, with its shocking masses of desperate unemployed people, constituted almost as profound a challenge to the American sense of historical mission as slavery had a generation before. It was no longer possible to take for granted the fundamental classlessness of American society which once had distinguished the new world from the old.

A new crystallization of class identity was taking place at every level of American society. The burgeoning proletariat was at the core of both economic growth and class conflict, but life and consciousness at other points on the socioeconomic ladder were also changing. Spectacular displays of wealth rivaled civic stewardship as the appropriate posture of the very rich. And within that peculiarly self-conscious category, the American middle class, a similar and related crisis of identity was also taking place: whereas in the aptly named Gilded Age professionals and intellectuals followed and flattered their betters, they were increasingly seeing their place in society as understanding, serving, and uplifting the poor.

At each level of society—bottom, middle, top—the question of who and what constituted "the American nation" was particularly disrupted by the most spectacular social change of the era, the massive acceleration in immigration. The organized working class, the wealthy stewards of society, and the earnest citizens of the middle class—all responded to this development with ambivalence. One would have thought that the racial crisis of the last great national drama, the Civil War, might have prepared Americans to accept what was literally the changing complexion of their society, but it did not. As the United States became more and more multi-European in character, inclusiveness and exclusiveness were both in evidence.

Yet, despite the intensity of this economic and social crisis, the nation's mood inclined more to hopefulness and optimism than to dread and fear. This was, after all, not just any historical shift, but the beginning of an entirely new century. Everywhere there was widespread hope for the coming of a truly modern age. Whether captain of industry or militant labor activist, charity worker or urban immigrant, Americans believed that the rapid historical movement they could feel all around them could be made positive and personally beneficial, providing that the right people were in place to guide it.

Where this consensus ended and conflict began was over who such leaders should be. After many years of industrial hostility, nationwide strikes and demonstrations, against which unprecedented levels of police power were arrayed, the site of combat was shifting to the electoral arena. Even socialists, the alleged enemies of the capitalist system, established a U.S. beachhead only by following the political route. To be sure, the national ambitions of the People's party had collapsed in the 1896 election, but the deadening two-party stasis that had previously characterized politics from the presidency on down was decisively disrupted in the process. Fusion and reform groupings, some inside, some outside the major parties, were proliferating at the local and state levels. Especially in the cities, where these changes were concentrated, local political reform activism was vigorous and substantive. And whereas post-Reconstruction politics had concentrated on how to narrow and limit the use of governmental powers, making these years the pinnacle of the regime of laissez-faire attitudes, this turn-of-the-century political revival struck a different note. For the first time since the high years of congressional Reconstruction, and in a much more broad-based and sustained fashion, the constructive possibilities of government power were beginning to seize the political imagination.

No survey of the transitions of American society at the beginning of the twentieth century would be complete without including the dramatic changes in the lives of American women. College education for women, which Harriot herself had helped to pioneer, now involved many thousand women, more than one-third of the baccalaureate population. The sense of fundamental division between masculine and feminine, the so-called system of separate spheres, had by no means vanished but its peak had passed. Public life was opening up for women, powered by five million women wage-laborers and made visible by tens of thousands of club women, settlement workers, and civic reformers whose sense of female mission had grown very expansive.

Given these epochal transformations in the lives of women of all classes, it was astounding how backward and oblivious to change the New York suffrage movement remained. The heavy hand of the nineteenth-century pioneers of the movement was everywhere. The center of activism, if it can be called that, was in the western part of the state, in cities like Geneva and Rochester, once bustling, now conservative.[2] Toward the end of her long life, Susan B. Anthony had retained her energy and devotion but not her vision, and those suffrage leaders who had come into their positions under her supervision were far more complacent about the state of their movement and the adequacy of its structures to the changes about them. They were stubbornly unwilling to undertake any response to the new class dynamics. On the contrary, established suffrage leaders were sufficiently impressed with the charge that enfranchising women would favor the "unfit" at the expense of the "fit" that they spent much of their time trying to refute it.[3] Nothing is more illustrative of the class character of turn-of-the-century New York suffragism than its temporary abdication of the goal of full suffrage in favor of a campaign to win municipal suffrage for tax-paying women.[4]

The primary form that suffrage organization took in these years was that of the "political equality club."[5] Harriot's acerbic characterization of these old-fashioned (or as she called them "orthodox") suffragists, penned decades later, vividly conveys how out of step established suffragism was at the start of the twentieth century and is widely quoted by historians to evoke what are called "the suffrage doldrums" at century's end. "The suffrage movement was completely in a rut in New York State at the opening of the twentieth century. It bored its adherents and repelled its opponents. Most of the ammunition was being wasted on its supporters in private drawing rooms and in public halls where friends, drummed up and harried by the ardent, listlessly heard the same old arguments. Unswerving adherence to the cause was held in high esteem, but, alas, it was loyalty to a rut worn deep and ever deeper. . . . The only method suggested for furthering the cause was the slow process of education."[6] So long as Harriot was bound to the movement by the memory of her mother and the leadership of Susan B. Anthony, who continued as a defining presence in the suffrage movement until her death in 1906, she could not really act on her distaste for suffragism of this sort. But she was impatient for a different kind of movement. Her years in England had changed her, and unlike the more provincial leaders of the American movement, she was uncomfortable with a suffragism that "stood alone for the rights of property, [instead of] . . . for the highest democratic ideals."[7]

Meanwhile, Harriot's political imagination was captured by two other early twentieth-century developments, both of which had an important influence on the innovative leadership she was soon to bring to suffragism proper. Her attention was drawn, in the first instance, by the anticorruption municipal reform movement which was emerging among women at the turn of the century. For the same reasons that the suffrage orthodoxy kept its distance from the teeming metropolis and immigrant masses of New York City, the municipal reform movement centered there: working-class voters of all nationalities were turning electoral politics into an unpredictable process, which the "best people" could no longer control.

Despite their disfranchisement, women were almost as involved in this movement as men. In New York City, the most important women's political reform organization was the Women's Municipal League, organized by Josephine Shaw Lowell in 1894 to oppose Tammany corruption.[8] By the early 1900s, municipal political activism had spread to women of other classes and there were groups with links to the Democratic party and the labor movement, a Women's Henry George Society, and a female wing of Hearst's Independence League.[9] By 1903, Harriot was so caught up in enthusiasm for municipal reform that she suggested the National American Woman Suffrage Association suspend its suffrage activism for a year and instead "pursue and punish corruption in politics."[10]

The relation between municipal reform activism and woman suffrage, though ambiguous and imprecise, highlights the way that women were poised on the brink of political activity in the early twentieth century. From one perspective, women anticorruption activists accepted conventional notions of what was appropriate to woman's sphere. The primary issue around which the Women's Municipal League generated enthusiasm for independent mayoral candidates from 1894 through 1905 was sexual immorality; Tammany corruption was made real and dangerous by emphasizing the support of the police for organized prostitution. Moreover, the ladies of the Women's Municipal League expended much rhetorical energy in contrasting their own womanly "non-partisanship" to the self-serving ways of male politicians. The many references to "municipal housekeeping" can be seen as a way to reconcile—for women's sake as much as men's—political reform activism with appropriately womanly behavior. As one of their supporters put it, the battle for municipal reform was a contest between political parties with all their endemic corruption and "the side of decency, honesty and righteousness."[11] Women's alleged moral superiority was being mobilized in a crusade against men's self-serving politics.

Yet these gendered oppositions between politics and morality were a convenient route precisely for ushering women into politics. Even though women municipal reformers saw themselves as fighting a battle against "politics," what else are we to call what they did—campaigning for specific candidates, opening neighborhood headquarters to solicit voters, and writing and distributing campaign literature to affect the outcome of an electoral contest—except politics?[12] While late twentieth-century feminists have expanded the definition of "politics" so as to legitimate their activism, women at the beginning of the century followed the opposite strategy for the same reasons: they defined politics as narrowly as possible, so as to expand their range of acceptable public concerns.

Out of the ferment of municipal reform activism, a group of dissatisfied New York suffragists came together and began to search for a different and more promising route to votes for women. Harriot was a leading figure in this crowd. By 1902, they had formed the Equal Suffrage League of New York, for which Harriot briefly functioned as president.[13] Many of the elements that would later characterize modern suffrage activism in New York City existed here in protean form. At Equal Suffrage League meetings the importance of drawing different sorts of women into suffrage activism, especially wage-earning women and college graduates, was discussed. The beginning of what would soon be called "suffragette militance" in England was noticed and applauded. Above all, the women of the Equal Suffrage League were among the relatively few who recognized the link between women's growing interest in electoral politics and the future revitalization of the suffrage movement.[14]

The one factor that condemned to futility the Equal Suffrage League's aspirations to modernize New York suffragism was a constituency: it had none. The group remained small and unable to reach out to any appreciable number of women not already identified with the woman suffrage demand. Nonetheless, its members understood where the suffragists of the future would come from. "There are nearly six million wage-earning women in America today," explained Maud Nathan, president of the National Consumers' League in 1905. "Have they no interest in laws relating to factories, hours of labor, wages, holidays and other subjects vital to men workers?"[15] The challenge was to turn this rhetorical flourish into a genuine organizing strategy for American suffragism.

The second of Harriot's activist involvements in the early years of the century was the Women's Trade Union League (WTUL). This group, modeled after a British organization of the same name founded in the 1880s, was established in 1903 by a combination of elite settlement house workers and female labor activists to encourage the formation of trade unions among women. The Trade Union League differed from other efforts by women of the privileged classes to aid wage-earning women because in it elite women labored with working-class women rather than for them; their common goal of forming unions was intended not so much to uplift working-class women as to empower them. The difference was expressed in the deliberately modest term that elite WTUL members used to describe their relation with working-class women—rather than leaders or benefactors, they were "allies." When asked to represent the Trade Union League at the 1906 national suffrage convention, ally Gertrude Barnum gently reprimanded her audience: "Instead of asking me here to speak for the . . . laboring women, you ought to have asked someone among their own fine speakers."[16]

Harriot Stanton Blatch was one of the first allies to join the New York chapter of the Trade Union League, formed in 1904. It was a natural move given her emphasis on the importance of work for the modern woman. Using the techniques of social science research she had learned in England, she undertook an investigation of women workers in the New York City hat-making industry. Along with Mary Van Kleeck, labor journalist and social reformer, she investigated the extent of sweating, the existence of laws protecting women workers, the methods of acquiring skills, and other aspects of women's work in the millinery trade. The results were meant both to inform the public and to help draw women into unions.[17] Harriot also spoke frequently for the WTUL. She hosted a meeting for male trade union leaders, at which she assured the veteran unionists that she understood their wariness of the young, uncommitted women workers who "watered the stock" of their unions.[18] She sat on the New York chapter's Executive Council from 1906 through 1909, and was often called on to stand in for President Mary Dreier.[19]

Of all the friends and allies of the WTUL, Harriot was most closely identified with the woman suffrage movement. She was insistent in her conviction that securing the vote for women was crucial to the WTUL's purpose of organizing working women. "These young women need stirring up, need independence and some fight instilled into them," she wrote to Samuel Gompers in 1905 in preparation for a meeting among immigrant working women at which they both were to speak. "I am understanding of all that the vote would mean to them. It would help them as nothing else could."[20] The possibility of a mutually beneficial relationship between woman suffrage and labor organization was beginning to be recognized and encouraged by other advocates of both trade unionism and votes for women. In 1906, Gertrude Barnum argued before the national suffrage convention that "our hope as suffragists lies with these strong working women," and Florence Kelley and Jane Addams used their influential voices to insist on working women's special need of the vote to improve their own conditions.[21]

Harriot played the role that she did in reinvigorating twentieth-century American woman suffragism by combining the new political energies being generated by municipal reform with the numbers, militance, and progressivism of the labor movement. In January 1907, she announced the formation of an independent suffrage organization, the Equality League of Self-Supporting Women. It may have been no accident that she took this move so soon after the 1906 death of Susan B. Anthony, after which she no longer felt personally obligated to defer to established suffragism.

For the short but influential life of the organization, its focus on working women distinguished the Equality League of Self-Supporting Women from the many other suffrage societies in New York City. Two hundred women were present at the initial meeting, including "doctors, lawyers, milliners and shirtmakers."[22] "We were pledged to serve the interests of women in the world of work, wherever help was needed." The organization was open to "any woman who earns her own living, from a cook to a mining engineer," Harriot insisted, "and we have both of them"—"The League is to take in women of all trade unions," but also "non union working women, professional women, in fact every class who earn their daily bread."[23] The Equality

League provided the medium for the introduction of a new and aggressive style of activism into the American suffrage movement. This modern political style was fueled by the energies of both politically sophisticated working-class women and elite, professional "new women."

According to Harriot, the idea for the Equality League emerged from a series of meetings that the Trade Union League had been having for more than two years with groups of immigrant women wage-earners on the lower East Side. At first, these meetings were confined to "social and industrial questions . . . but gradually as we came to know our ground better and our audience grew more accustomed to us, the question of citizenship for women was brought to the front. It was gradually borne in upon us that the enthusiasm of the suffrage movement in the future would come from the industrial woman, and that what she most needed was to be brought in contact, not with leisure women, but with women who, like herself, were out in the world facing life just as men do, and earning their own living."[24] Professional women flocked to the new suffrage organization, but attracting wage-earners into a movement long identified as middle class proved more difficult. "Members were instructed to keep recruiting cards always with them," Harriot recalled, "to approach everyone, always, everywhere, whether in workshop, office or social gathering." The group worked through the wage-earners' organizations themselves, and entire unions were listed as affiliates, which enabled the Equality League to claim a membership of nineteen thousand. Meetings attracted an average attendance of two hundred.[25]

Of the working-class members of the Equality League, the two best-known were Leonora O'Reilly, who was first vice-president, and Rose Schneiderman, who was its most popular speaker. O'Reilly was in her mid-thirties at the time and had been a member of the working women's society whose appeal to elite women resulted fifteen years before in the formation of the National Consumers' League. She was currently an officer of the New York chapter of the Trade Union League and had considerable—if frustrating—experience at trying to organize women in the garment industry, her trade. She was sensitive to condescension from elite allies, and although a friend and supporter of Harriot, she did not stay active in the Equality League. What she learned there, however, helped her several years later to form a wage-earners' suffrage society, undiluted by the professional women workers on whom the Equality League relied.[26]

Rose Schneiderman was twelve years younger than O'Reilly, Jewish rather than Irish, and a grassroots activist in the Cap and Hat Makers Union. She too was a Trade Union League activist, and at the time a member of the Socialist party. Like Harriot she was a great orator, and history remembers her for her bitter obituary for the Triangle fire victims of 1911: "The life of men and women is so cheap and property is so sacred. There are so many of us for one job it matters little if 143 [sic] of us are burned to death."[27] Schneiderman was featured at the Equality League's first public meeting at Cooper Union in April 1907, at which she was already unwilling to mince words: "We who provide everything that [leisured women] have are too nice about it. . . . These women live a tribal life. We want to be human. To be human is to think of the world as your country, not your little home."[28] The condescending *New York Times* poked fun at her "pathetic little appeal in odd English," but a suffrage paper was more impressed, describing her as "astonish[ing] everybody with her eloquence."[29]

The professional women workers who Harriot sought to join with industrial workers in the Equality League were college educated, and often pioneers in the few professional occupations as yet opened to women. Many were lawyers: Ida Rauh, Helen Hoy, Madeline Doty, Jessie Ashley, Adelma Burd, and Bertha Rembaugh. Others were social welfare workers, for instance the Equality League's treasurer, Kate Claghorne, a tenement housing inspector for New York City and the highest-paid female employee in the city government. Well-known figures such as Florence Kelley and Charlotte Perkins Gilman also participated in Equality League activities. These women were doing paid professional work, although many of them also had inherited incomes. They did not work solely or even primarily out of economic need, but from a desire for serious, public substance to their lives and as a way to make an impact on society.[30] Several of these women had tried to route their suffrage activity through the College Equal Suffrage League, formed in New York City in 1904. But conservative forces under the leadership of Dean M. Carey Thomas of Bryn Mawr College had taken control and this was driving the College League's more activist members into the ranks of the Equality League.

Nora Blatch was a perfect representative of these optimistic young professional Equality League members. She had graduated Cornell with distinction in 1905, and a year later was admitted into the American Society of Civil Engineers. Her first job was with the American Bridge Company, a subsidiary of the recently organized U.S. Steel Corporation. In contrast to her college experience, she was well received by her male coworkers. But if gender was not a problem here, class was. Workers without professional credentials were being miserably treated all around her. At a rolling mill in New Jersey, Nora saw underaged boys working twelve-hour shifts for piecework wages and when she protested was told it was none of her business. "The terrible injustice of it ground into my soul," she recalled, "and I never felt the same way toward the company again." A good progressive, she quit out of protest at the mistreatment of her fellows. At the time of the formation of the Equality League, Nora was working as an assistant engineer with the New York City Board of Water Works. Eventually she would leave this job, too, as unable to tolerate the endemic inefficiency of public employment as the rapacious standards of corporate profit.[31]

In bringing together wage-earning and professional women, the Equality League was grappling with two distinct but related aspects of "women's work": the long-standing exploitation of laboring women of the working classes and the newly expanding place of paid labor in the lives of all women in bourgeois society. Women thinkers and activists of the Progressive period struggled to understand how these two distinct processes were related. While most focused on the negative aspects of paid labor for women, Harriot emphasized the productive labor that women performed, both as it contributed to the larger social good and as it created the conditions of freedom and equality for women themselves. Women had always worked, she insisted. The new factor was the shift of women's work from the home to the factory and the office, and from the status of unpaid to paid labor. The question for modern society was not whether women should work, but under what conditions and with what consequences for their own lives.[32]

Harriot's vision of women in industrial society was democratic—all must work and all must be recognized and rewarded adequately for their work—but it was not an egalitarian approach or one that highlighted working women's material concerns. She stressed the common promises and problems work raised in women's lives, not the differences in how they worked, how much individual choice they had, or how much they were paid. As a young woman fresh out of college, she had dared to imagine that her desire for meaningful work and a role in the world need not deprive her of marriage and motherhood, but she also never earned her own living, depending instead on the income from her husband's family business. Within the ranks of the Equality League of Self-Supporting Women, she joked, she was the only "parasite" in the organization.[33]

The Equality League's special contribution was to focus on the bonds and common interests uniting industrial and professional women workers. The industrial women admired the professional ethic, if not the striving careerism, of the educated working women. For their part, the professional women admired the matter-of-fact way wage-earners went out to work. Above all, both classes of working women sought through paid labor a route out of marital dependence. Both the professional and industrial working women of the Equality League shared the conviction that for paid work to mean freedom, women could not abandon it when they got married, relying instead on their husbands for support.[34]

On the issue of marriage and work, Nora once again serves as a representative figure. Just as she was forming the Equality League along with her mother, she was getting ready to undertake what she hoped would be an egalitarian marriage. In early 1907, she had met and fallen in love with Lee de Forest, an engineer and inventor who had just introduced a crucial component for the development of radio broadcasting. Lee thought Nora was a "golden girl," a modern, energetic woman who would enrich his life without burdening it. For her part, Nora was dazzled by the fantasy of a partnership that brought together personal happiness and professional collaboration. Her plan was to leave her frustrating city job and together with Lee establish an independent radio corporation that would pioneer in this exciting field of technology. She expected not only the personal independence her mother had aspired to in marriage, but a continuing career of paid labor and professional satisfaction. In 1907 she was all hopefulness and optimism about becoming Lee de Forest's wife and marrying love and financial independence.[35]

Meanwhile, Harriot was absorbed in the Equality League. Her life was focused on breaking through the lethargy of the suffrage movement and linking her two fundamental concerns, working women and political equality. As Nora wrote in her own reminiscences, "there was no time for frivolity in those days—all day long work and the evenings devoted to speaking and organizing."[36] Harriot now lived at the Woman's University Club, a feminist equivalent of the midtown Manhattan men's clubs, which served as a residential hotel for women of means uninterested in maintaining their own households.[37] Harry remained in his cottage on the eastern end of Long Island, but Harriot visited him only on weekends and not always then. She preferred the city where, in the thick of New York's bustling political developments and female reform activism, she could throw herself into the work of the Equality League.

Harriot did not envision the Equality League of Self-Supporting Women as a single-issue organization focused exclusively on woman suffrage. True to its origins in women's municipal political reform, the league petitioned the City Charter Revision Committee to include women on the School Board. It also became involved in the battle of the city's female school teachers for equal pay, offering support and encouragement for the recently formed Interborough Association of Women Teachers.[38] But achieving the vote for women was always the league's distinguishing concern, its raison d'etre. In February 1907, the Self-Supporters made their public debut by sponsoring the first testimony ever delivered by women wage-earners on behalf of woman suffrage before the Senate Judiciary Committee of the New York legislature. The event made a stunning impression.

At the Judiciary Committee hearing, the Equality League was preceded by representatives of the National Association Opposed to Woman Suffrage, who repeated the now well-worn charge that the enfranchisement of women was undesirable because it would favor the "vicious" portion of the female sex.[39] The next day, Equality League members Clara Silver and Mary Duffy, both Trade Union League activists and organizers in the garment industry, spoke in favor of votes for women. The presence of these women before the New York legislature and the dignity and intelligence with which they conducted themselves constituted a repudiation of the antisuffragists' dire predictions about democratizing the franchise. Both Silver and Duffy linked suffrage to their trade union efforts: while they were struggling for equality in unions and through unions in industry, disfranchisement was undermining them, teaching the lesson of female inferiority to male unionists and bosses. "To be left out by the State just sets up a prejudice against us," Clara Silver explained. "Bosses think and women come to think themselves that they don't count for so much as men."[40]

The appearance of the two Equality League members before the New York legislature was greeted with enthusiasm in many suffragist quarters. Lillie Devereux Blake, whose own suffrage group had tried "one whole winter . . . to interest the working woman" but found that they were "so overworked and so poor that they can do little for us," congratulated Harriot on her success.[41] Helen Marot, organizing secretary for the New York Women's Trade Union League, was satisfied that the Equality League "is realizing the increasing necessity of including working women in the suffrage movement."[42] Even the New York State Woman Suffrage Association, with its conservative sense of suffrage possibilities, lined up behind the Equality League. Harriot Blatch, Leonora O'Reilly, and Rose Schneiderman were the star speakers at its 1907 suffrage convention. "We realize that probably it will not be the educated workers, the college women, the men's association for equal suffrage, but the people who are fighting for industrial freedom who will be our vital force at the finish," proclaimed the usually restrained newsletter of the National American Woman Suffrage Association.[43]

After an exciting first year, characterized by substantial growth in numbers and several large and successful public meetings, the Equality League co-sponsored with the College Equal Suffrage League a special event to welcome to the United States the British suffrage activist Anne Cobden-Sanderson.

Cobden-Sanderson had come to the United States at the Equality League's invitation to describe exciting new developments in the movement of which she was a part. In 1903, Emmeline Pankhurst, Harriot's old comrade from her Fabian days, had broken away from the established British suffrage organizations to form a new group, the Women's Social and Political Union (WSPU). This organization was distinguished by its willingness to confront the refusal of the Liberal party, still as obdurate as it had been in the 1880s, to support woman suffrage. Beginning in 1905, the WSPU began to garner worldwide headlines as its members were arrested for civil disobedience directed against the newly elected Liberal government. Proudly embracing the term of derision with which the press labeled them, the WSPUers became known as "suffragettes," to distinguish themselves from their moderate predecessors. Cobden-Sanderson was one of the first and most illustrious of the British suffragettes to be imprisoned.

She was also the daughter of the great British radical Richard Cobden and was herself closely connected with the Independent Labour party, formed in 1893. While the College League concentrated on getting young, professional women to attend the meeting, the Equality League made "trade unions . . . the special objects of [its] approach."[44] By emphasizing Cobden-Sanderson's labor politics and distributing free platform tickets to trade union leaders, the Equality League gathered an overflow crowd at Cooper Union, of which two-thirds were men and many were trade unionists.[45] In her memoirs of this period, Harriot remembered with special pleasure trudging through the snow up and down Fourth Avenue to secure the support and participation of large numbers of labor movement men for this event.[46]

The Equality League's meeting for Cobden-Sanderson was the first account that American audiences had ever heard of the new militance transforming the British suffrage movement. In describing the origins of the Women's Social and Political Union, Cobden-Sanderson emphasized its working-class origins and the formative role of Lancashire factory workers. After these factory workers were arrested for trying to see the prime minister, Cobden-Sanderson and other privileged women, who felt "we had not so much to lose as they did . . . and belonged to a class not so dependent on our own work," decided to join them and get arrested. She described in detail her subsequent two months in jail, living the life of a common prisoner and coming to a new awareness of the poor and suffering women there. Her simple but moving account conveyed the transcendent impact of the experience. "When you have a cause, the ideal seems real, and all the discomfort, all the ridicule, all the blame sink into nothing."[47] She especially addressed herself to American women of wealth, of whom she was very critical. "The opposition here is not from the men but from the women of the upper classes," she insisted, "who say they have everything they want, and do not care for the sufferings of others."[48]

In the wake of the Cobden-Sanderson meeting, many New York suffragists became fascinated by and eager to experiment with the British militant style. But contrary to what Harriot later claimed, she and her organization were not the first in New York City to imitate the British women's publicity-inviting tactics of open-air meetings and outdoor parades. Credit for this innovation goes to a small group of activists that was organized immediately after the Cobden-Sanderson meeting by a thirty-year-old British activist named Bettina Borrman Wells.[49] Borrman Wells wanted the American movement to go public and spectacular, in direct imitation of the dramatic developments in England. To signify this derivation, she declared herself the head of a new organization, the American Suffragettes. Various figures from the New York suffrage scene who were too unconventional for the established societies rallied to Borrman Wells's standard. Attracted rather than repelled by the contempt of the socially upright, the group took "as a badge of the order the slang term [*suffragette*] which was first used by the unsympathetic" to ridicule the British militants. America now had its own "suffragettes."[50]

The American Suffragettes were ready and eager—if not to get arrested as their British sisters had been, at least to outrage respectable opinion on behalf of their convictions. They were committed to "vigorous, forceful, aggressive agitation on lines justified by the position of outlawry to which women are at present condemned."[51] "Their policy," one sympathizer observed, "frankly is Publicity."[52] To win public attention to the cause, Borrman Wells insisted, "we have had perforce to use methods of a sensational nature, even methods involving personal danger."[53]

To the degree that suffrage militants had a more general goal above and beyond getting the vote, it had to do with challenging the existing standards of femininity. For the injunction that women be ladylike, helpless, and pleasing to men, they substituted a rebellious, daring stance. "The time has come when we must eliminate that abominable word ladylike from our vocabularies," Borrman Wells proclaimed. "We must get out and fight."[54] The ethic that the American Suffragettes wished to substitute for ladylike respectability—the new definition of femininity they were evolving—drew, on the one hand, on traditionally male behaviors, like aggression, fighting, provocation, and rebelliousness. On the other hand, they undertook a spirited defense of female sexuality, which had long been held to be the price for women of vigorous participation in public life. They wanted to demonstrate that "it is not only the masculine type of women who wants the ballot," but even more the feminine.[55] Inevitably, this led to contradictions. "Women are no longer to be considered little tootsey wootseys who have nothing to do but look pretty," suffragette Lydia Commander declared. "They are determined to take an active part in the community and look pretty too."[56]

The militant methods, taking suffrage out of the parlors and into the streets, were indicative of the new significance of working-class women in several ways. The WSPU had modeled its militant style after that of the labor movement.[57] Moreover, disrespect for the standards of ladylike respectability paralleled impatience with rigid standards of class distinction. Working-class feminists were eager to speak from the militants' platform. A socialist activist, Dr. Anna Mercy, organized a branch of the American Suffragettes on the lower East Side, which issued the first suffrage leaflets ever published in Yiddish in New York (and therefore probably in the United States).[58] Despite these democratic tendencies, however, it would be a mistake to confuse the radicalism of suffragettes with the different sort of radicalism that characterizes a working-class movement. The militant challenge to femininity and emphasis on publicity introduced a distinctly elite bias; a society matron on an open-air platform made page one while a working girl did not, because it was the former who was obliged by conventions and could outrage by flouting them. In their desire to redefine femininity, suffragettes were anxious to stake their claim to it, and it was with respect to the upper-class woman that femininity was ultimately determined.

The American Suffragettes held their first open-air meetings in Madison Square on New Year's Eve, 1907, and every week thereafter. The stiff wind and chill temperatures of midtown Manhattan in winter helped to underline the determination and commitment their suffragism was meant to express.[59] Speaking in public before a random crowd of men in the middle of New York City was a startling challenge to the conventions of respectable femininity. Mostly the suffragettes encountered curiosity about their political message but occasionally they faced open hostility. This was always a blessing, because female grit was what speaking in public was meant to test. A successful stump speaker was a woman who could take the hazing and return the male crowd's challenges with good humor. We might imagine a voice from the crowd yelling out, "Don't you wish you were a man?" A clever suffragette would retort, "Don't you wish *you* were."

In February 1908, the American Suffragettes announced they would hold New York's first suffrage parade, again in imitation of the British militants.

They were denied a police permit, but since "outlawry" was their position of choice, this opposition was just fine and they proceeded with plans for their march. Great numbers were predicted, but on the appointed day, only twenty-three women marched, greatly outnumbered by onlookers. In a public school auditorium in which they gave their speeches, the American Suffragettes told their sympathetic audience that "the woman who works is the underdog of the world" and needs the vote to defend herself. Socialists and working women alike stood up in support. "We are trying to work on public sentiment in favor of our demands," proclaimed one American Suffragette.[60] Despite the small crowds, the group had faced police opposition, generated press attention, and challenged an indifferent public. From a militant perspective, the event was a triumph.

Though the American Suffragettes represented a similar modernizing configuration to the Equality League of Self-Supporting Women, they lacked the kind of connection to working women which Anne Cobden-Sanderson had preached and which the Equality League's links to the Women's Trade Union League made possible. The American Suffragettes appreciated the importance of linking the suffrage movement up with the aspirations of women wage-earners.[61] But the association they made between new forms of propaganda and working-class suffragism was rhetorical and the group never became more than a small band of dedicated cadres. Borrman Wells in particular seemed to distrust any challenge to the traditional class character of the suffrage movement; like so many other advocates of women's equality before her, she believed that association with any other politics—from socialism to free love—would divert attention and energy from the main issue of woman suffrage.[62]

Rhetorically, the American Suffragettes positioned themselves less in class terms than with respect to conventional women and established suffrage methods, which they wanted to challenge. "The suffragists believe in milder and more conciliatory methods sitting in comfortable parlors and halls," the organization's provocative monthly, the *American Suffragette*, declared. "We on the other hand believe in standing on street corners and fighting our way to recognition, forcing the men to think about us. We glory in the reproach that we are theatrical. Dignity to the winds!"[63] The focus of the American Suffragettes was cultural. Their purpose was the creation of spectacle, their self-understanding was as "insurgents," their watchword was "novelty," and their first principle, to quote the editor of their newspaper, was "advertising."[64] When conventional suffragists began to adopt their methods and style, victory as they understood it had been won. By 1910, the *American Suffragette* magazine was able to declare, "How times have changed! The name 'suffragette' has become a by-word and today is associated with progressive womanhood. . . . Our suffragist sisters have now adopted the very methods which in the beginning they spurned and disapproved." With victory so defined secured, the group disbanded in 1911.[65]

In the repeated accounts of "suffragist versus suffragette" around which so much of the new publicity accruing to the movement was organized in these early years, the Equality League of Self-Supporting Women was usually positioned as a third tendency, neither a "gist" nor a "gette," but distinguished by its unique emphasis on working women.[66] Nonetheless, Harriot was sympathetic to the methods of Borrman Wells and her group. She got her first experience with outdoor speaking on the American Suffragettes' stump. In April 1908, she spoke along with Borrman Wells at an outdoor meeting in Harlem, at which time, according to the newspapers, the two women "were kicked and thrown down" by a rowdy crowd.[67] Nora was also an enthusiast. On her honeymoon with Lee de Forest in England, she participated in giant suffrage parades in London, and after her return in August, she presented the American Suffragettes with the stunning banners she had brought back, including a beautiful purple and gold banner with her Queenmother's likeness on it.[68]

Both Nora and Harriot went on to become accomplished outdoor suffrage speakers. A newspaper photograph from a few years later shows Harriot, wearing a fur hat and raising her fist, forcefully delivering her suffrage message while being swamped by men and boys gathered around her on Wall Street. Nora proudly told her children stories about her experiences on the stump. Her favorite anecdote related to the small portable stool that she would unfold when she got to her assigned corner, and from which she would aggressively declaim: a young man offered to carry the stool, innocent of its purpose, as he walked alongside her and tried to strike up a conversation; when they got to the appointed spot, Nora unfolded the stool, stepped up onto it, and began her suffrage harangue; the would-be suitor, realizing with a shock exactly what kind of woman he had tried to pick up, disappeared.[69]

In May 1908, the Equality League made its first sustained foray using modern suffragette tactics with a "trolley car campaign" between Syracuse and Albany. Harriot planned to travel with several women but in the end her only companion was Maud Malone, a librarian and longtime activist. They concentrated on the upstate corridor of counties in which Elizabeth Stanton had lived and worked and Harriot had been born and raised. The campaign began in Seneca Falls, and from there moved on to Auburn and Syracuse.

They traveled "so far as possible by the cheap aid of the democratic trolley, stopping for open-air meetings. All along the way, they concentrated on working-class audiences. In Troy, home of the Laundry Workers Union, one of the oldest and most militant independent women's trade unions in the country, they held a particularly successful meeting.[70]

Albany was a crucial stop. Although an antisuffrage and antilabor stronghold, this was the state capital and eventually suffragists were going to have to concentrate their energies here. The mayor tried to keep the suffragists from holding their meeting, but by this time Harriot was "full of wisdom as to how, when and where to hold an open-air meeting successfully" and outwitted him. The best places for gathering a crowd, she had learned, were "the busy marts of trade, on main streets competing for the ears of listeners with the rattling of trolley cars and horns of autos." "To this day, the memory of that trip makes the cold chills run down my back," she recalled in her memoirs. "However, I am grateful for all it taught me about the open-air meeting, that ideal auditorium for those who are trying to push an unpopular cause, who have in their pack no drawing cards, and lack money to 'go hire a hall.'"[71]

The final stop on the trolley tour was Poughkeepsie, home of Vassar, Harriot's alma mater, and of a rising generation eager to participate in a more modern and militant suffrage movement. President James Monroe Taylor forbade any woman suffrage activities on Vassar grounds, so senior Inez Milholland (who later became a famous suffrage speaker) arranged for the meeting to be held off-campus. For this final rally, Charlotte Perkins Gilman came up from New York, but it was Rose Schneiderman, the labor suffragist, who was the star speaker.[72]

As a result of "these two weeks spent experimenting with open-air meetings" the Equality League began a steady campaign of suffrage propaganda in New York City. "The out-door meeting is the popular method of reaching the people," Harriot preached. A speakers' bureau was set up to train women in public speaking. They concentrated on working women's clubs and trade unions, "audiences . . . of people who have never heard the subject discussed before." By the summer of 1909, the Equality League was holding regular outdoor meetings all over the city and recruiting steadily. A permanent headquarters was opened in a downtown building shared with the Women's Trade Union League.[73]

Suffragette methods brought much-needed publicity to the New York City suffrage movement. Suffrage activities had long been ignored in the mainstream press; if a meeting was reported, mention of it was usually buried in a small article in the back pages, which focused on the absurdity of women trying to organize a political campaign. The prejudice of the newspapers was compounded by suffragists' acceptance of the Victorian convention that respectable women did not court public attention. The Equality League's emphasis on the importance of paid labor for women of all classes struck at the heart of the conventional reverence for domesticity as the marker of femininity; publicity no longer held a special horror for its members—they invited it. By 1908, newspaper coverage had increased substantially and even the sneering *New York Times* reported regularly on the suffrage movement.

Militant tactics broke through the "press boycott" by violating standards of respectable femininity, making the cause "newsworthy," and embracing the subsequent ridicule and attention. Speaking at the National American Woman Suffrage Convention in 1908 on behalf of the new methods, Harriot explained the principle of publicity by a clever meditation on Lucretia Mott's famous objection to her mother's determination to raise the issue of political equality at the 1848 Seneca Falls Convention: "Why Lizzie, thee will make us ridiculous!" Like modern militants, the women of Seneca Falls "were not afraid of ridicule, nay they courted ridicule, for ridicule would spread the knowledge of the truth," Harriot insisted. "That is the pith of the movement we see to-day in England, our cause has been made known by the suffragettes. . . . Ridicule, ridicule, ridicule, blessed be ridicule."[74]

It is a measure of the complexity of the class relations within the suffrage movement that Harriot Stanton Blatch, who pioneered in bringing in working-class women, was simultaneously one of the leaders in recruiting women of great wealth. Many of the upper-class women who eventually became prominent in New York suffragism were her political protégés. As Caroline Lexow said of Harriot many years later, she formed "a connecting link between the two economic extremes of the suffrage movement . . . joining under one banner the forces of labor and wealth united for the common object of enfranchisement."[75] While Harriot's suffrage leadership initially grew out of her links to wage-earning women and to labor, her association with wealthy women underwrote her more ambitious plans and the route she saw to political victory. The resources upper-class women brought to suffragism—their wealth, connections to men of power, and cultural capacity to signify changing femininity—eventually gave them the wherewithal to control the movement, as against the historical initiative and numerical strength of working-class women. Unique among the suffrage leaders of the period, Harriot was situated at this point of contradiction, encouraging the aspirations to power of both classes.

Harriot's first exposure to elite suffragism had been in 1894 when she had joined her mother in the failed New York suffrage campaign. From the beginning, elite suffragism had complex motivations: an awareness of the changing standards of womanhood as they affected the upper classes through higher education and professionalization; aspirations to join with elite men in making government more "responsible" and politics more orderly; expectations that women of the lower classes would take political direction from their "betters"; and a sincere conviction that women would bring more harmonious class relations to American politics.[76] The high society suffragists of 1909 and 1910 followed in these paths, but were even wealthier than their 1894 predecessors; their class status rested less on their family and cultural standing than on their—or rather their husbands' and fathers'—mammoth fortunes. The magnitude of their wealth, what it could buy for the suffrage movement, the political influence associated with it, and the cultural power to set standards of what counted as "womanly"—all of this was new to the suffrage movement and profoundly altered it.

The first "queen of society" to associate herself with the twentieth-century New York suffrage movement was Katherine Duer Mackay, society beauty and wife of the founder of the International Telephone and Telegraph Company.[77] Mackay made her suffrage debut at a December 1908 public meeting of the Interurban Woman Suffrage Council, a loose federation of New York City suffrage groups under the leadership of Carrie Chapman Catt.[78] Katherine Mackay's suffragism was ladylike in every way. Her goals were to cultivate support for suffrage among men of wealth and power, and make prosuffrage sentiment socially acceptable in the best circles. Nonetheless, her woman suffrage ambition almost immediately overran the staid Interurban Council, and she turned to Harriot to help her set up her own woman suffrage fiefdom.[79] With Harriot's help, Mackay formed her own exclusive suffrage group, the Equal Franchise Society, which provided a conduit for other elite women to enter the suffrage movement.[80] Among these were Florence Harriman, Mrs. William Vanderbilt, and most important, the wife of urban railway magnate O. P. Belmont (and divorced wife of Mr. Vanderbilt), Alva Belmont.[81]

If Mackay demonstrated that a woman could be fabulously wealthy and a moderate suffragist, Alva Belmont made it clear that she could be a millionaire and a militant as well. Belmont quickly became impatient with Mackay's conservatism. After a trip to England, she returned a fan of the Pankhursts and an advocate of the militant style. "I do not think it is necessary to go so far as the English suffragettes do," she told reporters, "but I do think that we shall have to struggle to gain what we want. I most emphatically believe in street meetings for one thing."[82] Belmont's attraction to "suffragettism" had several sources. As a divorced woman already outside the pale of respectability, she dealt with her notoriety by embracing, even reveling in it. She had personal grievances against male power and female inequality which were deeply felt and found expression in her militant suffragism.[83] She angrily repudiated the status assigned to women of her class as idle, powerless ornaments of their husbands' wealth. Finally, she and Mackay were engaged in an energetic competition for prominence in the suffrage movement—rival society queens that they were: Mackay staked out the ground of "dignified" suffrage advocacy, whereas Belmont asserted her militance on behalf of the cause.[84]

It is curious that Harriot allied herself with Mackay, despite her tactical conservatism, and not with Belmont, who shared her attraction to the militant style. But from Mackay, Harriot could get financial support, access to wealthy women, and yet be left on her own when it came to the arenas in which she expected to set the agenda—the spectacular and the political. "There was an unspoken gentleman's [sic] agreement between Mrs. Mackay and me," Harriot recalled. "She never mentioned parades, Votes-for-Women balls, and other beating of the drums of public propaganda. And I, on my part, never suggested she might wander forth on these thorny paths."[85] By contrast Alva Belmont, who considered herself quite the militant, intended to wield her authority in these areas, thus assuring a clash of titans with Harriot.

Moreover, Harriot might well have recognized the differences between her and Belmont's versions of militance. The less terms such as *militance* and *suffragette* were tainted by socialist radicalism the more comfortable Belmont was in using them.[86] Her attitude to democracy was disdainful, to say the least. Much later, while preparing her autobiography, Harriot recorded a disturbing story about an unnamed wealthy suffragist, who was probably Belmont. This woman, she recalled, intended to use her wealth to "buy up the [State Senate] Judiciary Committee" to secure a favorable report on woman suffrage. Harriot was appalled and concluded that the woman "was unbalanced," an assessment that was strengthened when the woman implored her to "be the heroine and blow up the capital [in Albany] with a bomb!" Harriot recalled that she took counsel with Katherine Mackay and secured the aid of other suffrage leaders "to steer the lady back within the proper lines."[87]

Throughout 1909, the doings of the society suffragists fascinated the popular media. The involvement of these women heralded what a few years before would have been unimaginable: suffrage had become fashionable!

The newspapers and popular magazines took a particularly active role in declaring that the new high society converts had suddenly, single-handedly, made suffragism compelling to the modern woman.[88] A representative article trumpeted the fact that the movement had passed out of the hands of the "good gray women who have given their lives" to it, into the superior executive skill of the "women who are giving their influence and their check-books." The "near-rich" would become suffragists just to be able to follow the lead of the truly wealthy.[89] According to her private secretary, Katherine Mackay "realized that she had news value [which] would help the suffrage movement": the reporters came to cover her clothes and left with carefully prepared summaries of suffrage arguments.[90]

Veteran suffragists were thrilled with the high society suffragists; a woman like Mackay cast an aura of fashionability over everyone in the movement. "Snobbery is a sorry thing," wrote a correspondent to the *Woman's Journal*, "but the suffragist has for so many years been sniffed at by the Anti as an unfashionable, unpopular and unwomanly creature that she may perhaps be excused for breathing a sign of relief . . . to have smart people demanding your tickets." Inez Haines, a young Radcliffe graduate, had a similar reaction. "As for the suffrage movement, it is actually fashionable now," she wrote to a friend. "Oh God it's so good!"[91]

All this enthusiasm for what the newspapers characterized as the "bravery" that women like Mackay and Belmont had shown by stepping out of their "exclusive and fashionable" circles to support suffrage overshadowed the trade union women who had led in the revitalization of the suffrage movement over the prior two years.[92] Nonetheless, the involvement in suffrage of very rich women like Belmont and Mackay was a direct response to working-class suffrage activism. Because working-class women were beginning to demand the vote for themselves, wealthy women, who had long seen it as the prerogative of the elite to speak for the poor, were moved to demand it on their behalf. The politics of the "society suffragists" ran the range from conservative to liberal, but what they saw as their obligation to oversee working-class women figured prominently for all.[93]

Conservatives like Mackay acted in the old women's movement tradition of noblesse oblige, offering aid to the women of the poor, whom they never imagined as agents of their own amelioration.[94] Alva Belmont, by contrast, anchored her suffragism in the new ethic of self-activity for working-class women.[95] Belmont's suffrage organization, the Political Equality Association, actively organized wage-earning women from 1909 on, and was the first suffrage society in New York City to bring African American women into the mainstream (white) movement.[96] Even so, Mackay recognized the special need for the vote of "the wage-earning woman, who must express through the ballot what her working hours and wages should be."[97] And Belmont shared with Mackay the presumption that elite women were the natural leaders of their sex. Belmont was characteristically forthright in describing what the suffragism of the women of her class had to do both with the demands of working-class women and with their own ambitions for power. "Women of wealth and social power . . . now believe the suffrage to be a necessity for women wage-earners," she wrote. "And having once realized that the ballot means power, these women soon decided that they want this power for themselves, to protect their own interests and to enforce their own will in many directions."[98]

To Harriot, these society suffragists offered a solution to her persistent need for funds to support serious suffrage work, which the Equality League, with its self-supporter base, could not provide. While the principle of a democratically funded suffrage movement appealed to her, she had ambitious plans for public demonstrations and serious legislative lobbying that she could not pursue without financial help from other sources. A fundraising letter in early 1910 sent to eight hundred members of the Equality League netted only one hundred dollars. Charles Beard gave lectures on American politics and Florence Kelley organized a series of Sunday afternoon teas to raise money, but the returns on such efforts were paltry.[99] The suffrage establishment had always insisted on limiting its expenditures to the funds on hand. This financial conservatism exasperated Harriot. The notion that "the money for suffrage is a fixed quantity" which prudent leaders must expend carefully was in her opinion "as mistaken as the exploded theory held by the old Manchester school of economists as to the wage fund." On the contrary, "the money lying ready for suffrage is limitless. How to tap the reservoir is the only problem."[100] Millionaires like Katherine Mackay and her friends provided the answer.

At a more personal level, Harriot seemed to understand, even identify with the desire for power drawing these wealthy women into suffragism. Harriot's own sense of individual superiority, such a strong part of her character, led her to sympathize with women like Katherine Mackay. "Here was a beautiful and charming young woman, a social leader, longing for a broader stage to move upon than the usual outlet given by fashionable society," she wrote in her memoirs. "Naturally an office under a leader did not attract her in the least. She wanted to be on the top, running a show herself."[101] Harriot was quite an elegant woman herself and moved comfortably in these circles. Frances Perkins, then a settlement house worker, remembered her as "a kind of bridge" between the old style of suffragism and these elite women. She "had married well . . . [was] very stylish and good looking and had a flair and a style" that upper-class women appreciated.[102]

For the next few years, Harriot functioned both in Mackay's upper-class organization and with the Self-Supporters of the Equality League. Years later, writing from an explicitly socialist perspective, she was cynical about the alliances of this period, remarking that so long as she kept "the sheep and goats carefully separated," Mackay would help her reach conservative women and women of wealth, while she continued her work with trade union women and women with radical politics in the Equality League.[103] But at the time, she was hopeful about the unity that women could achieve on behalf of their own equality. At a 1909 mass meeting she organized at Cooper Union, millionaires and trade unionists shared the platform, as "society and labor joined hands" to demand votes for women.[104] This was the Progressive era ethic in its purest form: one could be prolabor in politics and yet move comfortably among the rich and powerful in personal life. Class conflict had to be acknowledged, but if it was addressed forthrightly, class harmony would be the result. Oppositions could be resolved.

With the exception of Katherine Mackay, many of the other wealthy women in the Equal Franchise Society were attracted to the modern and aggressive methods Harriot advocated. On at least one occasion in 1909, Harriot and some of these upper-class suffragists held an uptown version of the suffragette street meeting, agitating the crowds outside the Colony Club, to which they retired afterward for lunch.[105] Many of these wealthy women recalled later that it was Harriot Stanton Blatch who encouraged them to speak in public, address a rally, walk in a parade, and in general to develop new skills and a sense of public competence that they had never known. "It was Mrs. Blatch who insisted that I could speak; that I must speak, and then saw to it that I did speak," recalled Louisine Havemeyer, the wealthy art collector turned suffragist. "I think I spoke just to please her."[106] As a friendly journalist later observed, "Conservatives who had frowned on the outdoor method of campaigning as not quite—well they didn't use the word ladylike, but they meant it—adopted it with enthusiasm til [the kind of woman] who had lived the sheltered life of a petted protected woman would be seen talking freedom for women to huge swirling crowds on the most congested parts of the East Side."[107]

In 1910, when the Self-Supporters announced that they would hold their first suffrage parade, several of the elite members of the Equal Franchise Society indicated their interest in participating. Harriot later recalled how strongly Mrs. Mackay had objected to a public demonstration. "As she grasped the fact that her board was against her, she beat the table with her hands and in uncontrolled fury, as one after another voted to join the procession, buried her face at last in her hands."[108] Unlike the American Suffragettes' 1908 effort, Harriot had the resources to make this parade an expression of suffragism's power, rather than merely its daringness. Platforms for the speakers at Union Square, bands to entertain the crowd—such things cost money. With funds provided by its wealthy supporters, the Equality League was able to follow the example of the British suffragettes and have elegant banners made. Four hundred women marched, an unspecified number drove their cars (over Harriot's objection), and despite rain, ten thousand people crowded Union Square to hear suffrage speakers, including Blatch, Leonora O'Reilly, and Jessica Finch, headmistress of the exclusive Finch School.[109]

The suffrage movement, which had historically survived on many small donations, now became concerned with raising and spending money. With money, halls could be rented, newspapers could be published, lobbyists and organizers could be paid. The pursuit of publicity, that centerpiece of militance, became increasingly professionalized. Mackay paid three full-time workers to run a publicity office for her organization. Belmont personally paid the salary of Ida Husted Harper, Susan B. Anthony's official biographer, to act as a suffrage publicist, half-time for the suffrage movement, half-time for Belmont herself.[110] Suffrage newspapers, of which there had only been the *Woman's Journal* a few years before, began to proliferate. The first of these appeared in 1909 published by the American Suffragettes, and the next year the New York City branch of the state suffrage association began publishing its own paper, backed by Belmont money. Beginning in 1911, the Women's Trade Union League developed its own paper, *Life and Labor*. In 1913, just in time for the dramatic final push for woman suffrage in New York, Harriot finally got her own weekly newspaper, *Women's Political World*.

Increased funds also meant the possibility of paying women for their suffrage work. Wealthy women commonly hired young women as private secretaries, and as they became active in the suffrage movement, they extended the practice to hire other suffragists to work for them.[111] Initially, suffragists were paid for their work as stenographers and office workers, later as organizers. Among some of the college graduates, suffrage work was the first paid employment available to them. By 1910, Harriot had begun to pay a small office staff in her organization; by 1911, her budget, which had been eighteen hundred dollars in 1908, was seven times that amount, mostly for salaries.[112]

Paying women to do suffrage work led to complex changes in the relations between classes within the suffrage movement. Suffragists who earned wages for their movement work were dependent on the women of wealth who paid them. Moreover, no woman was ever paid a salary as an officer of a suffrage society, denying formal leadership to the self-supporting.[113] The pioneer militant Maud Malone, who might have been as important an innovative force as Harriot Blatch in the suffrage movement, had to work for a living and eventually became the personal employee of Alva Belmont.[114] Yet paid labor was the precondition for the spread of suffrage activism beyond women who could volunteer their labor to women who had to work for a living. "It is doubtful if any great movement can be carried through with scattered, interrupted volunteer effort," wrote one suffragist. "People have got to be paid so that they give up their whole time to it."[115]

In the midst of all this attention to the society suffragists, Harriot announced that Emmeline Pankhurst, the mother of British militance, would make her first speaking tour of the United States.[116] A year before, in December 1908, the Equality League had sponsored the visit of Anne Cobden-Sanderson, who had stressed the role of trade union women in developing militant tactics. Emmeline Pankhurst was bringing a different message for American suffragettes, the necessity of creating a militant movement for all women, in which the common bonds of sex were stronger than the class differences between them.

Pankhurst asked Harriot to arrange her U.S. tour for her. She was coming to America to raise money for both political and personal reasons. Her son, twenty-year-old Harry, had been diagnosed with infantile paralysis and money was needed for his treatment.[117] Harriot, who knew what it was to lose a child, responded immediately. Her sponsorship of Pankhurst earned her what she recalled as "a nice drubbing" from other leading suffragists on the grounds that the British leader was drawing off funds that by rights belonged to the U.S. movement, but the visit also strengthened Harriot's credibility as leader of American militance.[118] Throughout the tour, Harriot described herself as Pankhurst's "lifelong friend," and the Equality League basked in the credit for her decision to come to the United States.[119]

The news that Emmeline Pankhurst was coming to America caused quite a stir. While many were thrilled at her visit, Carrie Chapman Catt, the moderate leader of New York suffragism, was anxious lest Pankhurst's charismatic capacity to advocate militant methods would produce a "deluge of suffrage anarchy."[120] Anna Garlin Spencer, a veteran suffragist, refused to endorse the Pankhurst visit, though she feared that she had "placed myself in the category of the 'moral snobs' . . . in the eyes of my friend Mrs. Blatch."[121] While working to erase the lines of class in the suffrage movement,

Pankhurst was deepening the divisions of tactics and style between those who saw themselves as moderate and those who preferred the label "militant."

Harriot organized a grand opening meeting for Pankhurst at Carnegie Hall. Her goal was to bring together the disparate elements of the New York suffrage movement—especially the working and wealthy classes—under the British leader's mantle. At the rally, four hundred Self-Supporters were seated on the platform, representing "all shades and grades of professional and industrial work—lawyers, doctors, nurses, artists etc."[122] Hundreds of free tickets were distributed to wage-earning women, and Trade Union League president Margaret Dreier Robins welcomed Mrs. Pankhurst "on behalf of the organized working women" of the United States. But the meeting also featured high society suffragists, the women with the financial resources that Emmeline Pankhurst and Harriot Blatch sought to tap. Prominent wealthy women purchased banks of seats to offset costs.[123] Alva Belmont, who competed with Harriot for access to Pankhurst's militant cachet, hosted a reception in the luxurious office quarters she had just opened for the National American Woman Suffrage Association on Fifth Avenue.[124]

In planning Emmeline Pankhurst's first American tour, Harriot had to struggle to hold these class extremes together. Between upper-class women aspiring to exercise the power of their class, and working-class women struggling to realize the power of theirs, the bonds of common womanhood were stretched taut. To those elite women who were not yet willing to distinguish Pankhurst's radicalism from the radicalism of strikers and anarchists, Harriot offered reassurances that "the holders of the boxes and the occupiers of seats on the platform will put you in good company."[125] Conversely, to labor suffragists who were concerned that the form of suffrage which the British suffragettes were pursuing would exclude working-class women, she explained that the British freehold suffrage "would enfranchise a much larger number of wage earning women than women of the leisure class."[126] Both classes, however, were eager to see Emmeline Pankhurst, a powerful speaker, a beautiful and "womanly" woman, and an unparalleled feminist icon; especially in light of the challenge that the militant suffrage style posed to traditional femininity, she was a great relief to many women worried about what being a "suffragette" would mean for them.[127] The hall was filled to overflowing and the event netted a substantial sum, not just for Pankhurst but also for the Equality League coffers.[128]

After a month of touring the United States, Mrs. Pankhurst returned to

New York to take her leave. Helen Garrison Villard reported that she "never heard a mortal speech so appealing, so uplifting [as Pankhurst's farewell speech]. There were men in the audience who cried." Emmeline Pankhurst's militant appeal both emphasized class distinctions among women and urged the suffrage movement to transcend them. Faced with the inferiority of disfranchisement and the ignominy to which suffragettes had been subjected, women had learned "we are all born under a ban, and whether the wife or daughter of the rich man or the poorest man in the land, we are all outclassed because we are women." It was the suffragettes' great achievement, greater perhaps than political equality itself, to teach women "to trust one another . . . to value our womanhood before everything else in the world." "We have broken down class distinctions," Pankhurst proclaimed to wild applause.[129]

In describing the unity of women, Pankhurst assumed the leadership of upper-class women. If any class deserved to be singled out for special honor, Pankhurst argued, it was the elite, because their sacrifice was so great. "If there is any distinction of class at all," she told her audience, "it is the privileged women, the honored women [who] are doing the hardest and most unpleasant work [for suffrage] . . . who have never had to face the struggle for existence."[130] Her speech was filled with references to armies, wars, disciplined battle, and final victory, and the military metaphor was powered less by the enmity of men than by the comradeship of women. However, all armies, even of women, need an order of march; in hers, upper-class women found an expanded field of action by taking the lead, displacing working women as they did.

On December 5, the day Pankhurst sailed back to England, news of her departure was pushed out of the headlines by an event that embodied both the hope and the limits of her vision of "women for women now."[131] With great fanfare, the New York suffrage movement threw its considerable resources behind the month-and-a-half-long strike of New York City women shirtwaist workers.[132] Weeks before, in early November, striking workers at two of the city's largest shirtwaist shops had come to the activists of the Women's Trade Union League for help. Their pickets were being intimidated by hired thugs and arrested by police. Elite women reformers took over the picketing when an injunction banned the workers themselves from demonstrating. When Mary Dreier, president of the New York Women's Trade Union League, was arrested on the line, the newspapers finally gave the strike front-page coverage.[133] Two and a half weeks later, on November 22, the striking women and their sponsors in the International Ladies Garment Workers Union parlayed this publicity bonanza into a general strike of the entire shirtwaist industry.

On December 5, the day Emmeline Pankhurst left New York, Alva Belmont announced that she had rented the giant Hippodrome theater for a rally of suffragists and other supporters on behalf of the strike. Many other suffragists quickly followed suit with aid. Harriot offered the resources of the Equality League of Self-Supporting Women to the strikers, and its members walked the picket lines, addressed support rallies, and gave money. Even Anna Howard Shaw, the ineffectual president of the National American Woman Suffrage Association, spoke at Belmont's Hippodrome meeting and declared, "Our cause is your cause, and your cause is our cause."[134]

The story of the shirtwaist strike has been told many times, but the degree to which the transformation of the New York suffrage movement set the context for the strike has not been sufficiently appreciated.[135] For more than three years, forward-looking suffragists, chief among them Harriot Blatch, had been remaking the suffrage movement in ways that made suffragist support of the shirtwaist strike possible. Harriot had taken the lead in stressing the importance of reformulating the case for women's rights around the centrality of women's work, and had forged organizational links between organized working women and the woman suffrage movement. By 1909, the inseparability of woman suffragism and trade unionism, of political and industrial emancipation for women, had gained wide currency. Bertha Weyl, one of the Women's Trade Union League members most involved with the strike, declared, "The industrial and woman suffrage movement must go together in this strike."[136] The striking women themselves wore suffrage buttons on the picket lines.[137]

In addition, the increasingly familiar arsenal of suffragette tactics influenced the character of the strike support movement and reinforced the militant conduct of the strike itself. Suffragists supported the strike with open-air meetings, mass rallies, auto caravans, even a disciplined women's parade—tactics the New York suffrage movement had been using for the past two years.[138] The skillful focus on publicity that historians have noticed in the conduct of the strike especially built on the suffrage militants' theory and practice in this area. Harriot chaired the Women's Trade Union League's publicity committee and helped to manage the newspaper coverage.[139] Even the basic issue around which suffragists organized support for the strike—police brutality against the workers—reflected what American suffragists had just heard from Emmeline Pankhurst about the martyrdom of the British suffragettes at the hands of the police. Supporters' accounts of their experi-

ences with police on the picket lines and before night court judges emphasized sexual insult, "unprintable language," and dangers to the picketers'
womanhood; these themes were not simply unmediated reactions to the
events of the strike, but imports from Pankhurst's account of the arrest and
imprisonment of British suffragettes.[140]

Above all, the leadership role taken by wealthy women in the strike
support effort reflected developments in the suffrage movement. The enthusiasm with which upper-class women made the strikers' cause their own was
an outgrowth of their suffragism, in particular their eagerness to claim
political responsibility for the women of the poorer classes. Certainly
Belmont's role in the strike was a direct extension of her suffrage activity.
Other upper-class suffragist supporters of the strike ranged from wealthy
young college graduates like the Equality League's Inez Milholland, to whom
picket duty was a badge of honor, to dignified matrons, many of them
members of Mackay's Equal Franchise Society, who met the strikers over
lunch at the Colony Club and raised fifteen hundred dollars for them by
passing around one of their large picture hats. Most of the coverage that the
strike got was a result of the attention the papers paid to the rich women, for
it was their willingness to extend themselves into exotic environments
like night court or the picket line, rather than the strike itself, that was
newsworthy.[141]

These wealthy women were motivated to support the shirtwaist strikers, as
they were motivated to demand the vote, for many reasons: identification
with aspects of the strikers' experience, especially the contempt with which
public authority, the police and the courts, treated them; the feeling that the
young girl strikers needed their protection and the sense of importance this
gave them; and the power they felt at forcing the shirtwaist manufacturers
(most of them Jewish businessmen) to settle with the strikers. Most often, the
story of the shirtwaist strike is told as a great triumph of sisterhood over class
barriers, and the financial and political support of wealthy women certainly
helped the strikers to endure police and judicial harassment. But there was a
downside to the class relations of the strike as well, and from the larger
perspective of the suffrage movement, the outcome of the strike intensified
class antagonisms and deepened political divisions in the New York women's
movement.

As the strike progressed, the upper-class supporters took their guardian-
ship of the strikers literally, and moved to take control of the strike. Next to
Belmont, the most powerful strike supporter was Ann Morgan, daughter of
J. P. Ann Morgan brought in Eva Valesh, a conservative trade unionist, to try
to settle the strike.[142] In January 1910, Valesh urged the strikers to accept the

terms being offered by the larger shirtwaist manufacturers, even though the offer omitted union recognition. When the strikers refused, Valesh and Morgan went to the newspapers to blame "fanatical socialist doctrines" for this reckless act. Another strike support rally followed, but as the issue at the heart of the strike became an open conflict between workers and owners about who would control the conditions of labor, the limits of the emphasis on the abuse of police power became clear, and upper-class female support began to drop off.[143] By March, the strike was over. Although the union itself profited, the settlements the strikers made were quite weak and did not last the year. And the fact that the larger shops never settled left unchanged the dangerous conditions—especially barred exits—which just one year later, set the stage for the terrible fire at the Triangle Shirtwaist Company that killed 146 women.

Just as the suffrage movement helped to set the context for the shirtwaist strike, the course of the strike had its effect on the suffrage movement. In the beginning, the strike expressed the militant vision of women setting aside the distinction of class and standing "shoulder to shoulder" in defense of the least of their sex. Its outcome, however, showed how little control working-class women had over the terms of this collaboration. The outcome of the strike shifted the class dynamic of the suffrage movement away from labor and working-class influences, consolidating the power of wealth. Belmont's leadership claim was established beyond challenge by the role she took in the strike, and from there on it was a steady climb for her to national suffrage leadership. Furthermore, the final conflicts of the strike created new divisions and mistrust among suffragists. In the wake of Morgan and Valesh's attack on socialists, there was far more antisocialism among society suffragists, and more "anti-Belmontism" among socialist suffragists than before.[144]

The relation between the outcome of the strike and the consolidation of the political power of upper-class women within the suffrage movement affected Harriot's political position as well. Despite her long association with the Women's Trade Union League, when conflicts from the shirtwaist strike spilled over into the larger women's movement, she took the side of the wealthy supporters. When working-class members of the Women's Trade Union League called for the ouster of Eva Valesh because of her antisocialist remarks, Harriot was one of only two members to vote against the resolution.[145] In this antagonistic atmosphere, Harriot was formally censored for operating her organization's offices without union labor.[146] She may well have been the target for class antagonisms that could not be expressed more directly. It is curious, for instance, that she (and Valesh) were the objects of the wrath of working-class members of the Trade Union League, while Ann

Morgan was not. Similarly, Margaret Dreier Robins, who funded the Women's Trade Union League, emerged from the conflicts of the strike unscathed, despite her close collaboration with Morgan. Not a beneficent patron but a suffrage boss paying wages, Harriot was caught between capital and labor in her own organization, equally dependent on wage-earners for work and on wealthy women for the money to pay them.

As a consequence of these conflicts, the links Harriot had so carefully forged between the Trade Union League and the Equality League were broken. The Trade Union League formally terminated its three-year cooperation with the Equality League. Rose Schneiderman, a leader of the Equality League since its formation, was particularly angry at Harriot and charged that the Equality League no longer was "supported by working women."[147] Harriot was not reappointed to the Trade Union League Executive Committee and ceased attending meetings altogether.[148] The Trade Union League, which had made suffrage a priority in 1907 and 1908, turned away from the issue for the next few years, its interest not reviving until 1913.[149]

The erosion of Harriot Blatch's association with trade-union suffragists fed into her growing reliance on wealthy women. For the next several years, she continued to recruit talented upper-class women and to rely ever more heavily on their counsel in her suffrage work. Katherine Mackay, increasingly unable to tolerate the militant direction to which her own followers were tending, dropped out of suffrage work, but she was succeeded by others at least as wealthy and prominent. Vera Whitehouse, wife of a major investment banker and one of the wealthiest New York suffragists, was "discovered" by Nora and cultivated by Harriot. Another of Harriot's crucial upper-class advisers was Eunice Dana Brannan, daughter of Charles Dana, publisher of the *New York Sun,* and wife of John Brannan, head of the Board of Trustees for Bellevue Hospital. In 1910, Harriot announced that Eunice Brannan would chair a finance committee, the goal of which was to raise one hundred thousand dollars for suffrage agitation in New York.[150]

These two developments—the erosion of Harriot's alliances with working-class feminists and her growing bonds with wealthy suffragists—led her, in November 1910, to announce that the Equality League of Self-Supporting Women would henceforth be known as the Women's Political Union (WPU).[151] The change of name was a portent of deeper changes within her suffrage leadership. Within the new title there were three related references to Harriot's changing priorities. First of all, the name Women's Political Union was a direct reference to the Women's Social and Political Union, Emmeline Pankhurst's militant suffrage organization. On November 11, 1910—"Black Friday"—the British suffragettes of the WSPU had fought a violent and bloody battle with London police. The decision to change the name of the Equality League, coming so soon after this dramatic episode, was meant to indicate support of the WSPU, despite its escalating militance. The new Women's Political Union sealed this identification by choosing as its organizational colors white, purple, and green, the same colors as for the WSPU.[152] The WPU's inaugural public event was to sponsor the debut U.S. tour of Sylvia Pankhurst, Emmeline's twenty-eight-year-old daughter. Introducing her, Harriot declared that the British militants had done American suffragists an incomparable service: "They have wakened us to know ourselves."[153]

Second, the new title signaled Harriot's move away from her original class politics for suffragism—her special emphasis on working women and the priority she placed on trade union alliances. The 1911–12 annual report of the Women's Political Union explained the change of name in terms of the "desire to adopt a title for the society which should not carry the idea of discrimination against any class of people."[154] Here "discrimination" meant giving special emphasis to working-class women, instead of letting upper-class women take their "natural" place of leadership. "We didn't want the aristocracy, the snobbery if you will, of self support," Nora explained with unconscious irony. "We wanted to be absolutely democratic so we decided not to discriminate against the leisure classes."[155]

In subsequent years, the tactical disagreements between suffrage militants and conservatives would intensify, becoming so deep that historians still cannot see beyond this split to the larger forces at work in suffrage history. But there were no substantial class differences in this militant-conservative divide; both sides had come to reflect similar patterns of elite domination. The possibility of a woman suffrage movement in which working-class women were not subordinate elements but leaders, a movement which might have upended the class character of the organized woman's movement, which could have linked militant suffragette tactics to radical working-class politics, gave way to the consolidation of upper-class leadership. Harriot had been fundamental to all stages of this process, including the legitimation of the new upper-class leadership of New York suffragism.

Finally, the new name of the Women's Political Union was meant to signify the decision to concentrate on political work and to leave base building activities like the mass recruitment of new suffragists and the development of suffrage propaganda to other groups.[156] Harriot's new upper-class supporters not only brought with them financial resources, but also had access to and influence over politically powerful men. Elizabeth Selden Rogers was the sister-in-law of Henry L. Stimson, later U.S. secretary of war; Elizabeth Kent was the wife of a California congressman; and Dora Hazard had considerable influence with New York legislators in and around Syracuse. Harriot's new emphasis on electoral and legislative strategies—turning her organization into "an instrument keyed exclusively to the political aspect of the suffrage movement"—was the aspect of her suffrage work of which she was proudest, and it is to that we now turn.[157]

5

Politics

"There was not a baker's dozen who saw a connection between the advancement of suffrage and politics as they existed in our native state in 1910," wrote Harriot in her autobiography.[1] In 1910, New York politics was in the midst of a transformation from the structures that had dominated it since the Civil War into the form that it would take for the twentieth century. Two basic processes were at work. One was a conflict between reformers and regulars in both parties over whether and how various progressive demands for social justice would be introduced into legislation. The other was the shift of progressive political hopes and energies from the Republican to the Democratic party.[2]

Starting in 1910, the crucial task facing New York suffragism was to force the state legislature to pass a bill authorizing a voters' referendum on suffrage. For the next three years, Harriot lobbied and politicked tirelessly to this end. It would be easy to miss the importance of this part of the New York state suffrage campaign, sandwiched as it was between the dramatic modernization of the movement before 1910 and the spirited electoral drive conducted between 1913 and 1915. But Harriot understood these efforts were crucial to the victory of votes for women. Professional politicians held the fate of woman suffrage in their hands; they had the power to repeatedly delay, even permanently halt, the forward motion of women's demand for political equality. Moreover, in facing male political power head on, women effected the deeper cultural and psychological changes, the transformations of masculinity and femininity that were necessary if enfranchisement was ever going to signify the revolution in gender relations that suffragists had always said it would.

During her first session of concerted lobbying in Albany in 1910, Harriot concentrated on establishing her authority over the legislative campaign and assembling the necessary parliamentary knowledge. The next year, when Democrats took control of both houses, she was ready to move. The links to working women she had built through the Equality League helped her to address the prolabor forces in the Democratic party. Then, in 1912, when the Progressive bolt from the Republican party created a situation in which no party had full control, Harriot saw the first real possibility for passage. Finally, in 1913, reluctant state legislators were forced to accept the suffrage referendum and pass it on to the voters. It took Harriot four years of complex and sustained legislative lobbying to win this part of the suffrage battle.

From one perspective, her target was the New York legislature, but at least as often, she regarded the regular suffrage lobby, the conservative and circumspect group of mostly upstate women working under the rubric of the New York State Woman Suffrage Association, as the greater obstacle to progress. "The difficulties in the suffrage path, it seemed to me, were not so much the intricacies of amending State and Federal Constitutions," she wrote in her memoirs, "as that there did not seem to be a grain of political knowledge in the movement."[3] For over a decade, the state society had been sweeping into Albany, delivering its arguments at polite hearings, and allowing itself to be assured by friends in the legislature that the cause was slowly advancing. Its assumption was that its "educational" efforts would gradually create more and more support for suffrage until the legislature would pass the woman suffrage amendment out to the voters. Harriot believed this approach to be futile, a reflection of women's naïveté about the self-interest and negotiations over power that really moved politicians. "While all educational work is not necessarily political," she insisted, "all political work is educational. Every stroke on the political side educates."[4]

Even from the distance of so many years, her conviction of her political infallibility is irritating, and so it must have been to her contemporaries, who were as eager as she to get the state legislature moving on woman suffrage. Nonetheless, the Women's Political Union under her direction was indisputably the driving force in state suffrage politics in these years. It was not so much that Harriot's political instincts were always right, as that she was already functioning as a politician. In the face of disappointments and betrayals from individual legislators and entire parties, she was always ready to adapt to political circumstances, change tactics, negotiate with whom she must, and adjust her strategic direction. New York State was the most complex yet crucial political venue in the United States, and short of regarding the coming of woman suffrage as an inevitable force obliterating all political obstacles in its path, the centrality of Harriot's individual contribution must be recognized.

Harriot's own evaluation of her contribution to the woman suffrage movement centered on legislative politics; she experienced the 1913 legislative authorization of the suffrage referendum as a sweet and personal achievement. The political maneuvering and power-mongering, which women had traditionally repudiated as the unhappy consequences of the male monopoly of politics, challenged and invigorated her. Her reminiscences of this three-year campaign occupy almost a third of her autobiography, and her retrospective relish in remembering every parliamentary detail is evident; it is a good guess that she never felt more powerful or more the woman she wanted to be than in these years, when she was playing "the game of politics." "She had an exceptional comprehension of politics and government," Mary Beard wrote about Harriot just after her death, "and she worked steadfastly to root the suffrage movement in politics, where alone it could reach its goal."[5]

What does it mean to say that Harriot Blatch was distinctly "political" when the singular goal of the movement within which she worked was political rights and had been for over half a century? A decade later, after the Nineteenth Amendment had been secured, Carrie Chapman Catt made a distinction between "voting," into which women had at last been admitted, and "politics," from which they remained largely excluded.[6] Even as organized suffragism was nearing its goal of political equality, it still held fast to the rhetorical framework which identified the existing practice of politics with men, self-servingness, and corruption and counterposed it with women, morality, and social welfare. There was something about politics that made it harder for women to take than other male preserves, such as education or paid labor. Nor was it simply that men defended their monopoly over political power with all the weapons at their disposal, although that certainly was the case. The politicization of woman suffrage was as marked by women's hesitancy as men's hostility.

A fundamental element of suffragist aversion to practicing politics was women's horror of political parties. Even for suffragists, female nonpartisanship still had the status of a first principle. Men were also critics of excessive partisanship, but male and female nonpartisanship had different meanings. Traditional political partisanship was male to the core: to be a man you had to have a party. Men who criticized party excesses were vulnerable to charges of being "unmanly." By contrast, female nonpartisanship was compatible with, indeed constitutive of womanliness. "Women are different from men and their political methods will differ from those of men," explained Laura Clay in an important debate in 1897 on suffrage nonpartisanship.[7] Partisan politics seemed so inexorably "male" in the Victorian context because it involved conflict, opposition, contest. "Women at war with each other make particularly displeasing sounds, and their attitudes lack dignity and grace," editorialized the *New York Times*.[8]

Women's nonpartisanship was therefore more a statement about the system of gender that established and monitored boundaries between masculinity and femininity than an informed critique of how political parties thwarted the democratic will. Traditional female nonpartisanship complemented and reinforced male partisanship in a variety of ways. Inasmuch as most women lived in intimate and dependent relations with men, their proud female contempt for parties coexisted with class and family associations that inclined them toward a particular party. In New York, these inclinations were largely Republican. And when women did associate themselves with overtly political campaigns (for instance, when the Women's Municipal League advocated reform candidates for New York City mayor in the late 1890s), their involvement elevated their male allies by clothing their otherwise suspect political involvements in the selfless concern with community welfare associated with women's reform activism.[9]

The process to which Harriot had dedicated herself—finding a practical route to the realization of woman suffrage—led her to engage with parties as the basic structure of politics; but the character of New York politics in these years made it necessary for her to deal with both Republicans and Democrats, not to count on one or the other. Thus, her approach was neither nonpartisan in a traditionally female way nor partisan in a traditionally male way; she neither abjured the party system nor pledged loyalty to a particular party (though her own family inclinations were Democratic). When she spoke of herself as "nonpartisan," she meant that she was willing and able to take on opponents from any party; she did not mean that she would have nothing to do with the entire system of political parties. She recognized that parties were the necessary territory through which anyone with a serious legislative objective must move. "Any determined minority under the political system which we have in the United States can work its will," Harriot was concluding, "if marshalled by those who have at their command enthusiasm and political understanding."[10]

Harriot considered herself "a born politician,"[11] and she had the lineage on both sides for it. Her mother and Susan B. Anthony had immersed themselves in men's politics more than any other women of their generation. "Taught by two such veteran campaigners as my mother and Miss Anthony," she recalled, "I realized that women must adopt their own plan of action, shoulder the responsibility and be willing to accept temporary defeat."[12] But fundamentally she identified politics as masculine and associated her own deeply felt political tendencies with her father. The masculine character of politics drew her to it; she liked that the traditional practice of politics embraced the aspiration for power straightforwardly, unqualified and unashamed. Yet it was no simple task for her to claim this paternal inheritance. Men were contemptuous of women in politics, a response to which Harriot was regularly exposed.[13] The hostility of male politicians was like a gauntlet thrown in her face, a challenge she felt bound to answer and confident she could meet. She was driven by the desire to demonstrate to men that she was at least their equal in politics, hopefully their better.

Harriot trusted in the system of honor by which she believed that men conducted politics among themselves.[14] She fully expected that she and other women would be better treated once they forced themselves inside the world of men's politics than they were as excluded nonparticipants. She considered the chivalrous notion that women's dependence brought out men's best qualities absurd; men respected their equals, not their subordinates. Throughout her memoirs, she described politics as a "sport" she was determined to master, "a game that becomes infinitely more enjoyable the more evenly matched the opponents."[15] She believed in the rules.

The importance of introducing a more political sensibility into the woman suffrage movement was a crucial part of the militant message delivered by Emmeline Pankhurst to her American admirers in December 1909. Pankhurst gave a dramatic account of how British militants had campaigned against Liberal candidates in strategic by-elections for their opposition to woman suffrage. This, she explained, was what it meant to "create a political situation." In urging her American audiences to follow in this path, she was in no way calling for them to set aside their own demands in order to cultivate regular party support. On the contrary, Pankhurst's call to politics was basic to her reputation in America as a fighting militant. American women had to learn how to *force* politicians to do their bidding, to insist rather than plead.[16]

Most American suffragists were baffled by the political part of Pankhurst's message.[17] Conservative Katherine Mackay found the idea that women would "demand an expression of opinion" from politicians or force their way into politics reprehensible.[18] But the militant American Suffragettes were equally appalled and dropped out of the picture when it came time to shift the strategic emphasis from propaganda to politics. To them, lobbying state senators and assemblymen meant submitting themselves to the ignorance and hostility of male politicians and constituted an unacceptable affront to their feminist pride.[19]

By contrast, Harriot's response to Pankhurst's call to confront male politicians was one of sheer enthusiasm. "Welcome to the first political leader among women in the history of the world," she telegraphed Pankhurst on her arrival in New York.[20] Harriot had worked in British politics alongside Pankhurst for almost two decades. She believed that whereas American women had remained innocent of politics, British women's experience in party auxiliaries had taught them that parties structured political power and that only when women insisted would parties take up women's demands.[21] Overall, the political aspect of the militant strategy was even more compelling to her than its emphasis on propaganda or on interclass solidarity. The result of Pankhurst's visit was to strengthen her conviction that whatever other suffragists' hesitations, she was ready to make the move into New York politics.[22]

Pankhurst's visit coincided with the important 1909 New York City mayoral elections. Having discovered that New York's pollwatching law did not specify that one had to be a voter to serve, Harriot made her first incursion into American politics as a pollwatcher. She secured Prohibition party credentials and served as a pollwatcher on the upper West Side; other Equality League members watched on the lower East Side and in the Bowery. At a postelection meeting of suffragists, Harriot riveted her audience with the details of her absorbing day inside a polling place. "We have lifted the veil, we have entered the holy of holies," she declared to a hushed audience, "and yet the Republic is going on."[23]

At one level, women pollwatchers represented a relatively traditional female suspicion of political corruption. (Harriot and her pollwatching partner, Alberta Hill, had two drunken election officials removed by the police.) But pollwatching also functioned as a challenge to the political divide between the sexes. Polling places were set up in saloons, tobacco shops, and bootblack parlors, generically male sites that excluded women. After a day at these polling places, women were no longer as mystified by politics or the men involved in it. A condescending ward heeler told Harriot that a polling place "is no place for a woman," but after her pollwatching experience, she "laughed for the polling place was nothing but a candy store." It was the men at her polling place that she found to be weak and hysterical; she reported that one of them had nearly fainted, finding "the strain [of counting the ballots] too much."[24] She concluded that pollwatching brought women "behind the scenes" in politics, where men's ignorance and weakness could be observed and their claims to political infallibility exposed.[25]

Pollwatching desanctified the male preserve of politics. Female pollwatching had about it the air of a battle over the gender character of electoral culture. The *New York Sun* published a wonderfully expressive photograph of Cornell graduate and Equality League activist Elizabeth Ellsworth Cook at her polling place, a big picture hat on her head and a triumphant grin on her face; she is surrounded by a half-dozen stony-faced men, who seem amazed at the presence of this young woman and defeated by her invasion of their traditionally male preserve. "I was the only woman there," Cook told reporters. "But I'd got so used to being the only girl in a lot of my courses at Cornell that I didn't mind abit."[26]

Pollwatching was more than a symbolic threat, of course. A year later at the 1910 election, politicians had suffragists (including Nora) arrested. Eventually, Tammany leaders found women's pollwatching so disruptive that they had the privilege eliminated. By the same token suffragists saw that pollwatching would be an essential element in their eventual victory. The care that California suffragists took in that state's historic 1911 voters' referendum to patrol the ballot count seems to have been the only thing that protected their tiny, four-thousand–vote lead.[27] In New York, Harriot continued to fight for reinstatement of the pollwatching privilege for women, and by the time woman suffrage came before New York voters in 1915, women were once again at the polls on election day.[28]

Having entered the sanctum sanctorum as a pollwatcher, Harriot was now ready to become even more involved in "men's" politics. A series of special elections for New York state legislators had been called in the winter of 1909–10, the most important of which was to replace the recently deceased state senator P. H. McCarren, Democratic boss of Brooklyn. The Equality League raised a small budget, opened a storefront, and demanded that all three candidates for the seat come out in favor of woman suffrage.[29] The league declared it could influence the votes of enough men to make a difference in a three-way race, and they held regular open-air meetings at the Brooklyn end of the Williamsburg Bridge. Right before the election, two of the three candidates declared their support for the woman suffrage referendum bill.[30]

The special elections of 1909–10 convinced Harriot that she had hit on the "true method of gaining woman suffrage." In early 1910, the Equality League formally announced its determination "to change the legislature from an indifferent body into one responsive to our ideas." "We intend to question candidates before elections, not after . . . but with a fixed purpose to work against the man who is against woman suffrage."[31] The new policy foreswore reliance on any "knight errant" to come to suffragists' aid. Women must force the situation using their own power on their own behalf. "When we get the majority in a district on our side and make the connection between public opinion and the representative in the legislature," the league predicted, "we have Woman Suffrage for the first time on its way to victory."[32]

Harriot began her legislative offensive early in the 1910 session. Aware that the fate of the woman suffrage bill was always settled after the suffragists had conducted their hearings and left town, she knew that suffragists needed a constant presence in Albany throughout the entire legislative session. She negotiated with Katherine Mackay for the initial funds to open an Albany office and to assemble a staff to assist her there.[33] Determined to regularize suffragists' relations with the legislature, Harriot hired a professional woman lobbyist. "The State suffragists have many friends among the legislators, and we have never needed a lobbyist," Ella Crossett, state suffrage president, told reporters.[34] Harriot regarded this opinion as self-defeating, and the establishment of a regular suffrage lobby as essential.[35]

Hattie Graham, the woman Harriot selected as lobbyist, conducted the first systematic canvas of New York legislators and discovered that most districts had not one legislator who believed that women deserved the vote. Even legislators who had prosuffrage friends or relatives could not be counted on for support. The assemblyman who represented the state suffrage president's district did not support the suffrage bill.[36]

Graham submitted detailed and nuanced reports to Harriot of her findings. She was attentive to personal circumstances, and much of what she reported had to do with emotional aspects of legislators' positions, on which suffrage lobbyists could play. Of one representative from Queens, she wrote: "Wife and daughter [are] suffragists. Does not know any other women in his district wishing to vote. . . . Regrets lack of education. . . . In talking with him you feel that he is a good businessman. . . . He is full of inconsistencies. Says woman's place is in the home. . . . Said women teachers should receive more pay than men to enable them to marry and support a house." And of another man from a nearby district: "He thinks women should not vote because his sister does not want to. . . . On the 17th [of January] I introduced Mrs. Blatch and Mrs. [Helen Hoy] Greeley to him as experts who would furnish him with the information he desired. He refused to ask a single question, turned and walked to his seat where he sat and laughed. The next day he apologized. On the 17th of February I was told . . . that [he] was going to support our bill, that he was in favor of suffrage."[37]

The other woman who came to work in Albany with Harriot was a twenty-eight-year-old Barnard graduate named Caroline Lexow, who went on to become Harriot's close friend and her most reliable and indefatigable organizer. Caroline Lexow had the perfect background for the legislative side of suffrage work. She had strong paternal links to the political process, stronger even than Harriot's. Her father was Clarence Lexow, the attorney and state senator who had headed the eponymous Lexow Commission that tore into New York City police corruption in 1894, thus establishing the legitimacy of subsequent calls for basic municipal political reform. "Her gift, both by inheritance and the training of environment, lay supremely along political lines," Harriot wrote. "She loved the game of politics as much as I did."[38]

Graduating from Barnard in 1904 (reputedly the only advocate of woman suffrage in her class), Caroline founded and led the New York City chapter of the College Equal Suffrage League.[39] Harriot met her in 1907, when they collaborated on the Cobden-Sanderson mass meeting. From their first meeting, an obvious affection and common sensibility linked them. "Dear fellow president and slave," Harriot playfully wrote in her first letter to Caroline.[40] By 1908 Caroline had been replaced as the College League's organizing secretary by the more cautious Harriet May Mills.[41] Harriot, eager to secure Caroline's energies and talents, convinced Katherine Mackay to appoint her executive secretary of the Equal Franchise Society, so that they could work together in Albany.[42]

In assuming the role of Harriot's first lieutenant, Caroline Lexow was taking up many of Nora's roles and responsibilities. By 1910, Nora had become absorbed by personal concerns, first by her marriage to Lee de Forest, and within a year by its dramatic and contentious breakup. Nora's hopes for a life together combining conjugal bliss and scientific discovery were in no way shared by Lee. By the time their child was born in June 1909, they were living apart. Their divorce was delayed two years as they fought over how to raise their little girl, named after her grandmother.[43] Nora assumed that she would continue her professional and political work, helped by her mother and by Elizabeth Bransom, her own nurse who had come from Basingstoke. Lee was appalled at what he considered Nora's unnatural lack of maternal feeling. He wanted to take the child himself, although his own plans were to hire a nursemaid and in no way compromise *his* professional life. De Forest's disappointment with Nora, her fall from the preconnubial glory of being his "golden girl" to being an unnatural, unmaternal, asexual "suffragette," filled the newspapers, leaving Nora much preoccupied with fighting back his claims for custody, refuting his public attack on her, and earning a living to support her daughter and herself.[44]

In the winter of 1910, Harriot and Caroline Lexow set up political shop in Albany, and almost immediately Albany politicians began to close ranks against the acceleration of suffragist demands on them. Several legislators tried to set up new obstacles to bringing votes for women to the electorate. In the Assembly Charles Dana proposed that all constitutional amendments require a supermajority of two-thirds of the legislators before being passed on for ratification.[45] In the Senate, Republican Edgar Brackett proposed holding an "election" among women themselves to show how limited their support for their own enfranchisement was. Leaders of the state society seemed intrigued by the Brackett Bill, but Harriot was disgusted. She regarded it as a deliberate attempt to make woman suffrage look ludicrous. She and Caroline fought both proposals, neither of which made any headway in the legislature.[46]

Using Hattie Graham's legislative canvas, Harriot and Caroline Lexow identified suffragists' initial strategic problem. The bill to authorize the referendum was trapped in the Senate and Assembly judiciary committees, both of which refused to report it out for a full vote of the legislature. The state suffrage association believed that support on the judiciary committees was gradually growing, an evaluation that Harriot regarded as illustrating "the Egyptian darkness in which the orthodox woman suffragists worked" with respect to political matters.[47] She began to see that prosuffrage legislators benefited as much as opponents from avoiding a vote on the suffrage issue because the combination of support and inaction could satisfy both suffragists and antis.[48] Convinced that any report, including a negative one, would advance the cause, Harriot determined to find a way to break through this deadlock.[49]

"When we took up legislative action," she wrote in her memoirs, "I recognized fully our entire lack of knowledge of detail and determined to replace ignorance with the soundest of information." For help she arranged for a meeting with one of the most powerful politicians in the state, a man who not only lacked any sympathy for the cause but embodied backroom politics at its most sordid. James Wadsworth, Republican Speaker of the Assembly, was, in Harriot's words, "a past master in legislative procedure." She was oddly confident that he would give her the information she needed, even if it meant improving her chances in battling him in the legislature. She counted on his "sportsman's" instincts, hoping he "would probably enjoy instructing his enemy in skill." She convinced him to become her legislative mentor and to teach her how to force a recalcitrant committee to act. Wadsworth explained to her what kind of motion she needed to discharge the Judiciary Committee from the suffrage bill's consideration.[50]

With Wadsworth's help, Harriot got Republican state Senator Josiah Newcomb to secure a floor vote to discharge the referendum bill from the Assembly Judiciary Committee. In April 1910, the full Assembly voted—for the first time in fifteen years—on a measure affecting the fate of woman suffrage. Even though the discharge bill was defeated, Harriot was pleased. "I understand men pretty well because I had five brothers, all of them different," she told reporters. "All of these men will be all right as soon as they understand that they can't play with us and smooth us down any more. We must make them see that they must reckon with us as they do with men."[51]

The suffrage parade of May 1910 took place immediately after the adverse Assembly vote and was advertised as a "parade of protest against the Legislature for its indifference to our demands for woman suffrage."[52] Armed with the support of the numbers who turned out and with the newspaper coverage the parade received, Harriot returned to Albany to push for a vote of the state Senate to discharge the suffrage bill from its judiciary committee. Although the move failed in the Senate as it had in the Assembly, Harriot was confident that ground had been gained, debate had begun, and suffragists were in a position to target recalcitrant legislators.

Harriot also continued her efforts on the electoral side of politics. In November 1910 the Equality League and the Equal Franchise Society joined together in a campaign against Artmeus Ward, member of the Assembly Judiciary Committee, opponent of woman suffrage, and representative of the "banner Republican district" in New York City. William Ivins and Herbert Parsons, reform Republican leaders who were married to suffragists, tried to temper the suffragist campaign against Ward, but Harriot was determined.[53] The intensity with which Harriot and her allies worked against Assemblyman Ward suggests that they were engaged as much in learning the electoral process as in defeating a particular politician. In the campaign against Ward, the suffragists made use of every electoral technique, traditional and progressive. They organized torchlight parades, held openair meetings, and even conducted "dirty tricks." On election eve, in front of a crowd, they had a horse Ward was using seized by the city because it was abused. Harriot researched Ward's abysmal, reactionary voting record in Albany, and suffragists canvassed 90 percent of the district's registered voters with information on Ward and instructions on how to split a ticket. Ward was not defeated, but his margin of victory was whittled down to a few hundred votes and Harriot trusted that the campaign would have "an important effect on the attitude of the incoming legislature."[54] The thrill of a full-fledged political campaign was one more factor in Harriot's decision to redirect her focus from recruitment and propaganda to politics. The rechristening of the Equality League as the Women's Political Union occurred a week and a half later.

The irony of Harriot's second year of sustained lobbying, before the legislature of 1911, was that just as she was moving away from her original trade union base, Democrats took over both houses of the state legislature for the first time in seventeen years. A new generation of Democratic political leaders—men like Robert Wagner, Al Smith, and Franklin Roosevelt—began to reformulate progressive aspirations in terms of Democrats' working-class and immigrant constituencies. Democrats were not traditionally supporters of woman suffrage, which they tended to regard as a hobby of elite ladies and a Republican issue. For this to change, Democrats would have to be led to rethink suffrage in the context of their traditional labor politics. And yet the deepening necessity of a labor-friendly suffrage movement occurred just at the moment that Harriot was shifting from the Equality League and into the Women's Political Union. At the legislative hearings on the referendum bill early in 1911, Harriot invited the eloquent and authoritative Leonora O'Reilly to speak on behalf of working women's need of the suffrage. She arranged for O'Reilly's expenses to be paid by Katherine Mackay and promised her a ten-minute slot at the hearings. On arrival in Albany, however, O'Reilly found herself relegated to the end of the proceedings and limited to a few minutes. Overlooking the insult, she spoke with great effect.[55] "I represent 50,000 women in this State and over 800,000 in the country who have mauled in the mill, fagged in the factory, and worn out behind the counter," she dramatically proclaimed. "We can only strangle the organizations that want to make our hours longer at the ballot box."[56]

The conflict between the elite direction in which Harriot was moving and the necessity of cultivating Democratic political support can be seen most starkly in connection with the complex question of immigrant wives and their citizenship rights. As the prospects for the enfranchisement of women became more likely, careful observers were beginning to notice that the woman suffrage proposal before the legislature would allow immigrant wives of citizens to vote without having to go through the naturalization process that was required of all other immigrants. Under American law the wife's citizenship followed that of the husband, and thus an immigrant woman automatically became a U.S. citizen on marrying one. So far, citizenship had had little independent meaning for women, but with the coming of woman suffrage this would change. A practice that had had its origins in women's dependence and subordination would suddenly bring meaningful rights instead. Harriot knew the rule of wives' dependent citizenship well. In 1907, an act of Congress had clarified what she had long feared, that as an American woman who was married to a man who was not American, she could no longer claim to be a U.S. citizen.[57]

How Harriot responded to this curious legal juncture is telling: instead of supporting the original referendum bill because it granted political rights to women, she sought to have it modified so that it would not grant political rights to immigrants. Here her own inclinations coincided with that of her elite allies, who were not eager to bring more immigrant voters to the polls. Early in the session of 1911, the Women's Political Union submitted a new version of the enabling legislation for the woman suffrage referendum. The bill required that "women whose citizenship is derived solely from marriage with citizens" must go through a separate naturalization process in order to vote.[58]

Nativism was Harriot's democratic weak spot, as it had been her mother's. Suspicion of and contempt for old-world nationalities was the other side of her passionate Americanism. She was an active supporter of greater rights for African Americans, for they were Americans, but the unassimilated European immigrants with whom she came in contact throughout the New York campaign had no such claim on her sympathies. She favored "American" over "foreign" workers, as she had done during the shirtwaist strike.[59] And when disappointed in her hopes for popular support for woman suffrage, she was always ready to blame immigrant men. Up to the last vote of the legislature in 1913, this special clause regarding immigrant wives threatened Democratic votes for the enabling bill. In the end, it may even have cost woman suffrage crucial votes and contributed to the referendum's defeat in 1915.

Despite the energy and determination Harriot poured into the lobbying campaign during 1911, it was nearly impossible to get any political movement out of the new Democratic majority. Hopes for reform were starting out most inauspiciously. The leading demand for prolabor reform—a bill limiting the hours of working women to fifty-four—was being slowly gutted of all substance by powerful manufacturing interests.[60] Then, at the end of March, the legislature's attention was suddenly drawn to the conditions of the state's industrial workers, in particular its women. Late on a Saturday afternoon, at the end of a long work week, a deadly fire roared through the Triangle Shirtwaist Company in New York City, the site of the great women's strike fewer than fifteen months before. Within a few hours, 146 garment workers, mostly women, had either burned, fallen, or jumped to their deaths. The intrinsic horror of the event was enormous. But against the background of the Democratic ascendancy in Albany, the fire had special political meaning, intensifying the political prominence of working-class women and deepening conflicts about who spoke for them and what was said on their behalf.

In the aftermath of the fire, class tensions among New York women activists became heightened. Socialists, angry at the degree to which they had been overshadowed by bourgeois women during the shirtwaist strike of 1909–10, made sure they held the first public protest after the fire.[61] At a giant memorial meeting sponsored by society suffragists Alva Belmont and Ann Morgan four days later, upper-class patrons entered the hall early through a separate entrance to avoid confrontations with angry socialists and trade unionists. Once inside, they listened uneasily to Rose Schneiderman give her famous, fierce speech on the inadequacy of charity and "good fellowship" in the face of the squandering of working-class lives.[62] Two weeks after the fire, the International Ladies Garment Workers Union held a mass funeral procession which drew over a hundred thousand solemn marchers, the great majority working-class women. Those elite suffragists who participated, including Harriot, walked through the soaking rain in plain dress.[63]

Many political forces were positioning themselves to make political capital out of the Triangle deaths. The Women's Political Union was definitely among these and was determined to draw a straight line from the deadliness of the fire to the weakness of the state's factory inspection laws to the political powerlessness of working women. A month after the fire, in conjunction with the city's annual Labor Day parade, the WPU held a Sunday afternoon meeting on the lower East Side to make these connections. "Uptown women" were there to hear Leonora O'Reilly as the featured speaker, along with WPU Executive Board member Florence Kelley. "Your condition is no better than slavery, and as long as this slavery lasts you have got to work in firetrap factories," O'Reilly told her sympathetic audience. "The only way out is through the ballot and the only way to be sure of a good ballot is to cast it yourself."[64]

It was under these conditions—Democratic control of the legislature, the Triangle fire, and a well-organized suffrage presence in Albany—that working-class woman suffragism in New York can be said to have finally come into its own. Out of O'Reilly's concentrated focus on votes for women in the winter and spring of 1911, and perhaps directly out of the WPU East Side meeting on April 30, the Wage Earners Suffrage League was formed.[65] Like the now-deceased Equality League, it linked industrial and professional women, but it was led by the former rather than the latter. As O'Reilly proudly put it, the new league was "officered and controlled by women who work for wages."[66]

The primary goal of the WPU's East Side labor suffrage meeting was "to arouse the enthusiasm of the industrial women" for New York's second grand suffrage parade, the next Saturday, on May 6.[67] Perhaps inspired by the Triangle fire funeral procession, Harriot declared that this year, parade participants would not be allowed to ride in automobiles, protected from direct contact with the voting public: everyone would walk.[68] Everything was meant to highlight the link between labor and suffrage. The parade was led off by a series of floats depicting the history of women's labor, from the "home industry of our grandmothers' time" to the modern ranks of industrial and professional working women. The marchers were organized by trade and profession, to indicate the variety and complexity of twentieth-century women's work. Tradeswomen marched under signs of their crafts, college women in caps and gowns, and a hundred society women from the Equal Franchise Society walked under a hand-embroidered banner. The garment workers with their crimson banner draped in funereal black particularly drew applause.[69] Photos of the march show bands of women marching three and four abreast, many of them in simple dress and hats, with banners held aloft proclaiming, "Women Need Votes to End Sweat Shops" and "Suffrage Pioneers Gained for Married Working Women the Right to Their Wages."

By highlighting the working woman case for suffrage, the suffrage parade of 1911 was intended to put as much pressure as possible on the legislature. Three days after the march, dozens of members of the Women's Political Union reassembled, banners and all, at Albany. Harriot carried a banner that listed the names of legislators considered suffrage's major enemies along with the inscription, in Greek, "He who plots against the cause of women, may he miserably perish, both himself and his house." The suffragists tried to march right into the Assembly chamber itself but were stopped at the door, forced to relinquish their standards, and entered unarmed.[70] Nonetheless, slightly more than a week after the New York parade, the Senate Judiciary Committee, which had been eluding WPU pressure for months, voted to report out the suffrage measure affirmatively. Now the entire Senate was faced with the necessity of voting yea or nea on the referendum, a distressing prospect.[71]

For the next two months, the legislative opponents of suffrage succeeded in postponing the full Senate's vote authorizing a referendum. Robert Wagner particularly incurred Harriot's wrath by pushing the vote on the suffrage bill further and further back to the end of the session. While other suffragists left for their vacations, Harriot, Caroline, and a few other WPU stalwarts stayed upstate through the hot summer months, lobbying legislators during the week and following them to their districts on the weekends. In Syracuse, they pursued one man to his own doorstep, where they extracted a public promise that he would vote to discharge the suffrage bill from committee. In Schenectady, the Women's Political Union held rallies outside the gates of General Electric and American Locomotive.[72]

Finally, on July 12, the woman suffrage bill was forced onto the floor and the long delayed debate began. Popular and powerful Tammany figure Senator "Big Tim" Sullivan spoke movingly in favor of votes for women. "You can go down into my section of the city [the Bowery] . . . I think there are more women than men going to work [at 7:00 A.M.]. . . . [Woman suffrage] is going to come and you can't stop it. . . . It is a good proposition and I hope the bill is advanced." Despite his support the suffrage bill was defeated in the Senate by one vote.[73] Several Democrats who had pledged their support were absent from the chamber. Franklin Roosevelt was not present, thus avoiding having to take a stand on woman suffrage. Harriot never forgave him for the dodge.[74]

The legislative experience of 1911 left the Women's Political Union hungry for revenge.[75] The formation of a committee was announced, chaired by Eunice Dana Brannan, to raise a campaign fund of one hundred thousand dollars to defeat enemy legislators at the polls. Although "tricked by the politicians [and] treated with discourtesy," the women "mean to play politics in the masculine way," the *New York Times* reported ominously.[76] In October 1911, the WPU directed all its energies toward defeating two New York City Democrats, considered implacable enemies, running for reelection to the Assembly. "Each Democratic voter in the two districts was either personally canvassed or received a leaflet showing the legislative record of the candidate of his party and a card instructing him how to split his ticket against our enemy," the WPU reported—149,000 pieces of literature were distributed. One of the candidates, Ron Carew, was defeated; the other, Lewis Cuvillier, was returned to the legislature, his margin uncomfortably trimmed, now an even more adamant foe of the suffragists.[77]

The election of 1911 divided power between the Republicans, who took over the state Assembly, and Democrats, who kept control of the Senate and the governorship. Harriot was determined to do battle with her enemies in

both parties. The larger political environment underwrote the WPU's growing political confidence. In October 1911, suffragists in California, using
innovative political strategies and techniques much like those in vogue in
New York, narrowly but decisively won their own referendum and became
the sixth "suffrage state."[78] Meanwhile in England, British suffragettes were
undertaking new, more violent levels of militance, adding to American
women's sense that they too had the power to win the vote. "It is now good
politics . . . to vote [for woman suffrage]," Caroline wrote to her mother
about a former legislative opponent who had become a supporter. "They all
seem to be climbing on to the band waggon [sic]. I believe it is all over but
the shouting."[79]

The WPU began its third year of campaigning against the legislature with
a demonstration that drew on traditional notions of female patience and
endurance. Throughout the early weeks of 1912, pairs of suffragists stood as
"silent sentinels" outside the Judiciary Committee room, as WPU statements
put it, "typifying the patient waiting that the women of the Empire State
have done since Elizabeth Cady Stanton made the first demand for our
enfranchisement in 1848."[80] But despite this public demonstration of womanly virtues, Harriot remained convinced that the power to advance the
cause lay in behind-the-scenes masculine politics.

The terms in which Harriot described the legislative maneuverings in this
year were thoroughly pervaded by the metaphors of gender, often reversed to
give women the upper hand. In an episode that became a staple of suffrage
legend, Harriot, Caroline, and a few other WPU intrepids tracked down a
particularly elusive senator. "The chase led up and down elevators in and out
of the Senate chamber and committee rooms." They ferreted out his hiding
place and finally cornered him in the office of Senate Majority Leader Robert
Wagner. The official WPU account stressed that the senator, "of slight
build," was physically overpowered by the suffragists. "With Mrs. Blatch
walking on one side with her hand resting ever so slightly on his sleave [sic],
Miss Lexow on the other side and Miss Hill behind," they led him into the
committee room and got his vote. "I'll never forgive this," he told Harriot.
"Oh yes you will," she responded. "Some day you will be declaring with
pride how your vote advanced the Suffrage resolution."[81]

The WPU's battle in 1912 with Robert Wagner himself was similar.
Despite his otherwise progressive politics, Wagner emerged as one of the
most determined, serious, and critical opponents of suffrage in the New York
legislature. To prevent Wagner from repeating the delaying tactics he had
used to protect the Senate from having to consider the referendum the year
before, Harriot arranged for a special train of three hundred New York City

suffragists to go to Albany to pressure him to set a reasonable date for a vote.[82]

> Some fifty or sixty of us crowded into the committee room, the rest gathered in the corridor outside. There was but one door and that was on the corridor. . . . As the Senator passed down the wide, hospitable aisle from the door to the table and chair, the aisle space filled up just behind him solidly with delegates and even more delegates from the corridor. . . . At what point the Senator took in his predicament, I do not know. . . . There was not an anti-suffragist to rescue him, not an orthodox suffragist to show some human sympathy. There were only all about him, the convinced and ruthless members of the Women's Political Union.[83]

In this episode, the WPU's power lay not only in numbers, but in its willingness to exploit the gendered meanings of power. Harriot insisted that Wagner was not only physically but also politically trapped, for he could not afford for it to be known that he had been outmaneuvered by women. He agreed to a date for a vote of the full Senate on the referendum. Newspaper reports of the episode held to the fiction that the women requested and Wagner granted. But in Harriot's retrospective, the sense of sexual warfare, of women besting men, was close to the surface. Accounts of British suffragettes smashing shop windows ran in the newspapers at about the same time.[84]

The Senate debate and vote took place on March 19, 1912. Watching from the gallery, Harriot and Caroline ignored the speakers; they had heard it all before. They knew exactly who would vote for and against suffrage, and "were full of confidence that the bill would carry." Thus they were astonished when an antisuffrage senator "broke his pair," an agreement that he would not vote on the bill so that a prosuffrage senator could be absent; instead he registered his vote against the referendum bill. The senator had made one of those "solemn pledges" that were supposed to be inviolable in manly politics. Harriot was sure that Wagner was behind this "perfidy."[85] The result was a Senate vote of nineteen to seventeen against; suffragists had been fraudulently denied their victory.

Just at this moment across the hall in the Assembly chamber, suffragists were about to win an unanticipated victory. On a vote to accept or reject the Judiciary Committee's negative report on their bill, supporters of suffrage found themselves in the majority and voted sixty-eight to sixty-three to reject the report. Presumably this meant that prosuffrage forces had the votes to win on a subsequent vote to authorize a voters' referendum. Before a vote on the referendum bill could be arranged, however, Assemblyman Lewis Cuvillier, target of the WPU's unsuccessful election campaign of 1911, made a motion to reconsider and table the first vote. Cuvillier spoke bitterly of his experience with women as political opponents. "Talk about political trickery and man's political duplicity! Why gentlemen, the cunning and shrewdness, and the deception and underhanded way they will go round to secure votes to defeat a member for office! Woman is dangerous when she wants to gain a point. She will stop at nothing." Despite parliamentary irregularities, Cuvillier's motion was ruled in order and passed by one vote, consigning suffrage to oblivion in the Assembly for another year.[86]

The third annual New York suffrage parade was conducted in May 1912 against the background of what the WPU regarded as an undeserved defeat. "We never marched for nothing, on clouds of air," Harriot wrote. "This was to be a march of protest against the failure of the legislature to pass the woman suffrage amendment."[87] The parade of 1912 was by far the most carefully organized street demonstration in U.S. suffrage history. Efforts to recruit and educate marchers, to insure large numbers, and to alert the public to the meaning and significance of the parade accelerated once the legislative session ended in Albany. Pledge cards were circulated in large numbers, urging women (and men) to "show your independence, courage, self reliance, your pride in womankind, your recognition of the home to the state" and sign up to march on May 4.[88]

As the date neared, the WPU demonstrated its talent for publicity-grabbing "stunts," clever and humorous ways to advertise the suffrage cause that newspapers and their readers found irresistible. In the month before the parade, these included a WPU-sponsored suffrage society of the "ladies of Barnum and Bailey circus"; a "tally-ho" cart, drawn by horses decorated in the white, green, and purple of the WPU and driven by members of the Executive Committee; and recruitment booths patterned after the U.S. Army and set up behind the New York Public Library.[89] Perhaps the most successful stunt was the announcement that all marchers could purchase the same inexpensive hat in department stores, decorate it however they chose, and wear it for the parade. "The 39 cent suffragette hat" was the subject of articles for several days.[90]

Despite this democratic gesture, the parade was noticeably less focused on working women or directed toward prolabor forces than it had been the year before, when Democrats had controlled the legislature and outraged labor was on the move. Now that political power was split between Republicans and Democrats, the parade's message was the universality of women's demand for the vote. As Harriot explained to Leonora O'Reilly, "We want to mobilize a vast army of all classes from all districts. . . . To impress legislators we must show a mighty array. . . . The parade must not be for this class of women only or for that, it must aim to draw out the largest number of women of all sorts and conditions."[91] In particular, the parade was to bring together the extremes of wealth and poverty in a perfect representation of Progressive-era hopes for class cooperation. This had always been Harriot's vision of a winning suffrage movement, but over the years her emphasis had shifted. Upper-class women were more featured in the parade of 1912, and photos of them dominated the newspaper coverage.[92] And whereas in 1911 the parade route went downtown, ending at an outdoor rally in labor-associated Union Square, in 1912 the march went uptown, culminating in an indoor meeting at Carnegie Hall.

Class tensions showed up as issues of ethnicity, to which Harriot's response was defensive and conservative. All prior parades had been held on Saturday afternoon, which meant that many Jewish women, a sizable portion of New York's activist workers, would not attend. Pressure was building to shift the parade to Saturday evening to accommodate observers of the Jewish sabbath.[93] The idea of a night parade might have originated among socialist women, but it was soon being supported by a wide range of New York suffrage societies. Harriot was cold to the proposal and offered several justifications. "The vast majority of working women are under twenty alas, and I believe parents would discourage a night march for their daughters," she contended. By contrast, a day parade would make it possible "to show in the light of day the fine calibre of those of all classes who favor votes for women."[94] It was also important to hold the parade early enough on Saturday to get full coverage, including lavish photo spreads, in the Sunday papers. The compromise to which she finally agreed was to set the starting hour later in the afternoon, at 5:00 P.M. (the parade in 1911 had begun at 3:30), which would still keep many Jewish workers from full participation but allow them to join the parade toward its end.[95]

Harriot wanted the parade to give evidence of a massive, disciplined suffrage army. Great attention was paid to the details of the march, the numbers of marching columns, the spacing of lines of marchers. Women were instructed to dress simply, walk erect, keep their eyes forward, and under no condition to leave the march before they reached their destination. Timing and precision were crucial. This spectacle was to be an emotional and sensual evocation of women's power. "The enemy must be converted through his eyes," Harriot wrote. "He must see uniformity of dress. He must realize without actually noting it item by item, the discipline of the individual, of the group, of the whole from start to finish. . . . The enemy must see women marching in increasing numbers year by year out on the public avenues, holding high their banner, Votes for Women."[96] This event was to be a demonstration of women's collective power, their capacity for organization, and their willingness to subordinate themselves to a larger purpose, all of which were fundamental to proving women's right to enter the polity.

The *Times* numbered the marchers conservatively at ten thousand, the *Herald* reported closer to seventeen thousand, and the *Tribune* said there were twenty thousand, with four times that many watching from the sidelines.[97] As one reporter put it, "There is probably no one in New York who does not now know the meaning of the word 'suffragette.'"[98] In part because the long months of planning had built anticipation to a peak, in part because the numbers of both marchers and onlookers were so many times greater than in previous years, and in part because newspaper coverage was so extensive and complimentary, that year's suffrage parade in New York was an especially thrilling experience, resolving whatever ambivalences remained among women about undertaking public actions on their own behalf. "I wish you could have seen the suffrage parade this year. It was simply great!" one marcher wrote to a friend. "I marched the whole length. . . . The crowd to see it was beyond anything. Before very long there is going to be a woman suffrage landslide all over the country."[99]

The parade combined many of the elements that had been developed in prior parades, but in far more elaborate form. At the head of the rows of marchers was the Executive Committee of the Women's Political Union, a small group of women of distinguished bearing and conspicuous elegance of dress. Harriot marched with them in academic gown. Then came the marchers organized by trades, professions, and industries, followed by other divisions, many of them from upstate, organized by state senatorial district. Then came the contingents of other suffrage societies. After years of refusing to march, Alva Belmont finally joined the parade in 1912, at the head of her own organization. Photographs of Belmont, marching alone despite the crowd, capture her regal carriage.[100]

For the first time, men marched in a suffrage parade in significant numbers. Legend has it that Oswald Garrison Villard inadvertently carried a banner that read, "Men have the vote, why not we?"[101] Also present were women of color; this contrasted with later national parades, where race segregation was the rule. One of the divisions of Belmont's Political Equality Association, made up of African American suffragists, "turned out in all its strength."[102] Chinese women were featured, boosted into American suffrage awareness by the announcement that Nanking Province had declared equal suffrage for women. Several young Chinese "suffragettes" who were students at Barnard drew cheers, and Anna Howard Shaw, president of the

National American Woman Suffrage Association, carried a banner that read "Catching Up with China."[103] The Socialist party contingent brought up the rear, marginalized by the suffragists' increasing focus on the support of major parties. When the last marcher had passed, "chanting the Marseillaise with such fervor that its strains were caught up by the densely packed crowd of spectators," it was 7:30 P.M., two and a half hours after the parade had begun.[104]

One indication of the significance of the parade for the shifting political fortunes of suffrage was the reactionary upsurge of antisuffrage forces. The Catholic Church began to accelerate its opposition in response to the inroads that suffrage organizations were making among immigrant, working-class women.[105] The *New York Times* also intensified its attacks. A series of hostile editorials argued that the surprising strength of the woman suffrage movement necessitated a full-fledged male counteroffensive. The suffrage movement was far more dangerous than most men realized, the editors wrote, and women will "play havoc with [the vote] for themselves and society if the men are not firm and wise enough and . . . masculine enough to prevent them."[106] A handful of unnatural women led the movement, the newspaper argued, duping many times that number of unsuspecting women, who were drawn to suffrage activism by emotion and excitement; together they were challenging the entire order of the sexes on which society rested. Man, the *Times* warned, must retaliate. "With the opportunity afforded to him by the refusal of women to recognize his manhood as a title of supremacy in the world's affairs, he will be at pains to avoid some of the troubles which he has hitherto regarded as a part of his heritage."[107]

In her published response, Harriot assumed the reasoned, diplomatic tone she liked to use to disarm those who expected the outburst of an outraged woman. She ignored the calls to men to defend their supremacy and concentrated instead on elaborating the fundamental socioeconomic changes that underlay the suffrage movement. "The economic development which has taken millions of women from the home" lay at the root of the concerns of suffragists and antis alike, she contended. The difference between suffragists and their opponents was in their political response to those changes. Unlike antis, suffragists believed in a democracy of gender and refused to grant "man's title to supremacy in the world's affairs . . . the impelling idea of democracy being that each class can represent its own needs better than any other class, however able, benevolent and altruistic that other class may be." Suffragists also had greater faith in political power and legislative action. "Is it beyond the range of possibility that political power might be used by women in the future to make home life possible for all . . . [to] bring about a wise adjustment of work and maternal duties?"[108]

The formation of the Progressive party in the summer of 1912 involved both opportunity and danger for the New York woman suffrage movement. Women reformers had taken a major role in designing the social welfare planks of the party platform, and the rank and file of the party was decidedly prosuffrage. Theodore Roosevelt himself was more of a problem. His deep-seated masculinism manifested itself in embarrassing declarations that suffragists were "indirectly encouraging immorality with the appalling consequences . . . for hosts of absolutely innocent women and for the un-born." But party leaders took him in hand and, armed with arguments about the numbers of women voting in the upcoming election, notably in California, secured his endorsement of woman suffrage.[109]

On the basis of both their suffrage and their social welfare endorsements, Progressive leaders urged women to give the party their partisan support. "Women should make the fight within the Progressive party," Colonel Roosevelt declared. "They should help in founding a party which will represent the whole people in their fight for social justice."[110] Harriot may have been tempted at first, but she was so disappointed in the Progressives' role in the defeat of a woman suffrage referendum in September 1912 in Ohio that she publicly rejected the Progressives' invitation. "The Progressive Party was on trial in Ohio and it utterly failed," she told reporters. "Roosevelt flew around the state, but not one word did he say for suffrage. . . . The women have come out of this campaign decided not to trust any party, not even the Progressive or Socialist."[111]

Nonetheless, the Progressive party's support was crucial to the WPU's plans in New York because of the leverage it gave in prying support out of the Republicans, who were struggling to keep voters from bolting to the new party. Luckily, the state Progressive convention came first and the party's support for submission of the referendum was secured. "The question now is will Saratoga [the Republican convention] and Syracuse [the Democratic convention] act so as to make continued non-partisanship possible," Harriot explained.[112] At the Republican convention, the committee on resolutions approved a plank promising to submit suffrage to the voters.[113]

The culminating state party convention that summer was the Democrats' meeting in Syracuse. This event had great emotional and symbolic meaning because "Tammany" loomed so large in suffrage demonology. While other WPU representatives had petitioned the Progressives and Republicans, Harriot saved the Democratic convention for herself. In her memoirs, her meeting with Tammany head Charles Murphy at this convention functions as the narrative climax of the long battle to win legislative approval of woman suffrage. "The encounter was opened by my saying, 'I felt it was high time for me to come to the boss.' With a smile he queried, 'You are something of a boss yourself, aren't you?'" Murphy agreed to the plank. Harriot's sense of political triumph over the opposition was even sweeter once Wagner, as majority leader of the Senate, formally wrote her pledging to "do everything in my power to have passed through the Legislature as soon as possible the proposed amendment on woman suffrage. It is a plank in our platform and the Democrats carry out their pledges."[114]

The elections of 1912 swept Democrats into power nationally and strengthened them in New York State. It was also a good election for woman suffrage, which was approved by voters' referenda in Arizona, Kansas, and Oregon, making a total of nine states where women had full voting rights. As for New York, "the legislature is ours," declared Harriot. The solid pledges of all three party planks had seen to that. "Gentlemen, you can not escape us; capitulate while you can do so with grace and magnanimity."[115] To celebrate the new suffrage states, New York suffragists held a postelection victory parade, which Harriot left to others to organize.[116] It seemed all over but the final tally and bill-signing. "How smoothly the machine works when the leaders have been moulded to your liking!" she boasted.[117]

So completely did it seem that all the difficult political maneuverings were over that Harriot took a vacation. In late December, she sailed with her husband for a month-long trip to Cuba. Other WPU activists also took time out for a bit of personal life: four of the younger workers announced their engagements. Ethel Gross, Harriot's secretary, married a young social worker she had met named Harry Hopkins. Rose Winslow met her fiancé on the suffrage stump. He "fell in love with her instantly upon seeing her on a soapbox, speaking in front of the Tribune Building. Since then [he] invariably attended her meetings and carried her soapbox from corner to corner." The WPU recognized the value of these outcroppings of romance in the harsh landscape of political battle and invited the newspapers to cover them lavishly.[118]

No sooner had Harriot sailed off, however, than the Democrats in the Assembly revived their objections to the provision subjecting immigrant wives to special requirements for voting, and called for another bill without the clause. Even though the Democrats' action posed a serious dilemma for suffragists, it also indicated that both parties expected that suffrage might pass and were jockeying for favor among the women likely to become their partisans—Republicans among the nativists and the elite, Democrats among the immigrants.[119] Wagner, concerned that the Democrats would be accused of going back on their pledge to submit woman suffrage to the electorate, left it to the suffragists themselves to specify which form of the bill they favored.[120] The state society preferred the bill without any special clause, while "the Blatchites" reasserted the "great objection we have to letting the illiterate foreign women who have been here only a few minutes vote."[121]

Nora was serving as "big suffrage boss" while her mother was away, and this might have been an important call for her. Unable to sort out the situation on her own, however, she telephoned her mother in Cuba.[122] Harriot returned as soon as she could. The WPU rented a tugboat, baked a cake (to celebrate her fifty-seventh birthday), bundled up her granddaughter, now dubbed "the suffrage baby," and steamed down to Quarantine to greet their leader. There, her American citizenship still unrecognized by the courts, Harriot was being subjected to the same inspections and humiliations as the immigrants with whom she had so little sympathy.[123] As soon as the photographers had finished taking pictures of her kissing her granddaughter, she took the first train to Albany.

Faced with this last-minute complication, Harriot's own instincts were divided. On the one hand, she favored the naturalization clause, both because of her nativist prejudices and because she thought it would win the bill more upstate Republican votes than it would cost it downstate Democratic support. On the other hand, she understood that "in a democratic campaign such as a referendum" such an exclusionary clause was generally unwise.[124] In the end, she decided that shifting to a new form of the bill without the special clause was a mistake this late in the game, but she did hint that if she had more time, she might have chosen this route. On January 27, 1913, both houses signed legislation proposing an amendment to the state constitution striking out the word *male* and enfranchising "every citizen of the age of twenty one years . . . provided that a citizen by marriage shall have been an inhabitant of the United States for five years."[125]

Harriot had spent three years steadily working toward this moment. It was a long time to work for a single bill, and yet in the suffrage scheme of things, it represented a relatively brief struggle and a quick victory. Still, obstacles at least as great had to be surmounted before the women of New York actually won the right to vote. A state constitutional convention was likely to be held the same year as the suffrage referendum, greatly complicating suffragists' work and adding to the possibilities for politicians' duplicity. In addition, in order to get the legislature to submit the referendum to the voters, the WPU had deferred the question of how to secure party endorsement for woman suffrage itself, and this too would have to be confronted. Most difficult of all would be winning the referendum itself—organizing a movement that could convince a majority of New York men to vote for woman suffrage. When Harriot embarked on the referendum campaign, she was the most powerful figure in the New York suffrage movement. But she also approached her task with contradictory attitudes toward democracy and a fragile sense of cooperation among the several classes that made up the new suffragism, and this would lead her position to change.

Democracy

The referendum on woman suffrage in 1915 was a great democratic gamble. "The task which we must accomplish between now and election day, 1915, is a Herculean one compared to that we have just completed," the Executive Committee of the Women's Political Union declared. "Up to the present time we have had to convince the majority of an Assembly and Senate, together consisting of 151 men, that it was expedient to refer our question to the voters. Now we must convert the voters of the State of New York to woman suffrage . . . to the fundamental ideas of democracy, to a belief in the basis of republican government."[1] But the reward for victory would be great. "If we win the empire state," Harriot believed, "all the States will come tumbling down like a pack of cards."[2]

As leader of the WPU, Harriot faced the task of winning a voters' referendum with a faith in democracy that was almost bound to be dashed. Now that the politicians appeared to have been tamed, hopefully the election would be a fair fight pitting the passion, energy, and determination of the woman suffrage forces against the prejudices and curiosity of voters. "We have asked for a referendum and politicians have taken us at our word and granted our request and we must make good." She still harbored her nativist suspicions of the voters. "In New York . . . we have the biggest German city in the nation, the biggest Jewish city to convert from its Germanic and

Hebraic attitude toward women," she conceded.[3] But she was counting on the democratic logic of the situation, believing that men who were being invited to exercise their franchise, who appreciated its importance and its power, could be convinced to vote in favor of women's demand to share it. Politics prevailed in the legislature, and there she had shown her mettle; but democracy was the medium of the street corners and, she ardently hoped, of the polling places on November 2, 1915, as well.

The WPU faced the referendum of 1915 with genuine optimism. It expected that its innovative political approaches, its enthusiasm for spectacle and excitement, and its vision of the unity between women of all classes would win the support of the men of New York. But a significant tension existed between the demands of the referendum campaign and the nature of the WPU, with its proud tradition of being suffragism's avant-garde. In a rare moment early in the campaign, Harriot suspected that she and her organization might not be best suited to referendum work. "The dead, frontal attack of a referendum is heavy collar work," she wrote. "The labor is limitless, vague, unindividualized." Harriot was beginning to suspect that the realization of political democracy might well involve a less spectacular kind of effort than she was prepared to deliver. "There is no finesse possible" in a referendum, she worried. "It is plain, dead ahead slogging. There are no test votes to put spirit into the siege, no way of determining the weak and strong points of the enemy's entrenchment. The attack is carried on, day after day, over the whole contested territory, and there is but one final vote to determine the entire campaign."[4]

In reaching out to the democratic masses, therefore, the WPU sought modes that allowed it to play on its strengths. It based its suffrage advocacy on the proliferating devices of modern mass culture—forms of commercial recreation, methods of advertising, and the pleasures of consumerism. This modern approach to spreading the suffrage word had been pioneered in the California campaign of 1911, in which billboards, automobile caravans, and suffrage postcards had been successfully used in a swift, diverse campaign that was marked by decentralization, variety, and a lack of bureaucratic baggage.[5] The California workers had invited Harriot to participate in their campaign; she was "the ideal woman to take us in hand and make us more effective workers," but politics in New York had kept her at home.[6] She approved of the sort of approach used in California; it promised to democratize suffragism's appeal. "If we are to reap a victory in 1915, we must cultivate every inch of soil and sow our suffrage seed broadcast in the Empire state."[7]

Mass culture held out the promise of a new kind of democracy to Americans, quite different from the venerable republicanism of the Jacksonian era or the rowdy partisanship of the Gilded Age.[8] These traditionally masculine political modes had been closed to women. But the parlor politics and women's club culture of the late nineteenth-century suffrage movement were also inaccessible to many women. Nickelodeons and dance halls, department stores and advertising were comparatively more available to the uninitiated and the curious, among women and men both. Of all the dimensions of public life, commerce was the most opened to women; in the cities and towns of New York, commercial culture was opening up long-forbidden public spaces to them.[9]

Various criticisms have been raised against the democratic claims made on behalf of modern commercial culture. One is that to the degree that consumerism is a democratic structure, it is not an especially political one, reducing choice from meaningful public issues to interchangeable brand names. But nowhere were commercial choices as infused with political meaning as in the suffrage campaigns of the early twentieth century, where the link between popular culture and votes for women was so energetically made that commercial ventures sought to associate themselves with women's equality to sell their products.[10] Then there is the claim that consumerism has an inescapably bourgeois orientation, precisely because money is the route into it. This charge needs to be taken seriously, especially with respect to women. Shopping as a women's activity was much more limited to the leisured classes in the early twentieth century than it has become since. Harriot's personal objection to consumerism was just this: to her mind, it was associated with idleness and opposed to productive labor.[11] Again, the suffrage movement sought to correct in a democratic direction. Associating oneself with the suffrage movement was made deliberately inexpensive: buying a button or a postcard, going to a movie or a suffrage dance cost little. If anything, the commercial aspects of the suffrage campaign were more likely to expose women of the upper classes to aspects of the lives of women of the working classes than vice versa.

Above all, the impulsive, emotional, one might even say irrational aspect of consumer culture made it an especially rich source for a mass electoral campaign. Perhaps Harriot's most frequently quoted aphorism for organizers was that to be truly democratic, the appeal of politics must be made to the heart rather than to the intelligence; emotions were the key to popular democracy, not reason. "We learned over and over again as we toiled in our campaign," she recalled, "that sermons and logic never convince, that human beings move because they feel, not because they think."[12] This was not an expression of any special contempt on her part for either women or working-class voters; on the contrary, she considered men (especially politicians) more irrational than women and the rich more prejudiced and conservative than the poor. What she did believe, however, was that changes in women's status and in power relations between the sexes could never be reduced to rational argument and dispassionate appeal.

"Democracy was the keynote" of the grand suffrage ball that the Women's Political Union sponsored in January 1913, to celebrate the passage of the referendum bill through the legislature and to start off the referendum campaign. "Women well known in exclusive social circles, wearing rich ball gowns and jewels," the newspapers reported, "mingled with and chose for partners in the grand march young women workers in the factory and shops of the city." Wealthy women toured about town in their chauffeur-driven automobiles to advertise the ball, while free tickets were distributed to the International Ladies Garment Workers Union, which was on strike again.[13] The event was a politicized adaptation of urban working-class culture, a version of the heterosexual public recreation of working girls that was still under attack by conventional moralists. Popular dances like the Turkey Trot, which had been "put under the ban" the week before by the YMCA of Washington, D.C., were particularly popular at the ball.[14] The Seventy-first Armory was barely large enough to hold the eight thousand women and men who attended.[15] Even the fundraising aspect of the ball was democratic: everyone paid fifty cents to enter and the event raised five thousand dollars, the WPU's most successful money-maker of the year.[16]

In January 1913, the Women's Political Union also began publication of its own biweekly two-penny suffrage newspaper, the *Women's Political World*. Of the suffrage ball, the *Women's Political World* reported that a good time was had and an important lesson was learned by all: "Love of liberty and democracy did not belong to one class or one sex but is deeply rooted in human nature itself."[17] The *World* offered analyses of suffrage politics, notices of suffrage events, reviews of new books, controversies over sexual morality, and reports on women's labor activism. Its format was lively and its content was decidedly up-to-date. One issue featured a cartoon parody of cubist paintings at the Armory Show, a fractured drawing of an "anti-suffrage playgoer who says 'woman's place is home.'"[18] The *Women's Political World* was hawked on the street by suffragette "newsies," themselves a source of additional publicity for the cause.

Given Harriot's appreciation for the role of emotions in mass politics, she was especially intrigued by new technologies of mass communication. Her former son-in-law Lee de Forest was one of the pioneers of modern radio "broadcasting" (his biographer wonders whether he picked up the word from suffragists, who used it to characterize their mass propaganda work).[19] Nora's marriage to de Forest barely lasted a year, but it was long enough for Harriot to discover the political possibilities of the new medium. De Forest invited his mother-in-law to deliver a talk on woman suffrage from the newly opened radio-telephone station in the Metropolitan Life building and she eagerly accepted. "I stand for the achievements of the twentieth century. I believe in its scientific developments," she intoned over the wires in her classical oratorical style. "I will not refuse to use the tools which progress places at my command. I will make use of the telegraph with or without wires, the telephone with or without wires, anything and everything which to-day's civilization places at my command."[20] According to de Forest's biographer, her speech was "possibly the world's first taste of radio propaganda."[21]

Moving pictures represented another new technology with political possibilities. Working-class nickelodeons featured comedies that ridiculed the suffrage movement, and moral reformers attacked cinema as a salacious medium, but the same technology and popular tastes could be made to serve the movement, much as a working-class dance hall could be transformed into a suffrage ball. Nor was it only the form that was useful; the content could also be adapted. Romance, female beauty, sexual misunderstanding, and their emotional associations, rather than being ceded to the opposition, became tools for cultivating interest in votes for women. In 1912, the Women's Political Union arranged with a commercial movie company in Manhattan to produce *The Suffragette and the Man*, one of the first appropriations of cinematic technology on behalf of the suffrage cause. *The Suffragette and the Man* was a romantic comedy in which the beautiful young heroine, forced to choose between her suffrage principles and her financé, stands up for the former but wins back the latter—from a conniving anti![22]

In 1913, the WPU collaborated on a second movie, *What 8,000,000 Women Want* (the title was borrowed from Rheta Childe Dorr's 1910 prosuffrage book). This time the romantic triangle involved not good and bad men fighting for the heroine's heart, but good and bad politics fighting for the hero's soul. *What 8,000,000 Women Want* mixed studio players and a melodramatic plot with actual suffragists, including Emmeline Pankhurst, the movie's "star," in staged suffrage meetings; newsreel footage of suffrage parades was intercut. Harriot played herself with great animation and credible conviction, as real and fictional suffragists plotted to expose a corrupt politician. This second movie has survived and gives us a rare chance literally to see Harriot Blatch in action, a dynamic, attractive, commanding sixty-year-old debuting in a historic new medium. Even on the screen she conveys a sense of both self-confident authority and genuine pleasure at what she is doing.[23] Suffragists all over the state were urged to arrange for the movie to be shown in commercial movie houses, parks, halls, and other venues.

In everything it did in the campaign, the WPU rested its efforts on the principles of advertising: simplicity, repetition, subliminal appeal, and image. A suffragist account of the successful referendum in 1911 in California made this reliance on the strategy of commercial advertising explicit. "Although the proposition that women should vote is seriously and profoundly true, it will at first be established . . . much as the virtues of a breakfast cereal are established—by affirmation."[24] "Let us admit that this is a rushing, advertising age," Harriot wrote of the propaganda methods she sought to marshal on behalf of woman suffrage, "and that the suffrage movement has been drawn into the rapid[ity] characteristic of our times."[25]

One of the WPU's most original advertising devices was the "voiceless speech." A silent, disciplined suffragist stood in a shop window with a series of simple suffrage messages on large cards, which she displayed to the crowd one by one. WPU member Anna Constable introduced the voiceless speech in January 1913 on Fifth Avenue, in the window of a shop the WPU rented. Like the suffrage movie, the voiceless speech was called into service when there were no suffragists willing or able to do street-corner speaking. The success of the device, like most suffrage stunts, lay in its novelty. Like the Votes for Women Ball, the voiceless speech's success in gathering large crowds of women caused considerable public anxiety. After several warnings from police, Constable was arrested and "charged with causing a crowd to collect and block the sidewalk." A WPU spokeswoman went to the press insisting that women had just as much right to draw a crowd as men "when there's a ball game." The charges were dropped but the voiceless speech retained its useful notoriety.[26]

Modern suffrage propaganda had in common with the burgeoning world of modern consumerism both an appreciation for the strategies of advertising and a reliance on a female constituency. A good example of the intersection between consumerism and modern suffrage politics was the "suffrage hat," by which the New York City suffrage parades of 1912 and 1913 were advertised and which could be bought at a variety of local department stores.[27] The deliberately low price of the suffrage hat, however, was not enough to insure that the suffrage-minded consumer was everywoman. While midtown department stores were willing to lend their windows for the display of the hat and other suffrage items, they refused the request of a suffragist shop girl for time off to attend suffrage parades. "I have tried hard to organize the girls but could not do so because they were afraid of their positions or could not afford to lose the half day's pay," the shop girl wrote to the *Women's Political World*. "I hope in the next parade they will be with us," Harriot reprimanded. "The Department store is a woman's store and they must wake up to the fact of recognizing us."[28]

In late 1913, the WPU began to experiment with its own "suffrage shop." A downtown storefront was rented, a daily program of suffrage speeches and events was organized, "and the room was filled every day with working girls and men who gave up a large part of their noon hour to get more knowledge of suffrage."[29] The next spring, Harriot arranged to buy a used, horsedrawn lunch van and turned it into "a roving shop." The van was moved from place to place every few days, sold campaign paraphernalia—buttons, pencils, even suffrage cigarettes—and distributed suffrage literature. "A side of the van folded down, a little platform like a drawn bridge [was] let down," and speakers emerged to address the crowds that such an oddity drew. To Harriot the suffrage van reinforced the campaign's democratic logic. "The roving shop is to be a democratic affair," she explained to the press. "Young people move; the shop will move; democracy moves. . . . Youth harnessed to democracy is certainly a winner."[30] In late 1914, the shop evolved again, this time to a permanent site, farther uptown in a Fifth Avenue storefront. Management of the shop became one of the most prized jobs in the WPU. A series of wealthy suffragists—Vera Whitehouse, wife of an investment banker, Louisine Havemeyer, wealthy art collector, and Helen Rogers Reid, wife of the publisher of the *New York Herald*—energetically took charge of its daily activities.

The suffrage parade of May 1913, the last Harriot organized, embodied many of these new techniques of political advertising. The parade signaled the end of one phase of the suffrage movement, in which the goal was to impress politicians with the movement's power, and the beginning of another, in which suffragists concentrated on winning the support of the majority of male voters. "We will muster an army fifty thousand strong this year," Harriot predicted.[31]

To summon this kind of participation, the parade itself had to be advertised. For weeks ahead of time, a barrage of stunts increased coverage for the upcoming event. These efforts were clever and entertaining, successfully conveying a sense of suffragists as playful, light-hearted, even a bit self-mocking, a deliberate antidote to the stereotypical strong-minded woman. Big Bill Cody's Wild West Show, which was finishing its tour in New York, was announced for weeks as converting to suffrage, and it was promised that Native American women performers would ride in the parade (they did).[32] Then there was the suffrage hat-decorating contest, in which noted male artists were asked to judge individually decorated versions of the suffrage hat. This stunt illustrates suffragists' cultural ingenuity. It rewarded individuality and artistry, while lampooning the expensive, oversized hats for which women (especially wealthy women) were constantly being criticized.[33] The contest worked both with and against contemporary conventions of fashion, consumerism, and beauty, providing familiar territory for women even as it humorously dismantled confining conventions.

Visually the parade was especially powerful. It effectively represented both the diversity and the unity of modern women. "Spectators saw from the moment that the pageant started that it was different from those of previous years," reported the *New York Times*. While there was "uniformity of costume" within each division of the parade, the numerous banners and decorations "unfolded in such bewildering color that [they] . . . would have inspired a cubist painter."[34] At the head were two dozen female "marshals," mounted on horseback, dressed in stylish adaptations of men's evening wear, "black cutaways and silk hats," with streamers of green, purple, and white, the WPU's colors.[35] The herald was Inez Milholland, "the official beauty of the parade," clothed in white astride her "splendid chestnut." Her elegant, feminine image was extremely effective as a representation of the suffrage movement: for many observers, the memory of Milholland lasted long after all other recollections of the parade had faded.[36] Unifying the entire parade were fifty beautiful and expensive WPU banners. Taken together, the parade demonstrated, in Harriot's words, "the comradeship . . . the democracy, all sorts and conditions of women marching shoulder to shoulder together" for the vote. "In these times of class wars," she observed, could men really afford "to shut out from public affairs that fine spirit of fellowship" which suffragism represented?[37]

The visual inventiveness of the parade and its effectiveness as political advertising provoked an angry response from antisuffragists, who were wedded to older notions of feminine propriety, and for whom the spectacular aspect of modern suffragism was proof positive of the social and cultural upheaval that votes for women threatened. The antisuffragists charged that the bold stance of the marchers smacked of the deliberate exploitation of "sex appeal." "The National Association Opposed to Woman Suffrage came out in the open to-day," reported the *New York Times*, "asserting that the cause . . . was a phase of the modern tendency in dress, dancing and conversation, which marked a lowering of women's ideals." "It is high time [for] every thinking man and woman to realize that back of the woman suffrage disturbance is the question—or rather a distortion of the sex question," declared Mrs. Arthur Dodge, a leading anti.[38] Instead of a high-minded defense of suffragists' fundamental respectability, the response that the moralism of the antis invited, Harriot concentrated on the foolishness of the charge. This allowed her to defuse the controversy, absolve the suffragists of criticism, and yet continue to embrace the same modern, playful spirit in which the parade was conducted. "Funny idea of sex appeal," she joked. "Twenty thousand women turn out on a hot day—thermometer registered 87 degrees—and march up Fifth Avenue to the blaring music of thirty-five bands; eyes straight to the front; faces red with the hot sun. . . . If it had been mellow moonlight. . . . But a sex appeal set to brass bands! That certainly is a new one." Committed as it must be to the logic of the spectacle, the newspaper coverage, even by the *New York Times*, was on the suffragists' side in the "sex appeal" flap over the parade.[39]

The controversy illustrated the double bind within which conventions of female beauty had for too long placed women and how the Women's Political Union was finessing it. Suffragists were not immoral or disreputable; they were just too modern to abide by such outdated cultural modes any longer. "There was a time when suffragists were supposed to be antediluvian or at least antebellum frumps, or at best aggressively mannish in their attire," a New York activist wrote in response to the charge that suffragists were leaning on their womanly charms. "At that period the reproach of the suffragist was that nobody who stood for woman's rights could by any chance represent the charm and beauty of women, and it is interesting, and delicately consoling, to observe how completely defunct is that ancient argument against votes for women."[40]

Despite her historic role in diversifying the ranks of suffrage activists, Harriot's own record as a democrat within the suffrage movement was mixed. Among established suffragists, she had a reputation of being highhanded, dismissive of existing organizational prerogatives, and disrespectful of existing leadership. To her mind, the larger democracy into which she sought to bring modern suffragism was often in conflict with the narrow democracy which weighed it down. "We have ceased to put much energy into discussing the pros and cons of democracy with doubting women in the chimney corners," she wrote in 1913, "and have instead gone out on the street corner to appeal to men, to the voters."[41] She approved of circumventing existing structures of decision making, and relied on her unlimited faith in her own judgment to countermand the inclinations of others. A friend of Caroline Lexow warned her that "Mrs. Blatch, though resourceful and brilliant lacks balance, lacks real democracy, lacks the sense of 'teamwork.'"[42]

Nor did the criticisms of her high-handed ways come solely from those who felt that Harriot ignored jurisdictional niceties and organizational prerogatives. Some of the women who worked under her direction also objected to her peremptory ways. Laura Ellsworth, a Syracuse graduate, sister of WPU vice-president Elizabeth Ellsworth Cook, and herself head of the WPU Speaker's Bureau, was more than ready to tell an interviewer, sixty years after the fact, that she thought Mrs. Blatch was "terribly autocratic" in the way she treated the typists and stenographers in her office.[43] In the midst of the referendum campaign, the WPU, lineal descendent of the first New York suffrage society to champion union women, was cited by the Bookkeepers, Stenographers and Accountants Union for running an open shop and resisting unionization of its workers.[44]

But there were also many suffragists who found working under Harriot Stanton Blatch's leadership very much to their liking. Caroline Lexow "would have done anything" for her.[45] As a mentor to political operatives and organizers, Harriot was a demanding, effective, and revered boss. If she could sometimes be impatient with women as she found them, she could also be marvelously inspirational in getting them to move to a stronger, bolder, more courageous level. Proud of her own political fearlessness and defiant of convention, she expected the same high level of performance from other women. "She had a way," Mildred Taylor of Syracuse University recalled, "of making us novices deliver a job no matter what it was." Even though Mrs. Blatch was not generous with her praise—she did not want to "spoil" her organizers, Taylor "worshiped [her] to the point of adoration." "There was a spirit that took possession of us and it came through . . . Mrs. Blatch," Taylor wrote many years later. "What a privilege it was to work at late adolescence with such leaders."[46] These were not relations of equality, but that was not unique to the Women's Political Union: the suffrage movement everywhere was organized hierarchically. "You didn't argue in suffrage," Laura Ellsworth recalled. "You took orders!"[47] But Harriot did not soften her orders with unwarranted compliments or condescending encouragement.

Despite this domineering style, Harriot's suffrage leadership was fueled by her own strong sense of antiauthoritarianism. While the traditions of women's political culture encouraged, even required, adherence to an ethic of female solidarity, Harriot was eager to play the rebel to her sex. Not only was she willing to disagree with other women, she needed female opponents.

This stance of the rebellious daughter helps explain why the modern, militant suffragism she expounded flourished among women a generation younger. She was, in the words of a not particularly admiring contemporary, "brilliant and swift and independent in action, a guerrilla leader rather than a regular officer."[48] As a suffrage leader, she energetically denied that unity was good for its own sake or that organizational homogeneity was politically empowering. On the contrary, she was of the opinion that "rivalry is the best tonic for [political] workers."[49] She was less afraid of being separated off from the rest of her sex than of losing her identity by merging into the female mass. She believed that "women disagree and ought to disagree."[50]

During the legislative lobbying years from 1910 through 1913, Harriot did not face serious organizational opposition within the New York suffrage movement. The state suffrage association was disorganized, small, and ineffective. Occasionally its leaders protested when the Women's Political Union took off on some bold tactical shift of its own, but lacking any serious resources with which to challenge Harriot's leadership or to impose their own hesitant political judgments, they inevitably yielded to her initiative. Once the referendum campaigning began in earnest, however, the Women's Political Union found itself facing a serious organizational competitor in the Woman Suffrage Party (WSP), and Harriot's forthright political style came into direct conflict with that of the WSP's founder and leading force, Carrie Chapman Catt.

Harriot might well have butted horns with whomever headed the suffrage establishment in New York, but that said, Carrie Chapman Catt was still the perfect opponent and brought out all the hostility in her. While Harriot liked to take out ahead of the pack, Carrie Catt abhorred open conflict and believed that organizational unity and harmony of action must be strictly adhered to for suffragism to triumph. "The moment that rivalry enters into the situation, personal jealousies, antagonisms and all sorts of difficulties of that sort become part of the movement," she insisted. "To my mind, rivalry and competition within a state [suffrage movement] is deadly."[51] From the long view of historians, Catt is much revered for her work during the New York campaign and after for moving the lumbering National American Woman Suffrage Association into an active role in the final drive for suffrage. But to Harriot, a combatant in the struggle, these same characteristics designated her as a woman who resisted every new idea. It was precisely the intermediate quality of Carrie Catt's leadership—the way she situated herself between the militant and traditional wings of the suffrage movement—that infuriated Harriot; Catt was too cautious to be an ally but quite clever enough to be an opponent.

Within the women's movement, Carrie Chapman Catt embodied the Progressive-era faith in organizational rationalization and administrative centralization.[52] She and Harriot Blatch represented two distinct aspects of women's surging political energies during the Progressive era.[53] In contrast to Catt's emphasis on the corporate virtues of organization and efficiency, Harriot celebrated individual initiative, modern invention, and personal freedom. During the Progressive era, these two quite different historical developments, both of them simultaneously a gain and a loss for women, were in dynamic tension. Out of the discovery of female individualism came the dramatic changes in female sexuality of the period; out of the high value placed on unity and cooperation came the great political impact women made. The modern suffrage movement was one historical site where the two trends came together. Though the combination produced tremendous political energy, these quite different values, virtues, and styles clashed, often with great intensity. One of the ironies of these years is that even as women were effectively insisting on their unity to break into the male political monopoly and touting their genius for social harmony, their own political institutions were rife with conflict and competition. The Blatch-Catt rivalry was one such emblematic antagonism.

Carrie Chapman Catt had risen to suffrage prominence in the 1890s as the head of the newly formed Organization Committee of the NAWSA. She had been the major NAWSA organizer for the first successful state campaign for woman suffrage, the Colorado Referendum of 1893, and as a reward, Susan B. Anthony had chosen her over her protégé Anna Howard Shaw as NAWSA president in 1900.[54] Four years later, Catt resigned the presidency, according to her most recent biographer because she herself felt too constrained by established suffrage leadership (including that of Anthony).[55] In the subsequent years, Catt formed a series of other organizations, including an umbrella group in New York City called the Interurban Suffrage Council and the International Woman Suffrage Association. Her organizational initiatives always had a similar quality: she was more concerned to unify and reconcile all existing pockets of suffrage sentiment than to reach out and create new ones. One measure of her skill is that she was widely admired and made few enemies within the suffrage movement, in decided contrast to the resentments that frequently resulted from Harriot's leadership style.

Catt founded the New York City Woman Suffrage Party in 1909, on the eve of Emmeline Pankhurst's first visit to the United States. Her intent was both to take advantage of the excitement around Pankhurst's visit and to create a moderate center of suffrage activism to keep the New York movement from following too closely on the heels of the British militants.[56] Her attitude to Pankhurst's message of political involvement was similarly ambivalent. While Harriot was drawn to politics because of its traditional male associations and frank acknowledgment of the workings of power, Catt admired the capacity of parties to organize and discipline their members. Party organization, recognized structures of leadership, and the capacity to mobilize—to her mind, the suffrage movement needed just these elements to move steadily forward to its goal. The Woman Suffrage Party was to be, in her words, "a 'machine' . . . which has no 'bosses,' no 'graft,' no personal rewards to offer and whose sole motor power is self-sacrificing, conscientious service to a noble cause."[57] She formed a bridge between the traditional political culture of the women's movement and the politics of legislature and party to which suffragists such as Harriot were so drawn.

At first Harriot supported the WSP, which she thought would be a loose federation within which different suffrage societies could coordinate their activities.[58] But it soon became clear that Catt wanted to discipline all suffragists to her approach, which Harriot vigorously resisted on the grounds that it would limit her options and slow down her ability to respond. She charged that Catt's energies always went to creating internal order rather than tackling external obstacles, that her impulses were fundamentally bureaucratic, that she had no skill or taste for the intricacies of partisan politics and legislative maneuvering. In New York suffragism's early stages, there was considerable truth to Harriot's criticism that her own capacity to innovate was more important than Catt's impulse to consolidate. But Harriot's growing resentment may have reflected an intimation, as the drive to suffrage reached its final stages, that her rival's gifts would eventually overtake her own.[59]

After founding the Woman Suffrage Party in 1909, Carrie Catt spent most of the next three years outside of the United States. Characteristically, she preferred to leave the initial battles against entrenched suffrage conservatism in New York State to others, but just as Harriot was on the verge of getting the referendum bill through the state legislature in the winter of 1912, Catt returned from abroad, ready to assume what she saw as her rightful position as the head of the New York suffrage movement. Within a year, she was claiming responsibility for victory in the legislature.[60] Harriot resented the presumption. "In correcting Mrs. Catt's assertion in regard to the developments in the suffrage movement in recent years," she wrote, "I do not wish to be understood as implying that the inaccuracies are intentional or tinged with ulterior motive. We all realize that Mrs. Catt has been almost continuously abroad for some three years," she continued archly, "and naturally could not keep in touch with the newer developments in the suffrage movement at home."[61]

On her return to the United States in late 1912, Catt turned her attention to the Woman Suffrage Party, which had been flourishing in her absence. Under the leadership of women like Mary Beard and Harriet Burton Laidlaw, it had grown in size and ambition and had come to incorporate many of the bold public tactics and new suffrage constituencies pioneered by the Equality League of Self-Supporting Women.[62] When Catt returned, concerned that the organization she had founded had "nearly got on the rocks," she installed her ally and companion, Mary Garrett Hay, as the party's chair.[63] While Hay was attending to the city organization, Carrie Catt took on the reorganization and consolidation of the state suffrage society. Convinced that dissension and organizational "muddle" was New York suffragism's "chief handicap and not the opposition of our foes," she accepted the offer of the New York State Woman Suffrage Association to organize a statewide campaign committee to direct work for the referendum.[64]

Catt's plan was to combine the resources of all existing suffrage societies in New York under the umbrella of a single structure, to be known as the Empire State Campaign Committee (ESCC). Centralization, she was sure, would maximize resources, and her leadership would increase efficiency. Quickly, most of the independent suffrage societies in New York—including the College Equal Suffrage League, the Men's Suffrage League, Catt's own Woman Suffrage Party, even what was left of Katherine Mackay's Equal Franchise Society—fell into line and accepted the authority of the Empire State Campaign Committee. Only two organizations did not join. The Political Equality Association stayed outside, perhaps because Catt did not want its leader and sole benefactress, Alva Belmont, interfering in her organization.[65] The Women's Political Union, which Catt very much wanted within the fold, also refused to join.

From the beginning, the WPU Executive Committee was determined to stay independent.[66] Harriot had created the WPU in her own image, to cultivate innovation rather than consensus, and the women who ran it were determined to remain unfettered, autonomous, and innovative, which they felt excessive organization threatened and woman suffrage victory in New York required. They did not trust Carrie Catt to break free of "suffrage orthodoxy." Had they been able to see the situation from more of a historical distance, they might have said that without the Women's Political Union pulling on one side, there would be nothing to keep Catt's conciliatory style from slipping back to the overcautious timidity of the other.

For six months, the executive boards of the Empire State Campaign Committee and the Women's Political Union conducted a series of negotiations, extensively covered in the press, which never came close to finding a basis for consolidation. Between Carrie Catt's dedication to "perfection of the organization" and Harriot Blatch's "guerrilla methods" and preference for "friendly rivalry" there turned out to be no common ground.[67] Catt wanted the Women's Political Union, like all other suffrage societies, to "place its organization under the direction of the general committee . . . uniting in the creation of an organizational fund."[68] Harriot and the WPU Executive Board rejected the proposal.[69] "If to wipe itself out would insure victory in 1915, the WPU would willingly annihilate itself," Harriot explained. "But believing it has the same part to play in the future as in the past, it has decided in the interest of the referendum to continue to exist."[70]

Thanks to Harriot the WPU had the greatest concentration of financial resources in New York. According to the *New York Tribune,* "Probably there isn't another suffrage body in the country which has so large a budget in comparison to its size."[71] The rising young militant leader Alice Paul, soon to set her own sights on the WPU's wealth, wrote to Caroline Lexow that "we all feel that the WPU is one of the most successful societies in the country in the line of raising funds."[72] Given the seriously underfunded state suffrage association, which had nominal authority over the Empire State Campaign Committee, Catt needed the WPU's financial resources to conduct the kind of comprehensive effort she envisioned for New York. She wanted the Women's Political Union to fall into line, to be a solid division in the suffrage army, and to take its place in the complex and intricate political machine she was convinced was necessary.

Once local negotiations failed, Carrie Catt turned to the National American Woman Suffrage Association to pursue her efforts for consolidating the New York suffrage campaign. The national organization was itself in a state of great upheaval, as modern suffrage forces that had taken root in state campaigns were trying to force a change in national suffrage policy, and especially to push longtime national president Anna Howard Shaw out of office. At the NAWSA suffrage convention in December 1913, Carrie Catt chaired a committee charged with designing a new constitution for the national organization. Her committee proposed that all local suffrage societies become affiliates of their own state divisions of the National Association, and that they be taxed a percentage of their revenues to support national work.[73] Harriot objected to the new plan on the same grounds that she had refused Catt's proposals in New York: she believed that the future of her active and wealthy organization depended on maintaining both strategic and financial autonomy. The *New York Tribune* reported that "the plan which the National will try to put through the convention, taxing affiliated bodies according to their incomes, hits the opulent WPU right in the solar plexus."[74] Despite protest, the proposed constitution was adopted. A year later, the WPU, unwilling to submit to its terms, withdrew from NAWSA, a move that later weakened Harriot's capacity to offer leadership to suffragism nationwide even as it strengthened Carrie Catt's.[75] The WPU's withdrawal from NAWSA presaged later and deeper splits in the organization over militance.

By January 1914, it was clear that two parallel suffrage campaigns would be conducted in New York, one by Carrie Catt's Empire State Campaign Committee and the other by Harriot Blatch's Women's Political Union. Within New York City, there was a division of labor by class, with the Woman Suffrage Party taking over the immigrant and working-class agitation that the Equality League had pioneered years before, and the WPU concentrating on the wealthy and leisured women who lived uptown and who funded the rest of the organization's work. Upstate, however, these class valances were reversed and the Blatch forces demonstrated some of their earlier strengths in expanding suffragism's reach to working-class audiences. While the two organizations cooperated relatively well in New York City, upstate there were frequent jurisdictional battles.

By now, most of the working-class suffragists in New York City, including the influential Women's Trade Union League, were working in conjunction with the Woman Suffrage Party. There were several reasons for this shift. During Catt's absence before 1912, Mary Beard had brought labor suffragists, especially Leonora O'Reilly, into the Woman Suffrage Party ambit. Meanwhile, the decision of the women of the Socialist party to withdraw from any collaboration with bourgeois suffragists and to run their own suffrage agitation deprived the WTUL of its more militant members and moved it to the right, where it was compatible with the Woman Suffrage Party.[76] And finally, some trade union activists, notably Rose Schneiderman, still harbored resentments toward Harriot for her role in the settlement of the shirtwaist strike, three years before.[77]

Ironically, Carrie Catt herself was much less drawn to working-class politics than Harriot was. Her political history had not exposed her to the strategic importance and greater radicalism of either the labor or the socialist movements. She did not recognize anything special about the working-class contribution to the woman suffrage movement. She had no sympathy with socialists. "I've met a few fine ones," she advised a young friend, "but most of them are crazy."[78] Nor was she any more sympathetic to recent immigrants than Harriot, only more circumspect in revealing her nativism. She too was ready to blame "German Irish et al." for opposing suffrage, but only her friends were exposed to her xenophobia, not the newspapers.[79]

Meanwhile, the WPU concentrated its city efforts on the uptown districts. Here lived the wealthy, influential women who had migrated from the Equal Franchise Society to the WPU, many of them to serve on the organization's Executive Board. In anticipation of the referendum, they were reorganized as the seventeenth senatorial district and became the most active New York City division of the WPU. These women were charged with raising the funds to run an ambitious statewide referendum campaign. Harriot had long advocated "democratic" methods of fundraising (the suffrage ball for instance) both to support suffrage projects and to expand the movement's base of support. But to undertake a full-fledged political campaign, she understood that far more ambitious fundraising would be necessary. One of the excuses for inaction that most bothered her was that there was not enough money in suffrage coffers to undertake an initiative. "We knew by experience that waiting to get money for action was short-sighted policy," she wrote. "Do something and the money will come to foot the bill. That was our conscious conviction."[80]

After negotiations with the ESCC had collapsed, the WPU Executive Board announced its intention to raise its own special referendum fund of fifty thousand dollars. Placed at its head was Eunice Dana Brannan, wife of the head of Bellevue Hospital and daughter of newspaper publisher Charles Dana. Immediately on the committee's formation, as the newspapers reported, "the money roll[ed] in." On the first day of the drive, "Pledges for $2,300 came to Mrs. Brannan before she ate her breakfast."[81] The financial pitch that these wealthy fundraisers made was both class-conscious and democratic. Working-class women had contributed more than their share to the suffrage movement, they argued; now it was the turn of women of means. "The poor women pay the bills for suffrage," one of them declared. "The women of wealth, who could give lavishly, leave it to struggling girls in the shops and factories to go without their Easter hats that we may pay organizers."[82] Of the approximately $10,000 raised by the WPU in 1913 prior to the establishment of the referendum fund, contributions came from 370 donors, of whom two-thirds gave under ten dollars. But by the end of the year the special referendum fund had raised almost fourteen thousand dollars from fewer than one hundred donors, of whom less than twenty gave more than 60 percent.[83]

Vera Whitehouse, who eventually became the financial wizard for the second New York referendum of 1917, began her suffrage career under WPU auspices in late 1913. A young, beautiful, New Orleans–born woman, she had found through suffrage activism a sense of her own capacity. She was frequently quoted as saying that before she marched in the New York suffrage parade of 1913, "she could only dance and go to dinner." Six months later, when she made her first outdoor speech for suffrage, she declared it "the proudest moment in her life." Although relatively new to suffrage, she was made chair of the seventeenth district, where she quickly raised substantial moneys for referendum work. Her genius, it soon became obvious, was in fundraising.[84]

The money raised for the referendum fund was particularly important in securing speakers and organizers to tour the state.[85] Salaries generally ranged from fifty dollars a month for trainees to sixty-five dollars a month for well-tested workers. The top of the scale was set at one thousand dollars per year, reserved for the rare worker who had not only organized her district but put it on a self-supporting financial basis.[86] (Only Syracuse even began to meet this standard.) Presiding over the entire field effort was Caroline Lexow. As WPU field secretary, she worked herself to the point of exhaustion. "I travel, travel, travel! I never reed [sic]. Factory, sweat shop workers have more time than I and more energy left."[87] By the summer of 1913, she had politely suggested that she would withdraw her services if her wages were not raised; the Executive Board increased her pay to two thousand dollars per year.[88] Without Lexow, wrote Elizabeth Selden Rogers, a leading figure in the seventeenth district, "the WPU would just go to pieces and that cannot be."[89]

Paid political workers fell into two general categories. There were the experienced speakers and organizers, usually veterans of suffrage battles in other venues, whose reputations drew crowds all over the state. Helen Ring Robinson came from Colorado, where she had been elected a state senator. Helen Todd was a veteran of the California campaign of 1911. "I always called Helen Todd our 'primadonna,'" Harriot wrote, "so clever was she in talking our cause into the hearts of her audience."[90] Fola La Follette, daughter of Senator Robert La Follette of Wisconsin, also spoke for the WPU.[91] Special care was taken to secure speakers who had the credentials and know-how to address working-class audiences, either in their union meetings or at outdoor factory gate rallies. Rose Winslow, one of the only industrial workers in the WPU organizers' group, was a textile operative from Pennsylvania. After a tour of duty as a factory inspector that resulted in a physical breakdown, she recovered and devoted herself to suffrage.[92] Elizabeth

Freeman, a British socialist and longtime trade unionist, was a veteran of the WSPU campaign in London who also spoke effectively to factory audiences.[93]

Backing up these veteran suffrage speakers was a corps of young women who established regional headquarters around the state and spoke to groups of women and men in their localities. Caroline Lexow did this kind of work in Troy and Schenectady. In one month in 1913 she spoke at twelve meetings of women's organizations, including the Woman's Christian Temperance Union, women's clubs, and church societies, and eight groups of men, ranging from the Knights of Columbus to the Meatcutters' Union. A particular source of organizing talent was Syracuse University where, thanks to Dora Hazard, Harriot's wealthy supporter in the area, the WPU had what amounted to a direct pipeline to graduating seniors. One of these Syracuse women, Jane Pincus, was in Harriot's opinion "the most fearless, the most determined, and the most relentless of our young workers."[94] Another Syracuse graduate was Mildred Taylor, who was already a champion debater by the time she graduated. "I marvel at the facility I developed in handling heckling crowds," she recalled; "after that . . . there was no challenge in holding a polite crowd in an auditorium." For Taylor, as for many of these young women, suffrage organizing was the beginning of a career in social reform and politics.[95]

The energies of these paid organizers were concentrated in the small upstate towns and cities into which modern suffrage propaganda had never before reached. By late 1914, substantial regional WPU offices had been established in Troy, Syracuse, Schenectady, and Jamestown. For the most part, WPU organizers were effective in locating the pockets of suffrage interest and building working organizations of local suffragists. Jamestown, for instance, became a center for suffrage activism in the southwestern part of the state under the organizing talents of Jane Pincus.[96] But the real challenge was to be found in the tiny villages and centers of rural population surrounding the larger cities and towns. "People very hostile to suffrage," Lexow reported of her visit to Pattersonville, a small town on the Mohawk River. "Even Women's [sic] Christian Temperance Union refused us a hearing . . . organization at present is impossible. . . . This ground as far as we know has not been touched by suffragists before."[97]

In this upstate campaign, the WPU combined the "heavy collar" organizing drudgery that Harriot had predicted the referendum campaign would require with the group's distinctive flair for the spectacular. In the summer of 1913, Nora, now divorced from Lee de Forest, was back in the suffrage saddle, literally.[98] She and a suffrage apprentice, Harriet Porritt, undertook a horseback tour through twenty-eight towns in the eastern Mohawk valley. The newspapers loved them, especially the fact that their steeds were named Senator Root and Doctor Parkhurst, after two leading male antisuffragists in the state.[99] In the spring of 1914, instead of a parade in New York City, the major WPU march was held in Syracuse, where women from all over the state assembled. The parade featured WPU banners, equestrian marshals, and marching bands, all paid for by downstate funds.[100] Later that summer, the WPU toured the state's southern tier with a large tent which was billed as their traveling headquarters. Meanwhile, another WPU group toured the northern tier by automobile, concentrating on industrial centers.[101]

It was here, outside of New York City, that the greatest differences between the WPU and the ESCC were found. Upstate, the temperamental and ideological tension between Harriot Blatch and Carrie Catt was paralleled by tactical differences in campaign strategy and antagonism among the suffrage rank and file. Catt's commitment to organizational unity led the ESCC to defer to local suffrage establishments, to the women of the local elite who had been running the upstate suffrage movement since the 1890s and whose conservatism and timidity had long been the bane of Harriot's existence. The approach of the WPU, in contrast, was to sidestep existing suffrage organizations, set up separate offices and campaigns, and locate new activists and untapped constituencies, sometimes generating considerable resentment in the process.

In those places where no previous suffrage organization existed but there was significant untapped support, the WPU had an open field. This was the case in the working-class centers of Troy and Schenectady.[102] Conversely, where the suffrage establishment was strong, for instance in Susan B. Anthony's hometown of Rochester, the WPU was frozen out.[103] Early on, Catt had suggested that the two organizations divide up the districts of the state; given her rationalizing approach, this was a reasonable proposal, and perhaps the WPU, with its disadvantage of size, should have accepted. But the WPU Executive Board had no intention of being closed out of any part of the state and rejected separate organizational jurisdictions.[104]

As a result, in many places there were clashes between local suffragists with links to the ESCC and WPU organizers. In Jamestown, the leaders of the Political Equality Club and traveling organizers from the WPU engaged in a highly public and antagonistic battle of words. Local suffragists attached to the state organization insisted that the "powerful state campaign committee . . . with its endless chain of compact working forces" had the town fully organized and that WPU "free lancers" were engaged in "an unnecessary duplication of the work with great waste of time and energy." WPU sympathizers saw the situation differently: they had "ruffled somewhat the calm domain" of the local suffrage establishment, "a staid and conservative body which has never affiliated with the common people or with the so called working class."[105]

In Jamestown, the WPU forces won the skirmish and ran the local organization, but in Buffalo, a far more important center, the ESCC faction, led by local suffragists Nettie Shuler and Mrs. Dexter Rumsey, held on to their control. Star organizer Caroline Lexow led a WPU group into the city, despite the fact that the ESCC already had its own headquarters there. She dodged the local suffrage leaders and concentrated instead on meeting workers at factory gates. While the suffrage movement "want[s] one and all, rich and poor," she declared, "this cause is really of more benefit to the poor because the rich are protected against the conditions that exist regarding wage earning women."[106] Eventually, however, the WPU group was forced to close its offices and cede the city to Rumsey and Shuler.[107]

It is difficult to tell from the record which side was more responsible for this pattern of antagonism upstate. WPU workers swore that they never spoke publicly against "the State," but reported that they were regularly beset by ESCC efforts to take over their organizing efforts and woo away the local suffragists they had recruited.[108] Given the assumptions of each side about which was the greater danger to the campaign—for the ESCC, repetition and overlap of effort, for the WPU, hesitation and quashing of initiative—they were bound to see each other as threatening the victory of the referendum. When and where the consolidating logic of the ESCC was successful, particularly in places with strong and functioning suffrage movements, WPU women became even more resentful and antagonistic. But in the many parts of the state that had not had much exposure to suffrage propaganda, the innovative quality and energy of the WPU's approach was essential, and in the end the campaign could have used more of it.

Even though the focus of suffrage energies had shifted to the electorate, "the WPU [was] still on the alert, still active in the Legislature," and still on the watch for politicians' duplicity.[109] During these years, Republicans were again the stronger party and, despite residual pressure from the Progressives, becoming more conservative. Whereas Democratic antisuffragism seemed to have been tamed by the battle for the referendum bill in 1911–13, the Republicans' opposition to woman suffrage had intensified.

In the summer of 1914, a gubernatorial election year, suffragists concentrated on making a strong showing at the three state party conventions: Progressive, Republican, and Democratic. The legislature elected in 1914 was constitutionally required to pass a second bill reconfirming the action of the legislature of January 1913 in authorizing a voters' referendum in November 1915. This was not a pro forma action, and conservative Republicans were ready to use the opportunity to derail the entire referendum. The WPU and the ESCC basically agreed on what was necessary. Suffrage representatives went to all three conventions that summer with the intention of pledging each party at least to pass a bill resubmitting the referendum, and perhaps to pledge outright endorsement of woman suffrage in November 1915. "Our present problem is entirely concerned with securing a full Suffrage Plank from the Republicans on August 18th," Caroline Lexow wrote. "Should they adopt it, the Democrats will undoubtedly follow and our cause will be as good as won."[110]

Together the WPU and the ESCC headed off conservative Republicans' efforts to back away from a pledge to submit woman suffrage to the voters and got the party to pass a platform plank pledging to resubmit the necessary legislation. At Carrie Catt's suggestion, she and Harriot cosigned a letter to the Democratic Platform Committee, calling for a plank that not only promised to submit the matter to voters but also urged a yes vote on woman suffrage.[111] Although the Democrats were less hostile than the Republicans, they too only pledged to resubmit.[112] Even the Progressive party equivocated about endorsing woman suffrage outright. Although it reaffirmed its principled commitment to woman suffrage, its gubernatorial nominee was a longtime opponent of woman suffrage, Harvey Hinman.[113] Suffragists downplayed any disappointment that they felt. It was hard to tell from their public statements that they had lost their bid for outright party endorsement of woman suffrage, and perhaps they did not even register the defeat themselves, relieved merely not to have had the referendum withdrawn. "Victory has knocked everything out of my head," Caroline wrote to her mother after the Democratic convention in Saratoga. "I telegraphed you the moment the platform was adopted with our plank and went to bed. It was a wonderful success, the greatest we have ever had in New York."[114]

An upcoming state constitutional convention posed the next set of problems. The convention was scheduled to submit a revised state constitution at the same election as the woman suffrage referendum. Suffragists were worried about partisan contamination from the constitutional convention and that decisions made during the convention, which was sure to be dominated by conservative Republicans, would legally supersede the outcome of the woman suffrage referendum. Unless the constitutional convention made some arrangements to the contrary, Harriot feared, if the voters passed a constitution retaining the phrase "male voters" as well as a separate amendment enfranchising women, New York women might still find themselves without votes.[115] Eventually suffragists received shaky assurances from convention leaders that the revised constitution would not be used to finesse the action of the voters on woman suffrage.[116]

Despite such cooperation, the conflicts between Catt and Blatch and their two organizations grew ever more nasty and intense. The WPU declared its lack of faith in Catt's political leadership, and Catt characterized Blatch's behavior as "too childish to be worth the expenditure of any temper" in a letter to her own lieutenants.[117] Undoubtedly the WPU sensed that the ESCC was gradually assuming control over the entire campaign. It was one thing for endless, unexciting efforts to address the voters to be monopolized by the Empire State Campaign Committee, but quite another for intricate political maneuvering, which was the WPU's metier, to be as well. But the women of both organizations were also terribly worried about the referendum itself. Although she denied that she was predicting defeat, Catt admitted that she saw a "desperate fight" ahead.[118] And she may have seen this fight more clearly than Harriot, who was distracted by the political battles in which she always loved to engage. In late summer 1914, during the state political conventions, the *Women's Political World* even published a series of articles, written by Nora, entitled "How the Referendum Was Won."[119] Portentously, the series was never completed. After the seventh installment of a promised twelve, the *World* ceased publication, shifting all the organization's resources toward converting the electorate.[120]

In the last six months of the campaign, the WPU's flood of gimmicks and stunts accelerated. Suffragists played both ends of the gender divide to demonstrate that they could join in traditional male activities as good fellows and at the same time retain the dearest of feminine virtues. One of the big stunts of 1915 was Suffrage Day at the Polo Grounds, when New York suffrage organizations competed with each other to sell tickets to a benefit baseball game between the New York Giants and the Chicago Cubs. At the game they sold suffrage trinkets, sat in special boxes, and included advertisements in the score cards asking that they have their own "time at bat."[121] At the same time, to combat the charges that political women were desexed, they organized a series of events that emphasized their enthusiasm for the roles of wife and mother. The Women's Political Union held a Grandmother's Day at the suffrage shop, where grandmothers and granddaughters together advocated votes for women. They also repeated a successful publicity event from previous years, the suffrage baby contest.[122] To counter antisuffrage claims that suffragists were women who wanted the ballot as a compensation for their inability to find husbands, they held a series of "married couple days," in which husbands and wives declared that they were "happy though married and suffragists."[123]

In the last few months of the campaign, Harriot decided to concentrate on a mega-stunt around which attention could build until it climaxed on the day of the election. "Mrs. Blatch's fertile brain was already hatching a new scheme for publicity," Louisine Havemeyer, the wealthy art collector who became involved in the gimmick, remembered. Harriot's idea was a physical embodiment of the democratic claims of the suffragists, a "sacred token of liberty" that could be carried from meeting to meeting and function as the symbol of suffragists' transcendent political aspirations. Louisine Havemeyer especially devoted herself to the service of the Suffrage Torch. This torch, she told her Manhattan audience, "was like the one that lighted up our harbor . . . it stood for liberty and for freedom—the freedom we were seeking—and it greeted the strangers who came to our shores . . . men and women alike."[124] Newspapers followed the torch's progress "from Montauk Point to Long Island," and when its publicity value "began to get shop worn," a New Jersey affiliate of the WPU figured out a way to revive interest by announcing that it had stolen the torch. The torch also proved compelling to "the populace." At Chautauqua, "the audience rose en masse and began pressing towards the platform to get a new view of the symbol of enfranchisement and . . . to be allowed to hold the Torch, to touch it but for a moment."[125]

Three months before the election, in a development almost theatrical in its drama and timing, Harriot's single-minded focus on the woman suffrage referendum was shattered. Her husband, William Henry Blatch, Jr. was killed. Since moving from England to be with his wife and daughter, Harry had lived on the eastern end of Long Island. After her short-lived romance with Lee de Forest and radio broadcasting, Nora had built a large house for her father there. Harry kept himself busy gardening, receiving friends and neighbors, and generally living a private and modest life. He was visited frequently by Nora and her daughter, and occasionally by his wife when she needed to escape from the rigors of the campaign. After thirty years of marriage, their interests had diverged—his into the domestic and hers into the political.[126] Their marriage had become like that of Harriot's parents in late middle age, affectionate but not intimate.

On the evening of August 2, after a violent summer storm, Harry walked Nora and little Harriet to the train station to see them off to the city after a weekend visit. He stopped at a friend's house on the way back from the station. Outside the house, an electric wire had fallen down; presumably, he did not realize it was live when he bent down to pick it up. The newspapers reported that "under ordinary circumstances [the shock] might not have proved fatal," but there had just been a rainstorm, the ground was damp, and when he touched the wire, he died instantly.[127] Family friend Grace Channing Stetson, writing to Theodore Stanton, called it "an instantaneous and beautiful death."[128] There was poignancy in the fact that the husband of this famous modernizer had been the victim of an unanticipated surge of power of the most modern sort. Harry was sixty-five and Harriot had been married to him for thirty-four years.

While Nora, who was close to her father, was deeply affected by his death, Harriot kept her composure, either because they had drifted far apart or because she was habitually private with such feelings, especially the painful ones that exposed her buried vulnerabilities.[129] Perhaps Harry's sudden death recalled that earlier tragedy, the loss of her other daughter, which also occurred in the midst of a crucial political battle almost twenty years before. When she announced, two weeks after Harry's death (and ten weeks before the election) that she would have to go to England to settle her husband's estate, she was not so much grief-stricken as duty-bound. Emotionally, she was preoccupied with what her departure would mean for the referendum. "It is a sore trial to me to leave New York just now," she wrote to Caroline, whom she begged to take up her place, "for I know how terribly our campaign is in need of every worker, in need of live methods."[130]

Much to Caroline's later regret, she turned Harriot down. Once the summer party conventions pledged themselves to carry out the referendum, Caroline had married a young lawyer, Philip Babcock. Her husband did not object to her continuing to work with the Women's Political Union (although neither did he seem particularly thrilled with it), but when Harriot's request came, Caroline was pregnant. Harriot was philosophical. "It makes us see how life crowds death and death life," she wrote back.[131] Nora did not return to England with her mother, but she was too grief-stricken to assume the leadership of the WPU. Instead, Alberta Hill, another of Harriot's aides, agreed to act as a temporary steward until mid-October, when Harriot was scheduled to return.[132] Before leaving, Harriot took advantage of one of the benefits of widowhood and resumed, as the law allowed, her U.S. citizenship, which she had lost when she married an Englishman.[133]

For more than six years, Harriot had been working single-mindedly to an end which was only weeks away. Why was she willing to leave at this moment? After Harry's death, Nora was to receive the income from his stock in the family brewery and Harriot, who was cotrustee of the estate, was to inherit whatever else was left. She decided that she must go to England and see to matters herself. Not only was the estate small—only ten thousand pounds total—but British inheritance taxes were heavy. In the end, Harriot felt that widowhood left her "in financial embarrassment."[134] Later, after she returned to the United States, she initiated a suit against the Port Jefferson Long Island Electric Lighting Company for negligence in her husband's death, but she was awarded only five thousand of the one hundred thousand dollars she claimed.[135]

It seems highly likely, however, that Harriot could have gotten around the trip, or postponed it, or limited it to less than the six weeks she was away. She was on good terms with Harry's siblings, especially his sister Alice who was now married and well-connected. But she may have been growing weary of the unrelenting labor of trying to convert New York voters. And even more, she was ill-suited to such work and may have sensed that she was no longer at the leading edge of the campaign effort, that she was losing her position as New York's foremost suffragist to Carrie Chapman Catt. In her sudden trip to England so close to the election, there was an element of getting away from the stress of her conflict with Catt and her frustration at the growth and power of the Empire State Campaign Committee.

Surrounding and affecting Harriot's personal situation was global drama: England was at war with Germany. The British suffrage movement had split rancorously over whether to support its country's military efforts or ally with antiwar forces; Emmeline Pankhurst and her daughter Christabel were at the head of the prowar wing of the movement. A year and a half later, when the United States entered the war, the American suffrage movement would find itself similarly riven, and Harriot would follow the prowar path of her friend Mrs. Pankhurst. For the time being, however, American suffragists were still able to take the high and easy moral ground of pacifism in a nation not yet at war. In January 1915, Harriot joined with other prominent American suffragists at the founding meeting of the Women's Peace Party. That spring, however, the war was carried into the open seas and Americans were dying on torpedoed ocean liners. Prowar—or at least anti-German—sentiment in this country was growing and, despite her long years of connection to Germany, Harriot joined in.[136]

As she prepared to sail into waters under attack by German submarines, Harriot admitted that the "touch of risk" was not an "unwelcome sensation," that it mirrored how she felt: a new widow, an American citizen once again, on temporary reprieve from the biggest battle of her life. "I hope my ship will stand on end & the waves rage mountain high!" she wrote to

Caroline.[137] During her time in England, she was surprised with the pleasure the British women took in the hard work of a nation at war. "Bright-eyed, happy even when bearing personal bereavement," as she described it, a guide perhaps to herself for subsuming feeling in effort, which was the way she had always dealt with personal pain.[138]

When she returned, she had moved much closer to a prowar position. She had a chance to see wartime conditions for herself, not only in England but in France, where she went to see her brother and his family. On her return, she proclaimed an opinion that months before she would have regarded as heresy: war was good for woman suffrage. "Because of the service women of France and England are rendering this war," she told reporters when she returned in mid-October, "the men of those countries at the close of hostilities will be willing to grant suffrage to them." She also came back advocating universal compulsory military service, albeit with a feminist twist: while men fought, women should be mobilized to take up the homefront work and play an equal part in winning the war.[139]

Harriot returned to discover that Carrie Catt had extended her consolidating reach over the New York suffrage ranks. The WSP had announced that it would organize a parade at the end of the campaign; the WPU Executive Board angrily protested that this had been done "without . . . consulting those who had the widest experience in such demonstrations," a reference to its own pioneering role in the New York City parades. But the protest was ignored, and plans for the WSP-led parade went on.

On October 23, a week and two days before the election, Carrie Catt took the place that Harriot had once held, marching at the lead of the final suffrage parade. Under WSP's leadership, New York suffragists had the torchlight parade they had been wanting for years.[140] The ranks of the Woman Suffrage Party, now much more numerous than those of the Women's Political Union, led the procession, which was unified by giant banners of blue, gold, and white, the colors of the Empire State Campaign Committee. Under Alberta Hill's direction, the Women's Political Union, eager to retain some identification with the spectacular mode it had once spearheaded, organized its own subsidiary parade. Marching under the organization's colors of green, purple, and white, a few thousand WPU women paraded through the working-class lower East Side, and to further emphasize the WPU's self-supporting roots, featured a special division of municipal employees, headed by Katherine Bement Davis, head of the city Department of Correction.[141] Inasmuch as the WSP-organized parade was so enormous—the newspapers set its numbers at twenty-five thousand—and the WPU did not join up until the end of the line of march, it was dark by the time the WPU contingent turned from East Twenty-second Street onto Fifth Avenue.[142]

Meanwhile, Harriot was busy planning her own spectacular finale to the New York campaign. Carrie Catt had much greater organizational machinery behind her claim to leadership, but Harriot still had her own resources: a deeply dedicated cadre, wealthy supporters, and above all her unique maternal legacy. November 1915 was the hundredth anniversary of her mother's birth, and she was determined to link the event to the WPU's referendum campaign. Before Harriot left for England, she had begun to arrange a series of commemorative events. The first celebrations were held upstate—in Johnstown, where her mother had been born, and in Seneca Falls, Harriot's birthplace—with Nora and Harriot's sister Margaret Stanton Lawrence presiding in Harriot's absence.[143] From there the commemoration traveled to various sites around New York City where the Stanton family had lived, including the Forty-second Street brownstone where they had fled to escape the New York City draft riots in 1863.

The culmination was an enormous and elaborate Centennial Luncheon at the Hotel Astor on Saturday, October 30, three days before the election.[144] Harriot had been planning the event since April, when she began to assemble a long list of people for the Honorary Committee. She wanted names that demonstrated her mother was a "many idead woman," as well as ones that underlined the breadth of the suffrage coalition Harriot herself had forged.[145] Clara Colby and Helen Gardener, septuagenarians who had begun their suffrage work as Elizabeth Stanton's apprentices, spoke glowingly of her character and vision. A thousand people were anticipated, and the pictures of the event, taken using a panoramic camera lens, show more than a hundred tables of eight.[146]

Ever deliberate and purposeful, proudly disdainful of sentiment, Harriot insisted that the Centennial Luncheon was intended solely for propaganda purposes. "The occasion is not to be a meaningless laudation of a life that is passed," she wrote to Ida Harper. "At every turn it will be made to tell for the practical suffrage question before us at the moment."[147] But it is also clear that there were deep personal motivations behind the event, that it was Harriot's way of dedicating the entire, exhausting political effort of the referendum, and hopefully the victory of woman suffrage, to the memory of her mother. A yes vote for woman suffrage in New York on November 2 would be a "monument to the pioneers," chief among them Elizabeth Stanton.[148]

Winning votes for women had levels of meaning for Harriot Blatch that it had for few other women. It was a vindication of her mother's life; without the achievement of the franchise for women, her mother's life was at best unfinished, at worst misspent. It was also the basis for a profound kind of merger, a way for Harriot to amalgamate the purposes of her own life with those of her mother, which could mean variously submerging herself in her mother's greater significance or appropriating it for her own grandeur. Years later, when she compiled her records of the New York referendum campaign for deposit at the Library of Congress, she devoted an entire volume of clippings and memorabilia to the luncheon.

Harriot's emotional involvement in the event became even clearer when Carrie Catt announced that she did not think the Centennial Luncheon would do anything to help the referendum and that she would not attend. Although Harriot insisted that Catt was only showing what a small and jealous person she was, she was deeply offended.[149] To Harriot—and very possibly to Carrie Catt, too—Catt's refusal to attend was a refusal to acknowledge Harriot's special position in the suffrage movement, the leadership role she had inherited. To Harriot, it also underlined Catt's lack of political imagination, of any feel for "the drama of the event," and her refusal to acknowledge "the women who initiated the movement," meaning both her mother and herself.[150] Her open and explicit dislike of Carrie Catt, which grew stronger with every passing year, significantly deepened with this episode.

On election eve Tammany Hall declared itself neutral on the woman suffrage referendum. This was not a formal party endorsement, but it did mean that Democratic voters in New York City were officially free to vote as they wished on the measure. Everyone—suffragists, political pundits, journalists, politicians—recognized that, given the history of suffrage opposition among New York Democrats, neutrality was good news for votes for women.[151] Harriot seems to have regarded this as a personal achievement. "It is from a man who knows me, a man whom I can trust," she told newspaper reporters, referring to her highly publicized summit with Tammany head Charles Murphy the year before.[152]

All suffrage leaders predicted victory, though of significantly different dimensions. Carrie Catt, buoyed by the Tammany action, predicted a victorious margin of fifty thousand votes. Harriot was more circumspect: victory by less than ten thousand votes, with the winning margins coming from upstate, where her organization had concentrated its resources.[153] Anna Howard Shaw, just barely holding on to her position as president of the national suffrage association, was afraid to even guess the outcome. Meanwhile, the newspapers were engaged in a riot of predictions and polls. Newspaper editors around the state were polled, running almost evenly divided for and against suffrage.[154] Male workers at a large East Side factory showed similar margins.[155] The *New York Herald* found that women at uptown hotels tended to be indifferent or opposed, while wage-earning women in offices and in factories were more enthusiastic supporters.[156] Perhaps someone should have paid attention to the professional odds makers: New York bookies were giving two- and even three-to-one odds against passage.[157]

November 2, 1915, the day toward which Harriot Blatch and thousands of other New York women had been working for years, was the kind of warm and sunny election day for which hard-working campaigners pray. Arrangements had been made to insure that all suffrage workers woke up early enough to be at their posts at the crack of dawn, but the excitement of the event must have made this request superfluous. The polls opened at 6:00 A.M., by which time several thousand suffrage activists, mostly women but a few men, were in their places as pollwatchers, guarding against the chicanery that might cheat them of victory. The right for women to serve as pollwatchers had been lost in 1911, but in 1914 the WPU had won it back for this special election. Harriot had chosen as her own post a tailor's shop on a "thickly populated" lower East Side street.[158] The WPU shared with the Woman Suffrage Party the responsibility for training and coordinating the city's pollwatchers, and workers were instructed to gain the assistance of election officials while guarding against illegal voters.[159] Outside of the city, resources were not so ample or well deployed. In Oneonta, along the southern tier, hardworking Helen Ecker, who had been toiling with the Empire State Campaign Committee, reported herself "too weary to wiggle" and unable even to contemplate serving as a pollwatcher on election day. Instead, Oneonta suffragists relied on friendly men inside the polls and women on the outside to guard against illegal voters.[160]

In New York City voting was heavy: many polls reported that the majority of their votes had been cast before noon; the polls closed at 5:30 P.M.[161] Suffrage workers were instructed to observe the counting of ballots closely and then to phone in the results, either to the WPU's suffrage shop or the WSP's campaign headquarters. In some polling places, voting machines were being used for the first time, and since woman suffrage was at the end of the ballot, the results on the amendment came out first. This greatly accelerated the count, which turned out to a be a mixed blessing. By midnight, it was clear that the woman suffrage amendment had gone down to defeat. Of some small consolation, so had the proposed state constitution, which had been sponsored by conservative Republicans, opposed by Democrats, and defeated by almost a half million votes. By contrast, the woman suffrage amendment lost by less than two hundred thousand. All the boroughs of New York City voted against suffrage, although Manhattan and the Bronx did so by narrower margins, and around the state only six out of sixty-one counties showed up in the prosuffrage column.[162]

In any popular election campaign, especially one fought over such a long period and by so many activists new to the excitements and exhaustions of politics, any realistic sense of what might happen is overshadowed by the final drive necessary to get out votes and the belief, on which it must rest, that victory can be won. Most New York suffragists kept the disappointment they must have felt to themselves, an oddly private outcome to an intensely public event. The newspapers did not report any mass bemoaning or collective bitterness. On the contrary, there was a strong tendency to regard the referendum result as a kind of moral victory. "The suffragists have made a canvass to be proud of," the consistently antisuffrage *New York Times* beneficently wrote (especially given the results). "They are beaten, thoroughly and hopelessly beaten, but not for a neglect or mistake of theirs."[163] "On the whole we have achieved a wonderful victory," Carrie Catt wrote to her followers. "It was short of our hopes, but the most contemptuous opponents speak with newly acquired respect of our movement."[164]

The leaders of the Empire State Campaign Committee formalized this response by announcing, the day after the election, that a second referendum campaign would be mounted as soon as New York state law permitted. A fund of one hundred thousand dollars was pledged immediately (the amount was later found to be a bit inflated by the enthusiasm of the movement).[165] After the briefest of respites, the machinery Carrie Catt had forged began to grind its way toward a second referendum vote, scheduled for November 1917. Now these women were veterans; this time, they insisted, they would win. Catt heralded this move, although within a month she herself moved on to less well-worn and more portentous paths: fighting for woman suffrage at the national level. Vera Whitehouse and Gertrude Foster Brown, two of New York's wealthiest suffragists and WPU recruits, took over the second New York referendum campaign and rebuilt it on the twin pillars of money and steady organizational work.

Harriot Blatch was one of the few suffrage leaders who reacted to defeat with open anger. The morning after the vote she was ready to vent her spleen to the newspapers. Nor did she confine herself to restrained, womanly sentiments. Her two strongest feelings, reported the *Times*, were "disgust at the conditions which had forced women to campaign in the streets and radiant delight that . . . the arch enemies of the suffragists had lost even more heavily on the new Constitution." The fate of the conservative Republicans gave her perverse pleasure. "I never felt so vindictive in all my life and glory in it." But her anger at the voters, and through them, at democracy itself, was a different matter, sheer bitterness, with nothing consoling or compensatory about it. "Never again will I make an appeal to an individual voter," she raved. "No women in the world are as humiliated in asking for the vote as the American woman. The English, the French, the German women all appeal to the men of their own nationality. The American woman appeals to men of twenty-six nationalities."[166] She vowed she would never make another street-corner speech. "The men stand—not listening—but hypnotized by the sight and sound of a woman making a speech," she complained, ignoring what she had once preached about the importance and primacy of the emotional appeal to winning any campaign.[167]

Harriot's retreat to this extreme and underlying elitism was precisely the kind of reaction her mother had had to major defeat and crushing disappointment. After her failure to force Reconstruction Republicans to include women with freedmen in the Fourteenth and Fifteenth amendments, Elizabeth had indulged herself in vitriolic racist outbursts, charging that black men were less deserving than white women of the right to political power and might turn their unearned superiority over white women into unspeakable and immoral acts against them. After the failure of the campaign of 1893–94 in New York to get the legislature to authorize a referendum on woman suffrage, Stanton became an advocate of educational restrictions on the suffrage, on the grounds that the old-world ideas of immigrant male voters and the specter of a wave of "bad women" washing over the polls had together defeated woman suffrage. Then Harriot had criticized her mother for her reaction; now she echoed it.

"It is possible that Mrs. Blatch has been misinterpreted," Lillian Wald wrote to the newspapers in response to Harriot's interview, or that, "in the exhaustion following the extraordinarily active and capable campaign that she has led, she did not thoroughly analyze the vote that was cast on the East Side." Wald was the head of the largest settlement house in New York and a major spokeswoman for immigrants, and she was concerned to protect Harriot's record as an advocate for working women's suffragism from the consequences of this ill-considered nativist outburst. She was even more intent on setting the record straight about immigrant voters: with the exception of the seventeenth senatorial district uptown, where WPU workers were especially active, "no other part of the city did as well" for suffrage as the lower East Side. "I am quite sure that all of the women who participated in the election have a reassurance of their faith in democracy because of their experience on Tuesday," Wald wrote, with more hope than conviction.[168]

Calmer and with more time to consider, Harriot found two other targets to blame for the defeat of suffrage: the constitutional convention and Carrie Chapman Catt's leadership of the Empire State Campaign Committee. "Tammany's desire to defeat the proposed Constitution swamped us," she concluded in her autobiography. "Had the plan I suggested been followed, to refer the new Constitution to the voters at a separate election after the regular election [at which suffrage was voted on], I am confident the Suffrage Amendment would have carried in 1915."[169]

Harriot also demanded that the suffrage forces themselves answer for the defeat, and turned her wrath, predictably, on Carrie Chapman Catt. Two days after the election, she wrote to Anna Howard Shaw, whom Catt was poised to replace as president of the National American Woman Suffrage Association. "I sat up half the night last night analysing the vote, and I am convinced that New York State could have won if there had been anything worthy the name of a campaign up-state." Suffragists, Harriot continued, had always assumed that their small town votes would be better than their big city polling, but in New York, "the proportion of the vote in favor of us to the adverse vote was bigger in the city than in the country district." On reflection, she acknowledged the support that suffragists had won among the urban masses. But the obverse was also true: the vote had been terribly weak outside of the city. The Women's Political Union had campaigned hard upstate, but the ESCC had neglected that area, Harriot charged. The proof was that the few countries where suffrage had prevailed—Chautauqua in the far west, Schenectady midstate, and Rockland, north of the city (and home county to Caroline Lexow)—were all places "where the Women's Political Union was the dominating force." Catt's devotion to organization, Harriot insisted to Shaw, who was only too glad to hear it, was not the key to victory; quite the contrary. "Fiddle-sticks on organization! . . . Little groups of organized people here and there help mighty little. Big efforts . . . carried on in a state-wide campaign, are the things that achieve victory." But righteous indignation only went so far in removing the sting of defeat. "I am in the depths of despair," she confessed.[170]

Harriot thought the idea of waging a second state referendum to convince New York voters to endorse woman suffrage was a mistake. All the evidence of past state battles suggested that antis would work even harder against suffrage the second time around. She considered a second referendum in New York to be nothing less than "suicidal." With respect to the particulars of her home state, however, she turned out to be wrong: a New York campaign, held without her participation in 1917, was victorious, securing the most populous state in the union for the suffrage camp and winning an incalculable political prize in the larger struggle. But from the national perspective, the era of state suffrage referenda was over: with the exception of New York, no other state was won by this method after 1915. From this point on, attention, energy, and political initiative shifted to the federal amendment.[171]

Personally, Harriot knew that she could not go back to the simple democratic appeal, to ask men one by one to extend justice to women. "Those who have done the actual work of appeal to individual voters prefer henceforth to deal with legislators," she contended; she would rather play out the next engagement in an open political field where promises broken could be discovered and betrayal made costly.[172] Nor was she alone. The important irony of this turning point in the suffrage movement was that almost all of the activists who had pioneered the political and electoral work in New York, who had invented new techniques, reached out to new constituencies, and forged new attitudes to political action, reacted similarly. During the second New York referendum, what Harriot had called the "frontal assault" on the electorate was left to suffragism's second string, the hardworking masses of the movement who were willing to repeat and repeat until failure turned into success. But for their part the movement's radicals and militants needed to move on, to grapple with men's political power and to feel their own power more directly. The venue for this step up was the federal suffrage amendment, which had been languishing in the backwaters of the state-based reinvigoration of the movement for many years.

7

Victories

It is tempting to treat the last five years of the U.S. woman suffrage movement through a celebratory lens, as a greatly focused effort and satisfying victory. For Harriot, one would think it should have been the culmination not just of her own life's work but of her mother's before her, the vindication of two generations of labor, commitment, and passion. But in reality, the final years of the suffrage movement were at least as much a transition as a climax for Harriot. This final half-decade represented not only the height of the militant spirit and single-minded concentration of the suffrage campaign but the surfacing of the larger world of politics and citizenship, the wider range of concerns, beckoning on the other side of enfranchisement.

In the immediate aftermath of the New York defeat, Harriot threw her lot in with other suffrage radicals who were gathering around the young, charismatic militant Alice Paul and her determined campaign for a federal amendment. Harriot was drawn to the tactical militance of this rebel wing of the national suffrage movement, but even more to the political options opened up by a shift to the national stage. As frustrated as she was with soliciting men's votes on behalf of woman suffrage, she was fascinated by the possibility of appealing to enfranchised women in the growing number of "suffrage states" where women could vote in federal elections. From 1915 through 1917, she helped to organize the first women's voting bloc, which she hoped to direct against the ruling Democratic party to force it to support a woman suffrage amendment to the U.S. Constitution.

The core—and the weakness—of such a strategy was that it called on women voters to evaluate political options on the basis of a single issue: votes for women. The discipline of adhering to the single-issue mandate of organized suffragism was beginning to wear on suffragists. In a basic way this strategy was in tension with the high value attributed to the vote and the faith in political methods that suffragism so assiduously cultivated. This insistence that no other issue measured up in importance to votes for women finally gave way even before the last scene of the suffrage drama had played itself out. The entry of the United States into a world war—a matter simultaneously political and above politics—provided the perfect environment for many women, Harriot among them, to move, at long last, beyond suffrage.

Once the United States entered the war, Harriot moved away from Alice Paul and the militant battle for the federal amendment not so much because they differed over the war, but because Paul remained adamantly single-minded about the vote. Harriot spent from 1917 through 1920 paying only the most cursory attention to the final stages of the enfranchisement process. She participated in neither the campaigns of civil disobedience of the militant camp nor NAWSA's extraordinary lobbying effort to get Congress to pass the amendment, though either would have been consistent with her experience and her talents. By the time the Nineteenth Amendment was passed by Congress and ratified by the thirty-sixth state, Harriot Stanton Blatch was already living and working in a postsuffrage world.

When Harriot first came on to the American suffrage scene, the federal approach to woman suffrage—the approach her mother had championed so eloquently as "national protection for national citizens"—had been all but abandoned. The vigor and vision revitalizing woman suffragism in the early twentieth century were concentrated at the state and city level. While numerous independent suffrage organizations like the Equality League of Self-Supporting Women sprang up around the country, the National American Woman Suffrage Association, which retained control of national suffrage politics (such as they were), became increasingly irrelevant. Nonetheless, the numerous independent state-based campaigns of the 1910s, to which Harriot contributed so much, made the revival of a national campaign for woman suffrage inevitable.

Each time a state was won for suffrage, the women of that state began to vote in federal as well as state elections. If this new female voting power could be organized and directed, it could provide a way to force action on the federal level. By 1915, eleven states had amended their constitutions to enfranchise women: Wyoming, Utah, Colorado, Idaho, Washington, California, Oregon, Montana, Kansas, Arizona, Nevada. Added to this was the apparent success of "presidential suffrage" in Illinois; this was Catherine McCullough's brilliant strategy for securing the right of women to vote for presidential electors, and thus for president, by simple legislative action.[1] Everyone who was alive to woman suffrage strategic opportunities understood the link between the enfranchisement of women in particular states and the amendment of the U.S. Constitution.[2] Even the devastation of the New York defeat did not alter this fact. "With twelve states in which a large body of voting women are ready to act as levers in bringing pressure on Congress," Harriot wrote in late 1915, "an entirely new opportunity has presented itself to the suffrage movement."[3]

Three years before, the young Pennsylvania-born suffragist named Alice Paul had boldly taken on herself the flagging campaign to win a constitutional amendment at the national level. Under her leadership, the spirit of modern, militant suffragism, which had swept the cities and state referenda campaigns, began to flow into and transform the nearly defunct effort for amending the U.S. Constitution. Paul had participated in the British suffrage movement, been jailed and force-fed, and had come back to the United States with a powerful conviction about the necessity of militant action to win votes for women. From the start, Harriot was impressed with the younger woman's energy and commitment. The WPU held a reception for her immediately after her return from England, and Harriot tried to recruit her to the New York campaign. "People did not often say 'no' to Mrs. Blatch but Alice Paul said 'no,'" Caroline Lexow Babcock remembered many years later.[4]

Instead, Paul made it clear that she wanted to revive the campaign for a federal amendment. Harriot agreed to help her get appointed as chair of the NAWSA's Congressional Committee, to which no one had attended in years. She introduced Alice Paul to Jane Addams, who was then vice-president of the National American and who arranged for her to chair the Congressional Committee.[5] "Now, with young leaders of promise in Washington, trained in the Pankhurst school of dramatic direct action," Harriot wrote, "it looked as if things were going to happen."[6] As the new chair of the NAWSA's Congressional Committee, Paul announced that she would inaugurate her campaign with a grand suffrage parade in Washington, D.C., to coincide with the inauguration of Woodrow Wilson as president. Following the precedent of the WPU's work in New York, a suffrage parade was a virtual declaration of modern, militant methods. "I think the idea of having [a parade] at the capital is magnificent," Harriot wrote, "and I hope that the work . . . will bear rich fruit. You must feel ready to consult me in any way that you desire."[7]

As aggressive suffrage leaders, Harriot Blatch and Alice Paul had much in common. They were both alive to the potential of demonstration and spectacle, skilled at the uses of publicity, ready to go to battle with male politicians, and eager to challenge the authority of conservative suffrage leaders. But there were also important differences between them that the common category of militant tended to obscure. Alice Paul was the modern herald of the feminist principle of "the single issue," the contention that women had no business becoming involved with any other reform so long as their own freedom was incomplete. The origins of this strategic approach could be found in the years after Reconstruction and the disappointments of trying to anchor woman suffrage to black suffrage. Susan B. Anthony herself provided the historical precedent on which Paul rested her strategic claims. Dedication to the cause of one's sex, as Alice Paul preached it, was necessarily an exclusive faith. So long as women were the objects of the ultimate discrimination in the political realm, loyalty to their sex forbade involvement with any other cause. By contrast, Harriot identified with the "many idead" suffragism that had marginalized her mother in the last decades of her life and separated her from Anthony's path.[8]

From her apprenticeship to the Pankhursts, Alice Paul learned how to politicize the single-issue approach. Suffragists must direct unceasing pressure, be it either electoral or super-legal, against "the party in power" solely on the basis of that party's position on women's enfranchisement. This was an approach that Harriot had drawn on in her own work in New York, but there were problems with it. To begin with, there was the difficulty of translating the dictum of holding the party in power to the flame of suffragist anger from the British parliamentary system to the American federal system. After Wilson's election, when Paul began to pressure the Democrats to recognize woman suffrage as a national issue, the referendum campaign in New York was at its height. Harriot and most of the other New York suffragists urged Paul to keep clear of their state campaign, where Democrats were emerging as the more supportive party. Paul refused, unwilling or unable to adapt to the complexity of partisan politics in the American political environment.[9]

An even more fundamental problem with the single-issue approach was that it called on women to make political choices solely on the basis of votes for women. Harriot hewed to this requirement, but she had not begun her political career as a single-minded suffragist, and such restraint did not come naturally to her. For years she had resisted the temptation to connect herself with or even voice opinions on other issues. In response to a *New York Times* editorial page criticism in 1914 that suffragists refused to "discuss such issues as the tariff, the Mexican situation, or the political condition of the city," Harriot explained that responsible suffragists "avoid the discussion of such topics intentionally, but it does not follow that we have not opinions and even very decided views in regard to them. . . . We have to weigh at each point just what questions will and will not interfere with the advance of our cause." Even so, "it is not easy, when one has strong political views, to play the part of the oyster and it only becomes possible to remain silent when one considers the importance of the question of the enfranchisement of women."[10]

Tellingly, the "side issue" that first intruded into Paul's campaign for a federal constitutional amendment was the same problem that had generated Anthony's original conviction about adhering exclusively to a woman suffrage faith: African American claims to political equality. Early on in planning for the Washington, D.C., parade in 1913, Alice Paul was approached by representatives of the many educated, professional, and politically aware African American women of the district who wanted to participate. For African American women, the pursuit of enfranchisement required that they confront the obstacles of race simultaneously with those of sex. But Paul was unshakable in her insistence that it was "unwise to inject the Negro problem into the suffrage problem," and that the claims made by black women were solely a matter of race, not sex.[11] Paul's conviction in this matter was reinforced by the election of a Democratic president and Congress. The Democratic party's historic hostility to black political power had become opposition to all federal control of the franchise, and suffragists who were focused on suffrage at the federal level were going to have to either confront or finesse this position to win their amendment. After prolonged and contentious negotiations, African American women participated in the march, though in small numbers and on Paul's terms, at the back of the parade. Even so, Ida B. Wells-Barnett of Chicago succeeded in escaping the segregated place to which she had been relegated and marched prominently with white suffragists in the Illinois delegation.[12]

Harriot was not drawn into this controversy, but what her position might have been can be inferred from a similar conflict, seven years later. At the first conference of militant activists after the winning of the Nineteenth Amendment, African American suffragists urged that the organization support the passage of federal enforcement legislation to ensure that they not be deprived of the benefits of the recently passed Nineteenth Amendment. Harriot was contacted by the National Association for the Advancement of Colored People and the National Association of Colored Women about the proposal, and she wrote to Alice Paul that she thought it was a "splendid" idea. Attorney Emma Wold replied on behalf of Paul that the threat to these women's votes was not a "feminist" but a "racial" matter and therefore did not belong on the postsuffrage agenda.[13]

The Washington, D.C., parade in March 1913 inaugurated a new era in American suffrage history. Paul was able to parlay the public response to the demonstration—or more accurately claims of public outrage at the inability of district police to protect suffragists from rowdy onlookers—into a congressional hearing before the Senate Standing Committee on Woman Suffrage. Ten months before, Harriot had similarly transformed charges of crowd disturbances and police malfeasance during the parade in New York into widespread publicity and a formal apology from municipal authorities.[14] "The tide of condemnation [at the mistreatment of the Washington marchers] now sweeping the country will show how popular the cause of woman suffrage is," she confidently predicted of the Washington, D.C., "riot."[15] Immediately after, a special Senate hearing was held on the parade and the conduct of the police. One month later, senators from the suffrage states of Wyoming and Oregon introduced a resolution calling for passage of a woman suffrage amendment to the Constitution. The resolution was referred to the Senate suffrage committee, long dormant but now under the leadership of the senator from the premiere suffrage state of Colorado, who issued a favorable report. Thus the amendment was headed for a vote of the full Senate, the first since 1878, the year it had initially been presented.[16]

This achievement in turn precipitated a serious split between Alice Paul and the established leadership of the NAWSA. The fact that the vote in the Senate was likely to be negative gave no pause to a true militant; as Harriot had argued years before when "orthodox suffragists" had cautioned her to exercise greater caution before the New York legislature, even defeats moved the cause forward by publicly identifying supporters and opponents. But the NAWSA's Executive Board regarded the pending Senate vote as an unmitigated disaster. By the end of 1913, tensions between the National American leadership and its militant faction had reached the breaking point, and Paul was dismissed as chair of the Congressional Committee. Paul had earlier formed a separate entity entitled the Congressional Union, until then essentially a paper organization, and now she made it a genuine alternative to

NAWSA.[17] In early 1914, the National American refused affiliate status to the Congressional Union, which from this point on began to develop into a full-scale rival national suffrage organization. The split was intensified when the two organizations began to support different forms of constitutional amendment. While the NAWSA dallied with an elaborate and farcical plan which combined the worst of the state and federal methods—known as the Shafroth-Palmer amendment—the Congressional Union continued to advocate the constitutional language that had been used for woman suffrage since 1878.

Given the parallels in their situations, her own historic relationship toward suffrage militance, and her strong sense of herself as a suffrage rebel, Harriot was quick to take Alice Paul's side at the time of the break. Carrie Catt had been appointed by NAWSA to inquire into relations with the Congressional Union, and this gave Harriot another reason to sympathize with Paul. "Again and again, I have seen vigorous young women come forward only to be rapped in the head by the so called leaders of our movement," she wrote in support, clearly identifying with the opposition Paul and her cohorts faced. "When you and the Congressional Committee were in its infancy, the National ought to have known that it must either back you financially or choke you at birth."[18] She identified with the youth, the militancy, and the defiance of the Congressional Union. "The courageous spirits should be at variance with the timid, the determined with the faltering, the generous with the jealous," Harriot observed about the growing split at the national level. "Above all should variance prevail between the old and over-cautious," she insisted, "and the young and zealous."[19]

From 1913 through 1915, Harriot supported the work of the Congressional Union while concentrating her own energies on the New York referendum. Toward the end of the referendum campaign, Alice Paul, eager to gain access to the great financial resources of the New York suffrage movement, insisted on opening a Congressional Union office in New York City. Harriot angrily accused her of trying to undercut the referendum campaign.[20] "I have not changed one iota in my admiration for the splendid work that you and Miss Burns have accomplished," she wrote to Paul, "but it seems to me that your intentions in New York have become broader and more aggressive shall I say than I understood them in the first instance."[21] She nonetheless took Paul's part in the conflicts that continued to develop between her and established NAWSA leadership.[22] Between the timidity and caution she had come to expect of Carrie Chapman Catt and the militant vision, albeit sometimes too ruthlessly pursued, of Alice Paul, there was no question as to Harriot's preference.

In the aftermath of the defeat of the New York referendum, all expectations were that Harriot would throw her lot in with the Congressional Union. She was, after all, "the arch rebel of the suffrage army."[23] In addition, she had also made it clear that she was done with state referendum work and wanted to shift to the national arena.[24] But she was enough of a suffrage politician to want to preserve her own power base as she moved into the relatively unfamiliar waters of national suffrage politics. And her fiercely independent character would no more allow her to subsume herself under the leadership of Alice Paul, despite her great admiration for the woman, than to submit her organization, two years earlier, to the authority of Carrie Chapman Catt. She was still obeying her mother's mandate, never to put loyalty to individual or group above one's independent judgment. Thus, even though Harriot Blatch became an unflinching advocate of the federal amendment route to woman suffrage beginning in November 1915, she waited nine months to join the Congressional Union, and then stayed a member only briefly.

At first in the aftermath of her New York defeat, Harriot hoped to maintain the Women's Political Union, perhaps as an independent affiliate of the Congressional Union. However, her plans were rapidly undercut. Eunice Dana Brannan and Elizabeth Selden Rogers, two of her chief lieutenants, announced that they along with other members of the Executive Committee, were resigning from the WPU and affiliating themselves with the Congressional Union without their former leader. "Mrs. Rogers and Mrs. Brannan are pretty awful to Mrs. Blatch," Harriot's old friend Dora Hazard wrote to Caroline Lexow Babcock. "It was evident that neither Miss Paul or the old WPU board members wanted her . . . and it was quite heartbreaking."[25] The battle for a constitutional amendment was to be a completely focused effort, with no distractions and no extraneous issues to separate dedicated suffragists from each other. As Rogers confided to Babcock, the WPU Board along with the leadership of the Congressional Union "did not trust [Harriot] completely" and "feared that she would go off on side lines." As a result, Harriot would not be offered the chair of the New York branch of the Congressional Union, even though it would have been a fitting position for her and satisfied her desire for independent authority within the organization.[26]

"The decision of the WPU board . . . evidently made quite a change in Mrs. Blatch's plans," WPU secretary Mildred Taylor reported to Alice Paul.[27] Taken by surprise by this revolt against her leadership, Harriot announced that Nora would take over the WPU and make it into an upscale version of the Equality League, a suffrage society for business and professional women in New York City.[28] But within two months, Nora was reportedly too ill to lead the organization.[29] Perhaps like Harriot before her, Nora was unable to lay claim to her own authority so long as her mother was still acknowledged leader. Thus after six years of rambunctious life, the WPU came to an end. At a final meeting of the Executive Board, the WPU formally amalgamated itself with the Congressional Union, to which it transferred all its resources, including its priceless lists of New York suffragists.[30]

What were the reasons for the revolt against Harriot's suffrage leadership? At a general level, the militant wing of the suffrage movement was being reorganized as a single-minded phalanx, a disciplined army of women fighting for one and only one purpose: woman suffrage in the U.S. Constitution. Partly this was a way to focus and marshal suffrage energies for one last eagerly anticipated fight. But it was also a kind of defense against the splintering and dispersing forces that were waiting just the other side of enfranchisement to disrupt suffrage unity and tear women apart from one another at the moment of their greatest dedication to the cause. Talk of the danger of veering off into "side lines" could be heard increasingly.

In the opinion of Caroline Lexow Babcock, Harriot's residual links to working-class politics and the socialist premises which had informed her initial move into militant suffragism, as attenuated as these had become of late, went a long way in explaining the mutiny against her. "If they distrusted Mrs. Blatch," Babcock wrote many years later, "it may have been because she had belonged to the Fabien [sic] Society in England and she was a socialist. Her socialistic sympathies did not prevent her . . . pushing an endorsement of the amendment through both major political parties . . . and submitted to the voters in 1915 after decades of neglect," Caroline observed angrily. "But her socialism and labor sympathies were too much for the rich of the 17th Senatorial District."[31]

Her plans for the WPU thus thwarted, Harriot endorsed the Congressional Union's work, and especially praised the political possibilities of the federal amendment campaign. "We of the Women's Political Union are not strangers to the political methods used by the Congressional Union," she declared at the final meeting of her society. "In our work, when we were endeavoring to put the suffrage amendment through the [New York] Legislature, we used, and with success, the line of direct political action. We held legislators accountable for their vote at Albany and we sought to defeat our enemies when they were running for the Legislature. The work of the Congressional Union in Congress is our work transferred to a national field."[32] She urged all WPU members, many of whom were considering working on the second New York referendum, to affiliate with the Congressional Union instead.

Dora Hazard for one was convinced. "I want to send you word how wonderfully Mrs. Blatch told about the work and purpose of the Congressional Union," she wrote Alice Paul. "She was in her best mood—sweet, serene but keen and eloquent."[33]

Harriot now searched for an aspect of the national work to take up. She remained interested in the presidential suffrage route as a way toward an enhanced national suffrage presence, so much so that Rogers and Brannan asked Alice Paul to try to rein in her enthusiasm.[34] She also had what she called her "pet idea," to amend the Fourteenth Amendment so as to change the basis for congressional representation from the number of adult males to the number of voters. She thought that this would be a way to allow "the voting power of the colored race and of women [to be] pooled" and offered to the states as a reward for expanding the franchise. The suspicion and discomfort she felt toward immigrant voters did not extend to black people, whom she regarded as long-standing Americans, fully integrated into the democratic ethic. As the daughter of abolitionists, she liked the idea of a black-female alliance, but it made no sense in the context of a national political scene in which both Congress and the Executive were controlled by a party defined by its hostility to black enfranchisement.[35]

Instead she settled on a version of the work she had done in New York: the organization of political pressure on elected legislators on behalf of woman suffrage. Rather than staying in the east, where immigrant populations humiliated her by refusing to extend to her the rights that they had so recently been granted, she would go west, where she could appeal to genuine Americans, born of the same democratic blood as she. And even more liberating, instead of begging male voters to overcome their masculine prejudices and bestow women's rights, she could apply to women who were voters in the west to reach out and rescue their disfranchised sisters in the east. To this piece of work, she wrote Alice Paul, she felt both her "head and heart turn."[36] "Why should not the women of the East find champions among the politically powerful women of the West?" she wrote the month after the New York defeat. Making woman suffrage a national political issue would turn the "great power of the voting woman" to the benefit of her own sex.[37]

Organizing women voters in the west appealed to Harriot. Always interested in methods that used the weapons of electoral and party politics, she was one of the earliest strategists to recognize the possibilities of organizing women's votes on behalf of a constitutional suffrage campaign and was a strong influence on Alice Paul in this direction. The idea of organizing a women's voting bloc on behalf of suffrage seems to have first been broached by the National Council of Women Voters, a small group based in Washington State, at a conference it cosponsored in 1913 with the Congressional Union. "I feel very strongly that the voting women could do many things to help," Harriot wrote to Paul at the time. "I would like to tell them that if they would begin now to organize women to back a demand in 1916 for a plank in national party platforms pledging amendments of the U.S. Constitution with threat of losing the votes of women in ten states . . . they would be helping us in the most efficient way."[38]

The Congressional Union first campaigned among western women voters during the congressional elections of November 1914. In mid-September, Congressional Union organizers were sent to each of the suffrage states (including Colorado, still reeling from the massacre of women and children in the mining town of Ludlow) to urge women to vote against Democratic congressional candidates. Alice Paul invited Harriot to participate but she was involved with the New York referendum, and so the WPU instead sent Jane Pincus, the WPU's best organizer.[39] The Democrats lost the election and the Congressional Union claimed a role in bringing several Democratic congressmen down to defeat. Thus encouraged, the Congressional Union planned more extensive efforts to organize western women voters in 1916, a presidential election year.[40]

By 1916, Harriot was free of the personal and political constraints of the New York campaign and ready for an organizing tour of the suffrage states. After her husband's death, she had resumed her American citizenship. With the climax of the suffrage fight so near, she was eager to become a voter herself. "Ever since I was a young woman I have dreamed of qualifying as a voter in one of the western states if I could not get enfranchisement in the East," she wrote to Anne Martin in Nevada. "I have fully made up my mind to go West this spring." She chose Kansas. The state had so much intimate historical meaning to her, it must have seemed almost like going home. "From both my mother and father I heard no end of thrilling tales about the bravery of men and women in Kansas in making their state free soil."[41] Kansas was where her mother and Susan B. Anthony had led the first state referendum on woman suffrage ever held, almost a half-century before. Once Harriot announced her plans to establish political residence there, she began to receive letters from other women who shared her political dreams, and these in turn began to grow more elaborate. "There is no knowing how this will develop and there are all sorts of possibilities," she told reporters. "A few of us might build a house . . . we might build a town and then we would vote in the municipal elections. We will pay our personal taxes wherever we locate and that will take some money from New York. If many women should go, who could tell?—we might give Kansas another Presidential Elector and a greater representation in Congress."[42]

Having made herself into a voter, Harriot took her place at the head of the Congressional Union's 1916 electoral campaign. In early March, she was made "National Political Chairman" of the Congressional Union's "Suffrage Special," a train carrying two dozen eastern suffragists on a well-organized, highly publicized railroad tour of the west. This was the first phase of an elaborate plan that also included the creation of an organization of women voters, the application of sustained pressure on the major parties at their summer national conventions, and, if necessary, a return to the female voters of the west in September and October to make good on the threat of organizing their votes against recalcitrant politicians. Given her national stature, her speaking skills, her political acumen, and her movement seniority, Harriot's participation was crucial to the plan. "It would be a very great misfortune if you did not go on the trip," Paul wrote, offering to pay her expenses in full. "The expedition would mean little of course unless led by people who can make an appeal which will carry weight."[43]

Many other suffragists were clamoring to make the trip. Alva Belmont, whose money was being counted on to fund it, declared that she was going and bringing with her the dramatic suffrage radical Inez Milholland. Later Belmont withdrew, but Milholland was included, despite Paul's concerns that she was too associated with the peace movement and thus not single-minded about the vote, too "luxurious," and insufficiently "serious" for the tour's political purposes.[44] Elizabeth Rogers wanted to go, too, but Mary Beard recommended against it: "[She has] periodic break-downs when [she has] to be attended constantly." Beard was overruled, and Rogers joined the group without any problem.[45] As for Harriot Blatch, who had just turned sixty, no one raised any questions about her stamina and strength, which were assumed to be equal to the challenge. Hadn't her mother traveled every year to the west when *she* was in her sixties, at a time when conditions were much more arduous?

The pace that the suffrage envoys kept up was in fact grueling. In a week and a half, Harriot traveled by train to Los Angeles, Santa Barbara, San Francisco, Seattle, and Salem, Oregon. In Seattle, she headed a formal reception with the mayor, went to a luncheon with "pioneer suffragists," had tea in the afternoon with university women, dined with another group of prominent women, and in the evening was the lead speaker at a mass meeting in a downtown theater.[46] The next day she worked at the same pace. Harriot requested that wherever she spoke, the Congressional Union arrange for her to meet with women who remembered her mother and Susan B. Anthony.[47] "Everywhere I went, women would come up to me, to shake the hand of the daughter of Elizabeth Cady Stanton," she recalled in her memoirs. "I wanted to shake hands with you," one woman told her, "and tell you that you are not nearly as good looking as your mother."[48]

Away from New York, Harriot emphasized the humiliation she had experienced in the New York referendum of begging for enfranchisement from "foreign" men. "I have stood on practically every street corner in New York City . . . stood there pleading with men who had been given the right of self government simply for coming to the United States, stood there pleading with men who could not understand me and whom I could not understand," she declared in Arizona.[49] She struck this chord, over and over again, in almost every speech. "All day the men filed in to vote, three hundred of them . . . and only four Anglo Saxon names in the whole list," she told an audience in Colorado Springs. "They are from the other world, from Poland, Russia and Southern Europe and please understand one thing, I am glad they have self government and liberty . . . but I don't think they have the right in their self government to deprive me of my self government."[50]

The unrestrained nativism of these speeches was clearly a visceral response to the New York disappointment. But Harriot was also trying to craft an argument to appeal to western audiences who, she imagined, identified themselves as "real" Americans, proud of their birthright of liberty. Against the cesspools of eastern corruption, she contrasted the west, much as her mother's generation of Yankees had done: the seedbed of democracy, the natural home of true American political virtue, against which stood the debased cultures of Europe and the patriarchal peasantries of the old world. "In the mountains liberty has always found birth," she declared to an Oregon audience. "In the great west was the cradle and the fulfillment of the enfranchisement of the mothers of our race. We disfranchised women of the east turn to the west because its people are freedom loving and because its people have power to enfranchise us."[51] The good white citizens of the west had resolved their own "alien" political problems a decade or two before. Untroubled by political insurgency from Asians or Indians, the American women of the west would be free to rescue their sisters from the east, who were in thrall to old-world patriarchy.[52] On behalf of eastern women, Harriot appealed to "those of our own sex who are free to stretch out their hands and make the sacrifice and use their power to free one half the nation from political bondage." "I have faith. I believe in women," she declared. "The east calls to the west for succor."[53]

In June 1916, this phase of the Congressional Union's campaign culmi-

1. Harriot Stanton Blatch, her mother, Elizabeth, and her daughter, Nora, c. 1886. Courtesy of Rhoda Barney Jenkins.

2. The Stanton girls and their aunts, c. 1870. From left: Margaret, Harriet Eaton, Harriot, Tryphena Bayard, Catherine Wilkeson. Courtesy of Rhoda Barney Jenkins.

3. The "Two Harriots" at Vassar, c. 1877. Seated in the middle row, Ransom on the left, Stanton on the right. Courtesy of Alice and Arthur Milinowski.

4. Harriot as a young mother, with Nora, c. 1884. Courtesy of Rhoda Barney Jenkins.

5. Nora, Helen, and Harry Blatch, c. 1894. Courtesy of Rhoda Barney Jenkins.

6. The Basingstoke household, 1886. From left: Elizabeth Bransom (nursemaid), Harriot, the gardener, "Fraulein" (governess), Nora, Harry, and Elizabeth (housemaid). Courtesy of Rhoda Barney Jenkins.

7. Harriot (second from left) in the offices that the Equality League shared with the Women's Trade Union League, sometime after 1909. Note the elite women in hats and the working-class women in shirtsleeves. Courtesy of the Library of Congress.

8. Nora (left) and Harriet Porritt on horseback speaking to a street crowd, 1908. Courtesy of Rhoda Barney Jenkins.

9. Katherine Mackay and daughters. From *American Magazine*, v. 70, September 1910.

10. Caroline Lexow, 1914. Courtesy of Caroline Babcock Furlow.

11. Women's Political Union suffragists advertising the New York City parade in
1912. Front row, from left: Eleanor Brannan (daughter of Eunice), Jane
Schneiderman (sister of Rose), Mary Woods Smith, Elizabeth Selden Rogers, and
Elizabeth Mayer. Courtesy of the Library of Congress.

12. Elizabeth Ellsworth Cook serving as a pollwatcher, with policeman and
politicians, New York City, November 1909. Courtesy of the Library of
Congress.

13. New York City suffrage parade featuring working women, May 1911. Courtesy of the Library of Congress.

14. Suffrage delegation, led by Marcia Townsend, entering the Assembly chamber at Albany, March 12, 1912. Courtesy of the Library of Congress.

15. WPU Executive Committee on the march, in the parade of May 1913; Harriot is on the far right in academic gown. Courtesy of the Library of Congress.

16. Inez Milholland, equestrian marshal for the New York City parade in May 1913. Courtesy of the Library of Congress.

17. The Women's Political Union at the state legislature in Albany, March 1913. From left: Eleanor Irving, Harriot, Senator Stephen J. Stillwell of New York State, Marcia Townsend, Elizabeth Selden Rogers. Courtesy of the Library of Congress.

18. Harriot (center) with Women's Political Union star organizers, Jane Pincus (left) and Alberta Hill. Courtesy of the Library of Congress.

19. Harriot on the steps of the Women's Political Union traveling van, c. 1915. Courtesy of the Library of Congress.

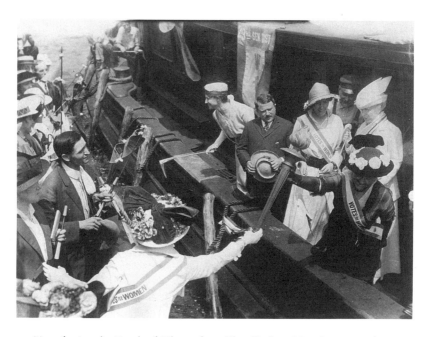

20. Transferring the Torch of Liberty from New York to New Jersey, on the Hudson River, September 1913. Courtesy of the Library of Congress.

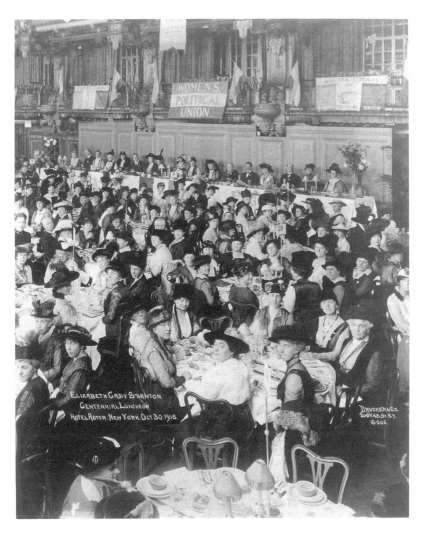

21. Elizabeth Cady Stanton Centennial Luncheon, October 30, 1915, Hotel Astor, New York City. At the head table, Alva Belmont is seventh from left, Harriot is eleventh from left, and Anna Howard Shaw is to her left. Courtesy of the Library of Congress.

22. From left: Harriet and Nora de Forest with Harriot Blatch, c. 1914. Courtesy of the Library of Congress.

Equal Rights

Vol. I, No. 1
FIVE CENTS

SATURDAY

Alma Lutz

Alma Lutz is nationally known as a biographer of famous women. Her first work in that field was a life of Frances E. Willard, the great temperance advocate, and one of the few women elected to the Hall of Fame; her most recent is the just-completed biography of Elizabeth Cady Stanton, co-worker in the suffrage movement with Susan B. Anthony, Lucretia Mott and Lucy Stone. The preparation of the latter work has led its author into pleasant by-paths, as shown by the delightful article on "The Bloomer Costume," reprinted in this issue from a recent number of the Christian Science Monitor Weekly Magazine.

Miss Lutz, whose home is in Boston, is a member of the National Council, and Chairman of the Literature Committee of the National Woman's Party. In addition to her achievements in the realm of biography, she is a frequent contributor to this and other magazines.

23. Alma Lutz. From *Equal Rights: An Independent Feminist Weekly*, January 1, 1915.

24. Harriot, behind grandson John Barney, in 1928 at the fiftieth reunion of Vassar College Class of 1878. Courtesy of Alice and Arthur Milinowski.

nated in a mass convention in Chicago. There the Congressional Union formed the world's first women's political party. In accord with the principles of a single-issue movement, the Woman's Party was to have only one plank in its platform—passage and ratification of a constitutional woman suffrage amendment—and no candidates. The goal was to create a bloc of women voters committed solely to woman suffrage, as a way of forcing the controlling parties to enact a constitutional amendment. Although reliant on the eastern-based Congressional Union for its financial resources, the Woman's Party membership was to be made up entirely of enfranchised women. "Amid scenes of wonderful enthusiasm," two thousand women and a handful of men crowded into Chicago's Blackstone Theatre, organized themselves by state delegations, and gathered under giant banners. Anne Martin of Nevada was elected chair of the Woman's Party, and Harriot, claiming Kansas as her residence, as head of the Committee on Resolutions.

Harriot delivered the major speech at the convention. Now a voter herself, she gave a thrilling address to this mass of enfranchised women. Drawing on her considerable rhetorical and strategic powers, she called for western women voters to put their political resources behind a woman suffrage amendment to the Constitution. "I stand ready to get a group of women about me who will go forth over the suffrage states. We will deliver against the party that blocks the progress of women, 500,000 votes. I intend to go into the West; I intend to use there every bit of energy and strength I have, to advance this cause of ours. . . . Women, you voters from every state, will you join with us; will you come?"

To underline the single-issue focus of the Woman's Party, she spoke as a woman with fully developed partisan inclinations of her own, which she was prepared to sacrifice for the good of woman suffrage. "I am by inheritance, by conviction, of the Democratic party," Harriot explained, "still I will vote in Kansas against that party if it does not, before November, do full justice to our federal amendment now before Congress."[54] Journalist Ida Tarbell, hardly a friend of woman suffrage, wrote in the *Chicago Herald* that "not even the most obdurate of anti-suffragists could have heard Mrs. Blatch last night without being moved. She had been so long a warrior for votes for women that to see her stand at last before a national body of women voters . . . sure it stirred your blood!"[55]

Harriot's speech came immediately after formal presentations to the women voters from representatives of the various "men's" parties. Some of their appeals were surprisingly strong. The Progressive party representative, Gifford Pinchot, confidently declared, "The Progressive party does not come before you as a suitor for your hand, because we married you in 1912," at which the audience laughed and applauded. "We were born as a party standing for every one of the things that every woman in this land wants: a fair chance for all the children to grow up and be decent men and women, a fair chance for every workingman, a fair distribution of all the good things of this life among all the people."[56] But given the nature of the Woman's Party, Harriot dismissed Pinchot almost offhandedly. "To the gentlemen of the minority parties," she explained, "We cannot of course stand for you because you have no power to give us what we want." The focus must be on the two major parties.[57]

The Democratic party was the ultimate target of the Woman's Party. The Democratic party, Harriot explained, "controls the White House, controls the Senate and controls the House of Representatives."[58] Suffragists' goal must be either to win the solid commitment of the Democrats for a woman suffrage constitutional amendment or to organize the votes of women against them. The emissary to the Woman's Party from the Democrats was Dudley Field Malone, an intimate of the president. Malone emphasized the issue which he believed must rival woman suffrage as a basis for women's political choices: that the spreading war in Europe was threatening to draw the United States into hostilities and that President Wilson would resist this. Doris Stevens, the Congressional Union activist who went on to marry Malone, recalled that he was so effective at the meeting with this approach that "it looked like a stampede to Wilson's 'he kept us out of war.' " But then Harriot, the party's "top gun," stepped up to refute Malone. "I remember two camps of women swirling on the platform after the meeting," Stevens wrote to Harriot many years after the incident, "one surrounding you, another surrounding Dudley. . . . He shook his finger at you and said: 'You took my audience away from me.' "[59]

The Woman's Party convention had been scheduled to coincide with the first of the major party conventions, the Republicans' meeting in Chicago. Maybe a western women's voting bloc could play a role in the battle between the party's conservative and progressive wings. The progressive wing was able to control the nomination for president, Charles Evans Hughes, chief justice of the Supreme Court and former governor of New York. However, the Resolutions Committee was chaired by the arch conservative Henry Cabot Lodge. Lodge's committee heard Carrie Chapman Catt speaking for the National American Woman Suffrage Association, Harriot Stanton Blatch representing the newly formed Woman's Party, and Mrs. Arthur Dodge for the antis. The suffrage plank which Lodge's committee passed was highly equivocating, intended to hold party progressives without driving away conservatives: it supported the "extension of suffrage" but also acknowledged "the right of each state to settle this question for itself." As the plank was passed, Harriot thought she saw Lodge sneer a bit, as if to indicate that this was all the women were going to get from his party and that it was not very much.[60]

A few weeks later, both groups of suffragists also addressed the Democratic convention in St. Louis. There, they got a similar resolution, calling for the extension of the franchise to the women of the country by the States upon the same terms as men."[61] As to the content of the party planks, Harriot conceded, "there is nothing to choose between the parties." But she thought that the manner of the Democratic convention had been "far more satisfactory than the Republican." Where Republicans had sneered, Democrats had been respectful. Perhaps the Democrats might come round after all, and she could cast her first vote for the party of her father.[62]

On July 24, Harriot and several other women of Democratic persuasion met with the president "to urge action on the suffrage amendment for our party's own good." "I am sixty years old, Mr. President," Harriot began (so was he), "I have worked all my life for suffrage." She led with the nativist approach she had been emphasizing all spring. Could not the president, as a man "who understand[s] what we are talking about and can speak to us in our tongue . . . accord to women a self-respecting method of working out their enfranchisement?" Perhaps encouraged by Harriot's anti-immigrant opener, Wilson parried with an overtly racist response of his own: "the negro question" made it impossible for him to do what she asked, for his party believed that enfranchising women would disproportionately strengthen the black vote. Harriot responded, as suffragists had been doing for some time, that "enfranchisement of women in the South would increase not decrease the proportion of white to black voters," but Wilson would have none of it. "The President smiled," she recalled, "and then added in a very low voice, 'In two states the blacks would still preponderate.'" "We left convinced that we could not change the President's mind," Harriot wrote of her July meeting, "that he would do nothing for the Federal Amendment. The only alternative was to change presidents."[63]

As senior suffrage politician, Harriot was also scheduled to lead the delegation to the Republican nominee, but at the last minute she demurred. She suggested that women with stronger connections to the progressive wing of the Republican party press Hughes, and Mary Beard took her place.[64] This delegation was more successful than those meeting with Wilson. Hughes surprised the suffragists by coming out with a clear endorsement of the federal route to woman suffrage. At this point, the Woman's Party path was set: it would go to the women voters of the west and ask them to stand for their sex, against their president, against the Democrats. Harriot, who had expected little from the conservative Republicans, now telegraphed Alice Paul, "Hurrah for Hughes!"[65]

Clear as the situation was when it came to federal woman suffrage— Hughes for, Wilson against—everything else about the elections of 1916 posed complications for the Woman's Party. While Hughes himself had a moderately good record on reform in New York, as a party the Republicans were moving in a more conservative direction. By contrast, Woodrow Wilson, on the basis of the achievements of his first term, could make a convincing case for the Democrats as the party of progress. In contrast to the election of 1912, third parties barely figured: the Progressives did not run their own candidate; the Socialists, internally divided and struggling to defend their loyalty to the United States, polled a fraction of their 1912 vote. Above all there was war in Europe. After two years of grueling combat in Europe, Wilson's gamble at keeping the United States neutral seemed to be paying off, and calls for preparedness were receding. Wilson went into the election as the candidate of "Peace, Prosperity and Progress." In such an electoral environment, faced with a choice between two major parties and dominated by the highly emotional issue of peace versus war, the Woman's Party campaign to organize women to vote as a bloc on the single issue of woman suffrage was an uphill struggle.

In October 1916, as she had vowed, Harriot traveled to Wyoming, and from there to Colorado, to organize women to vote against Wilson. From the beginning, however, this trip was a far cry from her spring tour, as dispiriting as the earlier tour had been inspiring. Threatening to organize women into a voting bloc was one thing; actually doing so was another. It was difficult for the Woman's Party to maneuver its way through the high-stake politics of a presidential election. In her insider's history, Doris Stevens insisted "that the Woman's Party did not attempt to elect Mr. Hughes. . . . The appeal was to vote a vote of protest against Mr. Wilson and his Congressional candidates. . . . That left the women free to choose from among the Republicans, Socialists and Prohibitionists."[66] But unlike 1912, a third-party vote was a luxury few voters were willing to take in 1916. Even Woman's Party activists were uneasy with what seemed like a call to vote for a Republican president and for war.[67] A suffrage sympathizer from California wrote that, despite her socialist politics and woman suffrage principles, she was going to cast her vote for Wilson, inasmuch as anything else would effectively be a vote for the Republicans.[68]

Throughout the tour, Woman's Party organizers found themselves repeatedly confused with another traveling train of eastern women speakers gone west, Republicans stumping for Hughes. The "Hughes Special," as it was called, deliberately included women well-known for their suffragism, such as Margaret Dreier Robins of the Women's Trade Union League and Rheta Childe Dorr, the first editor of the Congressional Union's magazine, the *Suffragist*. No wonder the press and the voters had trouble keeping the anti-Democratic Woman's Party speakers and the pro-Republican Hughes women distinct in their minds. Throughout the western tour, sloppy planning (or perhaps Paul's own Republican inclinations) resulted in Woman's Party organizers finding themselves speaking from platforms that were identified with Republicans. Harriot objected to speaking in Cheyenne under Republican auspices. "I was followed by a woman of the ultra partizan [sic] type," she complained to headquarters. "Next morning a Democratic woman called me up on the telephone and told me I had converted her, but the 'Republican lady had about driven her back again into the Democratic camp.'"[69] At the end of the tour, in Kansas to vote, she refused to speak at a Republican rally at which she had been scheduled.[70]

Nowhere were these problems worse than in Colorado. Not only had women been voting there longer than anywhere else in the United States—twenty-three years—and were strong in their partisan attachments, but also the state, in the words of one Woman's Party organizer, was "the most acutely union state in this country . . . where they even have a seven hour day in some trades."[71] A handful of the organizers in the field recognized the problem and urged that someone with good working-class credentials and obvious labor sympathies, Rose Winslow or Elizabeth Freeman for instance, be sent to present the Woman's Party case there. Harriot was grouped with all the other Woman's Party organizers, who were considered too tony to make a convincing appeal to the state's working-class women and men.

But the Woman's Party campaign as a whole was not organized around any real awareness of the importance of class alliances within electoral politics. Mary Beard had urged Alice Paul to "indicate our support of a Woman Movement that is big enough to include the efforts of women to organize in the industrial field," but she felt that her efforts had failed.[72] Vivian Pierce, one of the few prolabor activists in the Woman's Party, became livid at Paul for the "absolute blind complacency with which we've antagonized huge sections of the electorate in these states." Goodwill toward suffrage and potential working-class votes had been squandered. In the intensely prounion mining town of Bisbee, she angrily reported, the Woman's Party main speaker "was entertained for three days by some of the Company officials' wives and these women were in charge of the meetings," thus ruining any possibility of winning the votes of union men, who were the majority of the town's voters.[73]

Alice Paul acknowledged that Colorado was "a particularly hard nut to crack," but there were other concerns pulling at her and eroding her not especially deep appreciation for the importance of the working-class vote. Instead of the labor speaker requested for Colorado, she sent Louisine Havemeyer, one of Harriot's wealthy New York recruits. "Mrs. Havemeyer's husband has great sugar factories in many parts of Colorado," Paul explained, and she was impressed with Havemeyer's claim that "she has considerable influence in Colorado and that she could get a large audience."[74] The organizer in the field objected strenuously that Havemeyer's presence would exacerbate charges, already quite strong, that the suffragists were a dodger for the Republicans, "that we are anti labor in league with corporate interests [and] reactionary circles." But Paul had her eye on the pro-Hughes women as a future source of money and political clout for the Woman's Party.[75]

In addition to these political obstacles, the fall Woman's Party tour presented substantial physical difficulties. From the beginning, the weather and the altitude in the mountain states combined to take a serious physical toll on the Woman's Party women, of whom Harriot Blatch was the oldest.[76] Elsie Hill reported that Harriot's heart was "palpitating and her throat aching."[77] The difficulty of the natural conditions was compounded by poor arrangements. No hotel rooms were reserved and train schedules were unreliable; Harriot complained about having to find hotel rooms on her own and taking her meals in the unfamiliar Chinese restaurants that dotted the small western towns at which she was scheduled. "As to my trip in western Colorado, I can only say that if the conditions are like the ones I have lived in for the past week I could not stand up under them," she wrote to Hill. "I am absolutely worn out by . . . routing out at midnight and 4 o'clock in the morning. . . . Younger women must do that work."[78] Halfway through the itinerary, Harriot threatened to quit; given her pride at being a seasoned campaigner, she must have felt that the conditions were truly intolerable, and even more that her talents were being misused. "If I thought my leaving for Topeka would be known or cause comment, I would plow the forough [sic] to the unproductive end," she insisted, "but I've stolen into the West like a thief and I am certain my departure will not cause a ripple."[79]

Harriot was not the only one to complain about conditions. Organizers and speakers alike wrote back to the Washington office, which was coordinating the tour at a distance, to protest endemic mismanagement.[80] "With so few people and such an enormous territory to cover and almost no money to do it on," Alice Paul observed with her usual steely resolve, "the few who are working are absolutely worn out and in very bad physical shape."[81] Under these conditions it seemed inevitable that someone would fall seriously ill, and finally someone did.[82] In Los Angeles, Inez Milholland, whose reputation had earned her the tour's biggest billings, collapsed dramatically on stage. As legend has it, she cried, "President Wilson, 'How long must we wait, how long must this heart breaking struggle for justice go on?'" and then fainted. She was hospitalized but never recovered and died in late November of complications resulting from pernicious anemia, thus becoming American suffragism's first martyr.[83]

Harriot, now somewhat stronger herself, finished up Milholland's schedule. In Denver she spoke to an audience of one thousand and in Colorado Springs to fourteen hundred. "Let us punish the party that wishes to hand our political liberty over to forty-eight separate states to deal with as each sees fit," she thundered.[84] The exhausting tour ended in Chicago, where Harriot placed a transcontinental telephone appeal to Woman's Party activists in each of the suffrage states. Seated at the center of the stage of the Blackstone Theatre, surrounded by purple, white, and gold chrysanthemums, she sent her appeal out across the country: "Women voters! Remember. Wilson kept us out of suffrage. Be loyal to women. Do not return to power a President and a Congress hostile to political freedom for women. Vote against Wilson and the Democratic candidates for Congress."[85]

The Woman's Party had wanted to make woman suffrage the issue of the election of 1916 but this was impossible. On November 7, Woodrow Wilson was reelected by a narrow margin. Looming over everything and driving many voters into the Democratic column was war in Europe. Wilson's pledge to keep the United States neutral attracted many voters in general, and the widespread presumption—though impossible to test—was that women were especially drawn to his antiwar stance. The Democrats' slogan, that Wilson "kept us out of war," exerted a pull on the electorate that the militants' clever but paltry cry that "he kept us out of suffrage" could hardly counter. Even so, the closeness of the election might have cheered the Woman's Party, except that it was the western states where the militants had campaigned in which Wilson won his victory. California, with its crucial electoral votes, went for the Democrats by a mere four-thousand-ballot margin. Only in Illinois, where women's limited "presidential suffrage" required the keeping of separate ballots, was it possible to tell whether women voted differently from men; there, women had gone marginally more pro-Hughes than had men.[86]

The one consolation Harriot found in the election was that all assessments of the election paid close attention to how women voted. Although western women had been casting their ballots since the 1890s, in the election of 1916, she observed, their growing numbers, the closeness of the race, and the Woman's Party campaign led them to be "discovered" at last. "The Woman's Party did not accomplish all it would have liked to achieve, but believe me a sound foundation was laid," she concluded.[87] She was capable of a long view when it came to political organizing. The election had left the Democrats far less firmly in control of Congress than in 1912. She argued that this was exactly the moment to accelerate organizing efforts among voting women. She expected to continue the Woman's Party strategy in anticipation of the next election. Not so Alice Paul, who was ready to leave behind electoral drives in favor of a campaign of propaganda, publicity, and if necessary civil disobedience. In her years of work in New York, Harriot had demonstrated her conviction that propaganda preceded and gave way to politics; for Paul, the order was reversed.

The Congressional Union moved from politics to propaganda in January 1917, when it initiated a women's picket of the White House. A deputation met with the President to plead with him in memory of the martyred Inez Milholland. When Wilson refused to support the woman suffrage amendment, the delegation announced that picketing of the White House would begin immediately: suffragists would stand in speechless condemnation of the Wilson administration for its obduracy. At first, Harriot, who was a member of the delegation and furious at Wilson's recalcitrance, endorsed the picketing, which was modeled after the WPU's 1913 "silent sentinels" demonstration in Albany. "We can't organize bigger and more influential deputations. We can't organize bigger processions. We women can't do anything more in that line. . . . We've got to bring to the President, individually, day by day, week in and week out, the idea that great numbers of women want to be free, *will* be free, and want to know what he is going to do about it."[88]

Yet the next day, when picketing began, Harriot was appalled. She assumed the picketers would be eastern women protesting their disfranchisement, but prominent among them were western women who had the right to vote. "I thought it was to be clearly shown by choice of pickets that such a method of attack was adopted by weaponless disfranchised women," she wrote sternly to Alice Paul.[89] "To me it seems worse than foolish for a person with a battleax in her possession to use a toothpick as a weapon."[90] The picketing of the White House was an acceptable stunt for the months immediately after the election, when voting strategies had little effect, but hardly a permanent substitute for the political methods to which she had thought the Congressional Union had committed itself by forming the Woman's Party.[91] She tried to get other suffragist activists to object, a "betrayal" that Paul remembered and resented for decades after.[92] After an acrimonious exchange of letters, Harriot formally withdrew from the Executive Board of the Woman's Party, less than six months after she had joined. "Allow me to pass out as quietly as I passed in," she wrote to Paul.[93] Nonetheless, her resignation made the headlines.[94]

One month later, following this same logic, the members of the Woman's Party and the Congressional Union met together in Washington, D.C., to amalgamate into a single organization. Although the name of the new entity was to be the National Woman's Party, it was to follow much more closely in the mode of the original Congressional Union. The defining difference of the Woman's Party, that it was made up solely of women voters who would use their votes on behalf of the woman suffrage amendment, was set aside in favor of concentrating on protests and publicity. Harriot objected once again. "If you inject into the Woman's Party a large body of non-voting women, we would by just so much lower the political power of the woman's Party."[95] Paul responded that the election of 1916 had made the crucial point: women voters existed and supported woman suffrage; why pursue this tack any longer?

If the discussion at this meeting is any indication, the amalgamation of the two organizations was powered not only by frustration at the electoral methods of the Woman's Party and the need to consolidate resources, but by a widely felt desire for suffrage unity. The distinction between voter and nonvoter undermined women's unity, which fueled the fight for suffrage. "All of these remarks . . . have been made . . . from the material point of view, from the viewpoint of efficiency," Elizabeth Selden Rogers observed. "I should like to say that it seems to me there is a spiritual gain in the union of the Congressional Union and the Woman's Party just at this time. That for the women of the whole country to unite openly . . . uniting their spirit for freedom at this crisis, will give us a spiritual gain that will be perhaps more than the material gain."[96] Elizabeth Kent, a California voter and wife of Congressman William Kent, made a similar point. "Although I am very proud to have the word 'voter' on my badge here, I realize that it does not mean the same thing [for a woman] as it does to a man," she explained. "My feeling is far stronger that I belong to a disfranchised class rather than that I am a woman voter. I think that this feeling of solidarity of women is growing and that if we are all of us back of this movement it will have a greater push."[97]

Paul's advantage over Harriot was that she understood and spoke for this dimension of suffragist passion. "There does not seem to be any longer any necessity of taking these women voters and drawing a line around them so as to call attention to them," Paul observed. "That has been done."[98] Paul also appreciated suffragists' unsatisfied hunger for direct confrontation with the state as the embodiment of male power. A relative lack of interest in electoral methods was a curious position to be taken by one who was heading an all-out war for enfranchisement, but the truth was that Paul, who impressed everyone with the single-mindedness of her dedication to the vote, was not particularly interested in its power to shape events. When she turned to electoral methods, it was as a tactic, whereas for Harriot electoral politics was fundamental and strategic. It is possible that had Harriot's convictions about the power of electoral politics to force fundamental change prevailed among militants, the fervor that women expressed in their final drive for enfranchisement might not have stood in such stark contrast to their relative disinterest in using the ballot once it had been won. As the U.S. suffrage movement increasingly divided between Alice Paul's version of extrapolitical militance and the careful and conciliatory methods of NAWSA, from 1915 on headed by Carrie Catt, Harriot was left without a home for her special strengths of leadership.

Harriot's separation from the National Woman's Party coincided with the acceleration of hostilities between Germany and the United States. When Germany suddenly resumed its submarine warfare against allies and neutrals in February 1917, Harriot presumed that her differences with the National Woman's Party would fall by the wayside as Paul would surely see the absurdity of picketing the president in the face of war. "I presume now the bone of contention will be buried for picketing in the time of national crisis will not be pursued," she wrote to her friend Anne Martin the day that diplomatic relations with Germany were severed.[99]

But not even world war was enough to shake Alice Paul from her insistence that woman suffrage should be the sole conviction of women dedicated to the liberty of their sex. "The Congressional Union was organized for one purpose—to secure an amendment to the United States Constitution enfranchising women," Paul told newspaper reporters. "Some of us are militarists, some pacifists. We are united on only one ground—fealty to political liberty for women."[100] Even though Paul's declaration was not motivated by an antiwar stance, her declaration drew women who opposed the war because it allowed them to continue to function as suffragists. In addition, picketing the White House and challenging the authority of the president were ways of making a statement about the misguidedness of the war effort and the undemocratic nature of the government. It has even been suggested that the coincidence between opposition to the war and suffrage militance beginning in 1917 made the NWP seem more fundamentally left-wing than Paul intended it to be or than it was after the war.[101]

Meanwhile, Carrie Chapman Catt, speaking as head of NAWSA, took the opposite position on the war, announcing that suffragists would put their financial resources, their organization, and their patriotic passions at the service of their country.[102] Considering her prior credentials as a leading pacifist, Catt's declaration was no more determined by her preference for war than Paul's was by opposition to it; where she differed was in her judgment that the suffrage movement would gain more by anchoring itself to the energies of national mobilization than by keeping its focus and purposes pure of war fever.

To later historians and feminists, the radical suffrage methods of the National Woman's Party seem to be of a piece with its resistance to wartime hysteria; similarly, the National American's patriotic excesses appear consistent with its tactical restraint on behalf of the suffrage. But the fit was not so obvious or perfect at the time. Harriot was not the only suffrage militant who was prowar. The important and powerful New York chapter of the National Woman's Party caused great controversy by aligning itself with preparedness forces. Similarly, there were pacifists in NAWSA who objected strenuously to Catt's offer of suffrage service on behalf of the war; the New York Woman Suffrage Party, the NAWSA affiliate in the state, faced its own internal rebellion from antiwar suffragists, including large portions of its trade union wing.[103]

Much as an overly exclusive emphasis on the differences between the NWP and NAWSA with respect to suffrage strategy can oversimplify the conflicts that war brought into the movement, it can also obscure what was common to the entire suffrage movement in these, its final years. On both the pro- and antiwar sides, the passions engendered intruded into and threatened to crowd out an exclusive focus on the suffrage. The divisiveness that the war introduced into the suffrage movement—the first of what would turn out to be many such divisions among women—demonstrates that focused unity on behalf of the franchise was giving way to the diversity that was the consequence of the very political engagement for which suffragists fought. Perhaps there was such a taboo on difference among women, on partisanship and its conflicts, that it took an issue as total as world war to break through the prohibition against dissent within suffragism.

The conduct of the second New York referendum indicates the degree to which the discipline of focusing exclusively on suffrage was beginning to give way even as the vote was finally being secured, and that the war was a crucial context for allowing this to happen. New York suffragist energies were not nearly as concentrated in 1917 as they had been during the campaign in 1915. Younger women especially were becoming impatient with the obligation to "be silent . . . on the great political and social issues of the day."[104] Instead of repeating the mammoth organizing effort and spectacle of the first campaign, New York suffragists were using their resources and organization in other causes. In the summer of 1916, the Woman Suffrage Party volunteered its services to the New York City Board of Health to distribute antipolio literature. After April 1917, suffragist energies were concentrated even more on the war. Suffragists organized massive parades in the streets of New York, but they did so this time on behalf of Liberty Loans. "It was easy to enlist women, tired of the long drawn out suffrage campaign in the more exciting war work," remembered Gertrude Foster Brown, a major fundraiser for the campaign of 1917.[105] And if prowar sentiment powered the second referendum campaign, antiwar sentiment seems to have fueled suffrage victory at the polls in November 1917. New York City, with its strong Socialist party and antiwar vote, provided much of the margin of victory.[106]

The distractions of war may have been the context for Harriot's odd advice to the newly enfranchised women of her home state. Acknowledging that "since last February I have taken little part in suffrage work, having devoted my time mainly to matters connected with war service," she advised New York women not to bother with the electoral process for the war's duration. "Primaries and registrations and elections . . . are nonessentials in the present world crisis," she declared. Her advice was meant for both prowar and antiwar women. "Those who are in favor of the war can centre their strength on winning it, those who cannot see what the battle means can centre their energies on question of food, sanitation, education, health."[107] Was this the same woman who had lived for the thrill of electoral contests, and who had dedicated her own core years to winning the vote for women in New York? Harriot's advice to abjure politics had the character of a hypercorrection, an overreaction to her own long-standing exclusive dedication to woman suffrage. As she saw it, her country was enlisted in a bigger contest, where civilization itself was at stake.

Harriot's enthusiasm for the war was intense. "I am red hot for the war," she wrote. "I want ten million men put on the firing line as soon as they can be got there and I want women organized by women to enter on work here and free men for the army."[108] Her support for the war separated her from some of her most intimate friends. Caroline Lexow Babcock began what was essentially a second reform career as a leader of the women's pacifist movement. And Harriot Ransom Milinowski, Harriot Blatch's Vassar friend, was the wife of a Prussian army officer.[109] Theodore Stanton shared Harriot's prowar beliefs, and Grace Ellery Channing Stetson, William Ellery Channing's daughter and a friend of many years, added fuel to the fire of Harriot's anti-German sentiments.[110] Nora seems to have been preoccupied by personal matters, supporting herself and her daughter, and her opinions are not recorded, though she was by birth an Englishwoman.

On a larger stage, however, Harriot Blatch was representative of her generation of American reformers, including the majority of suffragists. Like most liberal activists, she experienced Wilson's decision to take the United States into the conflict not as a tragedy but as an opportunity for collective effort and deliberate social change.[111] Ignoring the destruction and sacrifices of war in favor of an eager vision of what could be accomplished in its aftermath, Harriot, like other prowar progressives, was swept away by ambitious hopes for national "reconstruction." The term harked back to the formative experience of her mother's generation and conjured up images of an activist, liberal government, dedicated to using its powers to sweep away oppression and remake society on egalitarian grounds.[112]

Harriot's particular contribution was to restate the prowar argument in women's rights terms, for which she now used the neologism "feminism." "To my mind feminism is at stake in the conflict between the allies and Germany," she wrote to Doris Stevens.[113] She recast the moral stakes of the war, civilization versus barbarism as it was commonly put, in gendered terms: "the nations in which women have influenced national aims face the nation that glorifies brute force."[114] Only the acceptance and utilization of women as workers, alongside of and equal to men, could mobilize the nation's full capacities and win the war. The corollary was that wartime work would be especially uplifting for women; it would draw them out of their isolated environments and primitive work conditions into a collective effort of national service. "When men go awarring, women go to work," she stated with brutal honesty. "War compels women to work. That is one of its merits."[115]

Harriot made her feminist case for war in a book published in April 1918 by the YWCA's Womans Press, *Mobilizing Woman Power*. The origins of the book lay in the trip she had made in 1915, after Harry's death, when Europe was already at war. She wrote passionately about the contributions that British and French women were making as workers to their nations' wartime mobilization. She had expected to find women broken down by the anxieties and shortages of war; instead she found them flourishing in their roles as citizens, workers, and national servants. The voice that Harriot assumed in *Mobilizing Woman Power* represented a return to the social scientific tone of her youth. The book was "objective," fact filled, and full of faith in progress. But she also wrote to urge Americans to recognize the importance of mobilizing their own woman power. With the cessation of European immigration and the enlistment of men into the military, the country's need for labor power could be met in only two ways: by "coolie labor," underpaid, nonwhite immigrant workers, or by American women. The choice for Harriot was obvious.[116]

The gender politics of *Mobilizing Woman Power* are curious.[117] On the one hand, Harriot adapted the common suffragist argument that women embodied "the protective side" of human nature surprisingly easily to her prowar purposes. "Men have played—all honor to them—the major part in the actual conflict of the war," she wrote in her concluding chapter. "Women will mobilize for the major part of binding up the wounds and conserving civilization."[118] But the deeper thrust of her argument ran in the opposite direction, away from the notion of a timeless female essence and toward the assertion that war would transform women, imbuing them with strengths Harriot liked to call "virile." The beauty of war for women, she argued, was that it brought them out of the isolated home and into the larger society, subjecting their labors to the same modernizing, specializing, and collectivizing processes through which men had passed and which she endorsed as "the manly method of work."[119]

To emphasize her argument that the demands of war would strengthen women and with them the nation, she asked that great advocate of modern virility, Theodore Roosevelt, to write an introduction, and he accepted. "I am a great believer in you and your work," he wrote.[120] "I join with [Mrs. Blatch] in the appeal that the women shall back the men with service," he wrote in his extended foreword, "and that the men in their turn shall frankly and eagerly welcome the rendering of such service and the basis of service by equals with equals for a common end." Reading Harriot's words in *Mobilizing Woman Power* had especially helped to quiet his anxieties lest women's presence lead to any "unhealthy softening of our civilization," a particular danger in wartime. So long as "women show, under the new conditions, the will to develop strength and the high idealism and the iron resolution," he assured Harriot's readers, "our nation has before it a career of greatness never hitherto equaled."[121]

In November 1918, when the armistice was announced, Harriot made plans for a second trip to Europe. She wanted to see the consequences of war, the plans for peace, and the great changes she had predicted in the status of women. She was part of a small army of activists, intellectuals, and reformers who made their way to Paris, to witness and hopefully affect the postwar treaty deliberations. The YWCA Womans Press, pleased with the reception of Harriot's first book, asked her to write a second volume, "dealing with the constructive outcome of the war for women."[122] This book was to include a section on the impact of war on Germany, where Harriot was to go as soon as possible after the borders were opened to civilian travelers.

Personally, she was in a period of transition. Only days before she sailed, Nora remarried. Harriot liked Nora's new husband, a naval architect named Morgan Barney, and was hopeful and happy for her daughter and grand-daughter, but she was also more distressed than she cared to admit. She had sold the house in which Harry had lived on Long Island, and now the large "string bean" apartment on the upper West Side where she had lived with Nora and little Harriet had to be broken up. In an odd sort of way, the situation harked back to her first ocean voyage to Europe, forty years before, except that now she was the bereft mother, holding on to her own daughter and feeling she was losing her. She wrote Nora five times before the ship even left New York harbor, and regularly when she was in England, France, Germany, and Switzerland. She complained that she was not receiving enough news from home, worried about how Nora and Morgan were doing, and sent back intrusive suggestions for where and how they were to live.[123]

The transatlantic journey added to Harriot's uneasiness. So soon after the cessation of hostilities, refugees of various sorts were eager to get back to Europe, and Harriot, who liked her creature comforts, complained that among "the lower middle class and upper working class folk" who crowded her ship, the HMS *Saxonia*, "the men are rude to the women and the women in turn take it out on the children." She was so beset by wailing babies on board that she thought she would have preferred the sound of gunfire to that of one more crying child. To escape the mothers and children, she spent most of her time on the ship in the smoking room, where it was "not customary to serve ladies," puffing away to the dismay of fellow travelers and shipboard personnel alike.[124]

The biggest disappointment, however, was still ahead and had to do with her confidence about the war's results. As soon as she landed in Liverpool, she began to see that England was a "war worn country." Everywhere, people were hungry and cold, lacking enough food or coal to take them through the winter. Her own sisters- and brothers-in-law, nieces and nephews, were exhausted and sick, and because she could not get any hotel accommodations, she shared their ill-heated homes and depleted larders.

"The weather is terrible and everybody is ill," she wrote to Nora before leaving London for Basingstoke. "Your Aunt Agnes [is] in bed with Bronchitis. I wonder everybody is not dead, the houses are so cold and damp." Sitting in a friend's house before a small parlor fire, she could see her own "breath curl off, like smoke from a cigarette."[125] She recognized that her entire way of thinking about the war was undergoing a radical change. "I have seen endless people & things & . . . realize more and more the serious effects of the war on England," she wrote to Nora. "We will talk it out later."[126]

What she saw after she crossed the channel was even worse. "The devastated regions of Europe must be seen to be comprehended," she later wrote. "No photograph, no description, can convey a realization of the actuality." She observed deserted villages, trenches that snaked along the contours of the hills, and battlefields. "Trees are wrenched off and splintered here, and there they stand straight and whole but dead and leafless, the bark peppered by shot until the trunk was ringed and life gone." The city of Rheims, heavily bombarded and nearly deserted, appalled her. Plaster dust from shattered buildings was everywhere. "Street after street of ruin, fallen roofs and walls littering the sidewalks, and jutting out into the gutter," she wrote in her diary, "a city of the dead."[127]

Under U.S. Army escort, Harriot crossed into Germany, traveling as far as the city of Koblentz. The evidence of prolonged food shortages, especially among the children, was everywhere and made her long for her nine-year-old granddaughter. She wrote to Nora of the undernourished children and the adult women who had not had milk in three years.[128] Occupying the city were American troops, sharp and soldierly but discontent and homesick. The devastation of the war was not even redeemed by a rejection of the follies of nationalism. On the contrary, narrow parochialisms seemed to have been fueled by the war. The U.S. doughboys spoke openly of their dislike of the French and, a heavy irony, claimed to prefer the Germans, their official enemies.[129] Repeatedly asked at every border her age, she told Nora that what she really wanted to say was "sixty three years old, feeling 100."[130] "The world is one big hate," she wrote once she had returned to Paris.[131]

Before returning home, Harriot had one more postwar obligation. Along with many other women reformers from Europe and America, she traveled to an international meeting of women peace activists in Zurich, a follow-up to the Hague Peace Conference of 1915, which the participants had vowed to call as soon as possible after the cessation of hostilities. Away from the controversies of the badly misnamed official Peace Conference in Paris, she was briefly able to find "peace and rest" for herself. "I see the reason why," she wrote Nora. "These women not being in trade or commerce have not felt the grip of international competition and so internationally tis easy for them to bury the hatchet."[132] She described to Nora how she and other conference participants helped to receive eight hundred undernourished Viennese children, who were to be taken care of and fed in Switzerland until they were strong enough to return to Austria. She wrote particularly about one little girl, who was left standing alone on the railroad platform after all the other children had been dispersed to their host families. Recalling her own childhood emotions of abandonment—"I can remember to this day how I felt"—Harriot stayed with the child, trying to amuse and comfort her, until her proper destination was located and she was sent on her way.[133]

With the Zurich conference behind her, Harriot began to make her way back home. The train to Paris was slow and crowded, and she was able to sit only because her traveling companion, Lillian Wald, bribed the conductor. From France, she went back to London, then to Falmouth, where she impatiently waited for her ship, the *Noordham*; on June 23, after some more delays, she sailed. She had been abroad a long five months. Waiting for her on her return were Nora, Morgan, and little Harriet—"I am looking forward, oh so longingly, to see you"—and the job of turning what she had seen and felt into a book that would no longer be on the constructive outcome of the war.[134]

Back in New York, Harriot quickly began work on the book, titled *A Woman's Point of View: Some Roads to Peace*. She wrote in a tone quite unlike that of *Mobilizing Woman Power*. She recorded her emotions as fully as her observations; what she saw had been "soul killing."[135] It is unclear whether the pressure of time came from her publisher or from her own conviction about the immediacy of what she had to say. In any case, the book was completed by the end of October and was published in early 1920, one of the first woman's memoirs of the drama of war and peace. "When I sailed to Europe to gather material for the book, I was full of confidence that I should find the roots if not the leafage of strong growths of sound constructive policies," she wrote in the preface. "I had been bitten with the propaganda of the war idealists, and went forth an optimist on a voyage of discovery. Circumstance honestly faced has changed a book, which was to have shown constructive results of the Great War, into a contribution of a volume to the library against all war."[136]

With enthusiasm for war banished, so it seems was her faith in "virility." More than any other time in her career, Harriot now emphasized the fundamental differences of the sexes, unambiguously privileging women's essential nature, which she regarded as constructive, protective, and humanitarian, while denigrating men as destructive, warlike, and selfish. "Women as women have a special contribution to make to the building of the nation," she insisted, "and I presume there is none so cynical as to assert the contrary."[137] Central to this assertion was her outraged maternalism and the haunting images of the underfed children of Europe, sacrificed by their own fathers to the masculine rituals of war. "It doesn't matter in the least whether the particular woman is married or not married, whether she has children or not," she wrote to the *Suffragist* in connection with her book's publication. "Her great responsibility in the world is to her dependents. If we are not the guardians of children then they have no guardians."[138]

And yet while *A Woman's Point of View* differs from *Mobilizing Woman Power* in crucial ways, it is equally striking how consistent Harriot's vision was with respect to women's future, suggesting that in some ways her prowar beliefs were a temporary vehicle for a more fundamental shift to a postsuffrage perspective and a feminism that was appropriate to it. The one "constructive outcome" of the war in which she still had faith was women's future. Even more important than the long-delayed coming of political democracy were changes the war had brought in women's economic position. Wage earning for adult women, wives, and mothers, was clearly here to stay. The war had shown beyond any doubt "that when it becomes necessary for [a woman] to raise the family income to a standard of decency, she will go out to earn a daily wage."[139] This irreversible trend raised profound questions about how children were to be cared for and families were to be tended that could not be resolved at the individual level. Here was a social problem, a governmental obligation, and a future political issue of immense significance.

By the time that *A Woman's Point of View* appeared in the spring of 1920, the woman suffrage amendment had passed through a reluctant Senate and the ratification process was well along. In late 1917, the National Woman's Party had resumed its picketing of the president, earning the militants arrest. Despite her continuing criticisms of wartime picketing, Harriot regularly sent telegrams and gave interviews condemning the imprisonment of NWP members.[140] After the armistice was signed in 1918, she returned to the National Woman's Party fold. For all her conflicts with Alice Paul, she believed that Paul's leadership had been crucial to suffrage victory. "I am perfectly certain," she wrote to Elsie Hill, that "if it had not been for the National Woman's Party we would not have had national suffrage in the U.S. for another fifty years."[141] She arranged to spend some time at the National Woman's Party headquarters. "I am really looking forward to a stay under your wing in Washington," Harriot wrote to Paul, "for I suppose that there is time for philosophizing now, that parades, picketing, hearing[s], and courts and jails are ended." She needed to recover from "the heart-ache of my European experience, my hurry in book writing and my turmoil of breaking up my apartment."[142]

One might have imagined Harriot to have been jubilant at this moment, the culmination not only of her life's work but of her mother's as well, or perhaps angry and frustrated at these last delays. But mostly she seems to have been impatient for the long, life-consuming struggle for woman suffrage to be over. Not one to mistake the radicalism of tactics for that of content, she observed that while "the method of conducting the battle may have been stormy at points," the goal had long before ceased to be "revolutionary."[143] One goal had been won, one enemy defeated; but as a career reformer, she knew that others lay ahead and she was eager to get on with them. "The next big battle for women," she predicted knowingly, "will be equality with men industrially."[144]

8

Feminism

Harriot Blatch in 1920, like other veterans of the suffrage movement, was asking herself what women had won now that they had won the vote. What were women supposed to do with their votes and how were they supposed to do it? With respect to both of these questions—the what and the how of postsuffrage feminism—the U.S. women's movement appeared to be offering ex-suffragists stark and opposing choices. Strategically, newly enfranchised women were either to plunge into the partisan structures of already existing politics, exchanging the unity of disfranchisement for the opportunity to participate across the wide range of their interests and inclinations, or to continue to hold together as a sex and remain aloof from men's parties, in recognition of the fact that enfranchisement had not ended the problem of their subordination.[1] With respect to substance, historians have described the postsuffrage women's movement as falling into an allegedly fundamental divide in feminist philosophy between the principles of "equality" and "difference": while one side called for the removal of all remaining legal distinctions between the sexes, the other gathered around the defense and expansion of protective labor and social welfare laws designed to address the special dilemmas of women, especially working women and specifically working mothers.[2]

But considering this moment from Harriot Blatch's perspective, neither set of choices seems to exhaust the feminist possibilities of the postsuffrage years. Along with a handful of other women, she sought a third way. From a strategic point of view, she could not regard the two goals of political autonomy and political engagement for women as antagonistic. In her understanding of the possibilities of the postsuffrage world, joining with men in the work of politics and continuing to pursue distinct goals as women were fully compatible imperatives for action. "I do not think it is wise for us to draw off into a corner," she declared just as the amendment was finally ratified. "Instead of forming all these committees and classes and things we ought to go right to work with the men and do our full share in practical affairs."[3] She had great hopes that ex-suffragists, armed with the rich experience of their recent struggle and motivated by a broader vision of human need than traditional politics, could play a major role in expanding, even revolutionizing political action. Harriot rejected *both* the notion that women must accept political priorities as men had long defined them and the obverse, that women must keep themselves separate from "men's" parties, organizing only other women and only to overcome the still thriving subordination of their sex. Women, working with men, could create a new kind of party, capable of incorporating a feminist political program in it.

With respect to substance, Harriot did not believe that enfranchisement had satisfied women's quest for emancipation. If anything, the winning of equal political rights had exposed even more clearly the root causes of women's subordination, notably women's continuing economic dependence on men. However, she regarded both "equality" and "difference" as unsatisfactory standards for a postsuffrage feminist program. As she complained to Nora early on, both sides in the growing split between advocates of equal rights and of protective labor laws seemed to her equally "niggling," proffering feminism in its least visionary manifestation.[4] Instead, along with a few other socialistically inclined feminists, she sought a "constructive" feminist program for the postsuffrage years. At the center of this approach was the pursuit of full economic equality for women. When groups of men had won the vote, they had usually done so in recognition of their growing economic power, but for women this had not been the case. For women, political independence had preceded economic independence, and now was the time to remedy this anomaly. As Harriot put it, with political rights secured, women had to achieve a level of economic independence to turn the "political possession" of the ballot into genuine "political power."[5]

At the core of the challenge of women's economic independence was the problem of motherhood. So long as women's relation to children threw them back into economic dependence on men, motherhood and autonomy would always be at odds and economic independence would be out of reach for the average woman. Harriot had pondered the problem of the working mother ever since her Fabian years, advocating sometimes an elevated system of domestic service, sometimes Charlotte Gilman's idea of socialized childcare, but always defending women's right to maintain and expand their labor force participation and through it their independence. Now, a new and more promising solution to the dilemma of the working mother was being advanced: universal motherhood endowments, state payments to all mothers, to compensate them for necessary absence from paid labor, while providing them with an alternative to absolute economic dependence on their husbands.

Harriot became acquainted with the idea of motherhood endowments in England in 1915. In 1895, she had lost her battle within the British women's movement to reject special labor regulations for women workers. But in 1915, when she returned during the war, she found a different and much more encouraging situation. The position that she had fought for and lost twenty years before—socialist in its acceptance of regulating the wage relation, but within the women's rights tradition in its opposition to doing so by virtue of sex—had become the generally agreed on approach of most progressive women, including Fabians.[6] Women war workers had forced both government and labor to recognize the futility of assuming that women's labor force participation could be undone or of regulating women's labor alone. At a meeting of trade union women in London, Harriot noted with pleasure that all the participants seemed to accept "the idea of the new workers being permanent factors in the labor market" and to recognize that policy proposals must rest on the principles of "equality of preparation and equality of pay with men."[7]

The most important element in British women activists' reevaluation of the place of women in the labor force was their newly aroused interest in the proposal that government compensate women workers financially whenever childbearing and childrearing kept them out of the labor force. In her important 1914 article, "The Economic Foundations of the Women's Movement," Fabian Women's Group member Mabel Atkinson wrote that the state endowment of motherhood offered the most promising way "to secure for women freedom and independence and yet make it possible for the same women to be wives and mothers."[8] The idea of the state paying women for their maternal work had been developed initially in Scandinavia and from there it had been picked up by British socialists, who advocated it from a masculinist perspective as a way to keep women from wage labor.[9] As such, it had been regarded by British women's rights activists with suspicion. By the mid-1910s, however, Fabian women were linking motherhood endowments with provisions for equal pay for equal work and a minimum wage standard for all adult workers, so as to make the reform compatible with, not antagonistic to, equality for women in the labor force.[10]

The wartime policy of the British government to authorize "separation allowances" to women whose husbands were taken away by national service significantly advanced the case for a permanent policy of state endowment of motherhood. Unlike the American approach to mothers' pensions established in the years right before the war, separation allowances were granted to all women with children, not just to widows or those who passed a need-based standard. In her 1918 book *Mobilizing Woman Power*, Harriot wrote extensively about the impact of the separation allowance program in wartime England. Allowances taught the women of England that "their work as housewives and mothers has a value recognized by government in hard cash."[11] Against charges that servicemen's wives spent their payments frivolously, she assured her readers that women had learned to use their money wisely, that children's health and welfare was improving as a result, and that this was being accomplished without the humiliating levels of supervision that American pension schemes involved. "One need not be endowed with the spirit of prophecy to foretell that 'allowances' in wartime will broaden out into motherhood pensions in peace time," she predicted. "The allowance laws may prove the charter of woman's liberties; her pay envelope may become her contract securing the right of self determination."[12]

When Harriot returned to Europe in 1919, she met with many of the leading advocates of motherhood endowments, including Eleanor Rathbone of England and Helena Stocker of Germany, founder of the Mutterschutz Movement. In Europe, it seemed to Harriot that most women reformers had come round to supporting both labor legislation without regard to sex and motherhood endowments, as a means for securing equality in the labor force and economic independence for women. So dramatically had things changed since the debates of the 1890s, so great an impact had women war workers had, Harriot found that even her old nemesis, Beatrice Webb, now agreed with her on every particular of economic policy for women, including motherhood endowments. To be sure, male labor leaders continued to defend the principle of a full family wage paid to a male breadwinner (and therefore of an economically dependent wife and mother), and she anticipated a major conflict between men and women over labor and social policy, not unlike that which had just been concluded over political rights.[13] But as for the community of women activists, from the European perspective the

battle seemed to have been won in favor of women's full labor force participation, economic autonomy, and sex-neutral regulation of wage labor.[14]
While U.S. labor legislation had always been relatively backward, there was
every reason to hope that U.S. feminists would now follow the same path as
their European counterparts.[15] But this was not to be.

During the war, as already existing labor legislation came under attack
from aggressive industrial interests and conservative political forces, American women reformers began to divide over how to defend hard-won labor
legislation that only applied to women. In 1918 in New York, a formidable
group of reformers, led by Florence Kelley of the National Consumer's
League and Mary Dreier of the Women's Trade Union League, went on the
offensive, organized a Women's Joint Legislative Committee, and proposed
an expanded legislative package of what they called "special welfare laws"
for women workers, ranging from maximum hours and minimum wage
legislation to prohibitions against night work and with respect to specific
occupations, such as elevator operators, streetcar conductors, and all-night
messengers.[16] The New York women's reform community was by no means
agreed on this move. Even the crucial New York chapter of the Women's
Trade Union League could not come to a resolution on the matter, with
working-class members themselves split over the desirability of special labor
legislation for women only. For the most part, however, debate went on
behind organizational closed doors.[17]

In January 1919, Harriot Blatch became the first major U.S. woman
activist to go public with her objections to the proposed package of welfare
laws for women workers.[18] She charged that special legislation for women
workers was incompatible with wage equality; that women in skilled occupations would be demoted or lose their jobs as a result; that in focusing solely
on dangers to women in the workplace, men were being left without any
protection from the same unacceptable conditions; and that the movement
for eliminating child labor was being fatally burdened by attachment to
women's protective legislation.[19] As she had in England twenty-five years
before, she tried to make it clear that she supported the principle of government acting on behalf of workers' interests, and objected only to protective
labor legislation that applied solely to women. Such laws rested on the false
premise that women were permanently weak and that men were inherently
strong. "Protection of women by state and national agencies" made her
"gorge rise," she wrote to her friend Anne Martin. "I am for special legislation for children to the limit and against such legislation for adult women
unless it applies to all adult workers."[20] Spokeswomen for the Women's Joint

Legislative Committee and the Women's Trade Union League wrote articles and gave interviews to refute her charges and defend their bills.[21]

By March 1919, when the New York legislature convened hearings on the proposed women's welfare package, Harriot had left for her tour of postwar conditions in Europe. In her absence, Nora surfaced as a leader of the opposition. At hearings in Albany, women supporters of the welfare bills came ready to speak for the entirety of their sex, only to find the chamber almost filled with women equally determined who wore purple badges with the word 'Opposed' on them." Most of the protesters were transit workers, members of the Brooklyn-Manhattan Transit Women's League, who had lost their jobs the year before from an earlier piece of sex-based labor legislation, the Townsend Bill, which had barred women from work as streetcar conductors. They were joined by supportive professional women, including several lawyers. Nora, described via her matrilineage as the "daughter of the erstwhile suffrage leader" as well as "herself a suffragist and professional woman," was among them. The group called itself the Women's Equal Opportunity League.[22]

Nora shared her mother's strong objections to sex-based labor legislation, but she had her own perspective on the issue. This was the first really independent political foray of her life. At the time, she was nowhere near the socialist that her mother was. Instead, her criticism of protective labor legislation was based on the liberal principle of guarding against excessive state regulation. Not only did she understand the dilemma of the working woman in more individual terms than her mother, but she was uncomfortable with the state maternalism, the need to oversee and protect workers, so prominent in Harriot's approach.[23]

Personally, Nora's feminism was also distinct from her mother's. While Harriot was a champion of working women, Nora supported herself most of her life and knew the contradictions and challenges of paid labor more intimately. For almost a decade, she had been struggling to raise her daughter on her own with little help from Lee de Forest, while establishing herself as an independent building contractor. Harriot, along with the aging family nurse Elizabeth Bransom, did much of the raising of her granddaughter. Harriot frequently criticized Nora for pushing herself too hard, and was especially annoyed that she did most of her own housework rather than rely on servants. Combining maternal solicitude with political territoriality, she all but ordered Nora to leave the battle over special welfare legislation in New York to her. "Its going to be a long and painful fight and unless you have time and energy to wage the war to the bitter end, I would pull out of it," she advised. "I [will] go through to the finish but you with your business, [daughter] Harriot, [husband] Morgan and all your new calls upon time and strength had better think twice before getting further involved."[24]

Furthermore, from the letters that Nora sent her in France, Harriot concluded that the opposition to the New York welfare laws was not in particularly good hands. Whereas Harriot advocated the expansion of protective labor legislation to include men as well as women, the leadership of the Women's Equal Opportunity League was opposed to all regulation of wage labor. Harriot was particularly distressed to learn that Ada Wolfe, chief spokeswoman for the group, opposed any ban on child labor. It was crucial to approach "the whole question . . . in a bigger and more constructive way," she chided Nora. "Be careful not to involve yourself in mere reaction. There is no use in trying to turn back. The laws for protection had only one fault in that they were for women only."[25]

Meanwhile, Harriot was learning about the New York conflict from another source. WTUL activists Rose Schneiderman and Mary Anderson were in Paris at the same time as she was, sent to represent working-class women's perspectives at an international labor conference held in connection with the peace treaty deliberations. All three were staying at a small hotel run by the YWCA, which was both Harriot's publisher and organizational sponsor of the package of women's welfare bills in New York. From Schneiderman, Harriot learned that the WTUL was moving toward a position of strong advocacy of sex-based labor legislation. Harriot came to the conclusion that the WTUL was following the lead of the YWCA, and that the impetus for this approach was coming from the upper-class backers of both organizations, rather than from their working-class members, who were more troubled over a program of protection. "Uninformed narrow minded bigots want to direct our labor movement as far as women are concerned," she wrote angrily to Nora. "Their whole stock in trade would be the safe program of restrictive legislation for women. Their subscribers would not stand for a democratic program."[26]

Harriot returned to the United States fired up over what she regarded as the disastrous turn that labor reformers and social workers were taking toward protective labor legislation. Even before she disembarked, she met with reporters and delivered her message about "the necessity for limiting the hours of adult men and women and of setting the same limitations for both men and women."[27] But as she had predicted to Nora, it was impossible to lead the opponents of the welfare package away from "mere reaction" to a more positive program of protection for all workers. Within a few months, she was drawn into an electoral contest between Thaddeus Sweet, the Republican Speaker of the New York Assembly and an opponent of the special welfare laws, and his female Democratic challenger, Marion Dickerman.[28] She could have hardly been comfortable on a platform that pitted her against other progressive women reformers and allied her with a conservative male politician who characterized all labor regulation as "Prussian" and "unamerican."[29] "Would that our differences could be laid aside," she wrote somewhat plaintively in defense of her involvement in the Sweet campaign, "and that there could be union on measures of unqualified constructive value . . . increased protection to our wards, the children . . . amend[ings of] our very inadequate widows' pension law . . . protective measures for the health of adult workers of both sexes in dangerous trades and poisonous processes."[30]

Within the next year, the conflict over special labor laws for women went nationwide via efforts by the National Woman's Party to forge a postsuffrage program for women's emancipation. Many issues, notably peace and birth control, were brought forward as appropriate to such a program. Harriot urged the NWP to take up the plan for universal mother-hood endowments. "Every woman, whether the wife of a millionaire or a day laborer," she argued, "will in the world builded [sic] by women, be made to feel that society honors motherhood sufficiently to raise it above all sordid dependence."[31] At its crucial convention in February 1921, however, Alice Paul led the NWP past all these proposals to a single-minded focus on removing all inequalities women faced before the law.[32]

Harriot was not present at the convention, having stayed away because of a disagreement over how to honor her mother, but Nora attended, and Paul took advantage of her notoriety from the New York controversy to have her introduce the platform on which she was pinning her organization's future, "absolute equality."[33] After the fact, Nora did not like how Paul used her at the convention. The morning after the convention, she wrote a letter to the *New York Times*, withdrawing her support for the NWP's single-issue program, ridiculing the narrow way that "pure feminism" had been construed in opposition to all other aspects of "human rights," and belittling the NWP's pursuit of a program dedicated exclusively to securing a "few little picayune legal rights."[34]

Because Nora had so notoriously opposed sex-based labor legislation two years before, Paul's choice of her to introduce the "absolute equality" slogan linked the New York welfare legislation controversy and the NWP legal equality program. Florence Kelley, who recalled with rancor "the mad-women who gathered under the banner of Nora Blatch" in Albany the summer before, was furious that Paul had given her such a featured role.[35] But in general, despite much discontent with the single-plank equality platform adopted, the convention of 1921 did not focus on the dilemma that was soon to rend the postsuffrage women's movement: whether to advocate labor legislation exclusively for women. This was only the beginning of the process by which Paul's vision of a single legal mechanism powerful enough to ensure that "absolute legal equality" and sex-based labor legislation were coming to be defined as mutually exclusive negations of each other, thus obscuring every other approach to postsuffrage feminism. Alice Paul remained willing to try to define the legal equality approach so as to exempt existing labor laws directed solely at women. Well into 1922, the NWP was still trying to shelter sex-based labor laws from its blanket equality legislation and the WTUL was still trying to identify an area, other than the industrial, where it could join in on a proequality campaign.

While defenders of special labor legislation for women were willing to wait to see if their program could be reconciled with the legal equality approach, Harriot was not. In general, she regarded the categorical (or "blanket") assertion of legal equality as so vague and abstract as to be useless. But she did think that there were particular forms of systematic sex inequality that called out for legal remedy, and prominent among these was the long tradition of legislating special regulations and limits for women workers. Paul's approach through 1921 and 1922, to try to combine a blanket equality bill with a specific exclusion of sex-based labor legislation, was, as far as Harriot was concerned, the worst possible solution, doubling rather than neutralizing the damage. For this reason, only eight months after she had rejoined, she resigned from the NWP for a second time. There is no evidence that she ever again resumed formal membership in the organization.[36]

Over the next two years, as the split accelerated between the NWP's legal equality program and the advocates of woman-only protective labor legislation, Harriot found it increasingly difficult to resist being drawn into the very negations she abhorred. In December 1922, the Consumer's League announced "that all efforts . . . to reach an agreement with the National Woman's Party with regard to protective legislation for women in the industries had failed" and that the two organizations would now go head to head before the New York legislature as to whether labor legislation should apply to men and women or to women alone.[37] "It is impossible for me to conceal my disappointment," Harriot wrote to the *New York Times*, "that women's organizations, with the honorable exception of the Woman's Party and a few minor societies, have assumed the selfish attitude of protecting only workers of their own sex."[38] She charged that her effort to articulate a prolabor critique of special labor laws for women was deliberately obscured, so that all opposition might seem to be coming from self-serving manufacturers. "Instead of wasting energy carrying on an internecine war," she pleaded from the pages of the *Nation*, "it might be well if those believing in protective legislation should unite."[39]

Harriot fought especially hard on the grounds of maternal responsibility, even though the protection of motherhood was the sturdiest ideological core of the defenders of protective labor legislation. She made especially telling points when it came to the floundering movement to ban child labor, which was consistently running afoul of both congressional and constitutional opposition in these years. The link between labor legislation for women and children was fatally burdening the latter, she contended. "I am quite sure that the Supreme Court's mind will not grow on the children question until we make a big and fruitful campaign in the separate states and never until we separate women and children," she insisted at a debate with Florence Kelley before the Columbia Sociological Society. "I would not have grown women hanging on the necks of little children."[40]

It cannot be emphasized too strongly that through all this controversy Harriot was also a critic of the NWP's single-issue program of "equal rights." "Please understand," she wrote in one of her analyses of the problems with sex-based labor legislation, "that I am not speaking for the Woman's Party. I hold no brief for that organization and am not even a member of it."[41] Perhaps this is why, when the NWP announced a gala beginning to its campaign for a federal Equal Rights Amendment, Harriot was not included, even though it was to be held in Seneca Falls on the seventy-fifth anniversary of the first women's rights convention in 1848. This was a curious omission, inasmuch as her mother had called the original convention, Harriot had been born in Seneca Falls, and the two previous anniversaries of 1848—in 1906 and 1915—had been organized under her aegis. Harriot's opposition to blanket equality legislation, especially as she was such an early and consistent critic of sex-based labor legislation, was precisely the kind of problem Alice Paul wanted to avoid in launching her campaign for the Equal Rights Amendment. "The thing is a marvel of simplicity," NWP publicity declared of its new program; "all misinterpretations, all legal complexities have been forestalled."[42] Nothing, least of all the complexity of women's subordination, must interfere with the proposed amendment's inaugural fanfare.

Harriot had to push to get herself included, and barely a week before the convention her participation was announced. On the morning of July 19, 1923, she stood on the banks of the Seneca River and delivered a brief, well-constructed address about her mother's life and achievements. She said nothing explicit about any conflict with the NWP leadership, but she did take care to establish a link not between woman suffrage and the shimmering new Equal Rights Amendment, but between her mother's goal of "political equality" and her own focus on "economic independence."[43] Once the convention was over, however, she took off after the Equal Rights Amendment, which she dismissed as a chimera, lacking the power to revolutionize the relations of the sexes that both supporters and opponents attributed to it. By contrast to the clearly understood meaning of "enfranchisement," no such general consensus existed as to the meaning of the concept of "equality" or of any constitutional amendment that mandated it. What, she asked, constituted "equality" of men and women within marriage? Even feminists were divided between "a left wing which urges that the wife should stand on her own economic feet" and "an extreme right wing . . . [which] would like to see the husband forced to pay the piper while the wife called the tune."[44] "Did you see a little screed of mine on the Equality Amendment?" she wrote to Carrie Chapman Catt, Paul's old suffrage rival. "I feel the proposal is an unqualified error."[45]

The only way to bridge the growing split within the ranks of women activists over sex-based labor legislation versus blanket legal equality was to change the larger political environment. Taking Florence Kelley and other defenders of protective labor legislation at their word—that laws for women could provide the wedge in the door of protection for all workers—Harriot sought to create a political vehicle for the pursuit of such a program around which the two sides might unite. Given the existing political options—the Democratic and Republican parties, the postwar mood of political conservatism—her notions of a truly "constructive" postsuffrage agenda and of an expanded battle for protective laws for all workers had to remain visionary. But why limit oneself to existing political options? While a great believer in electoral politics, she despised both existing parties as corrupt, antidemocratic, and closed to women's energies and perspectives. Here too there might be a third way: to work with men to create a new political environment, a new party if necessary, which would have room for the continued struggle against women's subordination.[46]

Even before the final ratification of the Nineteenth Amendment, therefore, Harriot announced her initial choice for a political home: the Socialist party. This was both an odd and an obvious choice: odd because the Socialist party, internally split and externally under siege, had passed its electoral heyday; obvious because of Harriot's Fabian background and long-standing social-democratic inclinations. Yet, as she explained in a long 1920 interview with party leader Anita Block, she had had to "set aside" her own socialist inclinations and concern with economic dimensions of women's emancipation to take up her "inherited job" of securing the right to equal political participation for women. Now, almost three decades after that initial deferral Harriot was impatient to resume her original agenda. "Long ago I made the choice inside," she explained, "and now I must make it openly."[47]

For Harriot, this move into the Socialist party constituted a major break with many elements of her work within the suffrage movement. As a suffrage leader, "convinced that only by a strict nonpartisanship could the result ever be attained," and particularly constrained by the Socialists' minority status, she had kept her personal political inclinations to herself.[48] That was no longer necessary. In addition, she had relied on the wealth and personal connections of upper-class women to underwrite her campaign to move suffragism into politics. But now, especially with economic aspects of emancipation in the forefront, she turned her back on the old cross-class structures of women's leadership. "We must make up our minds that altho all sorts and conditions of women were united for suffrage, that political end has been gained," she wrote to Anne Martin after a falling out with one of her wealthy suffrage supporters, "and they are not at one in their attitude towards other questions in life."[49] In particular, she charged, "women of the leisure class who were leaders in the struggle for the vote . . . are now trying to lead in industrial affairs, which is quite another matter and a dangerous one."[50]

The Socialists celebrated their new acquisition by distributing widely two leaflets Harriot had written. In *Why I Joined the Socialist Party*, she explained that the immediate context for her membership was a series of right-wing attacks on the party, which she regarded as dangerously unconstitutional. Wholesale deportations of those charged as Socialists and the imprisonment of party leaders, including Eugene V. Debs, appalled and frightened her. She was probably brought into the party by New York Socialist party leader Morris Hillquit, whose plan was to respond to these attacks by drawing in well-known progressives and liberals to protest violations of Socialists' civil liberties and defend party members' democratic rights.[51] Harriot was a willing recruit on these grounds. She wanted to help meet the charge that socialism was "un-American, alien" and was willing to "place my own thousand per cent Americanism at its disposal" to do so. "There's a war on," she wrote. "Socialism cannot amble along as in the days before 1914. The enemy is up and at us. It will crush every radical effort, if it can. My place is out in the open on the radical side."[52]

Harriot's other propaganda piece for the party was entitled *To Mother*. In it, she elaborated an economic and political framework for understanding maternity: mothers were workers, although unpaid and unrecognized as such. Yet for all women's burden of maternal labor, the only recognition they received was empty sentiment. "Society is so ordered that you receive no wage for your labor," she wrote. "Toil as you may, you remain a dependent." By promoting universal motherhood endowments, the socialist solution was "to confer on the mother full financial recognition of the values of her work to the state." She also wanted to see mothers recognized politically. Once mothers were liberated from economic dependence, their perspective was potentially a constructive, even visionary one. "You, mother, are a treasure house of knowledge about human nature. . . . Come into the Party that will take over the great industries that feed and clothe the people and change them from business schemes for profit . . . into cooperative plans . . . with the object of service for all."[53] In contrast to the defenders of protective labor legislation, she invoked motherhood as a source of women's power, not their vulnerability.

In *To Mother*, Harriot drew on her own source of power, her maternal heritage. She understood motherhood less through her personal experiences as a mother than because she had been tutored in these views by "a woman who years ago sounded in the hubbub of forgetfulness, a note of appreciation of mother." She never mentioned Elizabeth Stanton's name or even specified her relation to her, but the reader was clearly expected to understand that this unnamed appreciator of mothers was her own famous mother. Even the leaflet's title referred simultaneously to the generic mother of the working class and to her own mother, unnamed but hardly unknown.[54] Harriot and the Socialist party collaborated in using her mother as an effective symbol of an expansive postsuffrage socialist feminism. "My mother," she told Anita Block, "could not conceive of suffrage as standing by itself, as an issue unrelated to other issues. For her it was inseparable from the antislavery agitation, from women's demand for entry into the field of labor, into the universities and professions. Later when she saw how narrow the American suffrage movement had become, she was much disturbed and said, in a solemn warning, if the American suffrage movement does not develop broader interests, why then when women get the vote they will be totally unprepared for the part they ought to play in American political life."[55]

In becoming a member of the Socialist party, Harriot was returning to her Fabian political roots but with a difference. Her post-1920 socialism reflected many of the forces around which the political left's prospects were being reformulated in this period.[56] First was the impact of the war on workers, which she saw firsthand during her trip to Europe in 1919 and which deepened her faith in their political agency.[57] Along with the opening up of new economic opportunities for women, she regarded the rising expectations and growing discontent of the workers as the only "constructive" outcome of the war. Forced to bear the brunt of combat, called on to abandon every legislative "bulwark" they had achieved, the workers, like the women, were the true vanquished of the war. "But when peace came they rebelled. They aimed to throw off industrial autocracy," she explained. "They now wish democratic control in industry. . . . We may be seeing the beginning of the end of the wage system."[58]

The second factor was the Bolshevik revolution, which sharpened and clarified Harriot's faith in gradualism. As a manifestation of the worldwide uprising of the workers, she welcomed revolution in Russia, and she joined the protests of American liberals against U.S. refusal to recognize the new Soviet Republic.[59] But the methods of revolution and the Marxist ideology of inevitable class conflict and the violent overthrow of state power on which it was based were equally abhorrent to her. Revolution was, to her mind, of a piece with the war itself—destructive and barbaric.[60] As for Marxism, it offended her empirical sensibilities; far from its claim to being scientific, she regarded it as a modern form of superstition, what she called an "economic religion." In the margins of a book written to defend Marxism by her friend and comrade Morris Hillquit, she noted angrily, "Could there be a greater illustration of religious superstition! Just like the twentieth century Christian squaring everything with the Bible. Both attitudes are equally pedantic, equally narrow and superstitious."[61] Concern for what would happen to women's interests in an environment in which class loyalties became everything added to her suspicions of revolutionary communism. Under conditions of heightened class conflict, she feared that women would feel compelled to abandon any goals or demands of their own to ally with the men of their class. As she saw it, there were two fundamental historical conflicts going on simultaneously, and she was wisely concerned lest the monumentality of the battle between the classes overwhelm and obliterate the contest between the sexes.[62]

Her own understanding was that the failure of capitalism was not so much the inevitable suffering of the working class, which was not particularly obvious in the United States or Britain, but rather the total lack of "joy" in labor done within it. She detested capitalism for its "hot appeal to competition and . . . its encouragement to greed." On this point, she had been consistent ever since, at age twenty-four, she had read Charles Fourier and learned about the iniquities of "civilization." She thought that Hillquit's justification of communism as the final stage of the inevitable move from "small production to large scale" was "the error in a nutshell."[63] Whatever hopes she might have had for the Soviet Republic, therefore, were dashed when it turned against the movement for workers' control that had inaugurated it.[64] In contrast to the communist passion for state centralization and faith in production, she endorsed Guild Socialism advocated by the left wing of British Labour. "The form of present-day exclusive capitalistic management is showing itself to be unworkable," she wrote in *A Woman's Point of View*. "Through shop committees and like forms of democratic control, organized labor is taking part in business management. . . . And who that is capable of reading the times can doubt the certainty of such developments?"[65]

Here as elsewhere, the developments within British socialism had a profound influence on Harriot. The Labour party's decision to move from the margins of parliamentary politics to the center (and to build alliances with Liberals to do so) shaped Harriot's hopes for her own country. She regarded herself as one of the major proponents of the development of a "lib-lab" strategy for the United States.[66] "Not only the condition of the country generally, but, in part, the interests of women . . . seem to call for the organization of a third party," she contended.[67] The irony was that American socialism's great electoral moment was in the past. It had coincided with the height of Harriot's dedication to suffragism or, put another way, it had preceded women's enfranchisement and thus had been off limits to her. This was unfortunate, as she would have made a great Debsian.

Harriot's first service to the party was as codirector of the Political Amnesty Committee, which was working to win the release of Debs and all political prisoners still being held in federal jails under the wartime Espionage Act. As Hillquit and other Socialist party leaders had hoped, the demand for amnesty spoke to the strong civil libertarian strain among American radicals like Harriot. She drew on her entire repertoire of talents and contacts for the task. She solicited support from National Woman's Party members.[68] She threatened to stage a picket of the White House. She organized delegations of prominent petitioners to President Warren Harding and Attorney General A. Mitchell Palmer. For her troubles, she was rewarded with the surveillance of FBI operatives, who were expecting less constitutional methods and were disappointed at how "very conservative" her work was.[69] Although they never met, she and Debs corresponded at length. From prison in Atlanta, he wrote to her as "noble daughter of a great mother" and praised her for her "willing spirit . . . courage . . . splendid loyalty to the cause and . . . especially your uncompromising stand for amnesty for all."[70] After he was released in December 1921, she wrote, "Dear Leader: Before you and I pass on to the next world—we may go over Jordan together for we are the same age—we ought to exchange ideas face to face. I think we would find we had much in common even outside socialism."[71]

Harriot also served the Socialist party as a political candidate. In 1921, Anita Block withdrew from her position so that Harriot could be nominated for comptroller of the City of New York and from there help to "boom" the ticket.[72] She stressed children's welfare and education in her candidacy as well as the fundamentally economic nature of women's persistent subordination. The rise of the factory had displaced women from their central economic role. "Gradually robbed of her tools of production [and] robbed of the fruit of her toil . . . she has fallen into the grip of capitalism." There, dependence was the fate of women from the highest strata to the lowest, from the parasitical lady of the upper class to the unpaid drudge of the working class.[73] The Socialists were barely noticed in the election of 1921; but Harriot polled a respectable eighty-two thousand votes, almost as much as the party's mayoral candidate.[74]

The Socialist party, however, was not a sufficient carrier for Harriot's electoral ambitions or her socialist-feminist understandings. She remained a party member and sentimentally socialist for the rest of her life.[75] But the Socialist party was too damaged by the attacks on it, too defensive in its political orientation, perhaps even too male-dominated in its structures, to serve as a truly popular political vehicle for women.[76] In recognition of these shortcomings, in 1922 the party authorized an electoral coalition with non-Socialist labor radicals. In New York, Harriot helped to organize the American Labor Party (ALP), a fusion of Socialist and non-Socialist prolabor candidates.[77] Like many similar efforts, the ALP looked forward to a major third-party drive in the presidential elections of 1924. Harriot proudly claimed that she had helped to shape the platform of the American Labor Party and subscribed wholeheartedly to its tenets.[78]

Harriot's membership in the Socialist party won her a place on the ALP fusion ticket for 1922 as a candidate for the New York State Assembly.[79] She lost no time in elaborating her position with respect to labor legislation and sex equality. Whenever possible she emphasized that she was neither repudiating state interference in the wage contract nor accepting the necessity of woman-only labor laws; rather she was arguing for a distinct, third position, the importance of state regulation of wage labor for all vulnerable workers, without respect to sex. The American Labor Party offered her a satisfactory platform: it had gone "beyond the State [Labor] Federation's demand for an eight-hour workday for women and minors by favoring a maximum 44-hour week for minors under 18 years of age."[80]

Harriot's position on these issues immediately drew fire from advocates of sex-based labor laws, especially from the WTUL. Rose Schneiderman, whose name had been mentioned for the ALP slate, wrote angrily to ask how the position of Harriot and the ALP could be reconciled with the American Federation of Labor's support of maximum hour and minimum wage laws for women workers only.[81] Julius Gerber, acting secretary of the American Labor Party, wrote back to defend Harriot's position. He argued that the American Federation of Labor and the WTUL following it were adhering to a double standard of support for labor laws for women and opposition to government regulation in the wage contract for men. The larger issue, however, was not this or that piece of legislation, but what mode of political action the labor movement should pursue and how much control it could wield. "Our aim is to make Labor a factor in politics by Labor being boss of the political party," rather than constantly mounting "begging expeditions to Albany and Syracuse," he wrote. Once the WTUL agreed with this larger third-party strategy, Gerber was confident that Harriot Blatch's candidacy would present no problem, inasmuch as she was a strong supporter of state regulation of wage labor on behalf of all workers, male and female.[82]

Harriot followed up with her own letter, offered in a genuinely concilia-tory tone. She suggested that the differences between her position and that of the WTUL were primarily ones of "technique as to how to reach the end in view." But she trusted they were in agreement on the goal: protection for workers and equality for women. Maud Swartz, president of the New York chapter of the WTUL, responded that, on the contrary, she thought their differences were "fundamental" and had to do with "the conditions under which the woman who works lives." While Harriot claimed that her ap-proach unified men and women in their common needs as workers, Swartz claimed that it set them in competition. "Needless to say your letter is not entirely satisfactory," Swartz wrote back, "and we will have to accept your stand on legislation affecting women in industry as indefinite."[83] The WTUL, which had been waivering about participation in the American Labor Party effort, refused to endorse it.[84]

The drive for a labor-based third party accelerated in early 1924. The financial scandals that hit the Coolidge administration also splattered the Democratic front runner, William McAdoo, with the mud of corruption. Socialists, trade unionists, independent liberals, and feminists, who had been waiting and planning for a major political realignment, recognized their opportunity. Hopes centered on Wisconsin progressive Senator Robert La Follette, Sr., who was gathering support and seemed ready to make an independent run for the presidency. The prospect of a La Follette candidacy generated more activity among women activists than any of the other independent political initiatives of the decade, no doubt because of "Fighting Bob's" strong record on suffrage as well as the solid feminist credentials of his wife, Belle, and daughter, Fola (once a member of Harriot's Equality League). In April, Harriot put her name to the call of the Congress of Progressive Political Action for a convention in Cleveland on July 4 to launch a La Follette candidacy.[85] Here at last seemed a political development that might make all those years of fighting for women's right to vote worth something!

In anticipation of the July 4 convention, Harriot and a group of other women organized a Women's Committee for Political Action. Their goal was not only to advance Senator La Follette, but more broadly to lay out an independent, progressive alternative for American women voters, particularly those who might be hesitating on the verge of a fully franchised political identity. "We are particularly anxious to help women break through what might be called the 'organization complex,'" the chairwoman of the committee announced—"to stimulate women to direct political action in local, State and national politics on the basis of a sound economic program." The meeting did not linger long on the program, assuming it would include such obvious progressive elements as public ownership of basic utilities, action against corruption, and support for civil liberties. The only issue discussed at length was world peace, and there the only disagreement was whether to advocate the total abolition or gradual reduction of armaments.[86] The real business of this women's meeting was to draw women voters into the progressive movement and to insure a special presence and voice for them in the campaign's higher councils. A preliminary structure was established for women's groups in each state, so that women delegates could be sent to the July 4 convention, lest "the new liberal movement . . . like the old parties, will be largely a man made affair, doomed to fail because it lacks the support of the progressive women of the nation."[87]

Harriot spoke for this group at the July 4 meeting in Cleveland that launched La Follette's candidacy. La Follette had just been nominated and now different constituencies were seconding his candidacy. Morris Hillquit had spoken for the Socialists and George Lefkowitz for the Farmer-Labor party. William Pickens of the National Association for the Advancement of Colored People was waiting to give his endorsement. Harriot's job was to speak for the untapped energies and enthusiasms of the millions of newly enfranchised women.[88] "Fellow delegates," she began, "I felt . . . that I could not sit still without coming and offering to our candidate for President to this great platform which has been laid before us the services of the women of this nation." The moment offered a historic opportunity, she declared, the coincident appearance of a major political shift and a giant new electorate.[89]

Now that women could vote, both Democrats and Republicans were eager to claim credit for women's enfranchisement, but Harriot was there to set the record straight. In their platform, the Republicans had declared that their party "from the beginning has espoused the cause of woman's suffrage." No one knew better than she, the daughter of Elizabeth Cady Stanton, the absurdity of such claims. "From the beginning of what?" Harriot demanded. "From the beginning of their platform?" (The audience roared with laughter.) But it was the Democrats, increasingly credible in their appeals to those with progressive sympathies, whose claims to have been loyal supporters of woman suffrage particularly called out for refutation. Harriot spoke from her own experience. "Al Smith says he was always in favor of suffrage. Why, I knew Al Smith as a young Assemblyman when I used to lobby in the Legislature at Albany. Al Smith, with Elihu Root behind him on the one side, he on the other, Murphy pulling the wires from New York, defeating us again and again!"[90]

At its founding meeting, the Women's Committee for Political Action left in the background the potentially divisive question of sex-based labor legislation versus legal equality. But the more general convention in Cleveland did take on the issue, adopting a plank in its platform which called for the "removal of the legal discriminations against women by measures not prejudicial to legislation necessary for protection to women and for the advancement of social welfare."[91] This was the same compromise position taken by the 1921 equal rights provision passed in La Follette's home state of Wisconsin. The courts had begun to rule against this solution, and in less friendly situations both sides in the controversy had moved away from it; but in the context of a promising, independent, prolabor presidential campaign, dedicated to expanding rather than contracting social welfare legislation (and committed to breaking the hold of a conservative Supreme Court), attempts at compromise between the principle of sex equality and the existence of sex-based labor laws met with a much more friendly response.[92]

Evidence abounds that women who were both advocates and critics of sex-based labor law not only accepted but embraced the La Follette campaign. Mabel Costigan, who represented the women's group on the campaign's Executive Committee, belonged to the League of Women Voters, which supported sex-based labor laws, while Isabelle Kendig, the group's executive secretary, was a National Woman's Party member.[93] The editors of the magazines of the Women's Trade Union League and the National Woman's Party both gave the campaign good coverage.[94] Women's Trade Union League leaders were particularly enthusiastic about the La Follette campaign, which the AFL and even Samuel Gompers himself supported.[95] National Executive Secretary Elizabeth Christman attended the Cleveland convention and was thrilled with what she saw there. Ethel Smith, who was in charge of WTUL's legislative program, suggested that the WTUL formally endorse the La Follette ticket.[96] Progressive women had joined together in this campaign, Mabel Costigan explained to a women's club audience, "to see if they could not smooth over their differences and work for certain outstanding principles," particularly the welfare of children and "the placing of women on an equality with men in places of employment."[97]

After the Cleveland convention, the Women's Committee for Political Action became the women's wing of the La Follette campaign. Harriot was on the Executive Committee, where she was joined to her great delight by Caroline Lexow Babcock, who had been working since enfranchisement in the women's peace movement. There were twenty-six million women voters, and the La Follette campaign was going to make a serious bid for them.[98] The La Follette women assembled a Committee of One Hundred to appeal to a wide range of female political identities. The Socialists were represented by Meta Berger and Helen Keller. From the National Woman's Party came Zona Gale and Elizabeth Kent. Many WTUL figures were included: Rose Schneiderman, Mary Dreier, Elizabeth Christman. Florence Kelley, of the National Consumer's League, was there. Well-known independent feminists such as Freda Kirchwey, of the *Nation* magazine, and venerable figures such as Jane Addams and Charlotte Perkins Gilman also joined. Even Mary Dewson, on her way to leadership in the Democratic party, was listed. In fact, another way to approach the work of the Committee of One Hundred assembled by the La Follette women is to notice who was *not* included. Alice Paul, unwilling to distinguish between any "men's parties," was not listed, and Carrie Chapman Catt declined an invitation to join because she could not "see the aim" of an independent political effort.[99]

One of the special resources that the La Follette women had was Belle La Follette, the candidate's wife, herself a significant figure among progressive women and especially in the peace movement. The Women's Committee arranged for a giant meeting for her at Town Hall in New York City, as well as a smaller one at the Woman's University Club. At Town Hall, Harriot presided and Florence Kelley sat on the platform. Belle defended her husband "against the charge of radicalism and enmity to American institutions." (The focus of this charge was a plank in the platform, attractive to women reformers who were frustrated by conservative rulings on child labor and welfare legislation, to amend the Constitution to permit Congress to override the Supreme Court.) "I think Mr. La Follette is almost too old-fashioned in his worship of our institutions," his wife declared. "His belief in democracy, in the people and the ballot has given him patience, poise and endurance throughout the long fight to make government more truly representative of the people." She got her loudest applause when she defended her husband's stand "against militarism and imperialism."[100]

Whether women had any more power within the La Follette campaign than they did in the mainstream parties is an open question, but Harriot certainly did not act as if she were being shunted into a female auxiliary away from the main action.[101] She worked both within the Women's Committee and the New York State La Follette campaign, for which she served as cochair. She and more than a dozen other women made up a third of the campaign's National Committee.[102] When the senator himself went before New York City voters, at Madison Square Garden, Harriot was one of the speakers (although nearer to the end of the program than she was when Mrs. La Follette was featured).

Another way to appreciate the degree and nature of the influence of the La Follette women is to observe the counteractions they produced. Republicans and Democrats, male leaders and female loyalists both, seem to have been genuinely concerned that La Follette would inspire women and deprive the regular parties of control over the female electorate. A few weeks before the election, the women cochairs of the National Democratic, National Republican, New York Democratic, and New York Republican committees made a joint public announcement, more like a warning, that "the coming election is of as great importance as any which has occurred during the life of the nation." "The two historic political parties," they declared, "stand for government under the Constitution of the United States" and it was crucial for women to register and vote. It did not matter "to which party they are giving their allegiance," so long as it was not the Constitution-threatening third-party effort of the La Follette campaign.[103]

How great *was* the La Follette threat to the regular parties' aspirations to encompass women's postsuffrage political energies? Traditionally, organized suffragism had been vaguely pro-Republican since the 1890s, although the rising power of conservatives in the party was creating a decreasingly hospitable enviroment. Nonetheless, several former suffrage leaders were hopeful of establishing a position for women in the Republican party.[104] As for the Democratic party, its appeal to women voters via its historic claim as the party of labor was beginning to rise, and it had much to fear from the rise of a third party with a special appeal to progressive women. Emily Blair, the highest ranking Democratic woman, publicly reprimanded Florence Kelley, champion of women's welfare legislation, for choosing La Follette over the Democrats. A "seasoned campaigner" such as Kelley surely must understand that it is impossible to win a majority of voters *and* get a perfect political platform, Blair chided. In a letter released to the newspapers, Blair likened Kelley and other supporters of La Follette to children "who had left their homes to find the symbol of happiness and after much wandering and groping in the dark returned home to find it there."[105]

Intriguingly, the potential attraction to women voters of a third-party candidacy was experienced as a threat not only by the Democrats and the Republicans, but by some in the National Woman's Party, who also scrambled to counter the La Follette lure. Although some NWP women were in favor of the La Follette candidacy, Alice Paul clearly was not. While she claimed to be critical of all men's parties in equal measure, she had a decided bias toward the two dominant parties, and especially toward the Republicans. Within weeks of the July 4 convention, the NWP launched its own political offensive, the Woman for Congress Campaign. On the surface, this was an effort to elect women to Congress regardless of partisan affiliation, but its real focus was, in Paul's words, on "the two chief political parties." Paul acknowledged that other NWP activists had wanted to concentrate on a third party, but, like Catt, she did not see the point. "As a matter of fact, they are all about the same." All parties were equally male dominated; their only potential function was to provide legislative support for particular issues. Why then choose a weak and insurgent one? The NWP campaign endorsed women running as Progressives, as well as Democratic and Republican candidates, but the underlying orientation was mainstream. The major fundraiser was Democratic activist Mrs. Stephen Pell, and large donations came from Republican benefactors Phoebe Hearst and Mrs. Dupont.[106]

Harriot was hopeful and positive about the La Follette candidacy right through election day. On the Sunday before the election, she took the train to Baltimore to speak at a large afternoon rally. Her five decades of oratorical experience served her well. She began by contrasting the old parties and the new one: "I would like to picture the major parties as two old nags, each inviting the other to abandon the race . . . and help drag the load in a united contest against the La Follette motor." Far from threatening "the two party system," she believed, the emergence of the Progressive party was the only hope for reviving it, for offering voters a genuine political choice. For the past half-century, the Democrats and Republicans had become more and more similar, "differing not at all in political or economic principles," only existing to wage war for office.[107]

The La Follette campaign gave voters a genuine alternative to the Democratic and Republican consensus. While the established parties regarded the system of private ownership and profit as the natural order, "Fighting Bob" proposed a system of public ownership and management of the nation's basic economic resources, such as railroads, mines, and water power. Much as "the eighteenth and nineteenth century were largely given over to the growth of political democracy," Harriot predicted, "the twentieth century will have to solve the problems of industrial democracy." The Progressive party alone took up this challenge. As was so often the case for her, the abolitionist passions of her parents' generation provided the historic baseline for her understanding of herself and her own time. She stood for the party which believed "that it means slavery for a people to let a monopoly remain in private hands and be run for the profit of a few and not of the many."[108]

The Progressive party also offered women a real choice on the fundamental issue of peace and war. In 1915, La Follette had called for the United States to stay neutral and arbitrate between the warring parties, while Harriot had supported America's entry into combat. "I now see that his was the deeper view of the future," she acknowledged. In the postwar world, he remained a true visionary of global peace. While the Democratic party supported the League of Nations, La Follette knew that the Versailles Treaty must be scrapped and a genuine prescription for peaceful national coexistence adopted in its place. Harriot especially applauded his call for a constitutional amendment to take the power to declare war away from a few men in Congress and put it in the hands of the voters. The people deserved the right to make this decision, she insisted, "especially the young women who pay such heavy tribute to the war god [and] the young men who sacrifice their all."[109]

Fundamentally, though, Harriot would vote for Robert La Follette on November 4 in the interests of reinvigorating political democracy. The enfranchisement of women had been fought for and won in the name of democracy. Along with other Progressive-era political reforms—the direct election of senators, the mechanisms of initiative and referendum at the state level—the Nineteenth Amendment was a device to make politics more popular and elections more representative. Expanding the franchise did not complete the work of perfecting democracy, however; it was only the precondition for a truly popular politics and an effective electoral process. The challenge that democracy faced now was more subtle: voters were losing faith in the ballot, and with good reason. "The result of the one party system, with its contest over unrealities, has been not only the concentration of economic power in the hands of the few, not only corruption at the very centre of government," Harriot insisted, "but steady decrease of the interest of citizens in politics." Instead of genuine political debate, every four years American voters were offered "this game of hypocrisy" between Republicans and Democrats, and it "has made us a nation of political morons."[110]

Harriot cited the statistics of declining voter turnout to her audience: in the 1880s, 85 percent of those eligible had voted, whereas in 1920, less than half the possible voters went to the polls. Overly optimistic ex-suffragists were hoping that new women voters would reverse this decline, while misogynist political scientists predicted that they would accelerate it; but from Harriot's perspective, the greater danger was that women's votes would fall victim to creeping political demoralization.[111] In 1924, concern for how and whether women would use their votes was peaking, partly because this was the first presidential election in which they could be said to be fully involved, and partly because a three-way race was making politics much more exciting and less predictable. The approach of the League of Women Voters to this challenge was moderate and nonpartisan: neutral promotion of the electoral process to encourage voter participation among women. The campaign by the National Woman's Party to bring more women into Congress counted on women voters to turn out for women candidates. The framework of the Progressive party was very different: all Harriot's hopes were riding on the capacity of a third party to reinvigorate democracy at its core, to make women's and men's votes meaningful again. The same democratic purpose that had made her a woman suffragist now led her to work for La Follette: "only the presentation of real issues to the electorate can save democracy."[112]

When the votes were tallied, however, the La Follette candidacy had done nothing to stem the decline in voter turnout. Nor is there any indication that women voted for him in higher percentages than did men. Harriot was nonetheless pleased with the outcome: La Follette got approximately one-sixth of the popular vote. (In the electoral college, however, he carried only his home state of Wisconsin.) Until Ross Perot's run in 1992, La Follette's achievement stood as the strongest showing ever in a presidential race by a genuinely independent third-party candidate. As always, she was patient with the pace of political change. In a letter to Fola La Follette, the candidate's feminist daughter, Harriot treated the election as a substantial victory. "With our lack of funds and organization, I feel we did magnificently," she wrote. "Nearly five million votes . . . the future will mean bigger success."[113]

But the larger process of political realignment that Harriot hoped the 1924 election would initiate was not to be. In February 1925, she attended a conference in Chicago called to formalize the gains of the La Follette campaign by forming a permanent third party.[114] There the railroad brotherhoods, and following them the larger labor movement, withheld the support that was crucial to making the Progressive party permanent. Four months later, "Fighting Bob" himself died, fatally exhausted by his heroic presidential run. Without the support of labor, independents and socialists struggled to keep the hope of postwar progressivism alive. A network of exclusively male Progressive clubs was formed. Meanwhile, the Women's Committee for La Follette, determined to continue the struggle for a place for women in the waning movement, renamed itself the National League of Progressive Women and undertook a program of "intensive educational" work. Harriot was one of its members. Without a genuine party framework, however, the entire Progressive enterprise—male and female wings alike—lost its popular political possibilities, went from a small cadre to a minuscule band of committed activists, and within a few years disappeared altogether.[115]

In response to the La Follette campaign, ultra-right groups began to accuse women's organizations and leaders of being soft on Bolshevism.[116] Given her unapologetic socialism, it is interesting there is no record that Harriot was a named target of the red-baiting that plagued progressive women in the 1920s. Women such as Florence Kelley and Jane Addams were listed, but Harriot, arguably one of the most prominent women socialists in the 1920s and certainly the most important former suffragist to have declared her allegiance to the Socialist party once the vote was won, was not smeared. Possibly the fact that she was so open about her socialism spared her the attacks of the right, the object of which was not so much to silence socialists and communists as to frighten nonsocialist progressives and liberals from associating with them.[117]

Nonetheless, in the increasingly conservative political atmosphere of the late 1920s, politics such as Harriot's were thoroughly marginalized. Within what was left of the organized women's movement, the split between the National Woman's Party and the proponents of sex-based labor legislation became a permanent and defining feature of the political landscape, contributing to the silence of those like Harriot who aligned with neither side. She continued to adhere to a third position—motherhood endowments, the expansion of protective labor legislation to all workers regardless of sex— but in the larger world, no political context existed to make these realistic options. She did not take naturally to political quietude, and her name continued to grace the letterheads of progressive organizations. She protested

United States intervention in Latin America, unemployment, and the rise of fascism and supported relief for strikers, plans for a Socialist party radio station in Debs's memory, and atheism.[118] Every so often, she dashed off an angry letter to this politician or that newspaper protesting some offense against her sense of justice.[119]

In 1928, when it was reported (falsely) that she was going to support Herbert Hoover for president, she protested as forcefully as possible. The leadership of the National Woman's Party, betraying its fundamental political conservatism, had publicly announced for Hoover, and Harriot, although she was not an NWP member or a supporter of the Equal Rights Amendment, may have been tainted by this action. Also, apparently, some political dirty trickster had forged her name on a Hoover, petition, and the Hoover people rushed to publicize this fraudulent endorsement. Objecting to the NWP support for Hoover, another New York socialist feminist, Lavinia Dock, responded in graphic language: "I could no more cast a vote for the Republican party than I could swallow a large, smooth green caterpillar."[120] Harriot was just as disgusted. Mr. Hoover's place "is in the home, at the fireside, in the chimney corner," she wrote to the *New York Times*, in one of her classic political sex-role reversals. "Let him for his own good name and our safety play with little children, not with naughty men out in the rough and tumble world."[121]

After 1924, with politics, her normal stimulant, closed to her, Harriot found her excitement in the late 1920s in more private adventures. In 1878, while a senior at Vassar, she had been forbidden by her family from taking advantage of the opportunity to observe a solar eclipse in Colorado with her professor, Maria Mitchell. A half-century later, she still felt the pain of that subordination to the will of others. "It makes my heart stand still and my head whirl whenever I think of the utter lack of imagination in my guardians in allowing such an opportunity to slip away from a young student," she recalled. Now, on January 25, 1925, a total eclipse of the sun was going to be visible from the eastern seaboard, and she was determined to rectify that past wrong. Laypeople were being recruited to record the event, and she arranged to join, viewing the eclipse from her former teacher's observatory at Vassar. The experience of the eclipse itself and of undoing a past and very personal injustice was profound. She was "so impressed by this deeply moving miracle of the skies" that she vowed "to see every eclipse from then on that occurred within my reach."[122]

In 1927, she arranged to go to Sweden with an astronomer friend to observe a total eclipse there.[123] Two hundred and fifty miles to the northwest of Stockholm, she watched from a high hill as the clouds came and went, clearing away just moments before "totality." Despite her determination to observe and record every detail, the ecstasy of the event took her in. The first appearance of the corona was "overwhelming in beauty and suddenness," the reappearance of the sun from behind the moon was "blinding." Although exhausted, she jotted down her notes and posted them to Nora. "Burst of red at zenith of totality marvelous," she scribbled, "it burns in my memory."[124]

The deepest excitement of the trip was yet to come. Returning from Stockholm, she took a small commercial airplane flight, the first in her life, and was elated by the experience. "No six hours of my life were ever so packed with intense interest and joy." "The earth was an open book, the meaning of which he who flew could clearly read," she observed later. "No one knows the earth til he leaves it. . . . The beauties of mother earth are only realized when one looks right down into her heart." In flight, she was the transcendent one; finally she had found a way to soar above her origins. The day was July 4; as she wrote, she was celebrating Independence Day.[125]

Two years later, she arranged to take a much longer air tour of Europe. Sailing with Nora and her grandchildren to Paris, she took ground transportation from Paris to Hanover, and from there began a series of commercial air flights back and forth across the German-French border. She thought she might write an article which she would call "A Zenith View," "Flights of Reality," or "Escape." The area she explored by air was the contested territory that Germany had been forced to cede after the war and that she had visited in the early days of the armistice in the winter of 1919; her route from Hanover took her west across the Rhineland to Paris and then back east, across Alsace, to Frankfurt am Main. Later, the set of postcards she collected of aerial views of the region made their way to the U.S. War Department, to provide information about industrial facilities on the ground.[126]

By 1929, Harriot had logged sufficient time in the air to qualify for pilot's training, although there is no evidence that she ever succeeded in taking the controls of an airplane. Nonetheless, she habitually recorded the make and manufacturer of the planes in which she flew, and tried to learn as much as she could about contemporary aeronautical technology. She left it to her granddaughter and namesake Harriet to take up the vocation of pilot. Harriet de Forest remembered that "in those days for a woman to just get in an airplane and take off was just astonishing, but she loved it."[127] In her will she left her granddaughter enough money to buy two planes and to open a flight school, which is how she made her living for many years.[128] After 1929, Harriot Blatch does not seem to have flown again, but she continued to imagine herself in the clouds. In 1936, on the eve of her eightieth birthday, she told a reporter, "I don't think this dinner party will be my last appearance. I want to take long flights in small airplanes where you can sit right up to the windows and look down at the marvelous shadows."[129]

History

Under any conditions, Harriot Blatch's political program for postsuffrage feminism would have been ambitious, but the steady right-wing drift of American politics in the late 1920s made it an impossibility. As her frustration with the political present grew, she turned to the past, but not, as one might think, as an escape. On the contrary, feminism's past turned out to be fully as contentious as, and thoroughly implicated in, its present and future. As former suffragists battled among themselves for control over postsuffrage politics, they mobilized different interpretations of the past to legitimate their claims to the present. But Harriot had something at stake that other participants in these debates did not; suffragism's history was inextricably related to her own most personal life story, above all to the similarities and differences that linked her to her mother. In the political battles over the past, therefore, she had a dual involvement, representing her own political interests at the same time as she functioned as her mother's daughter. Her obligation to see that her mother's memory was rightly honored and her commitment to her own distinctive political vision are impossible to separate from each other. These were her concerns in her final years, up to the moment of her death on the eve of World War II.

Before we turn to Harriot's daughterly obligations to preserve and defend her mother's memory, her relationship to her own daughter, Nora, deserves some final discussion. Neither Harriot as daughter nor Harriot as mother is easy to observe from the outside; she had learned early on to draw a firm line between private, family conflicts and public matters. "One never criticizes one's family in public," she once told her granddaughter sternly.[1] If we take the view that there were patterns and traditions that ran through these several generations of strong-minded women, Harriot the mother can tell us about Harriot the daughter. There was, for instance, a kind of intensity between Nora and herself, a proud and exclusive sense of matrilineage that deprived as well as enriched; Harriot was passing on a determined model of unconventional womanhood which coerced even as it emancipated. Their relationship was one that outsiders, particularly men, found difficult to enter. At the same time, conflicts between the two women grew in later years, especially as Nora's own life became more complicated and her independent choices about how to lead it became more pronounced.

Throughout the 1920s, Nora and her children were a major presence in Harriot's life, and Harriot loomed equally large for them. Ever since the collapse of Nora's marriage to Lee de Forest in the early 1910s, Harriot Blatch had been closely involved in the upbringing of their daughter, Harriet de Forest. As she had done when Nora was a child, Harriot concentrated more on what would educate and uplift her granddaughter than what would comfort and nurture her. When little Harriet was four, her father, whom she had not seen since the divorce, came to see her and brought her a "beautiful china face doll"; the child adored the doll, which she named Helen, after the aunt she had never known and whom she had presumably learned about from her mother. For Harriot Blatch, the reference to her dead child and the involvement of the despised Lee de Forest merely reinforced what would have been her likely response to such frivolities. "My grandmother decided that I might turn into the kind of woman that would think of nothing but babies," little Harriet remembered, "so she took that doll and threw it out! . . . She thought she was doing me a favor . . . I thought it was a terrible thing to do."[2]

Despite it all, Harriet de Forest was quite clear that her grandmother cherished her and "loved her devotedly." Harriot Blatch gave her the time and attention that Nora, busy with her career, could not (as Elizabeth Stanton had done for Nora and Margaret Cady had done for Harriot). Harriet de Forest's warm memories of watching with childish fascination as her grandmother carefully fixed her hair each day seem remarkably similar to Harriot Blatch's own reminiscences of her grandmother smoothing on her silk stockings in her bedroom, providing her with an alternative to her own powerful mother. Harriet de Forest, who got enough feminist preaching as a child to last her a lifetime, later came to think that her grandmother was more "motherly" than her principles allowed her to acknowledge.[3] Despite a later rebellion from the family faith of women's rights, Harriet de Forest was deeply marked by her intimacy with her grandmother. Her profession as airplane pilot came from Harriot's thwarted ambitions. Even the date she chose for her wedding in 1932 had the family mark on it: November 12, Elizabeth Stanton's birthday, the same date which Harriot (incorrectly) remembered as the date of her own marriage, a half-century before.[4]

In 1922, Nora had two other children, another daughter, Rhoda, and a son John, both by her second husband, Morgan Barney. Because Morgan was a naval architect, they had moved to Long Island Sound, living first in Pelham, New York, then in Greenwich, Connecticut.[5] But by the mid-1920s, this marriage too had become troubled. Part of the problem between Nora and Morgan may have been Harriot, who after an initial affection for her son-in-law, came to dislike him intensely. "It is quite impossible for me to be near Mr. Barney," Harriot wrote to a friend a few years after the marriage.[6] "There was great rivalry between Harriot and my father Morgan Barney," Rhoda Barney remembered.[7]

One source of contention was childrearing. Harriot considered Morgan Barney's relationship with her grandchildren insufficiently high-minded. As a father, it seems, he was affectionate and playful, much as William Henry Blatch had been. Like Nora herself, Nora's children got from their father something they did not get from the women of their family, who were patrolling their own shores against the dangers of conventional femininity. Nora's children remembered their father, not their mother or grandmother, as the nurturing figure of their childhood. He showed them how to get around the New York City subway system by pretending that they were little tugboats that had to guide his big ship into port. He taught them to memorize poems, which they loved for the rhythms and rhymes; meanwhile their grandmother disapproved because they did not understand the words that they so obediently memorized and lovingly repeated for their father.[8] She still had a horror of mindless repetition, of devoted followership. While her grandchildren loved her and appreciated her efforts in their behalf, the emotional distance she maintained intimidated and mystified them.

Harriot continued to criticize Nora for the complexity of her life and her tendency to become overwhelmed by it. "She works too hard. . . . She has on her own shoulders her own expensive family and Harriet to help," Harriot complained to Grace Stetson. "She talks of needing a vacation and she does but it goes off in talk. Each time the verdict is that she can't afford it just then."[9] Their conflicts over authority and dependence were worsened by financial problems. Neither woman was wealthy and Nora was responsible for much of the support of her children herself.[10] She built and sold houses in Greenwich, and shared with her mother the income from the small inheritance that her father had left her. They disagreed over the management of this money, Harriot insisting that they buy stocks that preserved her sense of social justice and political responsibility; she would permit no investments in munitions companies or imperial profiteers. After the 1929 crash of the stock market, the income from their investments dropped, and Harriot began to borrow from her daughter for living expenses. For Nora, these financial pressures led to and were exacerbated by serious illness and a lawsuit with the city of Greenwich in the early 1930s.[11]

Harriot was no more accepting of dependence on Nora than Nora was on her. In the mid-1930s, Nora built a house for herself, her mother, and her children to live in together, but Harriot was not happy there and returned to New York City, where she once again took rooms at the Woman's University Club. She liked the simplicity, the freedom from domestic obligations, and the sense of living among like-minded people. She invited friends to meet her at the club, attended discussions and symposia there, and had her grandchildren stay overnight with her in the little bedrooms available for guests. She ate breakfast and lunch at the club, then went out to friends' homes or restaurants for her dinners. Her possessions were few; materially, she arranged it so that she could meet her own needs as efficiently as possible. "She had a room and bath," Harriet de Forest remembered, and "had dragged her own furniture along, her desk, her bureau and her bed."[12] Her other granddaughter, Rhoda Barney, remembers that she kept a portable coffeemaker in her room but took her meals in the dining room. As she had ever since she was a young woman, she used a portable canvas bathtub so that she could keep up her hydropathic habit of cold baths in the morning no matter where she was. In the summer, she left the city and either helped Nora with the rent in Greenwich or boarded out at guest houses in the country, as luxurious as she could afford. She did not seem to mind that, even though in her seventies, she sometimes had to scramble for accommodations.[13]

In terms of relationships, her life was also somewhat spare. In 1925, Theodore, with whom she had shared the responsibility of advancing and defending her mother's historical reputation, died. Harriot was proud that, like his mother, Theodore died hard at work, after a morning at his desk. "It is hard to imagine he is gone. The former abolition stock is falling away," she wrote to Oswald Garrison Villard (William Lloyd Garrison's son). "What is there to take its place? Only milk & water I fear."[14] Five years later, Maggie, her only sister and last surviving sibling, who had been attached to Harriot for many years, died.[15] As Harriot had done whenever someone close to her had died—from Helen to Elizabeth to Harry—she exhibited little grief or sense of loss. Of Elizabeth Stanton's seven children, now only she remained.

As for her friends, Caroline Lexow Babcock, who was now living with her family in Nyack, remained devoted to her, a fictive daughter whose affection was less complicated and more comforting than Nora's. Caroline's daughter remembered Mrs. Blatch from this period as "the most distinguished woman she had ever known," dressed elegantly, with a black ribbon around her neck, consuming cigarettes "like a chimney," the first reputable woman she had ever seen smoke in public.[16] Harriot's longest lasting and most important friendships were with people whose connections reached back to her youth, friends just beyond her immediate family with whom she was closest. One of these was Grace Channing Stetson, second wife of Charlotte Gilman's first husband, stepmother to her daughter Katherine, and—most important to Harriot—daughter of William Ellery Channing. "How precious are the friends who come down to us through generations," she wrote to Grace when they were both octogenarians. "Inherited friends are almost sacred one might say."[17] It was the link to Elizabeth Cady Stanton's generation, to "the old abolition stock," which made Grace so dear to her, indicating yet again how much this was the core of her personal identity, even more than the accomplishments and celebrity of her own long life. Her first friend remained her most enduring—Harriot Ransom Milinowski—who now lived with her own daughter, a music professor at Vassar, in Poughkeepsie. Perhaps this is why Vassar College became important to Harriot Blatch once again; she unsuccessfully tried to get one of her granddaughters to go there, and in 1928 she served as president of the class of 1878, in its fiftieth reunion year.[18]

For her final decade, Harriot's major concern was the restoration and preservation of her mother's historical reputation. Her goal was to make sure not only that the fact of her mother's leadership was acknowledged, but that its substance—Stanton's vision of a progressive, democratic, feminist women's movement—was understood. Defending her mother and asserting herself were, finally at this point in her life, fully compatible goals. Harriot's defense of her mother's historic reputation and her own dissenting vision for women's politics in the aftermath of suffragism's victory were intertwined. Now it was the two of them, standing alone: against other women whom Harriot felt stubbornly ignored them, and against the larger political forces of the period, which could not have been more hostile to their shared principles.

For some time now, awareness of Elizabeth Stanton's role in the long battle for women's emancipation had been fading, even as reverence for the memory of her comrade Susan B. Anthony was getting stronger and more widespread. As a relatively free-floating historical signifier, the figure of Susan B. Anthony continued to take on fresh meanings, while the historical Stanton, rigorously tended by her daughter, lost the power to invoke contemporary feminist associations. The first person to encourage public reverence of Anthony was her friend and protegé, Anna Howard Shaw. Shaw simultaneously apotheosized Anthony and linked herself to "Aunt Susan" as a way to strengthen and legitimize her own leadership. In Shaw's autobiography, the dramatic climax features Susan B. Anthony on her death bed, begging Shaw to promise to "keep the presidency of the association as long as you are well enough to do the work." Shaw, who portrays herself as lacking any personal ambition for office, reluctantly agrees, whereupon the dying woman kisses her hand in gratitude and lapses into unconsciousness, never to speak another word.[19] This tale of the divine transfer of power was intended to deflect charges, made almost from the beginning of Shaw's presidency, that she lacked the organizational talent and political vision to lead American suffragism.

In 1915 Shaw relinquished the NAWSA presidency to Carrie Chapman Catt, who was not as closely identified with Anthony. For a brief time, the Anthony cult lapsed, only to spring up again in 1918, in the dual context of the impending triumph of the woman suffrage movement and internal organizational factionalism. In the aftermath of the successful House of Representatives vote on the woman suffrage amendment in early 1918, both the National American Woman Suffrage Association and its militant organizational rival, the National Woman's Party, made claims to having led the way to victory, and both versions of suffrage history rested on the figure of Anthony. According to the NAWSA's version, Anthony, who had "the indefinable gift of prescience," had understood that the great victory of woman suffrage would require patience and quiet, systematic labors; "militance per se would not have interested her."[20] On the contrary, claimed Paul's camp, the successful vote proved the superiority of *their* Susan B. Anthony. (Anthony was linked to Paul through their common Quakerism.[21]) The House of Representatives vote "was a complete vindication of the theory of party responsibility, by which the Democratic party, as the party in power, was held responsible for the fortunes of the federal suffrage measure. . . . The theory of party responsibility . . . was recognized by Susan B. Anthony and advocated explicitly by her in the very first year of the first introduction of the federal suffrage measure, January, 1878."[22]

One wonders why the NWP, instead of fighting over control of Anthony's image, did not turn to the figure of Elizabeth Stanton, who had so frequently challenged the complacency of mainstream suffragism in her own lifetime, to provide an alternative historical precedent for their own proud militance. The answer is that Alice Paul's instrumental view of history and Harriot's serious stewardship of her mother's legacy were bound to come into conflict to the degree that their visions of the feminist future were different. An approach that was both specifically feminist and broadly progressive, to which Harriot looked forward, was quite different from the single-issue feminism and the tendency to separate gender issues from all other kinds of politics, which Paul favored. By contrast, Anthony had no immediate family who controlled the uses of her historical legacy. On the contrary, much of her posthumous power came from the fact that she appeared to have sacrificed herself totally to "the cause," that she was—as Gertrude Stein characterized her in the 1940s opera—"The Mother of Us All."

In the wake of suffrage victory, Harriot and Alice Paul first clashed on whether and how the memory of Elizabeth Cady Stanton could serve feminism's future. In connection with the NWP convention of 1921, Paul decided to have Adelaide Johnson's unfinished marble statue of Stanton, Anthony, and Lucretia Mott completed and dedicated under the Capitol Rotunda as a permanent memorial to the suffrage struggle, and she asked Harriot "as the daughter of Elizabeth Cady Stanton" to organize a committee to raise funds for the project.[23] Harriot began to assemble a wide-ranging committee that would symbolize the kind of politically inclusive women's movement to which she and her mother had always been committed.[24] But Paul wanted to focus exclusively on wealthy women donors; her plan was to raise five times the money it would cost to complete the statue, in order to fund the NWP's work.[25] Charging Paul with a "dangerous tendency to subterfuge," Harriot left the committee and refused to attend the convention.[26]

The core of their disagreement was not only over control of the committee or the uses of the statue, but over the historical interpretation of the long suffrage struggle and its message for the feminist future. For Paul, the only way to build a movement that could effectively unite all women and avoid being drawn into other ("men's") issues was to focus exclusively on a single legislative measure, symbolically identified with emancipation of the sex; this it was argued, was "the" lesson of the woman suffrage movement. From the perspective of Paul's single-issue feminism, both Harriot Blatch and Elizabeth Stanton were renegades, squandering precious feminist energies on superfluous issues. Many years later, Paul told an interviewer that the problem with Harriot was that she was "just like her mother, that she was just involved in too many things and could not commit herself steadily to one goal."[27]

Whether the NWP's interpretation accurately characterizes Anthony as a single-issue suffragist is difficult to assess, because of the many phases of Anthony's career and the interpretive accretions that are inseparable from her historical legacy. The NWP's versions of Anthony's life usually gave special weight to the 1860s, emphasizing her reluctance to set aside woman suffrage demands during the Civil War and her battle against the exclusion of woman suffrage from the Fourteenth and Fifteenth amendments. By contrast, little attention was paid retrospectively to her deep and prior commitment to the abolition of slavery. Later in her life, Anthony did focus more exclusively on the demand for the vote, for instance urging Stanton to downplay her militant critique of Christianity.[28] Yet even in the final phases of Anthony's career, there were other elements—her optimism for and support of the Populist party for instance—from which "lessons" contrary to those drawn by the NWP might have been learned.

Two years later, Paul tried to make use of Elizabeth Stanton's legacy but to bypass Harriot in doing so. To inaugurate the campaign for an Equal Rights Amendment, it was decided to return to Seneca Falls; the date chosen was July 19, seventy-five years to the day after Elizabeth Stanton's 1848 convention there. The point was to establish a strict continuity between the woman suffrage and the equal rights campaigns. The 1923 conference "will be linked up with that earlier one as one half of a whole is joined with the other," declared the editors of the NWP journal, *Equal Rights*.[29] "The National Woman's Party is the disciple of the pioneers, in the quest for true emancipation of women," another editorial, entitled "The Mantle of the Pioneers," proclaimed.[30] "Our researches showed that the movement for Equal Rights presents one continuous line of endeavor," the NWP insisted, "from the time of the first Equal Rights meeting in 1848 at Seneca Falls down to the recent Equal Rights Conference held by the Woman's Party at the same place on the seventy-fifth anniversary date of the first meeting."[31] Elizabeth's role in the original conference was downplayed, and Lucretia Mott, for whom the new amendment was to be named, was characterized in NWP press materials as the "prime mover" of the original convention. An even greater offense was to place Anthony at the 1848 convention, even though she did not meet Elizabeth Stanton until 1851.[32] Both Harriot and Theodore wrote letters to the *New York Times*, to protest. Contrary to the NWP's assertion, Theodore wrote, Susan B. Anthony had not "started" the women's rights movement. "The facts are that Miss Anthony had no more to do with the convention of 1848 than the man in the moon."[33]

The historical misattribution that most deeply galled Harriot concerned the woman suffrage amendment itself, the constitutional provision adopted in 1920 as the Nineteenth Amendment. In 1914, Paul's militant faction had redesignated the long-standing proposal for a woman suffrage constitutional provision as "The Susan B. Anthony Amendment" even though Stanton's children insisted that she was the one who had authored the measure and arranged for it to be first introduced into Congress in 1878.[34] At the time, however, Harriot did not publicly object, probably because she was a partisan of the militants and a strong supporter of their constitutional measure (as against the NAWSA's Shafroth-Palmer amendment). By the time she became more concerned with her mother's historical reputation, a decade later, the woman suffrage amendment had become permanently and exclusively associated with the memory of Susan B. Anthony. Up to the day she died, Harriot was angrily annotating articles in *Equal Rights*, which miscredited the woman suffrage amendment to Anthony.[35] To compound the insult, the NWP always referred to the Equal Rights Amendment, first introduced in 1923, as the Lucretia Mott Amendment. This move, which appeared to make Mott the historic partner of Anthony, buried Elizabeth Stanton's historical reputation even further.[36]

Nor did all the historic oversight emanate only from the National Woman's Party. The NWP's rival, the NAWSA, and its successor organization, the League of Women Voters, were also guilty in Harriot's eyes of ignoring her mother. In 1923, former NAWSA leader Helen H. Gardener began to assemble materials for a permanent exhibition at the Smithsonian Institution to commemorate the history of the woman suffrage movement. Harriot and Theodore were concerned that although the exhibit had been planned to honor the entire NAWSA legacy, no effort had been made to represent their mother's contribution, despite the fact that she had been that organization's first president; they feared that the project was becoming, in effect, a "memorial to Miss Anthony."[37] They offered to contribute a family portrait of Stanton, but had difficulty getting anyone to accept their gift. Eventually the portrait was included in the exhibit, and Harriot and Theodore issued a press release to insure their mother's leadership role in the woman suffrage movement got some notice. But eventually Stanton's place in these events drifted again into obscurity.[38]

Because of so many former suffragists' endemic blindness to her mother's significance, Harriot was alienated from most of their efforts to recall, preserve, and celebrate their movement's history. She did her best to identify her own arenas in which to bolster her mother's historical legacy. In 1922, she and Theodore republished their mother's 1898 memoirs, *Eighty Years and More*, along with an edition of her letters they had begun in 1902 immediately after her death.[39] At that time they had been too close to the pain of their mother's loss to complete the project, and also may have felt constrained by Susan B. Anthony's oversight.[40] They took up the letters in 1915, but again put them aside before completion.[41] Finally in 1922, perhaps in conjunction with Theodore's decision to archive his papers, they succeeded in publishing a collection of their mother's letters. By this time, Harriot and Theodore had full control of their mother's legacy. They wielded a heavy editorial hand, frequently combining several letters as if they were one and altering the meaning as they did so. Harriot's antagonism to Anthony worked its way into her editing decisions, which were meant to distinguish and highlight her mother's singular contribution. *Eighty Years and More* was also reedited, with significant substantive changes.[42]

In 1928, Harriot also deposited what was left of her mother's original papers—here Elizabeth had been the major censor, not her children—in the Library of Congress. That same year, Harriot wrote a 250-word biography of her mother for the *Encyclopedia of Social Sciences*, perhaps at the suggestion of Mary Beard, who wrote the entry on Anthony.[43] And in 1929, the *Woman's Journal*, which was associated with the League of Women Voters, got her to write a brief daughterly portrait, but the magazine edited out all her deliberate indications of Stanton's superiority of leadership.[44]

Acting on her own, there was little Harriot could do to reverse the tide of historical memory. Beginning in the late 1920s, however, a more modernist school of historical interest in the women's movement developed, which treated the official versions of suffrage history, including the accounts that so trivialized her mother, with skepticism and irreverence. These efforts cheered and encouraged Harriot even as they provided her with new resources to right her mother's historical wrongs. While dedicated to the principle of women's emancipation, these iconoclastic feminist historians were more concerned with the triumph of individual women over narrow social restrictions (including those imposed by their own sex) than with the inevitability of social reform. They were more interested in individual self-development than in the rising of the sex, friendly to sexual unconventionality rather than embarrassed by it, and psychological in method and focus. The heroines of prior generations, saintly and selfless leaders like Susan B. Anthony, were not compelling to them; they were looking for more flamboyant figures, women with chaotic, experimental lives who could serve as a source of both interest and inspiration. Their focus was thus more individual than collective, and—

of greatest importance to Harriot—they were fascinated with conflict, especially among women, rather than adverse to it.[45]

In 1928, Emanie Sachs burst onto the decorous women's history scene with her controversial biography of a figure long suppressed in suffrage memory, Victoria Woodhull.[46] Sachs was a feminist and a successful novelist, and found in Woodhull the perfect counter-heroine for a modern rereading of the history of the woman suffrage movement. Coming from an impoverished, unlettered background, Woodhull had risen to prominence after the Civil War. She was a stockbroker and a communist, a woman suffragist and a free lover, in other words, a standing reproach to all the oppositions on which Gilded Age culture was premised. The climax, if not the high point, of her career, was her decision in 1872 to publish in her newspaper, *Woodhull and Claflin's Weekly*, rumors that America's most revered minister, Henry Ward Beecher, had had an adulterous affair with Elizabeth Tilton, wife of his best friend Theodore Tilton, an important Republican newspaper editor. All three principals were active in the woman suffrage movement, and the ensuing scandal, Victorian America's most lurid such episode, embarrassed many suffrage advocates; later historians have even credited the Beecher-Tilton affair with rerouting the women's rights movement into more conservative, respectable channels for the next quarter of a century.[47]

After many other twists and turns in her amazing life, including marriage to a British banker and retreat into staid respectability, Woodhull died in 1927; Sachs began research for her biography immediately, which suggests that she had some personal knowledge of "The Terrible Siren," as she called Woodhull. Sachs placed a query in *Equal Rights* requesting help from people who had known Woodhull; this netted her an intimate reminiscence by the aging anarchist Benjamin Tucker, who had been one of Woodhull's many sexual conquests when he was a youth.[48] When published a year later, Sachs's controversial biography received considerable attention. Instead of a regular review, the *Nation* published an open letter from editor Freda Kirchwey to Woodhull herself: "Victoria, you were a terrible siren and a mad woman. But you were, I think, a useful and important one, for you flung open a dozen forbidden Bluebeard's closets, and the doors have never been entirely closed since. You were important for the noise you made and for the conventions you kicked over. Your madness was valiant and exciting and somehow consistent."[49] Even the *Woman's Journal*, which found the book "confused and burdensome in the telling," had to admit that Sachs's telling of Woodhull's story was "thrilling."[50]

In contrast to Elizabeth Stanton's shadowy role in the official accounts of suffrage history, Sachs made her a major figure in *The Terrible Siren*.

Borrowing from Paxton Hibben's biography of Henry Ward Beecher, published two years before, Sachs revealed that Elizabeth Tilton had told her sad
tale of adultery and betrayal to Elizabeth Stanton and Susan B. Anthony,
Stanton had told Woodhull, and Woodhull had told the world.[51] Then, the
merest whispers of involvement in the sordid Beecher-Tilton scandal had
sullied reputations, but now, a half-century later, Stanton's association with
Woodhull made her seem modern and up-to-date. Even her gossipy indiscretion, such an offense to Victorian sensibilities, gave evidence of passion,
unconventionality, and intolerance for sexual hypocrisy. Sachs painted a
uniformly positive portrait of Stanton, complimenting her even for her flaws.
She was a "splendid" woman, "a profound scholar and a brilliant speaker,
as wise as she was witty, but she was impulsive."[52]

It is unclear whether Harriot had anything to do with the Woodhull
biography, whether for instance, she responded to Sachs's research query. In
her acknowledgments, Sachs thanked Woodhull's "contemporaries and the
children of her contemporaries."[53] Catt reported that Ida Husted Harper,
Anthony's official biographer, who was horrified that the Beecher-Tilton
episode was once again coming to light, suspected that "it was Mrs. Blatch
who let that cat out of the bag" about the involvement of Anthony and
Stanton.[54] But any diligent researcher could have found this information
since most of the details of the scandal were in the public transcripts of the
several civil and ecclesiastical trials to which Beecher had been subjected at
the time; Paxton Hibben, who had first uncovered the story in 1927, had
been denied access to the private papers and discovered his facts through
published sources.[55]

Simultaneous with the appearance of Sachs's life of Victoria Woodhull, an
even more controversial contribution to suffrage history was published,
Rheta Childe Dorr's unauthorized biography of Susan B. Anthony. Dorr was
a long-standing member of the NWP and had served as the first editor of its
magazine, then called *Suffragist*. Her biography of Anthony, the first undertaken since the official three-volume life of Anthony written by Ida H.
Harper in the late 1890s under Anthony's own direction, was of a piece with
other NWP historical accounts in its determined efforts to link Anthony to
Alice Paul and to make of her a predecessor for modern suffrage militance.
Dorr, who had once been sympathetic to trade unionism and socialism in the
1910s but had become more narrowly focused on women's issues in the
1920s, praised Anthony above all for her single-mindedness toward women's
enfranchisement.[56]

Dorr had other objectives as well. Anthony, who was a lifelong temperance advocate, was hardly a natural heroine for women of the 1920s, and

Dorr wanted to bring her down from the Victorian clouds, to "humanize" her for a younger generation of feminists. She also wanted to explore the intrasuffrage controversies of the 1860s and 1870s, long buried in official movement accounts, to find precedents for the factional conflicts between suffrage conservatives and militants in her own time. Her book centered on the split, initiated in 1869, between the Boston-based suffrage faction, led by Lucy Stone and Henry Blackwell, and Stanton's and Anthony's group, located in New York.[57] While the actual substance of the conflict was over the Fourteenth and Fifteenth amendments and whether to support black suffrage without woman suffrage, Dorr, who was herself racist, located the essential difference between the factions elsewhere, over protomodern social and sexual issues such as prostitution, birth control, and divorce. The Boston wing "was as puritanically conservative as Plymouth Rock," according to her account, while "Susan and Mrs. Stanton in their whole social outlook were radicals."[58]

Dorr made extensive use of Sachs's biography of Woodhull and Hibben's account of the Beecher-Tilton scandal. Her portrayal of Woodhull was not flattering: she was described as "relentless, ambitious, implacable and as unscrupulous as Satan himself." Stanton, Dorr conceded, had been guilty of a highly unfortunate indiscretion when she passed on her knowledge of the Beecher-Tilton scandal to this opportunistic and manipulative woman, but Dorr contended that the affair, which was widely known in New York reform circles at the time, would have eventually been made public in one way or another. By contrast, Dorr portrayed Anthony's behavior as irreproachable: although hounded by reporters and lawyers to tell her story, she never relented. "They might as well have tried to interview the Great Sphinx," Dorr wrote. In her own way, however, Anthony made her views known on the underlying causes of this scandalous episode. Despite what Dorr called "the great taboo" that forbade Victorian spinsters from knowing about illicit sexuality, Anthony toured the country with a special lecture (for mixed audiences) on "Social Purity"; this, according to Dorr, demonstrated Anthony's "boldness" and provided social conservatives with one more reason to cast her beyond the pale.[59]

Yet another book on Anthony might have added to Harriot's irritation, but the evidence suggests, to the contrary, that she liked the Dorr book. "I happened to meet Harriot Stanton Blatch at the Women's [sic] University Club," Carrie Chapman Catt wrote to Alice Stone Blackwell in 1930. "She looked very old, sick and frail. I spoke to her and asked her if she had read Miss Dorr's book. She said 'no.' I told her I thought Miss Dorr had given her mother some pretty hard whacks. She smiled a little but looked as if she had no intention of reading that biography."[60] Harriot not only was familiar with Dorr's book but had contributed to it and was thanked in the acknowledgments.[61] Nor was the portrait of Stanton such as to offend her daughter. While Stanton is in the background, Dorr highlights her relationship with Anthony as "one of the most remarkable feminine friendships in history."[62] In the beginning of Dorr's account, Stanton converts Anthony from her initial "puritanical" belief in temperance reform to her mature faith in women's rights; later, their dynamic is reversed, and Stanton becomes Anthony's admirer and dependent. Dorr supplied the dialogue at the imaginary turning point: "Mrs. Stanton said to Susan, 'Do you see at last.' And Susan said, 'At last I see.' Thus women's rights made its essential convert." Catt may have presumed that Harriot would be as upset to see her mother tainted by association with Woodhull as she and Harper were on Anthony's behalf, but this was not likely to be the case. On the contrary, she was probably delighted to see her mother cast in an anti-Victorian light, modernized for a younger audience which approved of sexual controversy.[63]

The controversies stirred up by Dorr's unauthorized life of Anthony revived questions about Elizabeth Stanton's role and brought forward a potential biographer for her, a woman whose questions and perspectives were compatible with Harriot's, but who could do the scholarly work that Harriot could not to set the historical record straight with respect to Stanton's suffrage contributions. This was Alma Lutz, a forty-year-old writer and NWP activist. In late 1928, Lutz had published her first biography, a life of Emma Willard, the woman who had been Elizabeth Cady's teacher in the 1820s.[64] The Willard connection may have contributed to Lutz's interest in Stanton, but the timing suggests that the intriguing questions raised by Rheta Childe Dorr about the earliest decades of the woman suffrage movement were what sparked her curiosity.

In May 1930, Alma Lutz made her first visit to Harriot Blatch.[65] Although she had come to talk about the mother, she recorded in her notes how much she liked the daughter: "Liked HSB very much," she wrote in her notes of the visit. "Intelligent. Pleasant. Face lights up beautifully when she smiles. Decided opinions." A week after this first visit, she and Harriot were exchanging letters about intimate details of Stanton's life.[66] By early 1931, Lutz was fully embarked on a life of Stanton, working in close, almost collaborative, relation with Harriot. Without Harriot, in fact, a genuine biography of Stanton, as opposed to a hagiographic repetition of suffrage myths and legends, would have been impossible. As if she had been waiting for someone like Lutz, Harriot had made the necessary biographical resources available, albeit heavily marked with her own concerns. She helped Lutz to trace down other resources, for instance in her brother's papers, which he had left to Douglass College, and discussed with her at length various episodes in her mother's life.[67]

Two preoccupations particularly marked Harriot's vision for her mother's biography. First, she wanted to recast in a positive light her mother's un-Victorian concerns with divorce, birth control, and sexuality. These issues had brought Elizabeth much criticism and isolation over the long sweep of her nineteenth-century career, but now, in the context of the postsuffrage period, they made her seem presciently modern, a potential heroine for the younger generation of feminists so impatient with nineteenth-century suffrage virtues. With Harriot's help, Lutz concentrated on Stanton's position on divorce and her role in the Beecher-Tilton scandal, both of which were the subjects of separate chapters in the book.

The two women did not limit their concerns to public advocacy: Harriot confided in Lutz her suspicion that Elizabeth had been tempted to run off with Edward Bayard, her sister's husband, and that she had married Henry Stanton in part on the rebound.[68] Later, she wrote provocatively, either about this affair or another, that "owing to the death of certain persons," she was finally willing to talk "about the romance in my mother's life."[69] The hidden sex lives of all the suffrage saints were the objects of much curiosity in these years—Carrie Chapman Catt wondered about Susan B. Anthony's secret passions, for instance—as if the discovery of sexual secrets would humanize them.[70] But of all these Victorian paragons, Stanton alone, with her daughter's posthumous help, could offer anything to satisfy this need for buried sexual passion. In a nasty review of Alice Stone Blackwell's filiapietistic 1930 biography of her own mother, Harriot contrasted "dessicated saints," sexually inhibited, upstanding Victorian matrons, such as Lucy Stone, with "juicy radicals" like Elizabeth Stanton.[71]

Harriot's sexual agenda for her mother posed no problems for Lutz, but not so her other concern: Elizabeth Stanton's standing vis-à-vis Susan B. Anthony. At the beginning of the project, Harriot shared with Lutz her own interpretation of the political differences between the two women and why Stanton's approach was so superior. Anthony's devotees lionized her for her alleged devotion to the principle of a single-issue movement and criticized Stanton for her eclecticism, but Harriot saw it quite the other way. Dorr had claimed that Anthony had to "hold my mother to suffrage" to keep her from squandering her energies. On the contrary, Harriot insisted, "she warned Miss Anthony that if suffragists discussed nothing but the ballot, by the time they became full fledged citizens they would not have an idea how nor for what to use their weapon." In Harriot's eyes, of course, her mother's prophecy had been right, even if, like Cassandra, she had been tragically ignored.[72]

As the work on the biography progressed, Harriot became more and more agitated that Lutz was too deferential to Anthony's inflated reputation and insufficiently concerned to credit Stanton with the historical primacy she deserved. There was too much "dragging in Miss Anthony," Harriot complained, not enough challenge to the widespread misapprehension that "she was the only leader in the early days." Late in 1933, Lutz gave Harriot a full draft to read, which she found wanting particularly on this issue. The manuscript was "interesting and readable . . . but I am in doubt as to whether you have quite seen to the bottom of ECS and SBA." Lutz had not sufficiently communicated Stanton's "infinite superiority," especially her "unusual brain power." She had given too much credence to the claim, with which Harriot strenuously disagreed, that Anthony had special "executive ability." On the contrary, Harriot remembered, Anthony was "a nervous person, who couldn't sit still at a task, always wanted to be 'busy.'" Nor had Lutz done enough to correct the increasingly common misconception that it was Anthony rather than her mother, who called the first women's rights convention, and thirty years later introduced the woman suffrage amendment into Congress.[73] "In light of the fact that the Woman's Party . . . has completely misled public opinion about these events," Harriot wrote Lutz sternly, "history needs more than a mild statement to bring out the truth."[74]

The emotional meaning that historical restoration of her mother had come to have for Harriot, and in particular her historical vendetta against Anthony, created obstacles for Lutz in completing her book. Like other NWP loyalists, Lutz revered Anthony and naturally made gestures of inclusion and deference to her in her narrative, while Harriot wanted to take every opportunity she could to underline her mother's singular contribution and what she liked to call her "infinite superiority." This friction, no doubt aggravated by Harriot's imperious manner especially with respect to things touching on her matrilineage, at times made for a rocky collaboration. In response to some detail to which she felt Lutz was insufficiently attentive, Harriot wrote one of what must have been a series of abusive reprimands. "I am of the opinion [that] your mind . . . does not register when contentious matter is put before it," she wrote. "America needs a very aggressive biography of ECS, a stirring, fighting volume."[75]

Another factor complicating Harriot's longing to rehabilitate her mother's historical reputation was the overlap and confusion between the mother's career and that of the daughter. While Harriot was more than willing to defend her mother's historical stature and contributions, she was quite a bit more reticent about asserting her own. Yet at the same time, the rage she felt at the historical occlusion of her mother surely was fueled by her sense that her own contribution, leadership, and importance were being lost to history. She ended her critical review of Alice Stone Blackwell's book with a reminder about the significance of her own role in the suffrage split of the late nineteenth century: contrary to Stone Blackwell's charge that Stanton and Anthony's *History of Woman Suffrage* left out the whole story of the rival suffrage organization founded by Lucy Stone, Harriot pointed out that in 1882 she herself had written the long chapter incorporating this material into the book.[76]

One example serves to indicate Harriot's conflicted desire to assert her own historical importance. In 1930, to commemorate the tenth anniversary of enfranchisement, the League of Women Voters announced the establishment of a Suffrage Honor Roll, places on which were to be secured by state league nominations and the payment of "a suitable memorial fund . . . for each name proposed." This was not a serious act of historical remembrance, but a fundraising technique and a way, according to the league itself, to allow suffrage veterans to enjoy themselves by trading reminiscences.[77] However, as the major decennial commemoration of the suffrage victory by the successor organization of the National American Woman Suffrage Association, the Honor Roll got substantial media coverage. Harriot was one of many who were incensed by the venality of the league's plan. She was offended both on her mother's behalf and on her own. As she often did at such moments, Harriot prepared to write a letter of protest to the *New York Times*, but the several incomplete drafts preserved in her papers and the fact that nothing was ever published in the *Times* indicates that she could not quite figure out how to present her case.

On the one hand, she insisted on the magnitude of her own service to the cause and was outraged that this was not the criterion for inclusion on the Honor Roll. On the other hand, she wanted to take the high-minded road, "to deprecate the idea of honoring individuals at all" and credit instead the "vast suffrage army," all faceless servants to their sex. There is no question that Harriot was immensely proud of her own historical contribution—her special leadership—but she held back from claiming it, either because of the larger feminist ethic of selfless service or because of more personal prohibitions against self-pride. In this context, we can begin to see how much the preoccupation with her mother's rightful place was an expression and resolution of this conflict, but one that was going to have to give way in the face of the historical provocations that were piling up in Harriot's later years.[78]

The process of historical misrepresentation that Harriot began to suffer was strikingly similar to what she saw happening to her mother. Just as Elizabeth's contributions were being miscredited to Anthony, Harriot felt that her own historical role was in the process of being appropriated by her contemporary and rival, Carrie Chapman Catt. Catt, who never seemed to have trouble receiving historical honors, was being flooded with them in connection with the decade anniversary of the suffrage victory. In 1930 and 1931, she won several large monetary prizes, including an Achievement Award of five thousand dollars from the *Pictorial Review*, and was the subject of numerous, worshipful articles.[79] All this attention showered on this one woman—moreover, a woman she felt had held back the suffrage movement rather than advanced it—enraged Harriot. Her granddaughter Harriet de Forest, who knew little about her grandmother's historical accomplishments, nonetheless knew all about the details of Catt's many offenses and slights. "She stole the ball and made the touchdown," she recalled, "Oh my, get [Harriot Blatch] started on Carrie Chapman Catt and she would go on for an hour. . . . It wasn't just her coming on board but trying to take over if she did. Just sort of walked in the front row and said here I am and put her stamp of approval on it, which didn't go over very well. . . . I can't remember her damning anyone else."[80]

Like Anthony to Stanton, Catt appeared to be claiming acts of bold and innovative leadership for her own that really belonged to Harriot. A metaphor Harriot often used to challenge Anthony's historic displacement of Stanton applied to her own grievances against Catt. "You may admire above all women Mary Queen of Scots, & I Queen Elizabeth. . . . But this honest expression of personal taste enters quite another field when in order to secure adherents for your heroine, you take off the belongings of my queen and dress your queen up in them."[81] Carrie Chapman Catt was clothing herself in Harriot Stanton Blatch's historical achievements, and Harriot intended to get them back.

In a long, impassioned letter to Dora Albert, a journalist who was researching a muckraking, counter-celebratory article on Catt, Harriot detailed Catt's many offenses against her and against the historical record. Contrary to claims often made on her behalf, Catt had not initiated either suffrage parades or outdoor meetings; quite the opposite, she had constantly tried to dissuade Harriot and other unorthodox activists from any such innovations. She was a person "wholly lacking in imagination," a "self centered, conceited, pompous woman," and, despite her saintly demeanor, ambitious and untrustworthy. To prove this point, Harriot confirmed one of Albert's hunches, that in the 1890s, Catt had secretly worked against the election to the suffrage presidency of Susan B. Anthony.[82] And yet Harriot was still too conflicted to stand behind her own indictments and make her historical case in public. When Albert incorporated some of the details in Harriot's letter in her own draft article on Catt (especially the charge of betraying Anthony), Harriot angrily accused her of insincerity and deceit. Albert, understandably confused about what she had done to give such offense, sent back Harriot's original letter, purged her article of all references to it, and apologized, although she was not sure exactly for what.[83]

Despite such ambivalences, the work of correcting her mother's reputation nonetheless led Harriot to delve into her own historical memories and experiences. Her own life, career, and political commitments followed too closely on those of Elizabeth Stanton for her to separate the two subjects; it was simply not possible for Harriot to make large, public claims on behalf of her mother and not at the same time begin to plumb her own historical experience. The interconnectedness of history was built into her life. One of her basic questions about her mother was when and why she had begun to lose her vaunted place in the suffrage movement. When Harriot found "the reasons of the prevarications of history in woman suffrage," she found herself up against the rivalries and conflicts of her own suffrage leadership. "In 1895, my mother set forth all her heresies in Eighty Years and More, in important magazine articles on divorce, [and] in the Woman's Bible," she wrote to Alma Lutz, "and the then leaders began to bury her alive"—what an image!—"and to re-vivify Miss Anthony." The "then leaders" in 1895, chief among them Carrie Chapman Catt, were precisely the orthodox suffragists against whom Harriot herself came up, a dozen years later, with her Equality League insurgency. "They wanted a pure suffrage movement & killed it as dead as a door nail," until "the Women's Political Union with dramatic propaganda & political work began to revive it in 1907 in New York State."[84]

Within just a few months after Alma Lutz had begun the Stanton biography, Harriot was immersed in the researching and writing of her own autobiography. She began not at the beginning, but with the work of which she was most proud, the long, successful effort to get a bill enabling a woman suffrage referendum passed through the New York legislature. To do this, she had to reclaim for herself innovations and contributions that had become attached to other more celebrated historical figures. She was most concerned to establish that she and her organization, not Catt and her Woman Suffrage Party, had been responsible for developing the "political methods" that had revolutionized the New York suffrage scene. She wrote to Adelma Burd, who had been a young Equality League suffrage activist and was now a New York attorney, to confirm that while working for the Equality League, Burd had initially proposed that suffragists organize themselves into assembly districts in order to target state assemblymen who refused to sign on for suffrage. Burd agreed, and noted that, far from inventing political methods, "Miss Hays and Mrs. Catt were opposed to this idea on the ground that it savored of politics and might split our support from women."[85] A correspondence with Christabel Pankhurst from these years also suggests that Harriot was concerned to show that she was not merely a follower of the British suffragettes but rather a simultaneous inventor of modern militant methods.[86]

Harriot seemed to have adapted her method of work from the *History of Woman Suffrage*, at which she had apprenticed in her youth. The manuscript she was putting together, especially the important section on her work in the legislature was not so much an autobiographical narrative as excerpts from documents of the period—newspaper clippings, magazine articles, state legislative debates, organizational minutes and reports—linked together by a minimum of text, which functioned to identify time and place and personality. Also, the work tended to veer away from the autobiographical and toward the institutional. She kept burying herself in the larger entity of the Women's Political Union, or rather conflating her own perspective and that of her organization. Revising her manuscript, she would replace phrases such as "in my eyes" with "in the eyes of the Union."[87] Years before, she had jokingly suggested that Doris Stevens publish her 1920 history of Alice Paul and the National Woman's Party in a volume that was the same size and shape as the *History of Woman Suffrage*, as a way to get the historical jump on the *History*'s official publisher, the National American Woman Suffrage Association.[88] Now, it was almost as if she were writing her own last volume of the *History*, an account of the final phases of the movement in which she replaced her mother as editor and political leader.

Harriot Blatch's autobiographical efforts brought her close to Mary Beard, with major consequences for both women. Colleagues in the New York suffrage movement of the 1910s, they now had more in common than in the heyday of their activism. Depression-era conditions highlighted their common emphasis on political economy as well as the broadly based progressive political concerns they shared. From 1930 until Harriot's death in 1940, they pursued what Beard's most recent biographer calls "a remarkable correspondence and apparent mutual respect," ranging over current politics, historical scholarship, and family relationships.[89] While Harriot kept Mary's letters, her own suffered the ironic fate of most of Mary Beard's correspondence—destruction. In this period, Beard devised and began to execute her grand vision for a reinterpretation of history in which women's significant but distinctive contributions had a shaping role. In 1931, her *On Understanding Women* was published and two years later *America through Women's Eyes* appeared.[90] While Mary Beard provided Harriot Blatch with incomparable support and encouragement in a task that pushed her to the edge of her capacities, Harriot also was crucial in helping Beard to rethink her role as a pioneering historian of women. Their common preoccupation with the past involved not only its preservation but its critical reassessment in light of contemporary needs and realities.

They shared more than a perspective on the past. Politically, they both saw themselves as critics from the left of President Roosevelt and the newly elected Democratic administration. Beard found the president especially wanting on foreign policy. "Even worse than his mania for popularity is his mania for the Navy, isn't it?" she wrote to Harriot early in the first administration. "On all sides we hear the fear expressed that he is heading us straight to war. I was asked to campaign for him but refused because he would not come into the clear with a foreign policy." Nor was she particularly enamored of Eleanor Roosevelt, whom she described to Harriot as "chattering about a humanistic bent which in reality is non-existent."[91]

Harriot's dislike of Franklin Roosevelt had its roots in her years of hard lobbying before the New York legislature. While he claimed that "he was a believer in the cause," she remembered with clarity that "he was always absent when anything so raw as a counting of ayes and nays was taking place." When he became president, she found him especially disappointing with respect to domestic legislation. Because his administration was so energetically reviving prospects for labor and social welfare legislation, she was appalled to find that at the core of this project was her old nemesis, distinction by sex, now more clearly than ever discriminatory toward women workers. She was particularly enraged at the National Recovery Administration's setting of lower minimum wage standards for female than for male workers and at legislation prohibiting federal employment to the spouses of federal employees. "If those in social welfare had used their brains to solve the tangled problems appearing under the changed conditions of today—good not harm—would have been achieved," she insisted in 1935. "Oh that the hearts throbbing so sympathetically over women would come through with a constructive scheme for giving something to women, mother's pensions for instance, or a plan of social insurance or a wage equal to a man's for the same work instead of forbidding us to work at night, or to teach if we are married."[92] Never had her indictment of sex-based labor legislation been more timely or forcefully put.

As for their relations with other women reformers and activists, both

Beard and Blatch found themselves situated uncomfortably between the two successor factions of the suffrage movement, and equally longing, in Beard's words, for a "larger vision" of social change in which women had a fundamental role. On the one hand, there were the reformers, with First Lady Eleanor Roosevelt at their head, whom Harriot disparagingly called the "social workers" and Beard characterized as "Chicago women of the old regime" (the reference was to Jane Addams, Hull House, and the entire settlement tradition). Both Beard and Blatch found their female social reform approach simultaneously naive and pragmatic and lacking any complex sense of social change. "They believe in seeing and acting on 'one thing at a time,'" Beard charged, even if that "one thing" was as complex and multifaceted as "peace." Such women, she complained, "would crush my spirit if I saw them every day."[93]

On the other hand, neither of them felt that their position was represented by the National Woman's Party's ceaseless and abstract cry for "equality." Beard, who has been much misunderstood on this point, wanted Harriot to understand that it was not that she thought equality too much a demand, but too little. "The National Woman's Party mistakes my point of view about equality and I must do something to make that position clearer," Beard wrote to Blatch. "I am not against equality of course. I simply regard it as inadequate today."[94] Subsequent letters pursued the point. "What I was claiming is too bromidic for you and me alike to have to debate," she continued, "simply that the women of '48 were keyed to the opening competitive regime which seemed to offer immortality at that time." But now, in the modern era and in the context of a "competitive economy," Beard contended, defining women's emancipation as a matter of "sheer equality . . . had its economic, ethical and political limitations."[95]

Early in their renewed relationship, Beard and Blatch had an opportunity to explore some common political and historical territory. They, along with Maud Wood Park of the League of Women Voters, were invited to draft a manifesto for an ambitious National Council of Women's Congress, to be held in August 1933.[96] Both women felt that the congress, which was to be called "Our Common Cause: Civilization," had the potential for articulating a "third way," which could attract women affiliated with both the social welfare and the National Woman's Party camps. This optimism was framed, on the one hand, by the challenge and desperation of economic collapse, not just in the United States, but around the world, and, on the other hand, by the opening up of reformist possibilities in the election of Franklin Roosevelt and a new Democratic administration, after twelve miserable years of Republican conservatism.

The version of the manifesto that Blatch, Beard, and Park submitted to the National Council board in June 1933 employed a historical and feminist framework. It harked back to the spirit of Seneca Falls, which it was designed to commemorate and which it characterized as "the first Convention in the Revolution of our mothers." The manifesto's perspective on the generation of 1848 was admirably dialectical. Elizabeth Stanton and her collaborators were presented as working within an economic system—industrial capitalism—that was new and dynamic, but was depriving women of age-old occupations and authority; given their own historical constraints, the women of the period could not be expected to comprehend the limits of their vision, which those of the modern era could see. Yet the manifesto appreciated how much the '48ers were on the cutting edge of their age, determined to restore social and economic position to women, courageous, forward looking, and magnificently successful.[97]

Even while acknowledging that "most of the demands advanced in the Woman's Declaration of Independence [sic] have been gained," this historical retrospective was not meant to lead to complacency; on the contrary, the manifesto-writers wanted to show how social and economic conditions had changed since Seneca Falls and how the new political challenges that their own generation of women faced needed to be addressed. The message was to invoke the pioneering and progressive spirit of their foremothers while looking beyond their specific demands and particular perspectives. The authors argued that the factory system and production for private profit had, in the decades since 1848, led to such a "concentration of wealth" and a monopoly of power and privilege that an "emphasis on individual rights" had become almost meaningless. "The vaunted property rights, nominally ours as they are men's, prove meaningless" in such an environment. Even "the prized educational privilege, really ours as men's, turns out to be, too often, the mirror of an incompetent middle class overcrowding every market in which work must be sought, with white collar scholastics, filers and compilers." What was needed then was a "new manifesto adapted to the era of poverty," which challenged not simply the privilege of men, but the entire social system of unfettered individualism.[98]

By the time the congress was held, however, Harriot had pulled out of the project. She was discovering so many offenses against her mother's memory that she could focus on nothing else. This time she had become enraged because Elizabeth Stanton was not among the list of "twelve greatest American women leaders" chosen by the National Council of Women in connection with its congress. The list included Abigail Adams, Mary Lyon, Clara Barton, Emily and Antoinette Blackwell, Julia Ward Howe, Frances Willard,

May Wright Sewall, and the two most infuriating names, Susan B. Anthony and Carrie Chapman Catt. But Stanton was not included, despite the fact, as Harriot ceaselessly insisted, that it was she who had first conceived the 1888 International Council of Women out of which the present organization had grown.[99] In numerous letters to friends and enemies, and in furious articles she started to write but could not finish, Harriot could only say the same thing over and over again. "Women are making up history if not making it," was the way she put it in a letter to Alma Lutz. "I have corrected the errors but they go right on repeating them both in the press room of the Council and the Women's [sic] Party."[100]

Even so, Harriot's friendship with Beard survived the National Council of Women episode. More and more they realized they shared a common impatience with the received vision and smug self-satisfaction of so many other ex-suffragists that the past was merely a record of heroic victory, that it had nothing to teach the present, and no large unmet visions to bequeath to the future. As Beard began to pour her energies into her visionary Women's Archives project to identify and collect primary sources documenting women's far-ranging active contributions to history, Harriot became a major supporter. She, along with Dorothy Bromley, archivist at Howard University, initiated the meeting between Dutch feminist Rosika Schwimmer and Mary Beard out of which the Women's Archives project grew. Harriot was also a member of the Archives Board of Trustees, and helped in locating and acquiring groups of papers. "Try to have us in mind when you consider your personal papers," Beard wrote to Harriot in the thick of planning. "And do you think you could get Charlotte Gilman's papers for us from her executors?"[101]

For Beard, the connection to Harriot Blatch was crucial in helping her to understand that feminism was compatible with and could be incorporated into a comprehensive social justice framework, and that it was possible to be a comprehensive and forward-looking social thinker and at the same time to maintain an intense dedication to the equality of the sexes. For her, as for so many activist, progressive women in the decades after 1920, the NWP's insistence on a single-issue approach—as if women's equality could be considered "one thing"—had largely obliterated the capacity to draw simultaneously on feminism and all the other democratic passions. Here Harriot's link to her mother, which extended her historical memory so much longer than other suffrage veterans, had something special and unique to contribute. By and through Harriot, Mary Beard was deeply influenced by Elizabeth Stanton.[102]

Harriot initially thought that her friend lacked a genuine understanding of the positive contribution of women's rights to the larger project of American democracy, so that all she could see were the historical limits of the suffrage movement, especially in its later phases. When *America through Women's Eyes* appeared in 1933, Harriot protested that the book omitted Stanton and women's rights in general from its pages. "Think of leaving out the whole of the story of the struggle—a unique and striking struggle of a disfranchised class forming one half the human race—for enfranchisement," she wrote to Alma Lutz.[103] But as they pursued their historical labors together, Harriot succeeded in interesting Beard in Elizabeth Stanton and her generation. In response to what she was learning about earlier feminists' "criticism of Church and State," Beard wrote Harriot, she was thinking about "a final volume for my scheme" on women's history, an analysis of "the range and vigor of women thinkers."[104]

When at last Harriot succeeded in getting Beard to consult her mother's papers (which had been deposited at the Library of Congress in the late 1920s), to touch and read them, Mary was thrilled at the discovery. "I have longed to rush in upon you with my excitement over your mother!" Beard wrote from Washington. "Every item in those folders excites me. I have written you countless letters in my mind as I turned over the documents." Beard's greatest revelation was the breadth and radicalism of the large social vision that surrounded and informed Elizabeth Stanton's feminism. "I was so ignorant that I feared I should not find the fundamental economic thought. Thank god, it is there!" Now too she understood the roots of Harriot's own political perspective which she found so compatible. "It is very evident that you are a chip off the old block re social consciousness."[105]

For her part, Beard gently but relentlessly encouraged Harriot to complete her memoirs. She first broached the idea in 1930 as a way for Harriot to respond to the recently published suffrage biographies that so irritated her. "Your own picture of your own times . . . will certainly be worth a dozen second-hand tales by persons who may try to see it as they think you did," she wrote, a chilling reproach to any would-be biographer.[106] In one of her earliest acts of archival preservation, she encouraged Harriot to deposit her papers at the Library of Congress and facilitated negotiations with her friend, J. Franklin Jamieson, the chief librarian.[107] In almost every letter she wrote to Harriot, she inquired about the memoirs: "I will continue to prod you as you say I may," "I am ever solicitous about your autobiography," and "I am counting on you to provide the criticism of your times which so few women seem able to do."[108] When Harriot feared her opinions might be too controversial, Beard urged her not to hold back. "Dear Harriot Blatch, there is NO ESCAPE from drawing Mrs. Catt which you can find," she counseled in late 1934. "You will have to do it to make your perspective broad enough and your foundations deep enough."[109]

By late 1935, Beard must have known that Harriot was having trouble with what she called solicitously in one letter, "your big job." "I always want to put in my great query about your own memoir," she wrote. "But I must not be an abomination by seeming to nag you every day."[110] By this point, Beard was trying to provide the large, unifying themes and big questions that Harriot herself seemed unable to devise to organize her many memories into a coherent set of reminiscences. "I trust you will let nothing interfere with their preparation," Beard wrote, "and that . . . you will give a rounded-out picture of the suffragists, showing their ideas and their courage, their fears and their weaknesses, the youth and old age inner contest . . . the ordering and obeying, and as far as possible the content of the propaganda. What did the women think they were doing in very fact? . . . Unless you do set down your own relation to the public life of your time, dear Mrs. Blatch . . . young men and women will have no way of understanding these times or your place in them."[111]

Increasingly, Harriot found herself in need of help and support in doing this work of making sense out of her life: her memory was not always reliable, she wanted to talk over important episodes and issues, and the entire process of recollection and recording was unnerving and emotionally depleting. She was by now in her late seventies and could not reflect on the triumphs of a lifetime without also calling up the conflicts and disappointments. While Elizabeth Stanton had turned to Harriot during a similar period in her own life, Harriot did not move closer to Nora in this period. Instead, she chose Caroline Lexow Babcock, revisiting their closeness with a poignant intensity and expressing her needs with unusual vulnerability: "Could you, would you take me as star & paying guest from now on through the winter while I am finishing off this book?" she asked in September 1933.[112] She returned to Caroline's home in Nyack more than once, staying a few months at a time, always apologizing profusely for interferences she feared she was causing in the Babcocks' family life.

Harriot, who had lived all her life by the doctrine of absolute independence, now needed someone on whom she could depend to provide help that went far beyond lodgings and evening conversation, if she were ever going to complete this crucial, final task. She began to put pressure on Caroline, the only person she trusted sufficiently with her past, to take up the project and help her finish it. "I fear," she wrote in April, "that unless you put your capable shoulder to the wheel, that work will never be done."[113] But Caroline had her own economic problems, and all the many plans Harriot dreamed up—including securing her a Works Project Administration appointment—to pay her for the work, came to nought. "I should have preferred above all things to have helped Mrs. Blatch," she later wrote, "but I could not."[114]

By 1936, the year of Harriot's eightieth birthday, she had given up working on her autobiography entirely, discouraged and dispirited. Many factors were working against her. Depression conditions had depleted her income and she lacked the money she needed for basic stenographic help. Demoralized, she believed that the state of publishing was so abysmal that were she to complete the manuscript, she would be unable to find a publisher without some sort of private subvention (an accurate assessment). But her problems were deeper than economic hardship. Mary Beard, who was more familiar with her autobiographical project than anyone else, reluctantly concluded that Harriot would never be able to finish her memoirs on her own. Not only was her eyesight failing along with her memory, but she suffered an even greater handicap in "her apparent difficulty in making a synthesis of her ideas and interests."[115]

Faced with the necessity of making sense of her life, Harriot found herself fundamentally alone. "We come into the world alone, unlike all who have gone before us, we leave it alone, under circumstances peculiar to ourselves. . . . Alike among the greatest triumphs and darkest tragedies of life, we walk alone. . . . In that solemn solitude of self, that links us with the immeasurable and eternal, each soul lives alone forever."[116] Her mother had written these stark, comfortless words at almost exactly the same point in her life, on the brink of her eightieth birthday, confronted by political exclusion, as she was herself plunged into the challenge of self-history. But Elizabeth Stanton, who had been making propaganda from her own life for decades, was able to find an autobiographical voice and complete her memoirs.[117]

For her daughter, this kind of finality and closure proved maddeningly elusive. Here too historical epochs were changing. An older narrative framework for making sense out of an individual life—the heroic individualism of the nineteenth century—had passed into oblivion, but there was not yet a fully developed alternative for telling one's story. Just as her mother's generation had done the work to adapt political individualism to make room for women's rights, modern, psychological frameworks were going to have to be reworked to accommodate women's subjective complexities. In the future, such perspectives might help women to understand the implications of their complex relationships to the women who had come before them, especially to their mothers. But for now, Elizabeth Stanton's daughter was going to have to finish her life—living it as well as writing it—without these tools.

In November of 1938, Harriot suffered a bad fall. From this point on her decline was steep. So active all her life, she was now confined to bed and was, by her own description, "more or less confused in my mind most of the time." Letters from this period are in the unsure hand of someone very aged. Her income had fallen precipitously after the stock market crash, and she was living on less than two thousand dollars a year, much of which went for rent. Financial tensions continued to erode her relation with Nora, and their alienation grew worse in her final years. After her fall, she lived in a series of rented rooms in Greenwich and complained bitterly of the quality of the food and the intensity of the heat in the summer.[118]

By 1937, Harriot had given up trying to write her memoirs and was concentrating solely on organizing her notes and papers, with the hope that if she could not make sense of her life and defend the integrity of her historical contributions, someone else might. Encouraged by Mary Beard, she assembled the materials from her postsuffrage years, concentrating on peace, her pioneering critique of sex-based labor legislation, and the affronts suffered by her mother and herself at the hands of suffrage historians. Even this project was never completed, however, and the documentary record of her final years disappeared into the attic alcove of Nora's house.[119]

Ironically, it was Vassar College, which Harriot excoriated so mercilessly for its educational timidity and cloistered frustrations, that came to the rescue of her unfinished "Life." The college was assembling a series of publications to celebrate its seventy-fifth anniversary in 1940 and contacted Alma Lutz about the biography of Elizabeth Stanton she was writing. Lutz may have suggested to Vassar that she help Harriot Stanton Blatch, its illustrious alumna, to complete her autobiography, which could be included also in the publication program.[120]

In any case, when Alma Lutz appeared at Harriot's rooms in Greenwich to discuss what role she might play in the completion of her autobiography, the old lady was grateful. At first she demurred, insisting as in the past that her mother's life was more important and that Lutz focus exclusively on publishing the Stanton biography. "Then as we talked more she felt more like trying," Lutz reported to her Vassar contacts. Harriot gave her parts of the manuscript and they arranged to meet again.[121] "You could not overestimate my appreciation of your kindness in putting your shoulder under the burden," Harriot wrote back in her shaky hand. Even so, she wondered if it was really feasible to complete the project. "If made five years ago, your offer would [have] come as a godsend, for I could have shared in the demands on us. . . . [But] it seems clear to me now that Vassar has not funds to put behind the work and that you have not adequate resources to devote to enterprises outside your own sound ventures." She was still resisting her own inescapable limitations and the help she desperately needed.[122]

Alma Lutz's reasons for offering to take on the Blatch project were not primarily financial. Vassar agreed only to pay her expenses and to leave her what few royalties the book might earn. But Lutz was a historian because she was a feminist and saw this as a way to advance the cause of women's equality. She wanted to help Harriot to finish her memoirs for the same reasons that she had undertaken the Stanton biography, out of deep respect for their lifelong contributions to the women's rights movement and because both mother and daughter embodied a version of feminist politics that she wanted to advance and encourage.[123] "It is important that your mother's story be published," she wrote to Nora. "We need some of her spirit today."[124] She particularly appreciated Harriot's unflinching opposition to sex-based labor legislation, and was disappointed to discover that almost none of the manuscript dealt with this issue. The portions Harriot gave her at first, she reported to the head of the Publication Committee, were disappointingly incomplete, "about 30,000 words, about half a short book."[125] The fullest sections dealt with Harriot's childhood and her years in Europe before her marriage.

By their next meeting, Harriot had located a series of drafts that covered the crucial Women's Political Union years, and it now seemed to Lutz that the book could be finished in the few months that Vassar had allotted her and that it could be drawn for the most part from Harriot's own words. She arranged to have handwritten manuscripts typed up, to combine the various drafts into one readable narrative, and to submit what she had done to Harriot so that she could read it and correct any errors. She also asked Harriot to search her failing memory for recollections on subjects still missing from the manuscript—"your work for suffrage in England, your difficulties re nationality, the founding of the League of Self-Supporting Women, [and] your national work for suffrage." "I want you to enjoy this work and not let it worry you," she wrote kindly. "The point of my helping you with it is to make it easier for you and relieve you of the wear and tear of the tedious work. You have done plenty of it in the past."[126] For several weeks Harriot worked well with Lutz, who was excited about what she was finding. "This history of your suffrage work is going to be an eye-opener to many who think their organizations started the political ball rolling," she wrote in a clear reference to Carrie Chapman Catt. "You certainly did a grand job and I am having a beautiful time recording it."[127] And Harriot liked what her young coworker was producing. "My verdict is that your work has been excellently done," she wrote of the section on 1907–15.[128]

At this point, however, Nora, who feared that Harriot was losing control over her own history, became suspicious of Alma Lutz and communicated this. As a result, Harriot became much more resistant to collaboration, writing to Lutz that she needed a strict accounting of all the materials she had lent her for the book, and reprimanding her for slow and inaccurate methods of working. Despite her own obvious and growing incapacity, she insisted that she, "who had . . . done with the legislature intimate, personal work over the years, should put together the section on the New York campaign of 1915, not Lutz. "Admirable as I think your manuscript was, I do think it lacked the spirit of originality and spontaneity."[129] In one of those many eerie replays of her matrilineage's history, Nora's intervention echoed Harriot's efforts to rescue her own mother in 1881 from the exhausting work of writing the *History of Woman Suffrage*. But Lutz ably defended her intentions and integrity, making it clear to Harriot that she would not be treated peremptorily, and the work between them resumed.[130] By the end of August 1939, a manuscript covering Harriot's life through the first New York referendum was almost ready for the Vassar Publication Committee.

Harriot's last public act was for her mother's sake. In June 1939 she attended a National Woman's Party Mother's Day celebration in Washington, D.C., honoring Elizabeth Cady Stanton and Lucretia Mott. Five months later, she was unable to attend the dedication as a historical site of the New York house on West Ninety-fourth Street where she had lived with her mother during the late 1890's.[131] Five weeks before, in September 1939, Harriot had fallen a second time.[132] Alma Lutz was appalled at her condition. "I found Mrs. Blatch in a serious condition and really unable to talk about anything. She had broken her hip and the setting was an ordeal and the shock and the operation have been hard on her."[133] Now nearly totally immobilized in the nursing home wing of her former Greenwich boarding house, going blind (this too like her mother) she could not even muster the strength or clarity to review the manuscript Lutz was completing. Final chapters on the federal amendment, Harriot's reactions to world war, and her campaign against sex-based labor legislation had to be pieced together from other writings, ranging from her unpublished 1893 Fabian tract on women's wages to her pro- and antiwar books for the YWCA Woman's Press. One of Harriot's last acts may have been the decision to dedicate her book "to all the members of the Women's Political Union, in deep gratitude for their loyalty, earnestness and devotion to the cause of woman suffrage."[134]

At this crucial juncture, when it looked as if Harriot's life would expire before her "Life" could be completed, Caroline offered to read the manuscript. "When I told her you would read the chapters on the WPU," Lutz wrote to Babcock, "she said that it would be a great comfort to her."[135] The next month, Lutz was able to submit a finished manuscript to Vassar. The title she chose for the memoirs was *Challenging Years*; the choice echoed the title of her Stanton biography, *Created Equal*. Then as Harriot slipped deeper and deeper into incapacity, the project stalled again. The publisher for *Created Equal*, the John Day Company, turned down *Challenging Years*. Caroline also suggested that the manuscript be toned down a bit, particularly in its harsh tone toward Vassar and its biting criticisms of Carrie Chapman Catt. Lutz solicited additional comments and readings from Nora and Mary Beard and went to the Library of Congress to consult the WPU folios there.[136]

Challenging Years was finally brought out in May 1940 by G. P. Putnam's Sons, a publisher with a long-standing interest in women's rights. Harriot Stanton Blatch and Alma Lutz were listed as coauthors. Lutz was immensely relieved that Harriot had been able to sign the final contract, though she was also concerned that in her rush to complete and publish the memoirs in time for Harriot to know that they were done, the work would appear hurried and sloppy.[137] On this point, Caroline was reassuring. "What an achievement for you," she wrote. "You seem to have become Mrs. Blatch." Mary Beard was also pleased with Lutz's work, and agreed to write a foreword. More than anyone else, she knew "Mrs. Blatch's inability to finish her own work . . . and therefore how 'wellnigh' impossible it would be for anyone else to finish it." But Lutz had done just that. "You have done marvelously with this job! It does represent Mrs. Blatch, to an extraordinary degree."[138]

Fittingly, the last description we have of Harriot Stanton Blatch is from Mary Beard. It is a harrowing portrait, emphasizing not only Harriot's failing health and ignominious aging, but her final loneliness, the tragic side of the inescapable solitude of human existence that her mother had elevated to a glorious if harsh truth of women's emancipation. Neither family bonds nor public service could save her from dying alone. Beard wrote, "She lies flat on her back, blind, unable to read, in worse loneliness than a person who had nobody in the world, because her daughter lives in the same place but visits her only occasionally. . . . The owner of the Nursing Home seems to take good physical care of her, as far as service and cleanliness go, but doesn't seem to have the slightest idea of the psychological need of a woman with Mrs. Blatch's active mind."[139]

Still, the woman Harriot Blatch had been showed through. "Her body is entirely wasted, all wrinkled skin," Beard continued, "only her face shows remnants of her great beauty and though her eyes are not quite clear, she doesn't realize that she can't see." This is a haunting observation, an apt metaphor for one of the most enduring dimensions of Harriot's character.

All her life, she had looked far ahead into the future, seeing what others could not. Nothing was more regularly observed by her admirers in these last years than her capacity for "great vision," her far-seeing insight into political and historical affairs.[140]

It is hard to escape the sense that these last months of Harriot Stanton Blatch's life and the final arrangements for the completion and publication of her memoirs were moving toward some sort of intertwined climax: as one was ending, the other was at last coming into being. As Harriot was leaving life, Alma Lutz and Mary Beard and Caroline Babcock were ensuring that she would enter history. Despite her almost total immobilization, she wanted to attend the celebration at Vassar of the seventy-fifth anniversary publications, including both her mother's biography and her own memoirs. Of course this was not possible, and while the books were being put before the public in Poughkeepsie, Harriot was in her nursing home bed in Greenwich.[141] Hopefully she was aware of what was happening and the completion of her memoirs provided her a with blessed sense of closure in her last months.

Six months after *Challenging Years* was published, Harriot Stanton Blatch died in the middle of the night, on November 20, 1940, in the Alcorn Nursing Home in Greenwich, Connecticut, just a few days after the 125th anniversary of her mother's birth. She was buried beside Elizabeth Stanton in Woodlawn Cemetery in New York City. The *New York Times* obituary highlighted her role as "leader of the radical wing of the woman's suffrage movement in the United States," her political inheritance from her mother, and her own stature as "one of the most fearlessly and rationally 'advanced'" of twentieth-century suffragists. Surprisingly, there was none of the common tendency of these years to understate the achievement of votes for women, to trivialize the passion and intelligence that the women of Harriot Blatch's generation had brought to politics, or to overlook the breadth and depth of their long lives of public service.[142] It was a summary of her life and work that she would probably have found satisfactory. And yet, if she had been able to have the last word (and she would have liked that very much), it would probably have been to name women's prospects in the era to come and to identify the tasks that a fighting feminist and democrat would need to undertake on their behalf.

Conclusion: Significance

In the mid-1930s, Mary Beard recalled "the old three-cornered struggle of Blatch-Catt-and-Paul" and wondered how best to capture it in the women's archives she was assembling.[1] Sixty years later, this is not how the last decade of the suffrage movement has come down to us. Rather, we learn of a two-way struggle between the militant Alice Paul and the moderate Carrie Chapman Catt, an antagonism so stark and compelling that it still holds historians in its partisan grasp. While the tension between two points can be powerful, the notion of a "three-cornered struggle" defining this period may be more productive. In contrast to two points, three corners allow for a full historical fabric, with patterns and strains that go in multiple directions. Inserting Harriot Stanton Blatch and all that she stands for into the history of suffragism breaks open the frequently repeated and oversimplified narratives of sexual solidarity, democratic triumph, and feminist heroism around which that history is structured and through which it still influences feminism in our time.

What was it, then, that Harriot Stanton Blatch represented in the history of woman suffrage and feminism more generally? Let us begin with a comparison of Blatch and Catt, since Harriot herself was so passionate and voluble about their differences. Both Catt and Blatch were skillful politicians. They understood the importance of bringing legislators around to their position, though Blatch was more willing to take on political opponents in open electoral contests, while Catt preferred behind-the-scenes lobbying to overt electoral challenge. These similarities of method, combined with great differences of temperament, help to account for the intensity of Harriot's criticisms of Catt. Blatch charged her rival with being unable or unwilling to strike out in new directions when suffragism was stalled, but eager to claim responsibility for changes once others had pioneered them. Perhaps the best way to distinguish the two is that for Harriot, feminism required challenging female conventionalities as well as male; by contrast Carrie Catt worked within established notions of womanliness. One historian has characterized the former as an innovator, the latter as a consolidator.[*]

When compared to Carrie Chapman Catt, Harriot Blatch seems to fit comfortably within the militant pole of twentieth-century suffragism. Yet when Alice Paul is introduced into the picture and Harriot Blatch's more subtle differences with her are considered, that simple, linear opposition gives way to a more complex set of relationships. While equally militant in style, Blatch and Paul had many differences. The most important is their relationship to other social movements of their time. Unlike Alice Paul and the tradition of single-issue feminism which she did so much to advance, Harriot Blatch insisted on the necessity of linking women's emancipation and other movements for social justice of her time. This is why she so frequently and proudly cited her mother's abolitionism: the mid-nineteenth-century bond between women's rights and antislavery embodied her conviction that women's rights grew along with the larger movement for democracy, drawing energy from ever new definitions of social equality and human liberty and extending its own sense of freedom for women in the process. Yet she was under no illusions that the relation between feminism and its parallel movements for social change would be harmonious. She expected women's demands to be ignored unless they struggled to have them recognized, and she understood that an independent feminist presence was necessary to bring women's concerns into the larger political picture. Even as she embarked on the campaign for economic equality that characterized her postsuffrage years, she knew without doubt that "the next big battle for women will be equality with men industrially" and she prepared herself for the conflict.[3]

From this perspective, Paul and Catt show similarities with each other (and differences from Blatch) since both kept their distance from contemporary progressive movements. For Catt it was the entanglements of external radicalisms that threatened feminism—as in her careful association of woman suffrage with prowar patriotism from 1915 through 1917. For Paul the threat was the male-centered nature of other movements, which she believed inevitably pushed women's issues to the sidelines; as other historians have argued, she was not so much against World War I as determined to remain neutral toward it.[4] But both Catt and Paul agreed that feminism must avoid linking itself too closely to other political challenges to the status quo. The distinction that separates Catt and Paul from Blatch can be seen most clearly with respect to class. The recognition of the importance of working-class women, which was so strong in the early years of the suffrage revival, all but disappeared in the final half-decade of the movement. Neither Paul nor Catt was nearly as influenced as Blatch by the labor movement in her understanding of women's reasons for suffrage activism.

By the 1930s, Mary Beard saw the fault lines of the history of suffragism this way: "Wasn't your mother's group far more radical than the Shaw-Catt-Paul brigade?" she wrote to Harriot.[5] Beard was making two points: that there was a distinct and continuous tendency running from the earlier suffrage period through the later, represented first by Stanton and then by Blatch; and that this strain was the "more radical" tendency in suffrage history. Through Harriot Blatch's life story, I have tried to show the development over time of this tendency, to trace the process of adaptation and modernization by which the liberal convictions of the mother—the equal rights understanding that underlay her far-seeing analysis of women's political, economic, marital, and religious subordination—became the socialist leanings of the daughter. The complex attachment Harriot had to her mother's legacy helped her to understand how the feminist aspirations that they shared must nonetheless change to fit with the times. This is undoubtedly what Mary Beard meant when she wrote to Harriot that she took comfort from their common conviction that the women's movement must always be rooted in the "fundamental economic thought" of the moment.[6] While Harriot revered her mother's thought and her contribution to women's rights, she recognized that, to stay vital and inspiring, twentieth-century feminism must go beyond the individualist, competitive vision of even the best of the nineteenth-century movement to reflect a more socially based understanding of women's freedom.

The limits of feminism are as historically specific as its aspirations. Those of us who come after can—and must—see these constraints more clearly than do the leaders of earlier eras. In Harriot's case, she recognized and worked hard to correct the class limits of her mother's vision. But her own consistently ethnocentric perspective, especially her discomfort with recent immigrants, is just as disturbing to us with our late twentieth-century perspective. The haughtiness and sense of Yankee superiority that she inherited from her mother underlay this tendency, but it was the larger shape of her era that allowed it such unlimited play. The exuberantly biologist thinking that flourished in the Progressive years, which feminists made such rich use of by way of their maternalist rhetoric, provided excellent soil for her ethnocentrism to flourish. By contrast, her abolitionist heritage and the revival of the black freedom movement in the early twentieth century ensured that her suffragism was much more inclusive when it came to African Americans. She had learned from the past, and in considering her place in history, so should we, in setting our sights on a more inclusive feminism.

Beard's comment also helps us to make distinctions within the radicalism of the final years of the suffrage movement and, because that movement looms so large as precedent for us, in our own stage of feminism. Paul's reputation for radicalism lay in her tactical inclination toward civil disobedience, in her willingness to break the law on behalf of women's rights. In addition, her single-mindedness, on behalf of first suffrage, then the Equal Rights Amendment, adds to her reputation for fierce feminism. Harriot Blatch's radicalism, in contrast, was less short-term tactical, more long-term strategic. Her radicalism was fundamentally rooted in her adherence to a general progressive sensibility, to the large vision of social change as it was articulated in her era. Her feminism rested in her insistence on the radical revision of women's lives and options as part of this social transformation, not in her conviction that changes in women's lives must be pursued separately and with absolute purity of commitment. This view, along with her passionate commitment to liberating women's untapped possibilities, was the essence of her suffragism, and of the feminism that invigorated it.

Thus, "radical feminism" may well be too imprecise, too apolitical a category to help us understand history or learn from it. Elsewhere I have used the term *left feminism* and I invoke it here too as the best framework for appreciating Harriot Blatch's historical significance. In writing about the pioneering women's historian Eleanor Flexner (whose book published in 1959 was the first to highlight Harriot Blatch's suffrage leadership), I defined left feminism as a combination of the "recognition of the systematic oppression of women," the "appreciation of other structures of power underlying American society," and "an understanding that the realization of genuine equality for women, all women, requires a radical challenge of American society."[7] The term is related to the 1970s category of socialist feminism with which I identified my own feminism at its origin. But I think left feminism is a more useful concept, because it is more historically expansive, more helpful in analyzing the past, and hopefully more productive in understanding the future.

Though Harriot Blatch was more intimately linked to the history of women's struggle for emancipation than most of us, it was a remarkably complex process for her to find her own place and her best voice in it. Her struggle to make the past speak to the future thus is an example for the struggle we all must make.

Abbreviations for Manuscript Collections

AC-NY   Mrs. Robert Abbe Collection, Rare Book Room, New York Public Library

AL-NY   Alma Lutz Papers, Vassar College, Poughkeepsie, New York

AP-CA   Alice Park Collection, Huntington Library, San Marino, California

BH-Mass   Babcock-Hurlburt Papers, Schlesinger Library, Cambridge, Massachusetts

CC-CA   Clara Colby Papers, Huntington Library, San Marino, California

CCC-LC   Carrie Chapman Catt Papers, Manuscript Division, Library of Congress

EBH-CA   Elizabeth Boynton Harbert Papers, Huntington Library, San Marino, California

ECS-LC   Elizabeth Cady Stanton Papers, Manuscript Division, Library of Congress

ECS-NY   Elizabeth Cady Stanton Papers, Vassar College, Poughkeepsie, New York

HBL-Mass Harriet Burton Laidlaw Papers, Schlesinger Library, Cambridge, Massachusetts

HSB-LC   Harriot Stanton Blatch Papers, Manuscript Division, Library of Congress

HSB-NY   Harriot Stanton Blatch Papers, Vassar College, Poughkeepsie, New York

IHH-CA   Ida Husted Harper Papers, Huntington Library, San Marino, California

LOR-Mass Leonora O'Reilly Papers, Schlesinger Library, Cambridge, Massachusetts

NAWSA-LC National American Woman Suffrage Association Papers, Manuscript Division, Library of Congress

NWP-ERA National Woman's Party–Equal Rights Years, Microfilming Corporation of America

NWP-SY   National Woman's Party–Suffrage Years, Microfilming Corporation of America

NYWTUL   New York Women's Trade Union League Papers, Research Publications Microfilm

RBJ-CT   Rhoda Barney Jenkins Papers, Greenwich, Connecticut

SBA-CA   Susan B. Anthony Memorial Collection, Huntington Library, San Marino, California

SBA-LC   Susan B. Anthony Papers, Manuscript Division, Library of Congress

TS-NJ   Theodore Stanton Papers, Douglass College, New Brunswick, New Jersey

WSP-NY   Woman's Suffrage Party Papers, Columbia University, New York City

Notes

Introduction

1. The call was published in its entirety in the National Woman's Party journal, *Equal Rights*, January 4, 1935, pp. 347–49. All subsequent quotations not otherwise identified are taken from it. A typescript can be found in BH-Mass.

2. Alma Louise McGraw to Carrie Chapman Catt, December 7, 1935, reel 3, NAWSA-LC.

3. Harriot made a similar point in an interview she gave after the anniversary celebration. Hope Ridings Miller, "Lecturer Sees Women Losing Hard-Won Rights," *Washington Post*, April 18, 1936, n.p., HSB-NY.

4. "Mrs. Blatch, at 80, Hits at 'Mossbacks,'" *New York Times*, January 21, 1936, p. 25.

5. Harriot Blatch to Caroline Lexow Babcock, June 23, 1938, BH-Mass.

Chapter One: Daughter

1. Harriot Stanton Blatch and Alma Lutz, *Challenging Years: The Memoirs of Harriot Stanton Blatch* (New York: G. P. Putnam's Sons, 1940), pp. 2–3, 4.

2. Angelina Grimké Weld to Elizabeth Cady Stanton, December 9, 1852, TS-NJ.

3. Elizabeth Cady Stanton to Lucretia Mott, October 22, 1852, enclosed in a letter from Elizabeth Cady Stanton to Margaret Stanton Lawrence, c. 1882, RBJ-CT.

4. Elisabeth Griffith, *In Her Own Right: The Life of Elizabeth Cady Stanton* (Oxford: Oxford University Press, 1984), p. 88.

5. Blatch and Lutz, *Challenging Years*, p. 3; Elizabeth Stanton to Antoinette Brown Blackwell, March 13, [1861], Blackwell Family Papers, Schlesinger Library, Cambridge, Mass.

6. Stanton to Elizabeth Smith Miller, [January 24, 1856], ECS-NY.

7. Stanton to Martha Coffin Wright, [December 17, 1855], Garrison Family Papers, Sophia Smith Collection, Smith College, Northampton, Mass.

8. There are several extant versions of this letter, none of them the original. This version, identified as a letter from Stanton to Anthony, June 10, 1856, comes from Theodore Stanton and Harriot Stanton Blatch, eds., *Elizabeth Cady Stanton as Revealed in Her Letters, Diary and Reminiscences*, v. 1, (New York: Harper & Brothers, 1922), p. 66. All versions can be found in Patricia G. Holland and Ann D. Gordon, eds., *Papers of Elizabeth Cady Stanton and Susan B. Anthony* (Wilmington, Del.: Scholarly Resources, 1990); I am grateful to this mammoth project for its detailed and dependable work at discovering, identifying, and dating multiple versions of this and many other Stanton-Anthony documents. Stanton destroyed many of her papers, and those that were left were subject to an even more severe winnowing and editing by Harriot and Theodore.

9. Stanton to Anthony, [April 1855], "Early Letters of Elizabeth Cady Stanton," ed. Ida Husted Harper, *Independent*, v. 55, May 21, 1903, p. 1189.

10. Elizabeth Stanton to Anthony, November 2, 1857, TS-NJ.

11. Elizabeth Stanton to Anthony, July 4, 1858, TS-NJ.

12. Henry B. Stanton to Elizabeth Stanton, January 18, 1857, ECS-LC. A more typical letter, dated January 7, 1862, focused entirely on admonitions to his sons.

13. Margaret Stanton Lawrence, "As a Mother," *New Era*, November 1885, p. 323.

14. Interview with Harriet de Forest, Londonderry, Vt., July 14, 1985.

15. Stanton to Anthony, August 20, 1857, quoted in Alma Lutz, *Created Equal: A Biography of Elizabeth Cady Stanton, 1815–1902* (New York: John Day, 1940), p. 104; Anthony to Antoinette Brown Blackwell, September 4, 1858, quoted in Griffith, *In Her Own Right*, p. 96.

16. Stanton to Anthony, April 10, 1859, reprinted in Ellen Carol DuBois, ed., *The Elizabeth Cady Stanton—Susan B. Anthony Reader*, 2d ed. (Boston: Northeastern University Press, 1992), p. 68.

17. Blatch and Lutz, *Challenging Years*, pp. 5–6.

18. In 1885, in a birthday message to her mother, Margaret observed that "to write of a mother loved, honored, worshiped, as mine is by me, is so like viewing one's self subjectively and unveiling to others what is most sacred in the solitude of individual life, that I will leave the recording angel to write down all that is best of her" (Lawrence, "As a Mother"). Note the phrase about "the solitude of individual life," which anticipates the powerful, and very psychological, feminist message of Stanton's "Solitude of Self" (1892). Even so Margaret had more to say about her relationship with her mother (and Elizabeth's with Margaret) than did Harriot. See Margaret Stanton Lawrence, "Elizabeth Cady Stanton," speech, 1915, AL-NY.

19. Lawrence, "As a Mother."

20. Ibid., p. 322.

21. Blatch and Lutz, *Challenging Years*, pp. 10, 14.

22. For one rather acerbic opinion on Stanton's prejudice in favor of girls, see the unpublished "Reminiscences" of Robert Brewster Stanton, New York Public Library.

23. "The Lectures," *Greenfield [Iowa] Transcript*, January 24, 1880, n.p., ECS-LC.

24. Robert B. Stanton, "Reminiscences."

25. Stanton to Elizabeth Smith Miller, December 1, 1858, ECS-LC.

26. Blatch and Lutz, *Challenging Years*, p. 27.

27. Harriot characterized Margaret as too "loyal" to the opinions of others (ibid., p. 18).

28. Ibid., pp. 25–27.

29. In a letter to a young friend, Elizabeth Dwight Eaton, Elizabeth Stanton good-naturedly wished to be relieved of "the children, who continue to romp & scream, to laugh & joke, to fight & bite, to be witty & fitty, to teaze [sic] each other & ridicule their mother" (August 14, 1861, Alice Paul Papers, Schlesinger Library, Cambridge, Mass.).

30. Elizabeth Stanton to Elizabeth Smith Miller, spring of 1870, TS-NJ.

31. Blatch and Lutz, *Challenging Years*, pp. 4–5.

32. Harriot Stanton, speech to National Woman Suffrage Association meetings in Omaha, Neb., September 3, 1882, as reprinted in Elizabeth Stanton, Susan B. Anthony, and Matilda J. Gage, eds., *History of Woman Suffrage*, v. 3 (Rochester: Susan B. Anthony, 1886), pp. 247–49.

33. Elizabeth Stanton to Elizabeth Miller, January 24, 1856, ECS-NY.

34. Lawrence, "As a Mother."

35. Thanks to Rhoda Jenkins, Greenwich, Conn., for showing me Margaret's copy of Harriot's *A Woman's Point of View: Some Roads to Peace*, which is full of these clippings.

36. Blatch and Lutz, *Challenging Years*, pp. 17–18.

37. Interview with Harriet de Forest.

38. Harriot Eaton Stanton, diary, July 1881, RBJ-CT.

39. Interview with Harriet de Forest.

40. Blatch and Lutz, *Challenging Years*, p. 6.

41. Ibid., pp. 8–10.

42. Ibid., p. 6.

43. Elizabeth Cady Stanton, *Eighty Years and More: The Reminiscences of Elizabeth Cady Stanton, 1815–1897* (New York: T. Fisher Unwin, 1898), p. 3.

44. Blatch and Lutz, *Challenging Years*, pp. 16–20.

45. Laura Bullard, "Elizabeth Cady Stanton," in *Our Famous Women*, ed. Bullard, 1888, as quoted in Griffith, *In Her Own Right*, p. 223.

46. Margaret Stanton Lawrence, "Elizabeth Cady Stanton, 1815–1902, a Sketch of Her Life by Her Elder Daughter and an Afterword by Her Younger Daughter," 1915, p. 2, AL-NY.

47. Blatch and Lutz, *Challenging Years*, pp. 18–20; Stanton, *Eighty Years and More*, pp. 32–33.

48. Blatch and Lutz, *Challenging Years*, p. 20.

49. Ibid., p. 6.

50. Ibid., pp. 6–7, 20.

51. Harriot Blatch to Alma Lutz, June 27, 1937, AL-NY; Lutz, *Created Equal*, pp. 16–17.

52. Blatch and Lutz, *Challenging Years*, pp. 10–11, 22.

53. Ibid., p. 14.

54. One of many examples is the letter from Harriot to Elizabeth of October 29, 1885, published in the *Woman's Tribune*, v. 3, December 1885, p. 2.

55. Blatch and Lutz, *Challenging Years*, p. 13.

56. Ibid., pp. 13–15. These same biases characterize Harriot and Theodore's editing of their mother's letters and autobiography, which minimizes Anthony's role in the women's joint political efforts; see Amy Dykeman, "To Pour Forth My Own Experience: Two Versions of Elizabeth Cady Stanton," *Journal of Rutgers University Library*, v. 44, June 1982, p. 9.

57. Blatch and Lutz, *Challenging Years*, pp. 13–14.

58. Griffith, *In Her Own Right*, p. 107.

59. Samuel Wilkenson to John, May 31, 1865, Wilkenson Family Collection, Buffalo and Erie County Historical Society, Buffalo, N.Y.

60. Griffith, *In Her Own Right*, p. 116.

61. Blatch and Lutz, *Challenging Years*, p. 17.

62. Elizabeth Stanton to Nancy Smith, July 20, 1863, TS-NJ.

63. Blatch and Lutz, *Challenging Years*, p. 15.

64. Ibid., p. 13.

65. Ibid.

66. Florence Kelley, "My Philadelphia," *Survey*, October 1, 1926, p. 7.

67. Jane Addams, *Twenty Years at Hull House* (New York: Macmillan, 1910), p. 31.

68. Elizabeth Stanton to Gerrit Smith, January 29, 1869, George Arents Library, Syracuse University, Syracuse, N.Y.

69. Stanton to Martha Coffin Wright, March 21, 1871, TS-NJ.

70. Anthony to Isabella Beecher Hooker, November 16, 1872, reprinted in *New York Tribune*, September 19, 1874, p. 2. Harriot may have known a great deal of internal women's rights scandal and gossip that she never divulged, even in her final decade, when she was preoccupied with the history of the woman suffrage movement.

71. Elizabeth Stanton to Margaret, December 1, 1872, TS-NJ; also cited in Lutz, *Created Equal*, pp. 202–3.

72. Blatch and Lutz, *Challenging Years*, p. 24.

73. Ibid., p. 31.

74. Ibid., pp. 31–32.

75. Margaret Stanton Lawrence, "Life of Mrs. Harriot Stanton Blatch," *Johnstown Herald*, September 20, 1915, p. 145, HSB-LC; Elizabeth Cady Stanton to Elizabeth Miller, summer of 1870, TS-NJ. Harriot left this episode out of her autobiography.

76. Blatch and Lutz, *Challenging Years*, pp. 32–33; Vassar College Alumnae Association Biographical Records Questionnaire, College Archives, Vassar College, Poughkeepsie, N.Y.

77. Blatch and Lutz, *Challenging Years*, pp. 10, 21–22.

78. Lawrence, "Life of Harriot Stanton Blatch," and recalled by both Rhoda Barney Jenkins and Harriet de Forest in interviews with the author.

79. Florence Kelley, "When Coeducation Was Young," *Survey*, February 1, 1927, p. 557.

80. Stanton to Kate Field, September 1, 1877, TS-NJ.

81. Helen Horowitz, *Alma Mater: Design and Experience in the Women's Colleges from Their Nineteenth Century Beginnings to the 1930s* (New York: Knopf, 1984), p. 56; Barbara M. Solomon, *In the Company of Educated Women: A History of Women and Higher Education in America* (New Haven: Yale University Press, 1985), p. 62.

82. Horowitz, *Alma Mater*, p. 56.

83. Marjorie Housepian Dobkin, ed., *The Making of a Feminist: Early Journals and Letters of M. Carey Thomas* (Kent, Ohio: Kent State University Press, 1979), September 23, 1877, p. 121.

84. Elizabeth Stanton, "Coeducation," *Woman's Journal*, November 1873, n.p.

85. Stanton to Elizabeth Smith Miller, August 10, 1870, in *Stanton as Revealed in Her Letters*, pp. 128–29.

86. Edward Hicks Magill, *Sixty-five Years in the Life of a Teacher, 1841–1907* (Boston: Houghton Mifflin, 1907), p. 149.

87. Charlotte Wilson Conable, *Women at Cornell: The Myth of Equal Education* (Ithaca: Cornell University Press, 1977), p. 36.

88. Elizabeth Stanton to Ezra Cornell, February 13, [1872], University Archives, Cornell University, Ithaca, N.Y.

89. Blatch and Lutz, *Challenging Years*, pp. 34–36.

90. Dobkin, *Making of a Feminist*, November 21, 1875, p. 107.

91. *Seventh Annual Catalogue of Vassar College* (Poughkeepsie, N.Y., 1871–72), p. 14; Harriot was also listed in the eighth and ninth catalogues as a preparatory student and did not enroll in the regular collegiate program until 1874.

92. Blatch and Lutz, *Challenging Years*, p. 36; interview with Harriet de Forest.

93. In a passage in the *History of Woman Suffrage* (v. 3, p. 398), presumably written by Elizabeth Stanton after her daughters had graduated from Vassar, Cornell is contrasted as "more richly endowed than Vassar and in every way superior in its environs."

94. Horowitz, *Alma Mater*, p. 41.

95. Solomon, *In the Company of Educated Women*, p. 89.

96. James Monroe Taylor and Elizabeth Hazelton Haight, *Vassar* (New York: Oxford University Press, 1915), p. 72; Professor Backus's obituary for Raymond, as quoted in Horowitz, *Alma Mater*, p. 59.

97. Taylor and Haight, *Vassar*, p. 93.

98. Horowitz, *Alma Mater*, p. 39.

99. Blatch and Lutz, *Challenging Years*, pp. 34–36.

100. Mary Beard to Alma Lutz, April 15, 1940, AL-NY.

101. Blatch and Lutz, *Challenging Years*, pp. 32–38. Elizabeth to Harriot Stanton, March 11, 1877, TS-NJ. Although Harriot's lack of student activity in her freshman and sophomore years at Vassar constitutes corroborating evidence of her alienation, it still seems possible that she exaggerated her hatred of Vassar in her autobiography. She taught a course there in the 1890s, was active in alumnae activities in the 1930s, and her granddaughter remembers that her grandmother wanted her to go there (Harriet de Forest interview). Also see her correspondence with Helen Kendrick, February 21 and April 19, 1886, Vassar College Library.

102. Elizabeth wrote to Theodore in 1873 that "the ordinary young girls are not worth your thought or attention" (TS-NJ).

103. Blatch and Lutz, *Challenging Years*, p. 36.

104. In a public statement to a women's rights audience (her first) in 1882, Harriot wrote, "Having been reared in a large family of boys where we enjoyed equal freedom, and having received the same collegiate education as my brothers, it is not until lately that I have felt the crime of my womanhood." Stanton to the National Woman Suffrage Association, Omaha, September 3, 1883, quoted in *History of Woman Suffrage*, v. 3, pp. 247–49.

105. Denise Riley calls this a "virtuous apartheid of sex" (*"Am I That Name?" Feminism and the Category of "Women" in History* [Minneapolis: University of Minnesota Press, 1988], p. 54).

106. From Harriot Eaton Stanton's grade records, 1874–88, thanks to Dean Nancy Schrom Dye and the registrar's office, Vassar College, for help in locating and interpreting the records.

107. Blatch and Lutz, *Challenging Years*, p. 39.

108. Sally Gregory Kohlstedt, "Maria Mitchell: The Advancement of Women in Science," *New England Quarterly*, v. 41, no. 1, March 1978, pp. 39–63.

109. Anthony to Rush Ries, president, University of Rochester, November 20, 1900, AL-NY.

110. Blatch and Lutz, *Challenging Years*, p. 30.

111. Ibid., pp. 36–39.

112. Alma Lutz notes, interview with Harriot Blatch, June 15, 1939, AL-NY.

113. Elizabeth Stanton to Harriot, November 8, 1876, TS-NJ.

114. "Home Matters," *Vassar Miscellany*, v. 6, no. 4, July 1877, p. 243; ibid., v. 6, no. 2, January 1877, p. 107; "Poems, Prophecies and Histories: Class of 1878, Vassar College during Fresh, Sophomore and Junior Years," and Miss Rollins, "Vassar Class of 78, The Past," *Vassariana* 1878, pp. 38–39, 57–58.

115. Blatch and Lutz, *Challenging Years*, pp. 36–38.

116. "Poems, Prophecies and Histories," pp. 38–39.

117. Blatch and Lutz, *Challenging Years*, p. 42.

118. "Home Matters," *Vassar Miscellany*, v. 6, no. 4, July 1877, p. 229 and v. 7, no. 2, November 15, 1877, p. 265.

119. See Harriot Ransom's Vassar notebooks and travel diaries, Buffalo and Erie County Historical Society.

120. I am very grateful to Alice and Arthur Ransom Milinowski of Fort Erie, Ontario, for information on Arthur's grandmother, and for sharing their photographs of the two friends with me.

121. Harriot Stanton, 1881 diary, RBJ-CT.

122. Elizabeth to Harriot, January 8, 1879, TS-NJ; see also Elizabeth to Harriot, March 25, 1879, ECS-NY.

123. Elizabeth to Harriot, August 1877, TS-NJ.

124. Elizabeth to Harriot, March 12, 1878, TS-NJ. Note that we have these letters because Harriot, along with Theodore, saved and transcribed them. They obviously meant something important to Harriot in later years, although exactly what we cannot know.

125. Elizabeth to Margaret, autumn 1878, TS-NJ.

126. Harriot Stanton Blatch, review of *Two College Girls* by Helen Brown, in *Englishwoman's Review*, May 15, 1885, p. 214.

127. Lawrence, "Life of Harriot Stanton Blatch," p. 146.

128. "H. E. Stanton," from Rollins, "Vassar Class of 78," pp. 57–58.

129. Elizabeth to Harriot, March 12, 1878, TS-NJ.

130. Lawrence, "Life of Harriot Stanton Blatch."

131. Rhoda Barney Jenkins to the author, September 7, 1995.

132. Elizabeth Stanton to Lucy Stone, October 26, 1878, May-Goddard Papers, Schlesinger Library, Cambridge, Mass.

133. Elizabeth to Harriot, March 25, 1879, ECS-NY.

134. Elizabeth to Harriot, March 1879, TS-NJ.

135. Notice, *National Citizen and Ballot Box*, July 1879; thanks to Ann D. Gordon for this reference.

136. Advertising leaflet for "Transcontinental Tour of Harriot Stanton Blatch," HSB-NY.

137. "The Lectures," *Greenfield [Iowa] Transcript*, January 24, 1880, ECS-LC.

138. Alma Lutz interview with Harriot Blatch, n.d. [c. 1939], AL-NY; also Lawrence, "Life of Harriot Stanton Blatch."

139. Notice, *National Citizen and Ballot Box*, April 1880; "Edmund Burke," *Daily Nonpareil* (Council Bluffs, Iowa), February 17, 1880, n.p., scrapbook 10, SBA-LC; "Woman's Kingdom," *Inter Ocean Chicago*, March 6, 1880, n.p., from *Papers of Elizabeth Cady Stanton and Susan B. Anthony*.

140. Lutz interview with Blatch, c. 1939.

141. Susan B. Anthony to Mrs. Spencer, n.d. [spring 1880], in Ida H. Harper, *The Life and Work of Susan B. Anthony*, v. 2 (Indianapolis: Bowen-Merrill, 1899), pp. 515–16.

142. Susan B. Anthony to Margaret Livingston Stanton Lawrence, after January 24, 1880, Blanche Ames Papers, Schlesinger Library, Cambridge, Mass.

143. Blatch and Lutz, *Challenging Years*, pp. 45–46; the episode begins the long chapter on Harriot's years in Europe. The only corroborating evidence of any of these interviews is a letter from Elizabeth Stanton referring to Harriot's request for her mother to arrange for her to see Ralph Waldo Emerson and Thomas Higginson. The correspondence makes no mention of an interview with Garrison. Apparently, Harriot also asked to see several women, including Edna Dow Cheney and Louisa May Alcott (Elizabeth Stanton to Lucy Stone, October 26, 1878, May-Goddard Papers; and Elizabeth to Harriot, January 8, 1879, TS-NJ).

144. Blatch and Lutz, *Challenging Years*, p. 46.

145. Alma Lutz to Harriot Blatch, November 20, 1931, with Blatch answers, AL-NY.

146. Elizabeth Stanton to Amelia Bloomer, July 25 [1880], Amelia Bloomer Papers, Seneca Falls Historical Society, Seneca Falls, N Y.

147. Elizabeth to Harriot, July 15, 1880, TS-NJ.

Chapter Two: Vocation

1. Addams's classic account can be found in *Twenty Years at Hull House* (New York: Macmillan, 1910). My own research into Harriot Blatch's life has been paralleled closely by two new major biographies of Thomas and Kelley: Helen Lefkowitz Horowitz, *The Passion and Power of M. Carey Thomas* (New York: Knopf, 1994), and Kathryn Kish Sklar, *Florence Kelley and the Nation's Work* (New Haven: Yale University Press, 1995). Also see Mary Church Terrell, *A Colored Woman in a White World* (Washington, D.C.: C. Ransdell, 1940).

2. Theodore Stanton, ed., *The Woman Question in Europe: A Series of Original Essays* (New York: G. P. Putnam's Sons, 1884).

3. Harriot Stanton Blatch and Alma Lutz, *Challenging Years: The Memoirs of Harriot Stanton Blatch* (New York: G. P. Putnam's Sons, 1940), pp. 45–46.

4. Elizabeth Stanton to "my precious chicks," June 11, 1880, TS-NJ.

5. Elizabeth Cady Stanton, *Eighty Years and More: The Reminiscences of Elizabeth Cady Stanton, 1815–1897* (New York: T. Fisher Unwin, 1898), p. 325.

6. Elizabeth Stanton to Harriot Eaton Stanton, November 12, 1880, TS-NJ.

7. Blatch and Lutz, *Challenging Years*, pp. 48–52.

8. Ibid., p. 46.

9. Elizabeth Stanton to Professor William Channing Russell, April 26, 1881, in the possession of Lisa Unger Baskin and reproduced in Patricia G. Holland and Ann D. Gordon, eds., *Papers of Elizabeth Cady Stanton and Susan B. Anthony* (Wilmington, Del.: Scholarly Resources, 1990).

10. Harriot Ransom, diary, November 28, 1880, Buffalo and Erie County Historical Society, Buffalo, N.Y.

11. Blatch and Lutz, *Challenging Years*, p. 46.

12. Ibid., pp. 48–50.

13. There are two leather-covered, handwritten diaries, which are in the possession of Rhoda Barney Jenkins, of Greenwich, Conn., who kindly allowed me full access to them. The first diary runs from November 1880, six months after Harriot arrived in Berlin, through her travels in Italy, Switzerland, and France, and ending in August 1881 in Paris. The second diary begins soon after, ceases during the time that Harriot was in the United States, and concentrates on the period from June through August 1882, when she returned with her mother to Toulouse. Elizabeth began a diary at just about the same time as her daughter, in November 1880. Although Elizabeth's diary is only available to us in edited form, and Harriot herself was the editor, there are enough correlations between the diaries of mother and daughter, similar subjects and opinions appearing at similar times, to suggest a regular exchange of ideas between them (Theodore Stanton and Harriot Stanton Blatch, eds., *Elizabeth Cady Stanton, as Revealed in Her Letters, Diary and Reminiscences* [New York: Harper & Brothers, 1922]).

14. "The Solitude of Self" (*Woman's Column*, January 1892, pp. 2–3) remains Stanton's fullest statement of this philosophy; but also see her opinions on the sexual scandal surrounding the Irish patriot Charles Parnell ("Patriotism and Chastity," *Westminister Review*, v. 135, 1891, pp. 1–5).

15. Harriot Stanton, diary, n.d. [c. October 1881], RBJ-CT.

16. Ibid., July 19, 1881.

17. Ibid., September 10, 1881.

18. Ibid., May 31, 1881.

19. Blatch to Maria Mitchell, September 2, 1883 (in *Vassar Miscellany*, October 1883, p. 573): "I offer my pittance to the Observatory not only because it is presided over by one for whom I have the highest esteem but because at its head is a woman."

20. Harriot Stanton, diary, July 24 and 26, 1881, RBJ-CT.

21. Elizabeth Stanton to Hatty (also spelled Hattie), July 15, 1888, IS-NJ.

22. Harriot Stanton, diary, n.d. [after August 4, 1881], RBJ-CT.

23. Ibid., June 30, 1881.

24. Ibid., July 2, 1881. In her concern to find an aspect of "the ideal" that would not wilt under inspection, Harriot was influenced by Kantian thinking, perhaps as filtered through the ideas of one of her mother's favorite spiritual thinkers, Felix Adler (Horace L. Friess, *Felix Adler and Ethical Culture: Memories and Studies* [New York: Columbia University Press, 1981], p. 53).

25. Harriot Stanton, diary, n.d. [c. August 1, 1881], RBJ-CT.

26. Ibid., August 19, 1881.

27. Like many other Anglo-Americans who rejected Christianity, Harriot was intrigued by Eastern religions, which seemed exotic and mysterious without being familiar and foolish. Her personal library contained a copy of *The Wisdom of Wu Ming Fu* (New York: Henry Holt, 1931), ed. Stanford Cobb (RBJ-CT).

28. A fine account of this change, from the perspective of British feminism, can be found in Denise Riley, *"Am I That Name?" Feminism and the Category of "Women" in History* (Minneapolis: University of Minnesota Press, 1988), ch. 4.

29. Harriot Stanton, diary, July 19, 1882, RBJ-CT.

30. Ibid., June 25, 1881.

31. Ibid., November 26, 1880. Harriot devoted one of the longest sections of her first diary to her translation of an unpublished essay by Charles Fourier, in which human difference, complex social organization, and antiauthoritarianism are idiosyncratically combined in an elaborate blueprint for a fantastic, cooperative society. For an anti-Catholic comment, see June 25, 1881, diary entry.

32. Cynthia Eagle Russett, *Sexual Science: The Victorian Construction of Womanhood* (Cambridge, Mass.: Harvard University Press, 1989).

33. Harriot Stanton, diary, May 20, 1881, RBJ-CT.

34. William Leach traces this shift in Stanton's thought in *True Love and Perfect Union: The Feminist Reform of Sex and Society* (New York: Basic Books, 1980), pp. 133–57.

35. Harriot Stanton, diary, n.d. [c. December 1880], RBJ-CT.

36. Ibid., August 4, 1881.

37. Ibid., June 23, 1881.

38. Ibid., November 26, 1880.

39. *Elizabeth Cady Stanton as Revealed in Her Letters*, November 26, 1882, p. 198.

40. Blatch, "Unsolved Problems," *Woman's Tribune*, June 1887.

41. Harriot Stanton, diary, September 1881, RBJ-CT.

42. Ibid., n.d. [c. December 1880].

43. Ibid., November 26, 1880.

44. Elizabeth Stanton to Elizabeth Smith Miller, June 3, n.y., TS-NJ.

45. Elizabeth Stanton to Amelia Bloomer, July 25 [1880], Amelia Bloomer Papers, Seneca Falls Historical Society, Seneca Falls, N.Y.

46. Harriot Stanton, diary, November 26, 1880, RBJ-CT.

47. Ibid., November 15 and 26, 1880.

48. Ibid., November 26, 1880.

49. Ibid., November 26, 1880. A letter from Elizabeth to Harriot speaks of sending Harriot a letter from Channing considering this relation between sex and religion (April 17, 1881, TS-NJ).

50. Wolf Lepenies, *Between Literature and Science: The Rise of Sociology* (Cambridge: Cambridge University Press, 1988).

51. Harriot Stanton, diary, n.d. [before May 5, 1881], RBJ-CT. At about the same time, Elizabeth wrote to her cousin Elizabeth Smith Miller that she had just read the life of Eliot, and was greatly moved by the story of her love affair with George Henry Lewis (Stanton to Elizabeth Smith Miller, June 3, n.y., TS-NJ).

52. Theodore Stanton, *The Woman Question in Europe.*

53. Blatch and Lutz, *Challenging Years*, p. 56.

54. Ibid., p. 57.

55. Ibid., p. 60.

56. Thomas R. Osborne, *A Grande Ecole for the Grands Corps: The Recruitment and Training of the French Administrative Elite in the Nineteenth Century* (Boulder: Social Science Monographs, 1983).

57. Harriot Stanton, diary, September 10, 1881, RBJ-CT.

58. Ibid.

59. Blatch and Lutz, *Challenging Years*, p. 61.

60. Osborne, *A Grand Ecole*, p. 85.

61. Harriot Stanton, letter to suffrage convention, September 3, 1882, in Elizabeth Cady Stanton, Susan B. Anthony, and Matilda J. Gage, eds., *History of Woman Suffrage*, v. 3 (Rochester: Susan B. Anthony, 1886), p. 247.

62. Blatch and Lutz, *Challenging Years*, p. 61.

63. Harriot Stanton, letter to suffrage convention, September 3, 1882, *History of Woman Suffrage*, v. 3, p. 247.

64. Addams, *Twenty Years at Hull House*, p. 119.

65. Blatch and Lutz, *Challenging Years*, p. 61.

66. Ibid., pp. 64–65. Harriot's only other description of the meeting is in a questionnaire she filled out for Alma Lutz (n.d. [c. 1935], AL-NY) in which she describes Harry as terribly seasick, the most "hopeless case" she had ever seen, and that his illness "interested" her.

67. Ibid.

68. Theodore Stanton to Elizabeth Boynton Harbert, July 17, 1881, EBH-CA.

69. Elizabeth Stanton to Lillie Devereux Blake, n.d. [December 30, 1881], Lillie Devereux Blake Papers, Missouri Historical Society, St. Louis.

70. Susan B. Anthony to Harriot Hanson Robinson, February 21, 1882, Robinson-Shattuck Papers, Schlesinger Library, Cambridge, Mass.

71. Blatch and Lutz, *Challenging Years*, pp. 61–62.

72. Ida Husted Harper to Carrie Chapman Catt, November 10, 1930, reel 4, CCC-LC.

73. Blatch and Lutz, *Challenging Years*, pp. 62–63.

74. Leach, *True Love and Perfect Union*; Marjorie Spruill Wheeler, "Sex, Science and the 'Woman Question': The *Woman's Journal* on Woman's Nature and Potential," unpublished paper, 1980.

75. Harriot Blatch to Alma Lutz, n.d. [c. 1933], AL-NY.

76. Anthony, as quoted in Ida H. Harper, *The Life and Work of Susan B. Anthony*, v. 2 (Indianapolis: Bowen-Merrill, 1899), p. 536.

77. *Elizabeth Cady Stanton as Revealed in Her Letters*, November 18, 1880, p. 179.

78. Susan B. Anthony to Elizabeth Boynton Harbert, May 23, 1882, EBH-CA.

79. Elizabeth Cady Stanton, *Eighty Years and More*, p. 337.

80. Blatch and Lutz, *Challenging Years*, p. 63.

81. Elizabeth Cady Stanton, *Eighty Years and More*, p. 341.

82. *Elizabeth Cady Stanton as Revealed in Her Letters*, July 20, 1882, p. 192.

83. Blatch and Lutz, *Challenging Years*, pp. 63–64.

84. Harriot Stanton, diary, July 19, 1882, RBJ-CT.

85. Ibid., September 2, 1882.

86. Blatch and Lutz, *Challenging Years*, p. 64.

87. Ibid., p. 65.

88. George Washburn Smalley to Elizabeth Cady Stanton, October 27, 1882, TS-NJ.

89. Blatch and Lutz, *Challenging Years*, p. 58.

90. William H. Channing to Elizabeth Cady Stanton, November 3, 1882, ECS-LC.

91. Priscilla Bright McClaren to Elizabeth Stanton, October 29, 1882, ECS-LC.

92. Harriot Eaton Stanton to Moncure Conway, November 3, 1882, Conway Collection, Columbia University, New York.

93. Priscilla Bright McClaren to Elizabeth Cady Stanton, November 14, 1882, ECS-NY.

94. Elizabeth Stanton to Marguerite Berry Stanton, April 20, 1881, TS-NJ.

95. Elizabeth Cady Stanton, *Eighty Years and More*, p. 351.

96. Conway to Elizabeth Stanton, November 13, 1882, ECS-LC.

97. *Elizabeth Cady Stanton as Revealed in Her Letters*, November 13, 1882, p. 196. The date, supplied by Harriot as editor, is wrong. See note 99 of this chapter.

98. Harriot Ransom Milinowski to Paul Ransom, n.d., Buffalo and Erie County Historical Society.

99. Blatch and Lutz, *Challenging Years*, p. 65. The actual date of the wedding as November 15 was verified by a copy of the marriage certificate from the General Register Office, London.

100. Interview with Harriet de Forest, Londonderry, Vt., July 14, 1985.

101. Anthony, diary, March 10 and 11, 1883, SBA-LC.

102. The breakfast menu can be found in a scrapbook in TS-NJ. Ann D. Gordon was kind enough to examine this collection for me and discover this particularly delicious historical morsel.

103. Blatch and Lutz, *Challenging Years*, pp. 77–79.

104. Elizabeth Stanton to Ann Miller, January 1, 1883, TS-NJ.

105. Interview with Harriet de Forest.

106. Blatch and Lutz, *Challenging Years*, p. 66.

107. William Henry Blatch, Sr., obituary, *Hants and Berks Gazette*, May 14, 1892; he was mayor of Basingstoke in 1880. An extraordinarily detailed will reveals his desire to control his children, even after death (Public Record Office, Central London). The mother of all of William Henry, Sr.'s children was named Catherine Mary Edney; the genealogy does not list her death date. Subsequently, he had three other wives. All this information comes from the Blatch family genealogy, prepared by Derek Conran and provided to me by Rhoda Barney Jenkins.

108. Blatch and Lutz, *Challenging Years*, p. 86.

109. Ibid., pp. 69–70. Harriot told her children and grandchildren a story about Alice that reflects her criticism of the subordination of unmarried women within their families. Because Alice was not expected to marry, all of the family silver was left to her, Harriot's daughter Nora recalled, "as on her death it would all come back to roost." But then she married, predeceased her husband, and all of the family treasures ended up the property of another woman when he remarried. "And not a teaspoon of the old 18th and 19th century silver or even grandfather's portrait remains in the family," Nora gloated many years later (Nora Stanton Barney, unpublished autobiographical manuscript, 1971, RBJ-CT; an edited version of these reminiscences was published as "Spanning Two Centuries: The Autobiography of Nora Stanton Barney," *History Workshop*, no. 22, autumn 1986, pp. 131–52).

110. This description was provided in 1971 by Katherine Stetson, daughter of Charlotte Perkins Gilman, describing her 1898 visit to the Blatches with her father and stepmother, Charles and Grace Ellery Channing Stetson. By this time Harriot and Harry had separate bedrooms. Katherine recalled that the curtains in Harriot's bedroom were so heavy that when drawn, "one could not even make out one's hand within an inch of one's face" (Stetson to Harriet de Forest, April 17, 1971, RBJ-CT). The Blatches rented the Mount at seventy-five pounds a year (Barney, autobiography, p. 2).

111. Bransom, known by the children as Beffet, "got one pound a month. . . . The cook was the aristocrat and got two pounds a month, a German governess was imported later at one pound. . . . The gardener (got) two pounds and the stable boy practically nothing" (Barney, autobiography, p. 2).

112. Elizabeth Cady Stanton, *Eighty Years and More*, pp. 136–37.

113. Elizabeth Stanton to Margaret Stanton Lawrence, October 15, 1890, RBJ-CT.

114. Barney, "Spanning Two Centuries," p. 136.

115. Barney, autobiography, pp. 12–14. Reflecting on this episode many years later, Harriot's daughter thought that everyone would have been happier if the marriage had been allowed to dissolve, and that her "mother could have tipped the scales the other way very easily," but "this was the 19th century not the 20th." The child, who grew up to be the travel writer Freya Stark, reported in her own autobiography that she had been

born in Paris, presumably the daughter of her mother's husband and not the hapless American who was her true father (*The Freya Stark Story* [New York: Coward-McCann, 1953]). Nora also recalled a cook who "got into difficulties" and how her mother arranged for "a proper marriage" soon after the baby was born (Barney, autobiography, p. 10).

116. Matilda Joslyn Gage to Lillie Devereux Blake, June 29, 1883, Blake Papers.

117. Elizabeth Stanton to Eliza Garrison, n.d. [1870s], Garrison Family Papers, Sophia Smith Collection, Smith College, Northampton, Mass.

118. *Elizabeth Cady Stanton as Revealed in Her Letters*, September 18, 1883, diary entry, p. 211.

119. Elizabeth Stanton to Susan B. Anthony, August 20, 1883, TS-NJ.

120. Elizabeth Cady Stanton to Elizabeth Smith Miller, October 13, 1883, TS-NJ.

121. Rhoda Barney Jenkins to the author, July 12, 1979.

122. *Elizabeth Cady Stanton as Revealed in Her Letters*, October 7, 1883, p. 211.

123. Typescript, Elizabeth Stanton to Susan B. Anthony, October 17, 1883, TS-NJ.

124. *Elizabeth Cady Stanton as Revealed in Her Letters*, November 15, 1883, pp. 212–13.

125. Elizabeth Stanton to Margaret Stanton Lawrence, October 15, 1890, RBJ-CT.

126. Elizabeth Stanton to Harriot Stanton Blatch, April 2, [1901], ECS-NY.

127. Barney, autobiography, p. 8.

128. Elizabeth Stanton to Margaret Stanton Lawrence, October 15, 1890, RBJ-CT.

Chapter Three: England

1. Carol Dyhouse, *Feminism and the Family in England* 1880–1939 (Oxford: Basil Blackwell, 1989); David Rubenstein, *Before the Suffragettes: Women's Emancipation in the 1890s* (Brighton: Harvester, 1986); Patricia Hollis, ed., *Women in Public: The Women's Movement* 1850–1900 (London: George Allen and Unwin, 1979).

2. R. Wilson to Millicent Garrett Fawcett, June 1889, Manchester Central Library Woman Suffrage Collection; thanks to Gail Malmgreen for this document. Copy of Blatch note, on leaf of Stanton scrapbook from Library of Congress, AL–NY.

3. One member of parliament advocated woman suffrage as a "countervailing" force to votes for agricultural workers and an act of justice, rectifying the disfranchisement of the only "property holders now without a vote" (Caroline A. Briggs, "Woman Suffrage in Britain," in Elizabeth Cady Stanton, Susan B. Anthony, and Matilda J. Gage, eds., *History of Woman Suffrage*, v. 3 [Rochester: Susan B. Anthony, 1886], p. 886).

4. "Women and the New Reform Bill," *Hants and Berks Gazette*, May 10, 1884, p. 5.

5. Account of Basingstoke meeting, *Women's Suffrage Journal*, June 2, 1884, pp. 127–28. There was a persistent rumor that "Blatch" was a corruption of "black" and that the family had somehow gotten its start in the slave trade (interview with Rhoda Barney Jenkins, June 1979, Greenwich, Conn.).

6. Moncure Conway, "The Present Opportunity of Women," *Pall Mall Gazette*, May 26, 1884, pp. 1–2.

7. Edith Simcox, letter to the editor, *Pall Mall Gazette*, May 27, 1884, p. 2. The *Gazette* also began a long, detailed series of reports on working women in connection with the defeat of the Reform bill. In 1885, Eleanor Marx and Edward Aveling published their two-part essay, "The Woman Question, from a Socialist Point of View"; although it focuses more on marriage than on suffrage, the authors are basically friendly to the bourgeois women's rights movement and reflect the emergence of a socialist voice in the growing debate over the woman question (*Westminster Review*, v. 6, 1885, pp. 209–19).

8. Theodore Stanton and Harriot Stanton Blatch, eds., *Elizabeth Cady Stanton as Revealed in Her Letters, Diary and Reminiscences* (New York: Harper & Brothers, 1922), December 15, 1884, p. 221.

9. "Letter from Elizabeth Cady Stanton," *Women's Tribune*, April 1887.

10. Announcement that Harriot Blatch was scheduled to speak at Plymouth Workingmen's Liberal Association, *Women's Penny Paper*, November 22, 1890, p. 91; also *Women's Suffrage Journal*, May 1, 1890, p. 56.

11. H. B. T., "Central National Society for Women's Suffrage," *Women's Herald*, February 14, 1891, p. 26.

12. Harriot Stanton Blatch and Alma Lutz, *Challenging Years: The Memoirs of Harriot Stanton Blatch* (New York: G. P. Putnam's Sons, 1940), p. 70.

13. "About Headquarters," *Woman's Tribune*, April 19, 1890, p. 123.

14. Blatch, letter to the editor, *New York Times*, July 6, 1908, p. 6. Also see Patricia Hollis, "Women in Council: Separate Spheres, Public Space," in *Equal or Different: Women's Politics, 1800–1914*, ed. Jane Rendall (Oxford: Basil Blackwell, 1986), pp. 192–213.

15. Blatch and Lutz, *Challenging Years*, p. 70.

16. Blatch, "Not What I Have but What I Do Is My Kingdom," *Englishwoman's Review*, May 15, 1885, pp. 201–4.

17. Blatch and Lutz, *Challenging Years*, pp. 76–77.

18. Blatch to Susan B. Anthony, *Woman's Tribune*, April 1887, n.p.

19. "Mrs. Blatch Never to Vote," *New York Times*, March 26, 1913, p. 4. "I heard and cannot forget the impassioned speech of Harriot Stanton Blatch in Cooper Union when she described how she, the descendent of people who had founded America, was legally an alien because she had fallen in love with and had married an Englishman." Lillie Devereux Blake, quoted in Katherine Devereux Blake and Margaret Louise Wallace, *Champion of Woman: The Life of Lillie Devereux Blake* (New York: Fleming H. Revell, 1943), p. 215.

20. Prior to 1880, the British women's rights movement had focused its attention on the sexual and economic sufferings of unmarried women—from the genteel poverty of middle-class spinsters to the sexual exploitation of working girls. Victories in these areas, such as the opening up of higher education and the professions to women and the repeal of the Contagious Diseases Act, helped to shift attention to married women (Lucy Bland, "The Married Woman, the 'New Woman,' and the Feminist: Sexual Politics of the 1890s," in Rendall, ed., *Equal or Different*, pp. 141–64; Carol Dyhouse makes a similar distinction, although she does not date the shift as closely as I do [*Feminism and Family in England*, p. 56].

21. Dyhouse, *Feminism and Family in England*, pp. 69–72; Judith Walkowitz links this "discursive struggle" to the formation of the Men and Women's Club in 1885 (*City of Dreadful Delight: Narratives of Sexual Danger in Late-Victorian London* [Chicago: University of Chicago Press, 1992], p. 137).

22. Olive Schreiner, *Woman and Labour* (1911; republished London: Virago, 1978); Marx and Aveling, "The Woman Question." Mona Caird's essays were published as *The Morality of Marriage* (London: Redway, 1897).

23. Blatch, "Not What I Have but What I Do"; also see Blatch, "Unsolved Problems," *Woman's Tribune*, June 1887, p. 1.

24. Harriot Stanton Blatch, "Voluntary Motherhood," *Transactions of the National Council of Women of the United States, Assembled in Washington, D. C., February 22 to 25, 1891* (Philadelphia: J. B. Lippincott, 1891), pp. 278–85. Aileen Kraditor republished this piece in *Up from the Pedestal: Selected Writings in the History of American Feminism* (Chicago: Quadrangle, 1968), pp. 167–75.

25. Blatch, "Voluntary Motherhood," p. 283.

26. Ibid., p. 280.

27. Interviews with Rhoda Barney Jenkins and Harriet de Forest. This affection is evident in numerous letters Harriot wrote to Harriot Ransom Milinowski's children, in the collection of Arthur and Alice Milinowski, Fort Erie, Ontario.

28. Stanton to Harper, n.d. [c. April 1891], IHH-CA. Also see *Elizabeth Cady Stanton as Revealed in Her Letters*, March 25, 1891, pp. 272–73.

29. Nora Stanton Barney, autobiography, p. 13, RBJ-CT.

30. Ibid., p. 14.

31. Ibid.

32. Rhoda Barney Jenkins interview, June 16, 1982, Greenwich, Conn.; several of Elizabeth's letters mention playing with dolls with her granddaughters, which she, unlike Harriot, permitted (Stanton to Lizette Stanton, June 1891, and to Theodore, July 12, 1891, TS-NJ).

33. Katherine Stetson to Harriet de Forest, April 17, 1971, RBJ-CT.

34. E. Sylvia Pankhurst, *The Suffragette Movement: An Intimate Account of Persons and Ideals* (London: Longman Group, 1931), pp. 111–12.

35. The formation of the Women's Franchise League followed quickly after a split among suffragists over the infusion of party politics into the movement. In December 1888, at a meeting of the National Women's Suffrage Society, the loose national federation that coordinated local suffrage committees, Liberal party suffragists insisted on the right of overtly political women's organizations—notably, the Women's Liberal Federation—to affiliate. Anticipating that this demand would pass, Becker and other "orthodox" suffragists withdrew to form their own suffrage federation. The leaders of the pro-Liberal group, by far the larger faction, were the anticoverture warhorses Ursula Bright and Elizabeth Wolstoneholme-Elmy, and they were confident that the organization they now controlled would take a clear position in favor of women's enfranchisement without respect to marital status. However, they were outmaneuvered by a small group of London activists.

Now there were two suffrage federations, both of which limited their demand to votes for unmarried women. This led to a second factionalization, eight months later.

Although the Bright forces felt compelled to form a separate organization (the Women's Franchise League) they continued to function within the Women's Liberal Federation and to represent a dominant position within it. In fact, it might make sense to see the Women's Franchise League as a faction of the Women's Liberal Federation, which is why the former did not much outlive the latter past the early 1890s. See Pankhurst, *Suffragette Movement*, pp. 94–95, and Rubenstein, *Before the Suffragettes*, pp. 143–44.

36. Blatch and Lutz, *Challenging Years*, p. 73.

37. Ibid., p. 76.

38. Paul Ransom to Harriot Ransom Milinowski, October 3, 1886, from the collection of Arthur and Alice Milinowski.

39. Margaret Stanton Lawrence, "Reminiscences of Elizabeth Cady Stanton, 1815–1915: A Sketch of Her Life," ECS-NY.

40. Susan B. Anthony and Ida H. Harper, eds., *History of Woman Suffrage*, v. 4 (Rochester: Susan B. Anthony, 1902), pp. 166–67. Also see Blatch, letter to the editor, *Woman's Journal*, January 18, 1896, p. 18.

41. Women's Franchise League, *Report of Proceedings at the Inaugural Meeting, London, July 25th, 1889* (London: Hansard Publishing Union, 1889), p. 22; thanks to Gail Malmgreen and Mary Lyndon Shanley for copies. "Steadfast Blue Line," December 24, 1892, *Shafts*, p. 117.

42. Later, recalling her years in England for her biographer, Alma Lutz, Harriot recalled meeting Richard Pankhurst. As she frequently did of men, she commented on the fullness of his beard. Of his relationship to his wife, she wrote, "She had smoldering fire[,] he kindled the flame" (Blatch, notes in her copy of E. Sylvia Pankhurst's *Suffragette Movement*, RBJ-CT).

43. Pankhurst, *Suffragette Movement*, p. 105.

44. Blatch, *Married Women and Municipal Elections* (London: Women's Franchise League, 1891).

45. Helen Blackburn, "Great Britain: Efforts for the Parliamentary Suffrage," *History of Woman Suffrage*, v. 4, p. 1013. Also see E. Sylvia Pankhurst, *Suffragette*, p. 96, and Rubenstein, *Before the Suffragettes*, pp. 143–44. Sylvia Pankhurst follows these issues most closely in *The Suffragette Movement*, pp. 116–17. When parliamentary suffrage began to be extended to women, in 1918, it was initially limited, so as to keep the numbers of women voting below those of men, but the limitations were those of age, not marital status.

46. Sylvia Pankhurst, tribute to Harriot Blatch at eightieth birthday, New York City, January 1936, BH-Mass.

47. Pankhurst, *Suffragette Movement*, p. 119.

48. For the socialistic character of early Pankhurstian suffragism, see Jill Liddington and Jill Norris, *One Hand Tied behind Us: The Rise of the Women's Suffrage Movement* (London: Virago, 1978).

49. Barney, autobiography, p. 16c.

50. Ellen Carol DuBois, "Working Women, Class Relations, and Suffrage Militance: Harriot Stanton Blatch and the New York Woman Suffrage Movement," *Journal of American History*, v. 74, June 1987, pp. 34–58; *Report of the New York Campaign of 1894* (New York: New York Woman Suffrage Party, 1895).

51. Unidentified clipping, *Susan B. Anthony Collection Scrapbook,* 20, Manuscript Division, Library of Congress. *New York Times,* May 3, 1894, p. 9.

52. " 'My mother said something about the right to sue and be sued, and you all laughed at the idea of its being a privilege to be sued.' 'I meant in courtship,' said Mrs. Stanton. 'That was a joke' " ("Answering the Brooklyn Women," unidentified clipping, 1894, scrapbook 20, SBA-LC). Margaret Stanton Lawrence describes this period at length in her typescript reminiscences, "Elizabeth Cady Stanton, 1815–1915," pp. 120–21. While in New York in 1894, Harriot also received a master's degree from Vassar, based on her work on British rural poverty, which was published as "Another View of Village Life," *Westminister Review,* v. 140, September 1893, pp. 318–24.

53. Elizabeth Cady Stanton, "Educated Suffrage Justified," *Woman's Journal,* November 3, 1894, p. 348; Harriot Blatch, "An Open Letter to Mrs. Stanton," ibid., December 22, 1894, p. 402; Stanton, "Educated Suffrage Again," ibid., January 5, 1895, p. 5.

54. Stanton's clearest statement on socialism was made in 1898, reprinted in Ellen Carol Dubois, ed., *The Elizabeth Cady Stanton—Susan B. Anthony Reader,* 2d ed. (Boston: Northeastern University Press, 1992), p. 183.

55. Pankhurst, *Suffragette Movement,* p. 11.

56. Blatch and Lutz, *Challenging Years,* pp. 74–77.

57. Ibid., p. 81; Deborah Epstein Nord, *The Apprenticeship of Beatrice Webb* (Ithaca: Cornell University Press, 1985), pp. 148–52. Brooke initially opposed the formation of a separate women's group, but was a leader in its formation a dozen years later. In her excellent dissertation on feminism and the Fabians, Polly Beals argues that such women felt that "discussion of gender relations and differences between the sexes . . . might undermine their hard won image as capable contributors to intellectual life" ("Fabian Feminism: Gender, Politics and Culture in London, 1880–1930," Ph.D. dissertation, Rutgers University, 1989, p. 52); I am indebted to Beals for her careful scholarship on Fabian women in the early years.

58. Beals, "Fabian Feminism," p. 62.

59. Blatch and Lutz, *Challenging Years,* p. 78.

60. Rubenstein, *Before the Suffragettes,* pp. 110–34.

61. Boucherett, "The British Workingwoman in Danger," *Englishwoman's Review,* July 16, 1894, pp. 79–80, and in the same issue, "More Danger to the Workingwoman," p. 148.

62. See, for instance, Evelyn March-Phillips, "The New Factory Bill: As It Affects Women," *Fortnightly Review,* v. 329, May 1894, pp. 738–48.

63. Rubenstein, *Before the Suffragettes,* p. 123.

64. Karl Pearson, "Women and Labour," *Fortnightly Review,* v. 329, May 1894, pp. 561–77.

65. Ibid., p. 564.

66. Blatch, notes on Lady Commissioners' Report, HSB-NY

67. "The Implications of Collectivism," *Fabian News,* February 1894, p. 2.

68. There had been only seven previously: Annie Besant, Miss Grover, Miss Hoatson, Mrs. Mallet, Mrs. Sandham, Emma Brooke, and Mrs. Cameron.

69. *Fabian News*, March 1894, p. 2, April 1894, pp. 5–7, and June 15, 1894, p. 14; Beals, "Fabian Feminism," p. 90.

70. Harriot Blatch's draft for a women's rights tract, long thought to be lost, was discovered in 1988 in a set of her papers that had been left in her daughter's attic in Greenwich, at the time of her death in 1940. One part of the tract had been published, as "Specialization of Function in Women," *Gunton's Magazine*, v. 10, May 1896, pp. 349–56. Over the years, in fact up until the time of her death, Harriot recirculated portions of this material whenever she wanted to argue against sex-based protective labor legislation. Alma Lutz used some of this material in composing the last chapter of *Challenging Years*, especially pp. 320–32. The original drafts are now available in the Blatch Papers at Vassar College, which is where Harriot had wanted them to go at the time of her death.

71. Blatch, "Specialization of Function," p. 353.

72. Blatch, "Lecture IV: Factory Legislation," HSB-NY.

73. Blatch, "Specialization of Function," p. 350.

74. Blatch, "Lecture IV: Factory Legislation."

75. Ibid.

76. Blatch, notes on Lady Commissioners' Report.

77. Blatch, "Lecture IV: Factory Legislation."

78. Blatch, "Specialization of Function," p. 355.

79. Ibid., p. 354. "I said that servants did not mean high civilization but that cooperation did. . . . No one sees more clearly [than I] the evils of our domestic servants' system" (Blatch to Mrs. Hunt, March 19, n.y., HSB-NY).

80. This can be traced through the reports of the Women's Tract Committee, Executive Committee meetings of June 15, October 8, and December 18, 1894, and January 11, 18, and 25, 1895 (Brighton: Harvester Microfilms).

81. Sidney Webb, "The Alleged Difference in the Wages Paid to Men and Women for Similar Work," *Economic Journal*, v. 1, no. 4, December 1891, p. 657.

82. In 1898 she engaged in a particularly vitriolic exchange with Sidney Webb, who was sitting on the Technical Education Board of the London County Council. Harriot argued forcefully that the Education Board was supporting a system of vocational education that was channeling young women into low-paying, predominantly female occupations (Blatch, "Women and the London County Council Classes," *Woman's Signal*, February 24, 1898, pp. 125–26; and Webb's response, "Women and the London County Council Classes," ibid., March 3, 1898, p. 142).

83. Blatch and Lutz, *Challenging Years*, pp. 82, 77. Interview with Rhoda Barney Jenkins, July 1982.

84. Report on Women's Tract Committee, Executive Committee Minutes, January 24, 1895, Nuffield College, Oxford University.

85. Blatch, Brownlow, and Florence Balgarnie, letter to the editor, May 30, 1895, *Woman's Signal*, pp. 348–49. Beals also follows this episode; see her "Fabian Feminism," pp. 89–90.

86. "Women's Liberal Federation," *Shafts*, May 1895, v. 3, p. 37; "Women's Liberal Federation," *Woman's Signal*, May 23, 1895, p. 334; Rubenstein, *Before the Suffragettes*, p. 114.

87. This action was defended at a members' meeting, January 10, 1896. Beatrice Webb was not yet even an official member of the society when she wrote the tract.

88. Beatrice Webb, "Woman and the Factory Acts," republished in *Women's Fabian Tracts*, ed. Sally Alexander (London: Routledge, 1988).

89. Shaw to Webb, as quoted in Beals, "Fabian Feminism," pp. 64–65.

90. Within the Fabian Society, Blatch and Beatrice Webb never publicly debated their differences on sex-based labor legislation. However, at the International Congress of Women, held in 1899 in London, as part of a group of sessions entitled "Women in Industrial Life," both participated along with women from France, Sweden, and Germany in a discussion of "the attitude of different schools of thought to special labor legislation for women." Harriot restated the essence of her draft tract, emphasizing the negative impact of sex-based labor legislation on skilled women, the impossibility of effective labor protection when limited to women, and the importance of extending protective legislation to men as well. While holding to her defense of the Factory Acts of 1895, Webb conceded the desirability of maintaining women's presence in the labor force and the extremely limited number of cases in which labor legislation should focus on the distinction of sex as opposed to specialization. These concessions foreshadowed Webb's later change of heart with respect to sex-based labor legislation (*Women in Industrial Life: The Transactions of the Industrial and Legislative Section of the International Council of Women* [London: T. Fisher Unwin, 1899], pp. 40–43, 50–54).

91. Blatch letter to Fabian Executive Committee, Executive Committee Minutes, October 26, 1894; Barney, autobiography, p. 16c.

92. Blatch to Anthony, republished in *Woman's Tribune*, December 28, 1895, p. 161.

93. Harriot Stanton Blatch to Mrs. McIlquham, n.d. [sometime between December 1895 and January 1896], McIlquham Papers, British Library; thanks to Gail Malmgreen for her notes on this material.

94. Barney, autobiography p. 16c. The death certificate on file at the General Register Office in London says June 14, 1896, but the earlier date is from letters from Harriot (June 24, 1896) and Theodore (June 14, 1896) to Elizabeth, Clara Colby Papers, Wisconsin State Historical Society, Madison. These letters inexplicably ended up in the papers of one of Stanton's associates, safe from either Harriot's or Elizabeth's retrospective and privatizing eye. June 11 is also the date listed in Susan B. Anthony's diary, SBA-LC.

95. Harriot to Elizabeth, June 24, 1896.

96. Ibid., and Theodore to Elizabeth, June 14, 1896.

97. Susan B. Anthony to Harriot Stanton Blatch, July 3, 1896, ECS-LC.

98. Barney, autobiography, p. 16c.

99. Interview with Rhoda Barney Jenkins, July 1982. Harriot's preference for cold-water baths was particularly cited.

100. Blatch and Lutz, *Challenging Years*, p. 131. Helen's death is not mentioned anywhere in the autobiography.

101. Harriot Blatch to Grace Ellery Channing, February 28, 1897, Stetson Papers, Schlesinger Library, Cambridge, Mass.

102. Blatch to Salmon, March 22, 1898, Salmon Papers, Vassar College, Poughkeepsie, N.Y.

103. Nora's autobiography makes this contrast between England and America very clear (p. 23).

104. Barney, autobiography, pp. 17–18.

105. Ibid., pp. 22–25; "A Woman to Be Civil Engineer," unidentified clipping, September 19, 1902, SBA-LC.

106. Barney, autobiography, p. 23; interview with Rhoda Barney Jenkins, July 1985.

107. Blatch to Susan B. Anthony, September 25, 1902, ECS-LC.

108. "For some reason Mrs. Chapman Catt does not seem disposed to push her to the front, why, I do not know unless she is jealous of her as a speaker" (Stanton to Anthony, September 13, 1902, ECS-LC).

109. Blatch to Anthony, telegram, October 26, 1902, ECS-LC; Margaret Stanton Lawrence, "Elizabeth Cady Stanton," 1915, p. 134, AL-NY.

110. Gardener published Harriot's description in "Elizabeth Cady Stanton," *Free Thought Magazine*, January 1903, pp. 6–9; Lois Banner, Stanton's biographer, observed to me that this portrait of eighty-seven-year-old Elizabeth, on the verge of death, standing, is suspect to say the least, and wonders whether Harriot was engaging in a bit of dramatic license.

111. Anthony to Clara Colby, November 25, 1902, CC-CA.

112. "No, Not Mrs. Stanton's Brain," unidentified clipping, November 1902, SBA-LC; thanks to Ann D. Gordon for this citation.

113. Susan B. Anthony to Ida Husted Harper, October 28, 1902, IHH-CA.

114. Anthony to Colby, November 25, 1902.

115. Anthony, diary, February 17, 1904, SBA-LC.

116. Blatch and Lutz, *Challenging Years*, p. 86.

117. Harriot Stanton Blatch, "Woman as Economic Factor," delivered before Congressional Committee in 1898, excerpted in *History of Woman Suffrage*, v. 4, p. 311.

Chapter Four: Class

1. Nora Stanton Barney, unpublished autobiography, 1971, p. 23, RBJ-CT.

2. In his study of New York suffragism, David McDonald notes that these upstate cities did not vote strongly for the issue in either the 1915 or the 1917 referendum ("Organizing Womanhood: Women's Culture and the Politics of Woman Suffrage in New York State, 1865–1917," Ph.D. dissertation, SUNY–Stony Brook, 1987).

3. See, for example, the argument of Helen Rogers at the 1906 woman suffrage legislative hearing in Albany ("Woman Suffrage Hearing in Albany," *New York Times*, March 29, 1906, p. 9). Anna Howard Shaw was still trying to refute this charge in 1908 ("Woman's Suffrage a World-Wide Issue," ibid., December 6, 1908, p. 2).

4. Susan B. Anthony and Ida H. Harper, eds., *History of Woman Suffrage*, v. 4 (Rochester: Susan B. Anthony, 1902), pp. 860–64.

5. For example, see Robert A. Huff, "Anne Miller and the Geneva Political Equality Club, 1897–1912," *New York History*, October 1984, v. 65, pp. 325–48. Whereas Anthony had hoped that women's clubs would eventually come to look like

suffrage societies, these suffrage clubs were going in the opposite direction, increasingly influenced by the model of the women's club.

6. Harriot Blatch and Alma Lutz, *Challenging Years: The Memoirs of Harriot Stanton Blatch* (New York: G. P. Putnam's Sons, 1940), p. 92. Eleanor Flexner begins her analysis of the last phase of the suffrage movement with this quotation (*Century of Struggle: The Women's Rights Movement in the United States* [Cambridge, Mass.: Belknap Press of Harvard University Press, 1959], p. 250).

7. "Demand Vote for Women," *New York Times*, March 2, 1902, p. 8.

8. Joan Waugh, *Unsentimental Reformer: Life of Josephine Shaw Lowell* (Cambridge, Mass.: Harvard University Press, forthcoming); S. Sara Monoson, "The Lady and the Tiger: Women's Electoral Activism in New York City before Suffrage," *Journal of Women's History*, v. 2, fall 1990, pp. 100–135.

9. Oswald Garrison Villard, "Women in New York Municipal Campaign," *Woman's Journal*, March 8, 1902, pp. 78–79. The Gertrude Colles Collection, at the New York State Library in Albany, is particularly rich in evidence of the less elite, more radical side of female mugwumpery in these years.

10. Ida H. Harper, ed., *History of Woman Suffrage*, v. 5 (New York: NAWSA, 1922), p. 81.

11. Villard, "Women in the New York Municipal Campaign." There were antisuffragists among the membership (Maud Nathan to Alice Stone Blackwell, January 22, 1906, reel 14, NAWSA-LC).

12. Monoson, "The Lady and the Tiger," pp. 100–135.

13. Blatch to Mrs. Hunt, March 16, n.y., Sophia Smith Collection, Smith College Library, Northampton, Mass.

14. The Equal Suffrage League can be followed through reports to the *Woman's Journal*, for instance on December 31, 1904, p. 423, and January 21, 1905, p. 10.

15. "Discussed Women's Work," *Woman's Journal*, January 21, 1905, p. 10.

16. "Women as Wage Earners," *Woman's Journal*, March 17, 1906, p. 43. In general on the Women's Trade Union League see: Nancy Schrom Dye, *As Equals and as Sisters: Feminism, Unionism and the Women's Trade Union League of New York* (Columbia: University of Missouri Press, 1980); Meredith Tax, *The Rising of the Women: Feminist Solidarity and Class Conflict, 1880–1917* (New York: Monthly Review Press, 1980).

17. Dye, *As Equals and as Sisters*, p. 63. Harriot's handwritten notes can be found in the Blatch Papers, Vassar College, Poughkeepsie, N.Y. Van Kleeck published her own study of the industry, *A Seasonal Industry: A Study of the Millinery Trade in New York* (New York: Russell Sage Foundation, 1917), without acknowledging the WTUL study or Harriot's assistance; however, her biographer, Guy Alchon, assures me that the book was rooted in this earlier study. The millinery trade seems to have drawn much attention among students of wage-earning women, perhaps because as a high-fashion, seasonal trade, it generated a wide range of working conditions, wages, and quality of production.

18. "Laborers Sip Tea on Fifth Avenue," *New York Times*, April 11, 1907, p. 8.

19. Minutes, March 29, 1906, reel 1, NYWTUL.

20. Blatch to Gompers, December 30, 1905, as quoted in Dye, *As Equals and as Sisters*, p. 50.

21. Kelley, "Woman Suffrage: Its Relation to Working Women and Children," Political Equality Series pamphlet, published by NAWSA, 1906; "Jane Addams on Working Women," *Woman's Journal*, November 20, 1897, p. 297. Also see Addams's "Address to Wage-Earning Women," *Woman's Journal*, May 16, 1903, p. 369, and "Utilization of Women in City Government," in *Jane Addams: A Centennial Reader* (New York: Macmillan, 1960), pp. 116–17.

22. "Club Notes," *Progress*, June 1907, p. 3; *Woman's Journal*, April 1906, p. 79; "Self-Supporting Women," *New York Times*, January 3, 1907, p. 6; "Equality League of Self-Supporting Women," *Woman's Journal*, January 12, 1907, p. 8.

23. Blatch and Lutz, *Challenging Years*, p. 98.

24. "The Equality League of Self-Supporting Women: Report for Year 1908–1909," p. 5, HSB-LC. Also see "State Correspondence: New York," *Woman's Journal*, April 14, 1906, p. 60.

25. Blatch and Lutz, *Challenging Years*, p. 98.

26. The Wage Earners Suffrage League was established in 1911. By far the best portrait of O'Reilly can be found in Tax, *Rising of the Women*, pp. 95–112, 171–74.

27. Quoted in ibid., p. 235.

28. "Teachers Scorned Idea of Union," *New York Times*, April 5, 1907, p. 7.

29. Ibid.; "Self-Supporting Women," *Progress*, April 1907, p. 2.

30. Obituary for Kate Claghorne, *New York Times*, March 24, 1938, p. 23; obituary for Bertha Rembaugh, ibid., February 1, 1950, p. 30; obituary for Madeline Doty, ibid., October 16, 1963, p. 45; obituary for Helen Rogers Reid, ibid., July 28, 1970, p. 1; obituary for Jessie Ashley, ibid., January 22, 1919, p. 11. Those Self-Supporters of whom I have evidence of independent incomes include Nora Blatch, Lavinia Dock, Ida Rauh, Gertrude Barnum, Elizabeth Finnegan, and Alice Clark. In the case of Nora and Lavinia Dock and perhaps for others, the Great Depression destroyed their family incomes; when this was coupled with their refusal or inability to rely on the income of a husband, such women found themselves much more dependent on their own labor. Helen Rogers was one of the few college graduates in the Equality League who was under economic pressure to work, but the man she eventually married (she met him while working for his mother) was Ogden Reid, editor of the *New York Tribune*.

31. Barney, autobiography, pp. 32–33, RBJ-CT.

32. *Woman's Journal*, May 12, 1900, pp. 146–47; also see Blatch, "Woman Carves Her Own Way to Freedom," *Free Thought Magazine*, v. 14, April 1898, pp. 176–80.

33. "Buffalo Woman Suffrage Convention," *Progress*, November 1907, p. 1. Nora remembered it differently: "As the only supported wife, mother was barred [from membership]" (Barney, autobiography, p. 20).

34. "Think Husbands Aren't Mainstays," *New York Times*, January 7, 1909, p. 9. For wage-earning women's attitudes toward this problem, see Sarah Eisenstein, *Give Us Bread but Give Us Roses: Working Women's Consciousness in the United States, 1890 to the First World War* (London: Routledge and Kegan Paul, 1983).

35. Viola Justin, "Mrs. de Forest to Have Her Own Shop," unidentified clipping, January 2, 1909, AC-NY. This was Lee de Forest's second marriage; ominously his first had ended after less than two years. Jim Hijiya, *Lee de Forest and the Fatherhood of Radio* (Bethlehem, Pa.: Lehigh University Press, 1992). Also see Lee de Forest, *Father of Radio: The Autobiography of Lee de Forest* (Chicago: Wilcox and Follett, 1950), ch. 3. For a more general discussion of the heterosexual hopefulness of this period, see E. Kay Trimberger, ed., *Intimate Warriors: Portraits of a Modern Marriage, 1899–1944* (New York: Feminist Press, 1991).

36. Barney, autobiography, p. 29.

37. Olivia Howard Dunbar, "The Woman's University Club," *Harper's Bazaar*, v. 42, November 1908, pp. 1111–14.

38. "Woman Suffrage Notes," *Woman's Tribune*, January 26, 1907, p. 6; "Self Supporting Women," *New York Times*, January 3, 1907, p. 6. On the women teachers' struggle, see Robert Doherty, "Tempest on the Hudson: Struggle for Equal Pay for Equal Work in New York City, 1907–1911," *History of Education Quarterly*, v. 19, 1979, pp. 413–34.

39. "Women Discuss Ballots," *New York Times*, February 6, 1907, p. 6.

40. Harriot Stanton Blatch, ed., *Two Speeches by Industrial Women* (New York: Equality League of Self-Supporting Women, 1907).

41. "New York Legislative League," *Woman's Tribune*, February 9, 1907, p. 12, NYWTUL.

42. Minutes of the NYWTUL, April 27, 1909.

43. Program of the New York State Woman Suffrage Association Convention, Geneva, N.Y., November 1907, reel 12, LOR-Mass. "Buffalo Woman Suffrage Convention," *Progress*, November 1908, p. 1.

44. Harriot Blatch to Caroline Lexow, November 29, 1907, HSB-NY.

45. "Mrs. Cobden Sanderson in New York," *Progress*, January 1908, p. 1.

46. Blatch and Lutz, *Challenging Years*, pp. 100–101.

47. "Mrs. Cobden-Sanderson's Address," *Woman's Journal*, December 28, 1907, p. 1.

48. "Women Bar Suffrage Says Mrs. Sanderson," *New York Times*, January 11, 1908, p. 5.

49. Borrman (Boorman, the other spelling, sometimes hyphenated), Wells, "Militant Movement for Woman Suffrage," *Independent*, v. 64, April 23, 1908, p. 901; *Suffrage Annual and Women's Who's Who*, ed. A. J. R. (London: Stanley Paul, 1913), p. 390 (thanks to David Doughan of the Fawcett Library).

50. "Suffragists Hope to Capture Country for Equal Rights," *New York Herald*, March 8, 1909, p. 3. Later the group changed its name to the Progressive Women's Suffrage Union, PWSU being an anagram of WSPU.

51. Draft Constitution, American Suffragettes, Colles Collection.

52. Winifred Harper Cooley, "Suffragists and Suffragettes," *Hearst's International*, October 1908, p. 1067.

53. Borrman Wells, "Militant Movement for Woman Suffrage."

54. "Suffragettes Bar Word 'Ladylike,'" unnamed clipping, January 1909, AC-NY.

55. *American Suffragette*, March 1910, p. 3.

56. "Suffragists Hope to Capture County for Women's Rights." Commander was a veteran of the utopian socialist community in Ruskin, Tenn.

57. Dye, *As Equals and as Sisters*, p. 47.

58. *Woman's Journal*, May 30, 1908, p. 87, and *American Suffragette*, November 1909, p. 3.

59. "Suffragettes Open Their Campaign Here," *New York Times*, January 1, 1908, p. 16; "Suffrage in a Cold Wind," ibid., January 15, 1908, p. 6.

60. "Suffragist Parade despite the Police," *New York Times*, February 17, 1908, p. 7; there is also an account in Rheta Childe Dorr, *What Eighty Million Women Want* (Boston: Small Maynard, 1910), p. 298.

61. Lydia Commander, who went from the Equal Rights League to the American Suffragettes, described herself as "a socialist and a labor woman" who hated to see old-fashioned suffragists drive away wage-earners with their "smug middle class remarks" (Commander to Alice Park, February 13, 1909, AP-CA). Other independent socialist women active in the group included Drs. Anna Mercy and Maude Glasgow.

62. "Miss Malone Quits Suffragettes," *New York Times*, March 27, 1908, p. 4.

63. *American Suffragette*, August 1909, p. 3, and March 1911; "Suffragettes Also Meet," unidentified clipping, December 5, 1908, AC-NY; "Suffragist or Suffragette," *New York Times*, February 29, 1908, p. 6.

64. Sophie Loebinger, "Who Is a Suffragette?" *American Suffragette*, February 1911, pp. 3–4.

65. Sophie Loebinger, "Blazing the Trail," *American Suffragette*, September 1910, p. 16.

66. Cooley, "Suffragists and Suffragettes," p. 1070. The *New York Times* also distinguished "three different kinds of women suffragists: the 'old time' suffragists [who] don't want to get confused with the suffragettes . . . and then there are Harriot Blatch's 14,000 self-supporting women" ("Women Suffragists Plan Hot Campaign," October 25, 1908, p. 7).

67. "Suffragettes Protest," *New York Times*, April 30, 1908, p. 16.

68. "Suffrage Fight Trophies," *New York Times*, August 20, 1908, p. 7.

69. Thanks to Rhoda Barney Jenkins for this story. The photograph can be found in HSB-LC, reel 1.

70. Blatch and Lutz, *Challenging Years*, pp. 107–8; Equality League of Self-Supporting Women, *Report for Year* 1908–1909, reel 1, HSB-LC.

71. Blatch and Lutz, *Challenging Years*, pp. 107–8.

72. Equality League, *Report for Year* 1908–1909; Blatch and Lutz, *Challenging Years*, pp. 108–9.

73. Equality League, *Report for Year* 1908–1909; Blatch to Ella Crossett, July 15, 1908, AL-NY.

74. Typescript of speech to National American Woman Suffrage Association, October 16, 1908, HSB-NY.

75. "Women Unite to Honor Mrs. Blatch," *Equal Rights*, January 4, 1936, pp. 347–48.

76. Mary Putnam-Jacobi, M.D., "Address Delivered at the New York City Hearing," in 1894 *Constitutional Amendment Campaign Year: Report of the New York*

Woman Suffrage Association 26th Annual Convention, Ithaca, New York, November 12–15, 1895 (Rochester: Charles Mann Elm Park, 1895) pp. 17–26.

77. "Mrs. Clarence Mackay," *American Magazine,* September 1910, pp. 609–10.

78. "Equal Rights Society Aims to Advance Measures for the Extension of the Franchise," *New York Times,* February 21, 1909, pt. 5, p. 2; "Mrs. Mackay Comes out for Woman Suffrage," *New York Evening World,* December 4, 1908, p. 1; "Women of Fashion Aid Suffragists," *New York Herald,* December 4, 1908, p. 1.

79. Blatch, early draft of autobiography, p. 117, HSB-NY.

80. Blatch to Mrs. Robert Abbe, January 1909, AC-NY. "The membership dues were five dollars a year but you could be a life member for a hundred dollars. She had invitations engraved at Tiffany's" (Ethel Gross Hopkins Conant, an oral history interview conducted in 1964 by Roger Daniels for the Oral History Program, UCLA; thanks to June Hopkins for calling this interview to my attention and providing me with a partial transcript).

81. Mrs. Howard Mansfield to Blatch, October 16, 1915, HSB-LC. Harriot was on the Board of Trustees, a position she held for the life of the organization.

82. "Suffragist Armory at Mrs. Belmont's," *New York Times,* August 13, 1909, p. 7. For some of Belmont's ideas about suffrage and her leadership, see "Woman and the Suffrage," *Harper's Bazaar,* v. 44, March 1910, p. 170.

83. Margaret H. Rector, *Alva: That Vanderbilt-Belmont Woman* (Wickford, R.I.: Dutch Island Press, 1992). For Belmont's hostility to men, see her daughter's autobiography, Consuelo Vanderbilt Balsan, *The Glitter and the Gold* (New York: Harper and Brothers, 1952), p. 216. Belmont, "Woman's Right to Govern Herself," *North American Review,* v. 190, November 1909, pp. 664–74.

84. "What Mrs. Belmont Has Done for Woman," *New York Times,* March 9, 1910, p. 1.

85. Blatch and Lutz, *Challenging Years,* p. 130.

86. Kate Carew, "Asks Mrs. Belmont about the Baby and the Ballot," *New York World,* December 12, 1909, n.p., clipping in Colles Collection.

87. Blatch, draft autobiography. Harriot's account of this episode never saw the light of day. Even decades after the fact, suffragists did not expose their internal conflicts, and Harriot's biographer Alma Lutz removed the account from the published version of *Challenging Years.* A conflict described in "Lobbyist Splits Suffrage Ranks," *New York Times,* March 2, 1910, p. 5, probably refers to this episode.

88. "Mrs. Clarence Mackay," *American Magazine,* v. 70, September 1910, pp. 608–10; Olivia Howard Dunbar, "Mrs. Mackay at Work," *Harper's Bazaar,* v. 44, April 1910, pp. 240–41; "Equal Rights Society Aims to Advance Measures," *New York Times,* February 21, 1909, pt. 5, pp. 2–3.

89. Mabel Potter Daggett, "Suffrage Enters the Drawing Room," *Delineator,* v. 75, January 1910, pp. 37–38.

90. Ethel Gross Hopkins Conant oral history

91. "State Correspondence, New York," *Woman's Journal,* January 23, 1909, p. 15; Haines to Alice Park, December 7, 1910, reel 11, NAWSA-LC.

92. In the suffrage press, *Woman's Journal,* January 23, 1909, p. 15; and Reynolds

to the editor, *Progress*, January 1909; and in the general media, "Mrs. Clarence Mackay," *American Magazine*, v. 70, September 1910, pp. 609–10.

93. Jessica Garretson Finch, *How the Ballot Would Help the Working Woman* (New York: Equal Franchise Society, 1909).

94. "Mrs. Mackay Pleads for Equal Suffrage," *New York Times*, January 16, 1909, p. 18.

95. Belmont, "Woman's Right to Govern Herself," *North American Review*, v. 190, November 1909, p. 665.

96. On Belmont's work with African American women, see "Suffrage for Negresses," *New York Times*, January 9, 1910, p. 5; and "Negro Women Join in Suffrage Fight," ibid., February 7, 1910, p. 4.

97. "Gov. Shafroth Gives Suffragist Lecture," *New York Times*, December 4, 1909, p. 3.

98. Belmont, "Woman Suffrage as It Looks To-Day," *Forum*, v. 143, January 1910, pp. 264–67.

99. Blatch, draft autobiography, n.p.

100. Blatch, "Funds for Suffrage," *New York Times*, November 29, 1910, p. 10.

101. Blatch and Lutz, *Challenging Years*, p. 118.

102. Frances Perkins, Oral History Collection, Columbia University, N.Y., p. 401; thanks to Linda Gordon for this citation.

103. Blatch and Lutz, *Challenging Years*, p. 121.

104. "Society and Labor Join for Suffrage," *New York Times*, February 2, 1909, p. 6.

105. "Suffragists Hold a Street Meeting," *New York Times*, May 14, 1909, p. 5.

106. Louisine M. Havemeyer, "The Suffrage Torch: Memories of a Militant," *Scribners*, v. 71, May 1922, pp. 528–39.

107. Eleanor Booth Simmons, "Names of Suffrage Pioneers Now Forgotten," *New York Sun*, December 9, 1917, AC-NY.

108. Blatch, draft autobiography, p. 119.

109. Blatch and Lutz, *Challenging Years*, pp. 129–31. The American Suffragettes complained of being frozen out of the planning for the 1910 parade (Loebinger to Alice Park, May 21, 1910, AP-CA).

110. Belmont to Ida Husted Harper, June 9, 1909, IHH-CA.

111. Ethel Gross Hopkins Conant oral history.

112. Women's Political Union, *Annual Report 1911–1912*, IISB-LC.

113. New York State Woman Suffrage Association Minute Book, October 18, 1910, p. 10, WSP-NY.

114. Lucy Burns to Maud Malone, October 28, 1915, reel 20, NWP-SY. Malone has the curious distinction of being the first American woman arrested for her suffrage activism, more than a decade before Alice Paul did so to much greater publicity. Undoubtedly modeling her behavior after that of Christabel Pankhurst and Annie Kenney in England, Malone heckled New York politicians until an obliging policeman finally arrested her for disturbing the peace ("Arrest Maud Malone Again," *New York Times*, January 27, 1909, p. 16).

115. State Correspondence, *Woman's Journal*, February 13, 1909, p. 28.

116. Blatch, letter to the editor, *Woman's Journal*, September 11, 1909, p. 148.

117. Blatch to Christabel Pankhurst, n.d., reprinted in Christabel Pankhurst, *Unshackled: The Story of How We Won the Vote* (London: Hutchinson, 1959), p. 147.

118. Blatch, draft autobiography, n.p.

119. "Mrs. Pankhurst Due Today," *New York Times*, October 20, 1909, p. 5.

120. Catt to Millicent Garrett Fawcett, October 19, 1909, reel 4, CCC-LC.

121. Anna Garlin Spencer to Carrie Chapman Catt, October 1909, WSP-NY.

122. Blatch to Miss Jordan, October 6, 1909, Jordan Papers, Sophia Smith Collection.

123. "Mrs. Raymond Robins Welcomes Mrs. Pankhurst," *Woman's Journal*, November 4, 1909, p. 180; "Great Throng Hears Mrs. Pankhurst," *New York Times*, October 26, 1909, p. 1.

124. "Mrs. Pankhurst in New York," *Woman's Journal*, October 30, 1909, p. 174.

125. Blatch to Miss Jordan, October 6, 1909, Jordan Papers.

126. Executive Board Minutes, October 20, 1909, reel 1, NYWTUL.

127. "Womanly Mrs. Pankhurst," *Woman's Journal*, October 30, 1909, p. 173.

128. "We cleared on this meeting some $800. . . . We grew a little bit timid at the end, or we could have easily made $2000 or $3000" (Blatch, draft autobiography, n.p.).

129. "Mrs. Pankhurst's Farewell Address," *Woman's Journal*, December 11, 1909, p. 199.

130. Ibid.

131. Ibid.

132. "Suffragists to Aid Girl Waist Strikers," *New York Times*, December 2, 1909, p. 3.

133. "Arrest Strikers for Being Assaulted," *New York Times*, November 5, 1909, p. 1.

134. "Strikers Divide on Suffrage," *New York Times*, December 3, 1909, p. 6; "Throng Cheers on the Girl Strikers," ibid., December 6, 1909, p. 1.

135. Tax, *Rising of the Women*, ch. 8; Ann Schofield, "The Uprising of the 20,000: The Making of a Labor Legend," in *A Needle, a Bobbin, a Strike: Women Needleworkers in America*, ed. Joan Jensen and Sue Davidson (Philadelphia: Temple University Press, 1984); Leon Stine, *The Triangle Fire* (New York: Carroll and Graf, 1962); Philip S. Foner, *Women and the American Labor Movement: From Colonial Times to the Eve of WWI* (New York: Free Press, 1979).

136. "Strikers Divide on Suffrage"; Nancy Schrom Dye observes that even Helen Marot, who "usually took a hard line on workers' self-determination," shared these sentiments (*As Sisters and as Equals*, p. 93).

137. "Girl Strikers Go to City Hall," *New York Times*, December 4, 1909, p. 20.

138. "Strike and Votes in Open-Air Talk," *New York Times*, December 5, 1909, p. 11; Tax, *Rising of the Women*, p. 229; Executive Board Minutes, October 20, 1909, reel 1, NYWTUL.

139. See Executive Board Minutes, November 17, 1909, NYWTUL, for the role of the publicity committee.

140. "Police Mishandle Girl Strike Pickets," *New York Times*, December 10, 1909, p. 13.

141. "Girl Strikers Tell the Rich Their Woes," *New York Times*, December 16, 1909, p. 3. For the initial weeks, *New York Times* coverage of the strike was indexed not under "labor" but under "fashion."

142. "Strike's End Near, Both Sides Assert," *New York Times*, December 27, 1909, p. 9.

143. "The Rich Out to Aid Girl Waistmakers," *New York Times*, January 3, 1910, p. 1; "State Arbitrators in Girls' Strike," ibid., January 4, 1910, p. 20.

144. For an example of the increasing antisocialism, see Sophie Loebinger to Alice Park, March 1, 1910, AP-CA.

145. Executive Board Minutes, February 1910, reel 1, NYWTUL; the other negative vote was cast by Frances Kellor, life-partner of the New York chapter's president, Mary Dreier. Mary's sister, Margaret Dreier Robins, National WTUL president, was there, and spoke, both deploring Valesh's actions and urging that the Trade Union League give her the benefit of the doubt; but as a guest of the New York League she did not have to vote on Schneiderman's motion. Morgan was not present, but in April, when the final resolution for Valesh's expulsion came up, it was she who moved it.

146. Executive Board Minutes, November 7, 1910, reel 1, NYWTUL.

147. Executive Board Minutes, September 21, 1910, reel 1, NYWTUL. Sometime before 1917, Schneiderman and Blatch were back on friendly terms; they were in Paris together during the signing of the Peace Treaty.

148. The particular charge of obstructing unionization festered until 1914. Harriot objected that her organization was being targeted while the rival society, the Woman Suffrage Party, was allowed to proceed unorganized and unharassed (Blatch to Florence Wise, March 11, 1916, HSB-NY). In 1914, an accord was reached and the WPU's office workers were represented by the Bookkeepers and Stenographers Union and the office was unionized ("Suffragists Yield to Union's Demand," no citation, June 6, 1914, n.p., Rose Schneiderman Papers, Tamiment Library, New York City).

149. In 1911–12, the New York Women's Trade Union League did help to get a Wage Earners' Suffrage League, under the direction of Leonora O'Reilly and linked to the Woman Suffrage Party, off the ground. See Dye, *As Equals and as Sisters*, ch. 6.

150. Blatch and Lutz, *Challenging Years*, p. 137.

151. "New Headquarters for Suffragists," *New York Times*, December 11, 1910, p. 11.

152. *Woman Voter*, December 1910, p. 6.

153. "Proud of the Scars of Suffrage Wars," January 7, 1911, clipping from unnamed source, AC-NY.

154. Women's Political Union, 1911–1912 *Annual Report*, HSB-LC.

155. Mary Isabel Brush, "WPU 5000 Strong," *New York Press*, December 29, 1912, n.p., HSB-LC.

156. "Women's Political Union Open Headquarters Here," *Buffalo Courier*, April 10, 1914, n.p., HSB-LC.

157. Caroline Lexow Babcock, "The Women's Political Union: Its Organization, Achievement and Termination," in Isabelle K. Savelle, *Ladies' Lib: How Rockland Women Got the Vote* (Nyack, N.Y.: Historical Society of Rockland County, 1979), p. 51.

Chapter Five: Politics

1. Harriot Stanton Blatch and Alma Lutz, *Challenging Years: The Memoirs of Harriot Stanton Blatch* (New York: G. P. Putnam's Sons, 1940), p. 120.

2. Richard L. McCormick, *From Realignment to Reform: Politipal Change in New York State, 1893–1910* (Ithaca: Cornell University Press, 1981); Robert Wesser, *A Response to Progressivism: The Democratic Party and New York Politics, 1902–1918* (New York: New York University Press, 1986).

3. Blatch and Lutz, *Challenging Years*, p. 93.

4. Ibid., p. 111.

5. Ibid., "Foreword," by Mary Beard, p. vii.

6. Carrie Chapman Catt, "What Women Have Done with Suffrage," n.d., reel 7, CCC-LC; quoted in Melanie Gustafson's unpublished paper "Partisan Women: Progressive, Republican and Democratic Women in the 1912 and 1916 Elections" (delivered at the 1995 meetings of the American Historical Association).

7. Susan B. Anthony and Ida H. Harper, eds., *History of Woman Suffrage*, v. 4 (Rochester: Susan B. Anthony, 1902), p. 280. Although the shock of betrayal by the Republican party in the 1860s had given birth to an independent woman suffrage movement, it was not until the 1890s that the "lesson" derived from this history was that all political parties were the movement's implacable enemies. In a fine discussion of suffrage nonpartisanship, Aileen Kraditor argues that it was the experiences of the 1890s with Populists and Republicans that generated suffragists' obdurate antiparty attitudes (*Ideas of the Woman Suffrage Movement, 1890–1920* [New York: Columbia University Press, 1965], ch. 8). For an excellent consideration of women's suspicion of parties after 1920, see Nancy Cott, *The Grounding of Modern Feminism* (New Haven: Yale University Press, 1987), pp. 99–114. Conversely, Lori Ginzberg shows that there was substantial interest in party politics among women in the mid-nineteenth century (*Women and the Work of Benevolence: Morality, Politics, and Class in the Nineteenth-Century United States* [New Haven: Yale University Press, 1990]).

8. "Dissensions among Suffragists," *New York Times*, March 10, 1910, p. 8.

9. Gustafson, "Partisan Women." The pioneering discussions of gender and partisanship can be found in Michael McGerr, *The Decline of Popular Politics: The American North, 1865–1928* (New York: Oxford University Press, 1986), pp. 54–56, and Paula Baker, *Moral Frameworks of Public Life: Gender, Politics and the State in Rural New York, 1870–1930* (New York: Oxford University Press, 1991) ch. 2.

10. Blatch and Lutz, *Challenging Years*, p. 91.

11. "Mrs. Blatch's Address," unidentified and undated clipping (c. 1903) from Scrapbooks of Women's Club of Orange, New Jersey, v. 4, New Jersey Historical Society; thanks to Gail Malmgreen for this clipping.

12. Blatch and Lutz, *Challenging Years*, p. 127.

13. Ibid., p. 153.

14. The best account of the male system of honor by which Gilded Age politics were organized can be found in Baker, *Moral Frameworks of Public Life*.

15. Blatch and Lutz, *Challenging Years*, p. 111. Note the difference of language when she describes war, in her *Mobilizing Woman Power* (New York: Womans Press,

1918): "War is not a sport, it is a cold, hard science, demanding every energy of the nation for its successful pursuit" (p. 136).

16. "Suffrage Cheers for Mrs. Pankhurst," *New York Times*, October 21, 1909, p. 1; "Mrs. Pankhurst Has a Day of Triumph," ibid., November 30, 1909, p. 5; "Mrs. Pankhurst's Farewell Address," *Woman's Journal*, December 11, 1909, pp. 199–201.

17. "Mrs. Pankhurst Has a Day of Triumph," p. 3; "Womanly Mrs. Pankhurst," *Woman's Journal*, October 30, 1909, p. 173.

18. "Not a Suffragette," unidentified newspaper clipping, October 14, 1909, AC-NY.

19. Loebinger to Alice Park, March 16, 1910, AP-CA. When a suffragette was dismissed by her assemblyman, who suggested that she instead find a younger legislator, "give him a hug and a kiss . . . the way the girls on the street get what they want," it made the front page. "Insulted at Albany, Girl Delegate Says," *New York Times*, March 10, 1910, p. 1.

20. "Mrs. Pankhurst Due To-Day," *New York Times*, October 20, 1909, p. 5.

21. Blatch, letter to the editor, *Woman's Journal*, July 25, 1908, p. 4; also *New York Times*, December 7, 1907, p. 8. Early on, Blatch debated this point with Bettina Borrman Wells, the rival spokeswoman for British militance, who could not see the point of women's involvement in men's parties ("Suffragettes Show Mettle," *New York Times*, December 7, 1907, p. 8).

22. Harriot links her political emphasis to Pankhurst's example and encouragement in a letter to Dora Albert, July 30, 1930, AL-NY.

23. Blatch and Lutz, *Challenging Years*, p. 116; "Women Watchers at Polls Praise Ballot Casters," *New York World*, November 21, 1909, n.p., HSB-LC; "The Active Suffrage Movement," *Review of Reviews*, December 1909, pp. 653–54. She could still remember the details thirty years later, when talking to Alma Lutz (Lutz, notes from interview with Blatch, June 15, 1939, AL-NY).

24. "Fair Sex on Guard," *New York American*, November 3, 1909, n.p.

25. Lutz, notes from interview with Blatch, June 15, 1939.

26. "Miss Elizabeth Cook Watching at the Polls," *New York Sun*, November 21, 1909, n.p., HSB-LC.

27. "California Farmers Give Vote to Women," *New York Times*, October 13, 1911, p. 1. So close was the vote that the first reports in the *New York Times* were that the referendum lost ("Suffragists Gaining in California Vote," October 12, 1911, p. 3).

28. Women's Political Union Annual Report, 1913–14, p. 12, reel 3, HSB-LC.

29. "Want Suffrage Senator," *New York Times*, December 5, 1909, p. 11. The Independence League was also running a candidate.

30. "Women Complicate 7th District Fight," *Brooklyn Times*, December 9, 1909, n.p., HSB-LC; Equality League of Self-Supporting Women, *Enunciation of a Political Policy*, 1909, pp. 4–5.

31. Blatch, "Question the Candidates," *Woman's Journal*, January 15, 1910, p. 11.

32. Equality League, *Enunciation of a Political Policy*, p. 4.

33. "Mrs. Mackay Opens Campaign at Albany," *New York Times*, January 26, 1910, p. 4.

34. "Lobbyist Splits Ranks," *New York Times*, March 2, 1910, p. 5.

35. Blatch and Lutz, *Challenging Years*, p. 119.

36. Hattie Graham, manuscript report on 1910 New York legislature, HSB-LC. Graham also reported that the chairman of the Senate Judiciary Committee thought Blatch was "very wholesome to look at" but had no intention of supporting woman suffrage.

37. Ibid.

38. Blatch and Lutz, *Challenging Years*, p. 120.

39. "Twenty Years Ago Today in the New York Tribune," *New York Tribune*, June 4, 1924, n.p., BH-Mass.

40. Blatch to Lexow, November 1907, HSB-NY.

41. Thomas to Lexow, November 22, 1909, M. Carey Thomas Papers, reel 149, Bryn Mawr College, Bryn Mawr, Pa.; and Anna Howard Shaw to Maud Wood Park, May 28, 1909, NAWSA-LC.

42. Blatch and Lutz, *Challenging Years*, p. 120.

43. There were reports that Nora had offered her ex-husband five thousand dollars to give up all rights to the child; "100 Suffragettes Led by Baby, Greet Leader from Tug," *Evening World*, January 20, 1913, n.p., HSB-LC. The child was originally named Harriot but changed the spelling of her name to Harriet when she was a young adult; I use the latter spelling.

44. Jim Hijiya, *Lee de Forest and the Fatherhood of Radio* (Bethlehem, Pa.: Lehigh University Press, 1992), pp. 83–86; Lee de Forest, letter to the editor, *New York Evening Mail*, July 27, 1911, n.p., AC-NY; Ethel Avery, letter to the editor, *New York Times*, July 31, 1911, p. 6.

45. "Warning from Mrs. Blatch," *New York Times*, March 5, 1910, p. 4.

46. Blatch and Lutz, *Challenging Years*, p. 122; "Memorial of the Woman Suffrage Legislative Committees of the Senate and Assembly," *Progress*, March 1910, p. 2.

47. Blatch and Lutz, *Challenging Years*, p. 153.

48. The New York State Woman Suffrage Association journal, *Woman Voter* (April 1910, p. 2), reported that "the Committee was forced to kill the bill because of the urgent demands made by other members of the Assembly who wanted to be saved from their promises to support the measure if it got before the House."

49. Equal Franchise Society, "Report of the Legislative Committee," 1910, p. 11, reel 1, HSB-LC.

50. Blatch and Lutz, *Challenging Years*, pp. 111–13. Wadsworth, who became a U.S. senator, remained a staunch opponent of suffrage, and a failed effort to remove him from Congress was one of New York women's first major postsuffrage electoral offensives (Carrie Chapman Catt and Nettie Rogers Shuler, *Woman Suffrage and Politics: The Inner Story of the Suffrage Movement* [New York: Charles Scribner's Sons, 1923], p. 327).

51. *New York Sun*, March 1910, n.p., HSB-NY.

52. Blatch and Lutz, *Challenging Years*, p. 129.

53. Ibid., pp. 135–36.

54. Ibid.; "Women Make It Hot for Artemus Ward," *New York Times*, November 6, 1910, p. 8.

55. "Gowns Scared Solons Away," *New York Globe*, Feburary 22, 1911, n.p., HSB-LC.

56. Anne Herenden, WPU secretary writing for Blatch to O'Reilly, February 16, 1911, with O'Reilly's penned notes, LOR-Mass.

57. Sophonisba P. Breckenridge, *Marriage and the Civic Rights of Women* (Chicago: University of Chicago Press, 1931), p. 20. Her situation was further complicated by the fact that Harry had no intention of renouncing his own nationality. In 1909, after she had reestablished residence in the United States, Harriot began proceedings to reinstate her claim to U.S. citizenship ("Prepares to Cast Her Vote," *New York Times*, December 11, 1909, p. 8). Four years later, a federal district court judge ruled that so long as her husband remained a British subject, she would as well ("Mrs. Blatch Never to Vote," *New York Times*, March 26, 1913, p. 4).

58. "Suffragists' Bill Already," *New York Times*, January 5, 1911, p. 2.

59. On this division, see Elinor Lerner, "American Feminism and the Jewish Question," in *Anti-Semitism in American History*, ed. David A. Gerber (Urbana: University of Illinois Press, 1986), and Nancy Schrom Dye, *As Equals and as Sisters: Feminism, Unionism and the Women's Trade Union League of New York* (Columbia: University of Missouri Press, 1980), pp. 114–15.

60. Irwin Yellowitz, *Labor and the Progressive Movement in New York State, 1897–1916* (Ithaca: Cornell University Press, 1965).

61. "Faint in a Frenzy over Tales of Fire," *New York Times*, March 30, 1911, p. 1; Mari Jo Buhle, *Women and American Socialism, 1870–1920* (Urbana: University of Illinois Press, 1981), pp. 224–27. Two days later, the College Equal Suffrage League held a meeting at Cooper Union. "Public Indifference Held Responsible," *New York Times*, April 1, 1911, p. 3.

62. "Mass Meeting Calls for New Fire Laws," *New York Times*, April 3, 1911, p. 3.

63. "19000 Pay Tribute to the Fire Victims," *New York Times*, April 6, 1911, p. 1.

64. "Suffragists Sing New March Song," *New York Times*, May 1, 1911, p. 5; "Urging Women to Parade: East Side Invaded by the Suffrage Workers," *New York Sun*, n.d., n.p., reel 2, HSB-LC.

65. Lavinia Dock, "Suffrage on the East Side," *Woman Voter*, March 11, 1911, p. 3; Elinor Lerner, "Jewish Involvement in the New York City Woman Suffrage Movement," *American Jewish History*, v. 70, June 1981, pp. 442–61.

66. O'Reilly to Hettie Sherwin, May 12, 1913, reel 6, LOR-Mass. The organization of the WESL represents "the dream of my life come true," said O'Reilly ("Suffrage Demanded by Working Women," *New York Times*, April 23, 1912, p. 24.

67. Blatch to O'Reilly, April 19, 1911, reel 5, LOR-Mass.

68. "Parade Postponed," *Woman's Journal*, October 8, 1910, p. 165; "Suffragists Plan a Street Parade," *New York Times*, February 21, 1911, p. 5; "Suffragists March in Procession Today," *New York Times*, May 6, 1911, p. 13.

69. "Women of All Ranks in Suffrage Parade," *New York Times*, April 15, 1911, p. 13; "Women Parade and Rejoice at End," ibid., May 7, 1911, p. 1.

70. Typescript, "Political History of Women's Political Union," probably by Nora de Forest, p. 9, reel 1, HSB-LC.

71. Blatch and Lutz, *Challenging Years*, p. 143; Women's Political Union, Legislative Report, 1911–12, p. 8, HSB-LC; "Suffragists Off to Albany," *New York Times*, May 9, 1911, p. 11.

72. Women's Political Union, Legislative Report, 1911–12, p. 16.

73. Blatch and Lutz, *Challenging Years*, pp. 151–52.

74. "Legislative Doings and Legislators," *Woman Voter*, July 1911, p. 203; Savelle, *Ladies' Lib*, p. 30.

75. Eunice Dana Brannan, letter to the editor, *New York Times*, July 30, 1911, p. 8.

76. "$100,000 Campaign Fund for Suffrage," *New York Times*, May 17, 1911, p. 1.

77. Women's Political Union, 1911–12 Annual Report, pp. 23–24.

78. Ellen Carol DuBois and Karen Kearns, *Votes for Women: A Seventy Fifth Anniversary Album* (San Marino, Calif.: Huntington Library Press, 1995), pp. 20–23.

79. Caroline to Mamma, January 18, 1912, BH-Mass.

80. Women's Political Union, 1912–13 Annual Report, p. 1.

81. "Political History of Women's Political Union," pp. 13–14; Blatch and Lutz, *Challenging Years*, pp. 162–63.

82. "Suffrage Army to Albany," *New York Times*, March 9, 1912, p. 13.

83. Blatch and Lutz, *Challenging Years*, pp. 164–65.

84. "Promise to Speed the Suffrage Bill" and "Suffrage War Rules," both *New York Times*, March 13, 1912, p. 3.

85. Democratic senator Ferris's "pair" was with Republican Josiah Newcomb, the original sponsor of the woman suffrage bill in 1910, who was unable to attend the session. "Pairing" meant that Ferris promised to withhold what would otherwise be his vote against the bill, as a courtesy to Newcomb, so as not to cost the bill his vote by his absence. Blatch and Lutz, *Challenging Years*, pp. 169–70; Women's Political Union, 1912–13 Annual Report, p. 5.

86. Blatch and Lutz, *Challenging Years*, pp. 171–77; Women's Political Union, 1912–13 Annual Report, pp. 7–8.

87. Blatch, draft autobiography, p. 179, HSB-NY.

88. WPU, leaflet for march in May 1912, HSB-LC.

89. "Suffragists at Tea with Circus Women," *New York Times*, April 8, 1912, p. 7; "Women in Tally-Ho Advertise Parade," ibid., April 14, 1912, p. 7; "Seek Suffrage Recruits," ibid., April 24, 1912, p. 7.

90. "Suffragette Hats. 39 Cents Trimmed," *New York Times*, April 9, 1912, p. 7; "Suffragettes Rush for 39-Cent Hats," ibid., April 30, 1912, p. 8.

91. Blatch to O'Reilly, December 23, 1911, LOR-Mass.

92. "Servants for Suffrage," *New York Times*, May 19, 1912, p. 9, comments on rich women encouraging their servants to march with them.

93. "Suffragists Don't Agree on a Parade," *New York Times*, September 27, 1911, p. 13; "The Cooperative Committee and the Call for a Great Union Parade," *Woman Voter*, January 1911, p. 18; Lerner, "American Feminism and the Jewish Question," p. 317.

94. "Suffragists Don't Agree on a Parade"; Blatch to O'Reilly, December 23, 1911, LOR-Mass.

95. "One Big Suffrage Parade," *New York Times*, February 1, 1912, p. 6.

96. Blatch and Lutz, *Challenging Years*, p. 180.

97. "Suffrage Army on Parade," *New York Times*, May 5, 1912, p. 2; "20,000 Women in Suffrage March; 500,000 Look On," *New York Tribune*, May 5, 1912, p. 1; "17,000 Ardent Women Suffragists, Marching in 5th Avenue, Win New York's Plaudits," *New York Herald*, May 5, 1912, n.p., reel 3, HSB-LC.

98. "A Woman Marcher's View," unidentified clipping, n.d., HSB-LC.

99. Katherine Devereux Blake to Alice Park, n.d., Clippings v. 15, p. 6, SBA-CA.

100. In addition to giving front-page coverage, the *New York Times* devoted an entire pictorial section to the suffrage parade (May 5, 1912, pt. 9).

101. Caroline Lexow Babcock to Alma Lutz, December 28, 1939, AL-NY.

102. Mary Holland Kinkair, "New York's Suffrage Parade," no citation, n.d. [probably June 1912], Clippings v. 15, p. 29, SBA-CA.

103. "Chinese Women to Parade for Woman Suffrage," *New York Times*, April 14, 1912, pt. 7, p. 5.

104. "Suffrage Army on Parade," *New York Times*, May 5, 1912, p. 1.

105. "Suffrage Parader Loses Teaching Job," *New York Times*, May 22, 1912, p. 1.

106. "The Uprising of the Women," *New York Times*, May 5, 1912, p. 14; "For and against Equal Suffrage," ibid., May 11, 1912, p. 121.

107. "The Uprising of the Women" and "The Revolution of Woman," both *New York Times*, May 19, 1912, p. 14.

108. "Views of Men and Women on Suffrage," and Blatch, letter to the editor, both *New York Times*, June 2, 1912, pt. 7, p. 7.

109. "Roosevelt Is for Woman Suffrage," *New York Times*, February 3, 1912, p. 7.

110. "Woman Suffrage by States," *New York Times*, August 6, 1912, p. 2.

111. "Suffragists Fooled," *New York Times*, September 6, 1912, p. 2. The month before, Blatch was counting on victory in Ohio and arranging for Roosevelt to participate in a New York suffrage rally to celebrate it (Blatch to Jane Addams, August 12, 1912, Addams Papers, ser. 1, box 3, Swarthmore College Peace Collection, Swarthmore, Pa.).

112. Blatch, letter to the editor, *New York Times*, September 27, 1912, p. 12.

113. "Political History of WPU," p. 16. Historian Robert Wesser characterizes the suffrage plank as one of the few concessions to reformers in an otherwise conservative platform (*A Response to Progressivism: The Democratic Party and New York Politics, 1902–1918* [New York: New York University Press, 1986], p. 78).

114. Blatch and Lutz, *Challenging Years*, pp. 184–85, 187.

115. Blatch, "Legislature Is Captured," *New York Evening Sun*, November 9, 1912, n.p., HSB-LC.

116. "400,000 Cheer Suffrage March," *New York Times*, November 10, 1912, p. 1.

117. Blatch and Lutz, *Challenging Years*, p. 187.

118. "Cupid of the Cause Lurks in Soapbox," *New York Tribune*, October 1, 1912, n.p., HSB-LC.

119. Transcript of Assembly debate, January 13, 1913, p. 6, HSB-NY. Also see "Joker in the New Votes for Women Bill," *New York Globe* (a Republican paper), January 15, 1913, n.p., HSB-LC.

120. "Suffrage to Suit Women," *New York Times*, January 17, 1913, p. 22.

121. "Joy of Suffragists Tempered by Fear," *New York Tribune*, January 9, 1913, n.p., HSB-LC.

122. "Ready to Leave Albany," no citation, January 23, 1913, HSB-LC.

123. "Tug Load of Women Greets Mrs. Blatch," *New York Evening Press*, January 21, 1913, n.p., HSB-LC.

124. Blatch, draft autobiography, p. 14.

125. "Official Copy of Proposed Amendments," November 2, 1915, HSB-LC.

Chapter Six: Democracy

1. "The Referendum Policy of the Women's Political Union," p. 19, reel 1, HSB-LC.

2. Blatch to Alice Paul, August 26, 1913, reel 4, NWP-SY.

3. "Mrs. Blatch Plans Hot Fight to Win New York to Suffrage," *Chicago Tribune*, March 16, 1913, n.p., reel 2, HSB-LC.

4. "Political Possibilities," *Women's Political World*, July 1, 1913, p. 1.

5. *Winning Equal Suffrage in California, Report of Committees of the College Equal Suffrage League of Northern California of the Campaign of 1911*, 1913.

6. Mary Ware Dennett to Catherine Waugh McCullough, June 5, 1911, McCullough Papers, and Charlotte Whitney to Harriet Burton Laidlaw, June 19, 1911, Laidlaw Papers, both at Schlesinger Library, Cambridge, Mass.

7. Blatch, "Seed Time and Harvest," *Women's Political World*, June 16, 1913, p. 2.

8. My discussion here is indebted to the dissertation work of Margaret Finnegan, who graciously allowed me to read her work in time to profit from its research and analysis ("'So Much Color and Dash': Fighting for Woman Suffrage in the Age of Consumer Capitalism," Ph.D. dissertation, UCLA, 1995).

9. Mary Ryan, *Women in Public: Between Banners and Ballots* (Baltimore: Johns Hopkins University Press, 1990).

10. Finnegan, 'So Much Color and Dash'; Alice Park of California collected examples of such advertisements, which can be found in v. 2, Leaflets, SBA-CA.

11. Harriot Stanton Blatch, "Weaving in a Westchester Farm House," *International Studio*, v. 26, October 1905, p. 103.

12. Harriot Stanton Blatch and Alma Lutz, *Challenging Years: The Memoirs of Harriot Stanton Blatch* (New York: G. P. Putnam's Sons, 1940), p. 192.

13. "Suffragists Tour City to Boom Ball," *New York Daily Mail*, January 11, 1913, n.p., reel 2, HSB-LC.

14. "Society Mingles with Girl Toilers at Suffrage Ball," *New York American*, January 12, 1913, n.p., reel 6, HSB-LC. Harriot, still in the Bahamas, was not present. Kathy Lee Peiss, *Cheap Amusements: Working Women and Leisure in Turn-of-the-Century New York* (Philadelphia: Temple University Press, 1986).

15. Blatch and Lutz, *Challenging Years*, pp. 192–93.

16. Annual Report, Women's Political Union, 1913–1914, reel 3, HSB-LC.

17. "Charity Versus Votes," *Women's Political World*, January 15, 1913, p. 7.

18. *Women's Political World*, April 11, 1913, p. 1.

19. Jim Hijiya, *Lee de Forest and the Fatherhood of Radio* (Bethlehem, Pa.: Lehigh University Press, 1992), p. 159.

20. "Barnard Girls Test Wireless Phones," *New York Times*, February 26, 1909, p. 7.

21. Hijiya, *Lee de Forest*, p. 71.

22. Kay Sloan, "Sexual Warfare in the Silent Cinema: Comedies and Melodramas of Woman Suffragism," *American Quarterly*, v. 33, fall 1981, pp. 412–36. Sloan notes that from 1912 on, commercial movie companies were less inclined to parody and ridicule suffragists than they had been before, and found that there were audiences—and money—in prosuffrage films as well.

23. "Pay Dime and See Suffragist Leaders in Picture Drama," *New York Evening Mail*, June 10, 1912, n.p., reel 4, HSB-LC. The NAWSA also produced suffrage films, "starring" Jane Addams and Anna Howard Shaw. These films depicted their suffragists as noble reformers rather than romantic heroines. Alice Paul, less comfortable with these working-class cultural forms, decided against making a movie (Paul to William A. Ventner, May 9, 1913, reel 2, NWP-SY). Much thanks to Daniel Czitrom and Amy Kesselman, who helped me to locate the 1913 film, a copy of which is available from the University of Missouri at Columbia.

24. *Winning Equal Suffrage in California*, p. 11.

25. "Maternity and Woman Suffrage," *Women's Political World*, June 2, 1913, p. 3.

26. Blatch and Lutz, *Challenging Years*, pp. 191–92.

27. "Male Milliners Balk at Being 'Preserved,'" *New York Tribune*, April 28, 1913, n.p., reel 2, HSB-LC.

28. "Business Chivalry in Practice," *Women's Political World*, June 2, 1913, p. 2.

29. Helen Rogers Reid, untitled speech delivered at Fifth Avenue Suffrage Shop, 1914, typescript, Reid Family Papers, Manuscript Division, Library of Congress.

30. "The Winner: A Roving Shop," *New York Evening Sun*, n.d., [c. April 1915], AC-NY.

31. ". . . With Suffrage Workers," *New York Post*, March 7, 1913, n.p., reel 2, HSB-LC.

32. "Poor Lo Will Ride as a Suffragette," *New York Times*, May 1, 1913, p. 11.

33. "Male Milliners."

34. "Ten Thousand Marchers in Suffrage Line," *New York Times*, May 4, 1913, p. 1.

35. "Crowds Cheer Suffrage Host in Big Parade," *New York Evening Mail*, May 3, 1913, n.p., reel 2, HSB-LC.

36. "Eyes to the Front Will be the Parade Order," *New York Tribune*, May 3, 1913, p. 6.

37. Blatch, "A Reviewing Stand," *Women's Political World*, May 15, 1913, p. 1.

38. "Says Suffrage Idea Is Only Sex Fad," *New York Times*, May 12, 1913, p. 2.

39. "Answers Antis' Attack," *New York Times*, May 13, 1913, p. 3.

40. Elizabeth Newport Hepburn, letter to the editor, *New York Times*, May 15, 1915, p. 10.

41. Blatch, letter to the editor, *New York Evening Sun*, November 11, 1913, n.p., reel 3, HSB-LC.

42. Anna Garlin Spencer to Caroline Lexow, November 4, 1914, box 8, BH-Mass.

43. Sherna Gluck, interview with Laura Ellsworth Sellers, July 1973 and 1974, Claremont, Calif., copy provided to me by Gluck; edited version in Sherna Gluck, ed., *From Parlor to Prison: Five American Suffragists Talk about Their Lives* (New York: Vintage Books, 1976).

44. "Peace Finally Patched Up between Union and WPU," June 8, 1914, no citation, clipping from AL-NY. Harriot suspected that the Women's Trade Union League, which had grown closer to the organization of her rival Carrie Chapman Catt, was harassing the WPU unfairly for partisan reasons (Blatch to Florence Wise, March 11, 1916, HSB-NY). However, unlike the Women's Political Union, the stationery of the Woman Suffrage Party included a mark to indicate that it was prepared by union labor.

45. Interview with Caroline Babcock Furlow, Nyack, N.Y., July 1982.

46. Taylor to Caroline Lexow Babcock, January 4, 1940, AL-NY.

47. Gluck interview with Ellsworth Sellers, p. 31.

48. Mary Grey Peck, "Some American Suffragists," *Life and Labor*, February 1911, p. 5.

49. "We'll Win in '15 Says Mrs. Blatch," *Poughkeepsie Daily News*, n.d. [c. August 1913], reel 3, HSB-LC.

50. Harriot Blatch, "The Old and the New," *Women's Political World*, January 1, 1914, p. 1.

51. Catt to Sarah Algeo, April 9, 1915, reel 2, CCC-LC.

52. In my comparison of Catt's and Blatch's leadership styles, I am indebted to David McDonald, "Organizing Womanhood: Women's Culture and the Politics of Woman Suffrage in New York State 1865–1917," Ph.D. dissertation, SUNY–Stony Brook, 1987.

53. Catt is one of the representative figures for Robert Wiebe's examination of this subject (*Self-Rule: A Cultural History of American Democracy* [Chicago: University of Chicago Press, 1995]).

54. In the 1930s, while working on her autobiography and recalling her antagonism to Catt, Blatch told Alma Lutz, her mother's biographer, the following incident about the 1893 convention at which Anthony assumed the NAWSA presidency: "By courtesy I was allowed to be present at the Executive session of the Organizational Committee of which Mrs. Catt was chairman. No one knew revelations were to be made of Mrs. Catt's and Miss Hay's dirty work.... At a given point, Mrs. [Abigail Scott Duniway] ... whom everyone knew as the President of her State association, truthful, and frank to the point of cruelty, said as she rose that the chief work of the Chairman of the Organization Committee, Mrs. Catt, in Oregon was to send Miss Hay everywhere to urge in private the idea that Miss Anthony was too old to be president and should be persuaded to withdraw as a candidate in favor of Mrs. Catt. The old lady stood there and laid down in her forceful speech an overwhelming structure of facts Before she was half through with her statement of definite facts, Mrs. Catt was in tears. Imagine the scene—the old Oregon war horse whom Mrs. Catt in the chair did not dare to curb, in full charge, Miss Hay for once silenced. It was an awful scene, and neither

Mrs. Catt nor Miss Hay dared peep for several years" (Blatch to Lutz, July 30, 1930, AL-NY). There is no confirmation for this story.

55. Robert Booth Fowler, *Carrie Chapman Catt: Feminist Politician* (Boston: Northeastern University Press, 1986), p. 23.

56. Catt to Millicent Garrett Fawcett, October 19, 1909, CCC-LC; Eleanor Booth Simmons, "Suffrage Pioneers Not Forgotten," *New York Sun*, December 9, 1917, n.p., AC-NY.

57. Catt, letter to the editor, *Woman's Journal*, v. 16 (41), no. 8, February 19, 1910, pp. 30–31.

58. Women's Political Union, "Referendum Policy," 1913, p. 6.

59. Being Harriot's biographer has made it quite difficult to reach a balanced assessment of the Catt-Blatch conflict. I have been much helped by other historians, especially Sandra Ann Moats ("The New York Suffrage Campaign of 1915," Master's thesis, Smith College, 1994) and David McDonald ("Organizing Womanhood").

60. "The Woman's Suffrage Party [sic]," *Woman Voter*, May 1914, p. 23.

61. Blatch and Lutz, *Challenging Years*, p. 205.

62. The Wage Earners Suffrage League, formed by Leonora O'Reilly in 1911, had been brought into the WSP fold by Beard and Laidlaw.

63. Catt to Clara Schlingheyde, December 20, 1912, reel 4, CCC-LC.

64. Catt to Mary Grey Peck, December 12, 1912, reel 4, CCC-LC; New York State Woman Suffrage Association, Annual Report, 1913, p. 37.

65. Belmont to Catt, April 20, 1913, reel 3, NAWSA-LC.

66. Executive Committee, Women's Political Union, to Catt, January 8, 1915, HBL-Mass.

67. NYSWSA, Annual Report, 1913, p. 39. Blatch proudly describes her organization's independent, "militant" stance in "We'll Win in '15 Says Mrs. Blatch," *Poughkeepsie New Press*, n.d. [c. August 1913], reel 3, HSB-LC.

68. Blatch and Executive Committee, WPU to Chairman and Members of the Empire State Campaign Committee, December 31, 1913, enclosure of minutes of meeting of October 22, 1913, prepared by Elizabeth Selden Rogers, NAWSA-LC.

69. Elizabeth Selden Rogers, "Why We Withdrew," *Women's Political World*, November 15, 1913, p. 2.

70. Blatch, letter to the editor, *New York Tribune*, November 24, 1913, n.p., reel 3, HSB-LC.

71. "WPU Hard Hit in New Constitution," *New York Tribune*, November 14, 1913, n.p., reel 3, HSB-LC.

72. Paul to Lexow, November 8, 1913, reel 5, NWP-SY.

73. "NAWSA Convention," *New York Times*, November 9, 1913, p. 8.

74. "War Now Wrinkles Suffragist's Front," November 13, 1913, and "WPU Hard Hit in New Constitution," November 14, 1913, both *New York Tribune*, n.p., reel 3, HSB-LC.

75. Eunice Dana Brannan, letter to the editor, *New York Times*, March 1, 1915, p. 8. The two reasons she gave for the withdrawal were the WPU's desire to control its own funds and the NAWSA's new and disastrous congressional policy on behalf of the Shafroth-Palmer amendment.

76. "Suffrage Day," *New York Call*, May 2, 1914, n.p., reel 3, HSB-LC.

77. For an example of Schneiderman's suffrage work in these years, see "Suffrage Talks in Church," *New York Times*, June 7, 1915, p. 18.

78. Catt to Mary Grey Peck, December 12, 1912, reel 5, CCC-LC.

79. Catt to Mary Grey Peck, November 25, 1914, reel 5, CCC-LC. Robert Fowler, Catt's most recent biographer, argues that she prided herself in controlling and disciplining her anger and her emotional side altogether (Fowler, *Carrie Chapman Catt*, p. 41).

80. Blatch and Lutz, *Challenging Years*, p. 194.

81. "Money Rolls in on Suffrage Call," *New York Tribune*, December 9, 1913, reel 4, HSB-LC.

82. "Scolds Rich Suffragists," *New York Tribune*, March 23, 1914, n.p., reel 3, HSB-LC.

83. Contributions to Women's Political Union and Statement to Budget Committee, 1914, reel 4, HSB-LC.

84. "Soap Box Routs Society," *New York Tribune*, December 31, 1913, n.p., reel 3, HSB-LC.

85. Women's Political Union, Annual Report 1913–1914, reel 4, HSB-LC.

86. Caroline Lexow, Report on 1914 Summer Campaign, HSB-NY.

87. Lexow to Helen Owens, August 21, 1914, box 2, Helen Owens Papers, Schlesinger Library, Cambridge, Mass.

88. Lexow to Mamma, June 23, 1913, BH-Mass.

89. Rogers to Lexow, October 21, 1914, BH-Mass.

90. Blatch and Lutz, *Challenging Years*, p. 219.

91. Blatch to Fola La Follette, March 29, 1915, box E1, the La Follette Family Collection, Manuscript Division, Library of Congress.

92. "We'll Win in '15 Says Mrs. Blatch," *Poughkeepsie News Press*, n.d., [c. August 1913], reel 3, HSB-LC.

93. Elizabeth Freeman to Caroline Lexow Babcock, July 9, 1915, BH-Mass.

94. Blatch and Lutz, *Challenging Years*, pp. 216–17, 220.

95. Mildred Taylor to Caroline Lexow Babcock, January 4, 1940, AL-NY. Taylor went on to become an investigator of municipal politics with the People's Institute in New York.

96. Jane Pincus, Report of Work, March 1914, HSB-NY.

97. Report of Caroline Lexow [to Executive Committee] for the month of February 1913, HSB-NY.

98. "Mrs. Blatch Plans Hot Fight to Win New York to Suffrage," *Chicago Tribune*, March 16, 1913, n.p., reel 2, HSB-LC.

99. "Root Rejoices to Set Hoofs Back in Town," *New York Tribune*, August 19, 1913, reel 3, HSB-LC.

100. "Parade Starts at Court House," *Syracuse Post-Standard*, May 22, 1914, reel 4, HSB-LC.

101. Caroline Lexow, Report on Summer Campaign, May 1914, HSB-NY.

102. Caroline Lexow, Report to the WPU for January and February 1914, HSB-NY.

103. McDonald, "Organizing Womanhood," p. 175.

104. Typed copy of letter from Catt to Blatch, March 14, 1914, and Blatch to Each Member of the Executive Board, HSB-NY.

105. Mrs. G. Alfred Haynes, letter to the editor, "The Facts in the Case," February 26, 1914, and Clara Watson, letter to the editor, n.d., both *Jamestown Evening Post*, reel 4, HSB-LC.

106. "Fair Advocate of Suffrage Will Start Tour Today," n.d. [c. June 1914], unidentified Buffalo paper, reel 3, HSB-LC; Caroline Lexow to Mamma, April 19, 1914, BH-Mass; "Women's Political Union Opens Headquarters Here to Conduct Suffrage Educational Campaign," *Buffalo Courier*, April 10, 1914, reel 4, HSB-LC.

107. Lexow to Pinkus [sic], May 30, 1914, HSB-NY.

108. Pincus to Lexow, March 30, 1914, and Anna Etz to Lexow, February 14, 1914, both HSB-NY.

109. Blatch, draft autobiography, p. 81, HSB-NY.

110. Lexow to Pinkus [sic], May 30, 1914, HSB-NY.

111. Catt and Blatch, To the Members of the Platform Committee and Democratic Conference, August 22, 1914, BH-Mass. Even so, the newspapers reported with great delight intense rivalry between the WPU and the WSP ("Women Rivals in War for Vote," *Evening Mail*, August 24, 1914, AC-NY). And in their accounts, Harriot and Caroline Lexow both recalled obstructionism on the part of Catt (Blatch and Lutz, *Challenging Years*, pp. 225–26; Isabelle K. Savelle, *Ladies' Lib: How Rockland Women Got the Vote* [Nyack, N.Y.: Historical Society of Rockland County, 1979], p. 34).

112. Savelle, *Ladies' Lib*, p. 35.

113. Harriot recalled the WPU's tactics with respect to both the Progressives and the Republicans in detailed and dramatic form (Blatch and Lutz, *Challenging Years*, pp. 220–21, 224–26). Hinman refused to run solely on the Progressive ticket and was not nominated by the Republicans, who chose prosuffrage Charles Whitman ("Hinman Won't Run as Bull Moose," *New York Times*, August 18, 1914, p. 6).

114. Caroline to Mamma, September 14, 1914, BH-Mass.

115. "Find Suffrage a Puzzling Issue," *New York Times*, April 30, 1915, p. 1.

116. Blatch and Lutz, *Challenging Years*, pp. 231–32; "Root Pledges Vote in Fall on Suffrage," *New York American*, May 6, 1915, n.p., reel 4, HSB-LC.

117. WPU Executive Board to Carrie Chapman Catt, January 8, 1915, and Catt to Chairmen of Campaign Districts, January 20, 1915, both in HBL-Mass.

118. Catt to the Executive Board of the Women's Political Union, January 15, 1915, HBL-Mass.

119. "A Change in the World," *Women's Political World*, September 15, 1914, p. 4.

120. The last issue was dated September 15, 1914.

121. "Suffrage Leaders Get Their Innings," *New York Times*, May 19, 1915, p. 5.

122. "$5 Prize for Best Suffrage Baby," *New York Herald*, May 9, 1915, n.p., reel 3, HSB-LC.

123. "Suffrage Husbands Praise Their Wives," *New York Times*, February 25, 1915, p. 6; "Married Folk Talk for Women's Votes," ibid., February 28, 1915, p. 6.

124. Louisine Havemeyer, "The Suffrage Torch, Memories of a Militant," *Scribner's Magazine*, v. 71, no. 5, May 1922, pp. 528–39.

125. Blatch and Lutz, *Challenging Years*, pp. 232–33.

126. Interview with Harriet de Forest, Londonderry, Vt., July 14, 1985; Alma Lutz, notes on conversation with Mary Beard, December 27, 1939, AL-NY.

127. "Blatch Killed by Live Wire," *New York Times*, August 3, 1915, p. 4.

128. Grace Stetson to Theodore, August 23, 1915, TS-NJ.

129. Writing to Theodore, Grace Stetson described Harriot leaving for England "in her usual calm and courageous mood upon her sad errand . . . both your sister and Nora were very brave, tho poor Nora was a heart breaking sight, recalling to me my own step daughter after her father's death" (ibid.). Nora's daughter, Harriet de Forest, remembers that her mother never got over the tragedy but that her grandmother was not very upset by it (de Forest interview).

130. Blatch to Lexow Babcock, n.d., BH-Mass.

131. Lexow Babcock note, much later, on ibid. The engagement notice is in *New York Times*, October 8, 1914, p. 11, and lists Philip as associated with the Standard Oil Company.

132. "Suffragists Differ as to Their Course after Nov. 2," *New York World*, September 30, 1915, n.p., AC-NY.

133. "Mrs Blatch Takes Oath," *New York Times*, August 19, 1915, p. 18.

134. Both Blatch wills are on file at the Public Record Office in London; Blatch to Lexow Babcock, January 15, 1916, reel 23, NWP-SY; Harriet de Forest interview.

135. "$11,000 Verdict for Widow," *New York Times*, November 22, 1916, p. 7. (The $11,000 figure refers to another widow, not Harriot.) The local superintendent of the electric company was also served with papers, after which he committed suicide.

136. Grace Stetson to Theodore Stanton, August 23, 1915, TS-NJ.

137. Blatch to Lexow Babcock, n.d., BH-Mass.

138. Blatch, "English and French Women and the War," *Outlook*, July 29, 1916, pp. 483–90.

139. "Mrs. Blatch Urges U.S. Conscription," *New York Press*, October 19, 1915, n.p., AC-NY.

140. Executive Committee, WPU, to Carrie Chapman Catt, January 8, 1915, HBL-Mass.

141. "Giant Ballots to Plead for Women," *New York World*, October 12, 1915, n.p., AC-NY.

142. "Women Perfecting Plans for Big Suffrage Parade," *New York Morning Telegraph*, October 22, 1915, n.p., reel 4, HSB-LC.

143. "To Honor Memory of Mrs Stanton," *New York Tribune*, October 9, 1915, n.p., AC-NY; "Celebration Held in Honor of Elizabeth Cady Stanton," *Fulton County Democrat*, December 15, 1915, p. 1, reel 4, HSB-LC.

144. Stanton's actual birthday anniversary was November 12, but the celebration was held on October 30, before the November 2 election.

145. The phrase is from Helen Gardener's speech at the event, TS-NJ. Blatch to Mary Church Terrell, April 6, 1915, reel 3, Terrell Papers, Manuscript Division, Library of Congress.

146. Centennial Luncheon Scrapbook, reel 4, HSB-LC. Colby's remarks were published as "Commemoration of the Rights of Women," *New York World*, October 31, 1915.

147. Blatch to Ida Husted Harper, October 21, 1915, AL-NY.

148. Blatch to Anna Howard Shaw, November 4, 1915, AL-NY.

149. Blatch to Harper, October 21, 1915.

150. Lutz, notes on an earlier draft of Blatch autobiography, AL-NY. The version of the Centennial Luncheon that Lutz chose for inclusion in *Challenging Years* (p. 238) is much milder on Catt. Also see Blatch to Lutz, n.d., AL-NY ("You know Mrs Catt refused to attend the luncheon as she wished to work only for referendum efforts. She never saw anything except a woman suffrage convention serving the cause, not even the parades and votes for women balls").

151. "Tammany Neutral in Suffrage Fight," *New York Times*, October 27, 1915, p. 1.

152. "Vote as You Like on Suffrage Is Tammany's Order Says WPU Leader," no citation, October 28, 1915, n.p., AC-NY.

153. "Suffrage Campaign Leaders Confident of Victory," *New York World*, October 2, 1915, n.p., AC-NY.

154. "Literary Digest Poll," *New York Sun*, October 13, 1915, n.p., AC-NY.

155. "Tribune Poll Gives Suffrage Big Lead in New York City," *New York Tribune*, October 17, 1915, n.p., AC-NY.

156. "Shows Leisure Class Is Opposed to the Ballot," *New York Herald*, October 30, 1915, n.p., AC-NY.

157. "Betting against Suffrage," *New York Times*, October 29, 1915, p. 5.

158. "Suffrage Women Tame an Election," *New York Times*, November 3, 1915, p. 4.

159. Women's Political Union, "Summary for Watchers," reel 1, HSB-LC.

160. Ecker to Helen Owens, October 29, 1915, Owens Papers.

161. "Old Traditions Die as Big Vote Is Cast," *New York Times*, November 3, 1915, p. 3.

162. Broome, Chautauqua, Chemung, Cortland, Schenectady, and Tompkins counties.

163. "Defeat of Woman Suffrage," *New York Times*, November 3, 1915, p. 14.

164. Carrie Chapman Catt to Assembly District Leaders, November 6, 1915, HBL-Mass.

165. Catt to Assembly District Chairman, November 5, 1915, HBL-Mass.

166. "Mrs. Blatch Pours Out Wrath on Root," *New York Times*, November 4, 1915, p. 3.

167. "Women Start Triple Drive to Win Vote," November 15, 1915, unidentified clipping, AC-NY.

168. Lillian Wald, letter to the editor, "The East Side and Suffrage," *New York Tribune*, November 4, 1915, n.p., AC-NY. Also see Wald, letter to the editor, "The East Side Vote," *New York Times*, November 6, 1915, p. 10. In a later analysis of the vote, Nora contended that the only city districts that had gone for suffrage were "purely laboring class." The Italians, Serbs, and English had voted against the amendment, the Germans and French in favor, and the American, Irish, and Jews were divided (Nora Blatch de Forest, "The Lessons of the Suffrage Referendum," *Cornell Women's Review*, 1915, pp. 79–82).

169. Blatch and Lutz, *Challenging Years*, pp. 238–39. Historian Robert Wesser agrees that the constitutional convention hurt woman suffrage (*A Response to Progressivism: The Democratic Party and New York Politics, 1902–1918* [New York: New York University Press, 1986], p. 200).

170. Blatch to Anna Howard Shaw, November 4, 1915, HSB-NY. See similar observations in Blatch to Margaret Dreier Robins, November 4, 1915, Robins Collection, University of Florida, Gainesville. In her analysis of the vote in the *Cornell Women's Review*, Nora also argued that "the inadequacy of the upstate campaign killed us," but did not place the blame exclusively on the ESCC, contending that "the only districts that carried upstate were those in which two suffrage organizations had each been spurring the other on to further efforts."

171. Blatch to J. Hampden Dougherty, February 25, 1916, HSB-NY; "Suffragists Call the President Weak," *New York Times*, February 12, 1915, p. 6.

172. Blatch, letter to the editor, "The Suffragists' Lever," *New York Times*, December 2, 1915, p. 10.

Chapter Seven: Victories

1. The WPU commissioned a formal brief on the constitutionality of the presidential suffrage method, in the midst of the New York referendum (reel 3, HSB-LC). Carrie Catt later remarked that she thought presidential suffrage was crucial in the pressure put on Congress to pass the Nineteenth Amendment (Catt to Elizabeth Booth, February 25, 1941, reel 2, CCC-LC).

2. Blatch, letter to the editor, "The Suffragists' Lever," *New York Times*, December 2, 1915, p. 10.

3. Blatch, letter to the editor, *New York Times*, November 30, 1915, p. 10.

4. Isabelle K. Savelle, *Ladies' Lib: How Rockland Women Got the Vote* (Nyack, N.Y.: Historical Society of Rockland County, 1979), p. 43.

5. It was agreed that the Congressional Committee would have no budget provided it, but would raise its own funds. Paul to Dora Lewis, November 24, 1918, reel, 65, NWP-SY.

6. Harriot Stanton Blatch and Alma Lutz, *Challenging Years: The Memoirs of Harriot Stanton Blatch* (New York: G. P. Putnam's Sons, 1940), p. 195.

7. Blatch to Paul, January 31, 1913, reel 1, NWP-SY.

8. Ellen Carol DuBois, ed., *The Elizabeth Cady Stanton—Susan B. Anthony Reader*, 2d ed. (Boston: Northeastern University Press, 1992), pt. 3.

9. This controversy is covered in the National Woman's Party—Suffrage Years papers from November 1914 through January 1915. Mary Beard and other Congressional Union loyalists who understood the New York scene counseled Paul to hold back until the referendum was over. Paul's eagerness to get to New York seems to have been due, at least in part, to the fact that the state "is such an excellent field for raising money" (Paul to Beard, November 9, 1914, reel 13, NWP-SY).

10. "Women's Political Views," *New York Times*, June 5, 1914, p. 8.

11. Paul to W. E. B. Du Bois, July 12, 1913, reel 3, and Paul to Maud Wood Park, July 23, 1913, reel 4, NWP-SY. Paul was counseled on this approach by Alice Stone

Blackwell, who though uneasy because of her family's abolitionist background, nonetheless recommended that a large black presence in the first national suffrage parade would be unwise (Paul to Stone Blackwell, January 15 and 23, 1913, reel 1, NWP-SY). Mary Ware Dennett, corresponding secretary of the National American, disagreed, arguing that Paul's advice to the African American suffragists not to march "amounted to official discrimination which is distinctly contrary to instructions from National Headquarters" (Dennett to Paul, February 28, 1913, reel 1, NWP-SY).

12. Paula Giddings, *When and Where I Enter: The Impact of Black Women on Race and Sex in America* (New York: William Morrow, 1984), p. 127; Rosalyn Terborg-Penn, "Afro-Americans in the Struggle for Woman Suffrage," Ph.D. dissertation, Howard University, 1977. Christine Lunardini describes this incident from Paul's viewpoint (*From Equal Suffrage to Equal Rights: Alice Paul and the National Woman's Party, 1910–1928* [New York: New York University Press, 1986], pp. 26–27).

13. Mary White Ovington to Blatch, December 3, 1920, Blatch to Paul, November 20, 1920, Wold to Blatch, December 29, 1920, all reel 5, NWP-ERA. This incident is covered at length in Giddings, *When and Where I Enter*, pp. 164–69. Nancy Cott's judgment—that Paul's single-issue focus was at work—is not as harsh as mine (*The Grounding of Modern Feminism* [New Haven: Yale University Press, 1987], p. 70).

14. For Harriot's response to the New York violence, see her letter to the editor, *New York Times*, May 18, 1912, p. 12.

15. "Rowdies Helped Suffrage," *New York Tribune*, March 5, 1913, reel 2, HSB-LC; Blatch and Lutz, *Challenging Years*, p. 197.

16. Lunardini, *From Equal Suffrage*, pp. 36–37.

17. Eleanor Flexner, *Century of Struggle: The Women's Rights Movement in the United States* (Cambridge, Mass.: Belknap Press of Harvard University Press, 1959), p. 266. Caroline Katzenstein (*Lifting the Curtain: The State and National Woman Suffrage Campaigns in Pennsylvania as I Saw Them* [Philadelphia: Dorrance, 1955], p. 137) recalls that Paul had initially thought to call the independent organization the Women's Political League, a clear reference to the New York organization.

18. Blatch to Lucy Burns, December 22, 1914, reel 14, NWP-SY.

19. Blatch, "The Old and the New," *Women's Political World*, January 1, 1914, p. 1.

20. Paul to Beard, November 9, 1914, reel 13, and Blatch to Hill, January 19, 1915, reel 14, NWP-SY.

21. Blatch to Paul, February 1, 1915, reel 15, NWP-SY. Lucy Burns was cofounder of the Congressional Union.

22. In May 1915, Congressional Union activists pursued President Wilson to grant them an interview while he was in New York. Catt and other New York suffragists accused them of "harrying" the president and imperiling the referendum. In the incident, Blatch defended Paul. "I have always regarded Miss Paul as an enthusiast with good political sense. Getting an appointment for their interview was an important step" ("Woman Suffrage Wins Men," *New York Times*, May 29, 1915, p. 13).

23. "Women Start Triple Drive to Win Vote," November 15, 1915, no citation, AC-NY.

24. "Mrs. Blatch Now in Federal Fight," *New York Times*, November 7, 1915, pt. 2, p. 19.

25. Hazard to Babcock, December 13, 1915, BH-Mass. In a set of explanatory notes attached to this letter, Babcock later wrote, "Mrs. Brannan was a key figure because of her personal acquaintance with many rich people and her ability to pry large sums of money out of them."

26. Rogers to Lexow Babcock, November 25, 1915, BH-Mass.

27. Taylor to Paul, November 12, 1915, reel 20, NWP-SY.

28. "Mrs. Blatch Retires," *New York Times*, November 24, 1915, p. 5.

29. Blatch to Lucy Burns, January 2, 1916, reel 23, NWP-SY.

30. Blatch to Lucy Burns, January 22, 1916, AL-NY.

31. Caroline Lexow Babcock, handwritten notes relating to November 25, 1915, letter from Elizabeth Selden Rogers, n.d., BH-Mass.

32. This language is from the letter from Blatch to WPU members, explaining the meeting's conclusions, n.d., HSB-NY.

33. Hazard to Paul, January 31, 1916, reel 23, NWP-SY.

34. Brannan to Paul, December 14, 1915, reel 22, NWP-SY.

35. "The Rising Tide," *Women's Political World*, March 1, 1914, p. 1; "Statement by Mrs. Harriot Stanton Blatch," November 3, 1915, HSB-NY.

36. Paul to Blatch, November 16, 1915, AL-NY; Blatch to Paul, November 22, 1915, reel 21, NWP-SY.

37. Blatch, letter to the editor, *New York Times*, December 2, 1915, p. 10; speech for 1916 western tour, HSB-NY.

38. Blatch to Paul, August 6, 1913, reel 30, NWP-SY; "Woman Suffrage in Constitution," *New York Times*, April 14, 1913, p. 6; Beatrice Brown to Paul, July 28, 1913, reel 4, NWP-SY.

39. Paul to Blatch, September 3, 1914, and Blatch to Paul, September 17, 1914, reel 12, NWP-SY.

40. Eleanor Brannan and Elizabeth Rogers to Executive Committee and Advisory Council of the Congressional Union, June 16, 1915, NAWSA-LC; Christine Lunardini believes that the Congressional Union had an impact (*From Equal Suffrage*, pp. 67–68), as does Doris Stevens (*Jailed for Freedom* [New York: Liveright, 1920], p. 36).

41. Blatch to Martin, January 21, 1916, reel 23, NWP-SY.

42. "Women to Migrate to Suffrage Lands," *New York Times*, December 16, 1915, pt. 2, p. 13. Ironically, her success at casting her vote in Kansas in 1916 cost Harriot her right to vote in New York in 1918 (Blatch to Martin, October 3, 1918, Martin Papers, Bancroft Library, University of California, Berkeley).

43. Paul to Blatch, March 2, 1916, reel 24, NWP-SY.

44. Paul to Beard, March 18, 1916, reel 25, NWP-SY.

45. Beard to Paul, March 23, 1916, reel 25, NWP-SY.

46. Margaret Fay Whiteman to Paul, April 26, 1916, reel 27, NWP-SY.

47. Helen Hunt Weed to Blatch, March 23, 1916, reel 25, NWP-SY.

48. Blatch and Lutz, *Challenging Years*, pp. 259–60.

49. Blatch speech in Arizona, April 21, 1917, reel 26, NWP-SY.

50. Blatch speech in Colorado Springs, April 1917, NWP-SY.

51. Blatch speech in Salem, Oregon, n.d. [c. April 30, 1916], AL-NY.

52. I thank Rebecca Mead (of UCLA), who is writing a dissertation on suffrage in the west, for this observation.

53. Blatch speech, no title, n.d. [1916], AL-NY.

54. "Mrs. Stanton Blatch to the Woman's Party Convention, Chicago, June 6, 1916," *Suffragist*, June 17, 1916, p. 10.

55. Ida M. Tarbell, "Woman's Party Real Factor in US Politics," *Chicago Herald*, June 7, 1916, n.p., HSB-NY.

56. "Pinchot on Behalf of Progressive Party at National Woman's Party Convention," June 8, 1916, no citation, reel 28, NWP-SY.

57. "Mrs. Harriot Stanton Blatch to the Woman's Party Convention, Chicago."

58. Ibid.

59. Doris Stevens to Blatch, August 11, 1936, AL-NY. Stevens first met Malone at this event. As she explained to Harriot, "Admiration and profound respect after being defeated by a woman, overtakes men."

60. Blatch to Anne Martin, July 9, 1916, reel 29, NWP-SY.

61. Blatch and Lutz, *Challenging Years*, pp. 264–65.

62. Blatch to Paul, July 9, 1916, AL-NY; also Blatch to Katherine Fisher, July 6, 1916, reel 29, NWP-SY.

63. Blatch, "Points for Speech," HSB-NY; also Blatch and Lutz, *Challenging Years*, pp. 268–69. See Suzanne Lebsock, "Woman Suffrage and White Supremacy," in *Visible Women*, ed. Nancy Hewitt and Suzanne Lebsock (Urbana: University of Illinois Press, 1993), for a discussion of the constraints under which white suffragists responded to this staple claim of the antis. Nancy Cott has perceptively observed to me that when historians try to account for Wilson's reluctance to support the Nineteenth Amendment, they do not usually include defense of white supremacy as one of his motives.

64. Blatch to Paul, July 18, 1916, and Paul to Dora Hazard, telegram, July 22, 1916, reel 30, NWP-SY.

65. Blatch to Paul, August 2, 1916, reel 30, NWP-SY.

66. Stevens, *Jailed for Freedom*, p. 46. Inez Haines Irwin says the same thing in *The Story of Alice Paul and the National Women's* [sic] *Party* (Fairfax, Va.: Denlinger's Publishers, 1974), p. 177.

67. Louise Bryant to Sara Bard Field, n.d. [c. October 10, 1916], box 112, Charles Erskine Wood Papers, Huntington Library, San Marino, Calif.

68. E. M. Barker, Berkeley, Calif., to Paul, October 1916, reel 34, NWP-SY.

69. Blatch to Paul, October 15, 1916, AL-NY. Inez Milholland's husband, Eugene Boissevan, wrote to Paul to object to newspaper coverage that described his wife as having "gone west to speak for old 'tin whiskers' the same as the Hughesites" (Eugene Boissevan to Paul, October 26, 1916, reel 34, NWP-SY).

70. Paul to Katherine Mooney, October 31, 1916, reel 35, NWP-SY.

71. Vivian Pierce to Paul, October 21, 1916, reel 34, NWP-SY.

72. Beard to Paul, February 21, 1916, reel 24, and Beard to Paul, April 6, 1916, reel 26, NWP-SY.

73. Vivian Pierce to Paul, October 21, 1916, reel 34, NWP-SY. Winslow had been successful in appealing to workers in strike-ravaged Trinidad (Florence Hilles, report on Colorado Federation of Labor Conference, August 1916, reel 31, NWP-SY).

74. Paul to Elsie Hill, September 29, 1916, reel 33, NWP-SY.

75. Alice Carpenter to Paul, October 27, 1916, reel 34, and Paul to Carpenter, November 1, 1916, reel 35, NWP-SY.

76. Ella Riegel to Mrs. Mackaye, September 28, 1916, reel 33, NWP-SY.

77. Hill to Paul, October 17, 1916, reel 34, NWP-SY.

78. Blatch to Hill, October 13, 1916, reel 34, NWP-SY.

79. Blatch to Paul, October 15, 1915, reel 34, NWP-SY.

80. Alida Hammon to Paul, October 23, 1916, reel 34, NWP-SY.

81. Paul to Ella Riegel, September 21, 1916, reel 32, NWP-SY.

82. "Most of our organizers would receive a similar [negative] edict from a doctor if they consulted one" (Paul to Ella Riegel, September 21, 1916, reel 32, NWP-SY).

83. Stevens, *Jailed for Freedom*, p. 48.

84. "Eastern Appeal Carried to Women Voters," *Suffragist*, November 14, 1916, pp. 4–5.

85. Marjorie Miller Hitteman to Vivian Pierce, November 2, 1916, reel 35, NWP-SY.

86. "Reported the Women Voted Overwhelmingly for Hughes," *Chicago Tribune*, November 9, 1916, p. 4; Joel H. Goldstein, *The Effects of the Adoption of Woman Suffrage: Sex Differences in Voting Behavior—Illinois, 1914–1921* (New York: Praeger, 1983).

87. Blatch, "The Woman in the Case," n.d. [November 1916], HSB-NY.

88. Stevens, *Jailed for Freedom*, p. 59.

89. Blatch to Paul, January 14, 1917, reel 37, NWP-SY.

90. Blatch to Martin, January 14, 1917, reel 37, NWP-SY.

91. Blatch to Paul, January 27, 1917, reel 37, NWP-SY. Harriot was not the only militant to urge that picketing, while useful, should not replace the strategy of using the power of voting women to pressure the president and Congress (Ethel Adamson to Alice Paul, January 20, 1917, reel 38, and Mary Beard et al. to Mrs. Gardner, January 13, 1917, reel 37, NWP-SY). Ironically the White House "silent sentinels" device was the only one of the many militant activities that Harriot influenced for which historians of the Woman's Party have given her proper credit (Stevens, *Jailed for Freedom*, p. 58).

92. Amelia Fry, *Conversations with Alice Paul: Woman Suffrage and the Equal Rights Amendment, 1972–1973* (Berkeley: Suffragists Oral History Project, 1976), p. 338.

93. Blatch to Paul, February 5, 1917, and Paul to Blatch, February 6, 1917, reel 2, NWP-ERA.

94. "Suffrage Worker Resigns: Objects to Picketing," *New York Herald*, February 20, 1917, n.p., and "Mrs. Blatch Quits Suffragist Union," *New York Post*, February 20, 1917, n.p., reel 33, NAWSA-LC.

95. Proceedings, Congressional Union Convention, Washington, D.C., March 2, 1917, p. 5, reel 40, NWP-SY.

96. Ibid.

97. Ibid., p. 7.

98. Ibid., p. 3.

99. Blatch to Martin, February 3, 1917, reel 38, NWP-SY.

100. "Suffragists Deny Split," *New York Times*, February 24, 1917, p. 16. Crystal Eastman, one of the NWP pacifists, wrote to Paul that her statement "satisfies me absolutely" (Eastman to Paul, February 14, 1917, reel 39, NWP-SY).

101. This is how I read Nancy Cott's treatment of this period in *The Grounding of Modern Feminism*, p. 61.

102. Carrie Chapman Catt, "Organized Womanhood," *Woman Voter*, April 1917, p. 9.

103. Paul to Belmont, February 24, 1917, reel 39, NWP-SY; "Suffragists Fight Army Aid," *New York Tribune*, February 11, 1917, n.p., AC-NY; Minutes, February 27, 1917, WSP-NY.

104. "Sacrificed to Suffrage," reprint from *New Republic*, in *Woman Voter*, June 1916, p. 21.

105. Gertrude Foster Brown, unpublished manuscript, "On Account of Sex," ch. 16, p. 5, c. 1940, Sophia Smith Collection, Smith College, Northampton, Mass.

106. Elinor Lerner, "Jewish Involvement in the New York City Woman Suffrage Movement," *American Jewish History*, v. 70, June 1981, pp. 442–61.

107. "Mrs. Blatch to Women," *New York Times*, November 13, 1917, p. 12.

108. Blatch to Martin, March 30, 1918, Martin Papers. I am indebted to Nancy Cott for alerting me to this Blatch-Martin correspondence.

109. Blatch to Milinowski, April 8, 1917, HSB-NY.

110. Stetson to Theodore Stanton, August 23, 1915, TS-NJ.

111. David M. Kennedy, *Over Here: The First World War and American Society* (Oxford: Oxford University Press, 1980). See two new biographical accounts of prowar progressives: Robert Westbrook, *John Dewey and American Democracy* (Ithaca: Cornell University Press, 1991), and David Levering Lewis, *W. E. B. Du Bois: Biography of a Race*, 1868–1919 (New York: Henry Holt, 1993).

112. On the National Woman's Party tour in the fall of 1916, Blatch declared that "Europe is going through a baptism of fire and blood, being born again, born to fullest democracy" (speech, 1916, HSB-NY).

113. Blatch to Stevens, November 30, 1917, reel 41, NWP-SY.

114. Ibid., p. 12.

115. Blatch, *Mobilizing Woman Power* (New York: Womans Press, 1918), pp. 88–90.

116. If the book was unspectacularly received at the time, historians have since recognized it as the era's most comprehensive progressive-feminist case for war. See William L. O'Neill, *Everyone Was Brave: The Rise and Fall of Feminism in America* (Chicago: Quadrangle Books, 1969), pp. 187–89; J. Stanley Lemons, *The Woman Citizen: Social Feminism in the 1920s* (Urbana: University of Illinois Press, 1973), pp. 15, 25.

117. Molly Ladd-Taylor describes the varieties of maternalist rhetoric used during the Progressive era (in *Mother-Work: Women, Child Welfare, and the State*, 1890–1930 (Urbana: University of Illinois Press, 1994).

118. Blatch, *Mobilizing Woman Power*, p. 176.

119. Blatch, "War and the Work of Women," *Pearson's Magazine*, n.d., p. 103, from general clipping files, Smith College, Northampton, Mass.

120. Theodore Roosevelt to Harriot Blatch, March 22, 1918, HSB-NY.

121. The original, with corrections, of the foreword can be found in reel 309, Theodore Roosevelt Papers, Manuscript Division, Library of Congress.

122. Blatch to Anne Martin, January 10, 1919, Martin Papers.

123. This extensive correspondence can be found in the Blatch Papers, Vassar College, Poughkeepsie, N.Y.; see for instance Harriot to Nora, March 9, 1919.

124. Comment on shipboard classes, Harriot to Nora, February 25, 1919; "wailing children," Harriot to Nora, probably February 13, 1919; "not customary," Harriot to Nora, February 14, 1919, all HSB-NY.

125. The friend was Millicent Garrett Fawcett and Harriot describes the heavy clothes she was wearing against the cold. Harriot to Nora, March 19, 1919, HSB-NY.

126. Harriot to Nora, March 30, 1919, HSB-NY.

127. Diary entry, April 6, 1919, from Blatch, *Woman's Point of View*, pp. 30–31; Harriot to Nora, April 10, 1919, HSB-NY.

128. Harriot to Nora, April 26, 1919, HSB-NY.

129. See a similar observation in Jane Addams, *Peace and Bread in Time of War* (New York: Macmillan, 1922): despite the evidence of nationalism's destructive impact, everywhere "in that moment . . . the nation was demanding worship and devotion for its own sake similar to that of the mediaeval church" (p. 174).

130. Harriot to Nora, April 29, 1919, HSB-NY.

131. Harriot to Nora, May 22, 1919, HSB-NY. Harriot's May 25, 1919, letter to Nora (HSB-NY), written after her return from Switzerland, is particularly overbearing. She wants Nora, who is inclining to live in New York City, to settle in Greenwich, for young Harriet's sake. Harriot even goes so far as to sketch out a design for a house they should build in Connecticut, although Nora was an engineer and contractor.

132. Harriot to Nora, May 17, 1919, HSB-NY.

133. Harriot to Nora, May 26, 1919, HSB-NY.

134. Wald incident, Harriot to Nora, May 22, 1919; return voyage, Harriot to Nora, June 19, 1919, both HSB-NY.

135. Blatch, *Woman's Point of View*, p. 24.

136. Ibid., pp. 5–6.

137. Ibid., p. 78.

138. Blatch, letter to the editor, *Suffragist*, March 9, 1920, n.p., HSB-NY.

139. Ibid., p. 173.

140. Blatch to Doris Stevens, telegram, July 17, 1917, reel 45, NWP-SY; she was particularly critical of NAWSA public statements condemning the pickets.

141. Blatch to Elsie Hill, March 22, 1921, reel 7, NWP-ERA.

142. Blatch to Paul, November 13, 1919, AL-NY.

143. Blatch, *Woman's Point of View*, p. 74.

144. Blatch to Anne Martin, May 14, 1918, Martin Papers.

Chapter Eight: Feminism

1. As the NWP journal, the *Suffragist*, put it in 1920, women had the simple and stark choice of either "entering existing parties and boring from within" or "staying outside the parties . . . pursuing a campaign based on the political strategy used by the Woman's party to win suffrage." "Woman's Party Leaders Confer on Present and Future Plans," *Suffragist*, October 1920, p. 232.

2. The best account of this period is Nancy Cott, *The Grounding of Modern Feminism* (New Haven: Yale University Press, 1987).

3. "Urges Suffragists Not to Stand Alone," *New York Times*, December 7, 1917, p. 12.

4. Harriot to Nora, May 4, 1919, HSB-NY.

5. Harriot Blatch, *Mobilizing Woman Power* (New York: Womans Press, 1918), p. 48.

6. Carol Dyhouse, *Feminism and the Family in England 1880–1939* (London: Basil Blackwell, 1989); Jane Lewis, *The Politics of Motherhood: Child and Maternal Welfare in England* (London: Croom Helm, 1980); Polly Beals, "Fabian Feminism: Gender, Politics and Culture in London, 1880–1930," Ph.D. dissertation, Rutgers University, 1989.

7. Blatch, "English and French Women and the War," *Outlook*, June 29, 1916, p. 486.

8. M.A., "The Economic Foundations of the Women's Movement," in *Women's Fabian Tracts*, ed. Sally Alexander (London: Routledge, 1988), p. 276.

9. Dyhouse, *Feminism and the Family*, pp. 93–94.

10. Susan Pedersen, "The Failure of Feminism in the Making of the British Welfare State," *Radical History Review*, no. 43, winter 1989, p. 88.

11. Dyhouse, *Feminism and the Family*, p. 98; Blatch, *Mobilizing Woman Power*, p. 58.

12. Blatch, *Mobilizing Woman Power*, p. 117.

13. Harriot Blatch, *A Woman's Point of View: Some Roads to Peace* (New York: Womans Press, 1920), p. 67.

14. In England, the motherhood endowment scheme was eventually modified to family endowments, which were justified in terms of child welfare, not recognition of maternal labor. For a critical evaluation of this shift, see Lewis, *Politics of Motherhood*, p. 171.

15. Blatch, *A Woman's Point of View*, p. 166. Other American feminists who shared her enthusiasm were Crystal Eastman and Mary Beard.

16. Alice Kessler-Harris, *Out to Work: A History of Wage-Earning Women in the United States* (Oxford: Oxford University Press, 1982), p. 194. The impact of the victory of woman suffrage in November 1917 should also not be minimized; the women of New York were now in a position to advance their own legislative agenda, rather than depend on men to do it for them.

17. Nancy Schrom Dye, *As Equals and as Sisters: Feminism, Unionism and the Women's Trade Union League of New York* (Columbia: University of Missouri Press, 1980), p. 149.

18. This distinction was observed twenty years later in her obituary in the *New York Herald*, November 21, 1940, p. 32.

19. Blatch's charges are referred to in "More about Special Legislation," *New York Tribune*, January 26, 1919, sect. 3, p. 12.

20. Blatch to Martin, May 14, 1918, Anne Martin Papers, Bancroft Library, University of California, Berkeley.

21. "More about Special Legislation," p. 12.

22. "Women Fail to Agree on Welfare Measures," *New York Times*, March 6, 1919, p. 7; also "Women in Clamor over Labor Bills," *New York World*, April 18, 1919, n.p., AC-NY. Mary Dreier, the original proponent of the bills, had become a Republican. There was a prolonged contest between the progressive wing of the Republicans and the Smith-Wagner-Roosevelt Democrats about which party would get credit for the bills. See the letter by Sarah McPike to the editor, *New York Times*, January 6, 1920, p. 14.

23. On her later opposition to sex-based labor legislation, see Nora Barney's "Women as Human Beings: A Plea for Equal Opportunity" (1946) self-published in Greenwich, Conn., RBJ-CT. Nora was also closer to the NWP than was her mother, though she had her own battles with Alice Paul in later years.

24. Harriot to Nora, April 10, 1919, HSB-NY.

25. Harriot to Nora, May 4, 1919, HSB-NY.

26. Harriot to Nora, April 10 and June 2, 1919, HSB-NY. For an indication that Harriot and the WTUL women were on good terms during this visit, see Anderson's letter to her, November 12, 1920, reel 5, NWP-ERA.

27. Harriot to Nora, June 2, 1919, HSB-NY; "Studies Labor Abroad," *New York Times*, July 7, 1919, pt. 13, p. 3.

28. Elisabeth Israels Perry, *Belle Moskowitz: Feminine Politics and the Exercise of Power in the Age of Alfred E. Smith* (New York: Oxford University Press, 1987), p. 149.

29. "Predicts Repeal of Welfare Bills," *New York Times*, December 28, 1919, p. 20. After reelection, Sweet continued to lead the battle against maximum hour and minimum wage legislation for women workers, which became increasingly associated with conservative Republicanism. His most formidable opponent was Democratic governor Al Smith. The conflict among women supporters and opponents intensified, peaking in a charge by the League of Women Voters that Sweet was running an "unlawful lobby to kill social welfare bills" ("Urges Lobby Investigation," *New York Times*, March 26, 1920, p. 12). Eventually the night-work prohibitions as they affected women printers and conductors were repealed. The minimum wage and maximum hours bills were never passed. If anything, in the years after women got the vote, prospects for labor regulation by sex diminished in New York. See Elisabeth Faulkner Baker, *Protective Labor Legislation with Special Reference to the State of New York* (New York: Columbia University Press, Studies in the Social Sciences no. 259, 1925).

30. Blatch, letter to the editor, "The Welfare Bills," *New York Times*, January 12, 1920, p. 8.

31. "What Next," *Suffragist*, October 1920, p. 235. The other major NWP advo-

cate of universal motherhood endowments was Eleanor Taylor, who wrote frequently in the *Suffragist* on the issue ("Wages for Mothers," November 1920, p. 273).

32. Cott, *Grounding of Modern Feminism*, pp. 70–72.

33. Paul to Mrs. Morgan Barney, January 19, 1921, reel 5, NWP-ERA.

34. "Absolute Equality Women's New Cry," *New York Times*, February 17, 1921, p. 11; Nora Stanton Barney, "The Feminist Party," letter to the editor, February 22, 1921, ibid., p. 16.

35. Kelley to Elsie Hill, March 21, 1921, reel 7, NWP-ERA.

36. Blatch to Hill, April 22, 1921, reel 7, NWP-ERA. Many historians get this crucial fact wrong, no doubt because of Harriot's consistent opposition to special labor laws for women. At the very end of her life, Harriot associated with a breakaway wing of the NWP led by Edith Houghton Hooker.

37. "Women to Maintain Separate Lobbies," *New York Times*, December 15, 1922, p. 20.

38. Blatch, "Legislation for Women," letter to the editor, *New York Times*, December 18, 1922, p. 16. Alma Lutz wrote in the 1930s that when she was completing *Challenging Years*, Caroline Lexow Babcock told her that "indefatigable and fine as Florence Kelley was in the suffrage campaign, Blatch would say that again and again— when suffrage is won, Florence Kelley will go one way and we another" (undated notes for *Challenging Years*, AL-NY).

39. Blatch, "Do Women Want Protection: Wrapping Women in Cotton Wool," *Nation*, January 31, 1923, pp. 115–16.

40. Debate before Columbia Sociological Society, May or June 1923, BH-Mass. Also see Blatch, "The Industrial Woman," *New York Times*, August 22, 1922, p. 16.

41. Blatch to Mollie Ray Carroll, October 30, 1923, HSB-NY.

42. Lavinia Egan, "The Seneca Falls Conference," *Equal Rights*, August 4, 1923, p. 196.

43. Blatch's notations on Program for the 1923 Conference, ECS-LC.

44. Blatch, "Can Sex Equality Be Legislated," *Independent* v. 3, December 22, 1923, p. 301.

45. Blatch to Catt, January 8, 1924, reel 3, NAWSA-LC.

46. "Talk of a Third Party," *New York Times*, March 31, 1920, p. 17.

47. Anita Block, "Harriot Stanton Blatch Joins the Socialist Party," *Takoma Leader*, July 10, 1920, p. 1; thanks to Mari Jo Buhle for sending me this clipping.

48. Ibid.

49. Blatch to Anne Martin, June 18, 1920, Martin Papers. The woman was Louisine Havemeyer, whose husband was a sugar magnate, and the issue was the nationalization of basic industries, which Martin was advocating in her candidacy for the U.S. Senate.

50. "Opposition to Welfare Bills," *Christian Science Monitor*, January 5, 1920, n.p., SBA-CA.

51. Jessie Hughan to Alma Lutz, September 30, 1939, AL-NY; Hillquit to Blatch, June 14, 1920, Hillquit Papers, State Historical Society, Madison, Wisc.

52. Blatch, *Why I Joined the Socialist Party* (Chicago: Socialist Party of the USA, 1919), p. 1. Of course, Harriot had her own discomfort with the "foreignness,"

especially the Jewishness, of American socialism, which this boast betrays. To Caroline Lexow Babcock she wrote that she did not like how much the Socialists were controlled by "men who speak broken English and who show an old time attitude to women," who regard themselves as "'the chosen people of god'" (Blatch to Babcock, note probably October 19, 1920, on letter from Block to Blatch, September 20, 1920, HSB-NY).

53. Blatch, *To Mother* (Chicago: Socialist Party of the USA, 1920).

54. Ibid.

55. Block, "Harriot Stanton Blatch Joins the Socialist Party."

56. For a fine overview of the Socialist party after 1917, see James Weinstein, *The Left in American Politics* (New York: New Viewpoint, 1975).

57. On May 1, 1919, she was in Paris during the general strike. Harriot to Nora, dated April 29, 1919 (actually to May 3), HSB-NY.

58. Blatch, *Woman's Point of View*, p. 58.

59. Blatch, "Russian Bonds and American Ideals," *New York World*, February 27, 1920, n.p., HSB-NY. "Labor Leaders Ask Trade with Russia," *New York Times*, January 27, 1921, p. 17.

60. Blatch, *Woman's Point of View*, p. 141.

61. Morris Hillquit, *From Marx to Lenin* (New York: Hanaford Press, 1921), p. 30. Harriot's copy is in the possession of Rhoda Barney Jenkins.

62. Harriot to Nora, April 10, 1919, HSB-NY.

63. Blatch's notes on her copy of *From Marx to Lenin*, RBJ-CT.

64. She explained this at a National Woman's Party meeting in Boston, a report of which was carried in the anticommunist women's paper, the *Woman Patriot* ("Suffrage Meeting Turns into Bolshevist Convention," December 27, 1919, n.p., AC-NY).

65. Blatch, *Woman's Point of View*, p. 58.

66. Blatch to Rose Schneiderman, October 8, 1922, reel 12, NYWTUL.

67. "Talk of a Third Party," *New York Times*, March 31, 1920, p. 17.

68. Blatch to Elsie Hill, March 21, 1921, reel 6, NWP-ERA.

69. Report on Blatch, dated April 13, 1921, reel 912, Investigative Files of the FBI from 1908 to 1922, National Archives.

70. Debs to Blatch, April 24, 1921, HSB-NY. Also Blatch to Debs, March 21, 1921, Eugene V. Debs Papers, Indiana State University, Terre Haute.

71. Blatch to Debs, February 9, 1925, Debs Papers.

72. "Mrs. Blatch Opens Fight for Schools," *New York Times*, September 20, 1921, p. 10. In 1925 she was again the party's candidate for comptroller and in 1926 she was the Socialist nominee for the U.S. Senate ("Socialists to Run Woman for Senate," *New York Times*, July 5, 1926, p. 26).

73. Blatch, "The New Voter," *Socialist Review*, October 1920, pp. 164–66.

74. "Mayor Hylan Elected," *New York Times*, November 9, 1921, p. 1.

75. Blatch obituary, *New York Herald*, November 21, 1940, p. 32.

76. Socialist Jessie Hughan reported to Alma Lutz that Harriot found the party biased against women and thought "this is probably why she ceased active work for the party" (Hughan to Lutz, September 30, 1939, AL-NY). But other evidence suggests that Harriot was as likely to find fault with women members—for instance Block herself,

whom she thought had "got obstruction on the brain"—as men (Harriot note to Caroline Lexow Babcock, on letter from Block to Blatch, September 20, 1920, HSB-NY).

77. Not to be confused with the Labor party, the electoral dimension of the newly formed Communist party of the USA.

78. Blatch to Rose Schneiderman, October 8, 1922, reel 12, NYWTUL.

79. "State Labor Party Holds Ratification," *New York Times*, October 16, 1922, p. 2.

80. Blatch, "The Industrial Woman," *New York Times*, August 22, 1922, p. 16; "Say Two Parties Back 12 Labor Reforms," ibid., October 1, 1922, pt. 2, p. 2.

81. Schneiderman to Executive Committee of the American Labor Party, September 30, 1922, reel 12, NYWTUL.

82. Gerber to Rose Schneiderman, October 6, 1922, reel 12, NYWTUL.

83. Harriot offered to support an eight-hour bill for women nurses, but not for women workers in general. Blatch to Schneiderman, October 8, 1922, and Swartz to Blatch, October 24, 1922, reel 12, NYWTUL.

84. Certainly an additional factor was the fact that the American Federation of Labor, to which the WTUL was increasingly attached, remained adamantly opposed to political involvement so long as the Socialist party had a major role.

85. Circular, April 19, 1924, Morris Hillquit Papers, Tamiment Library, New York City.

86. "Women Seek Votes for Progressives," *New York Times*, April 7, 1924, p. 3.

87. Isabelle Kendig to Fellow Member, June 18, 1924, Alice Park Collection, Hoover Institute, Palo Alto, Calif. Socialist Meta Berger took the organizational lead. See *Report on the National Conference of the Woman's Committee for Political Action Held in Washington*, May 8–11, 1924, Park Collection; thanks to Nancy Cott for a copy of this document.

88. Kenneth Campbell Mackay, *The Progressive Movement of 1924* (New York: Octagon Books, 1966; original publication, 1947, as Columbia University Studies in History, Economics and Public Law No. 527), p. 121.

89. *Stenographic Report of the Convention of the Conference for Progressive Political Action*, v. 2, July 4–5, 1924, Cleveland, People's Legislative Service Records Manuscript Division, Library of Congress; thanks to Neil Basen.

90. Ibid.

91. Mackay, *Progressive Movement*, p. 272. It seems as if this plank, unlike the others of the platform, was introduced on the floor of the Cleveland convention on July 4 rather than in preliminary meetings. It was adopted unanimously ("Why Women Endorse La Follette," address by Mabel C. Costigan before Conference for Progressive Political Action, July 4, 1924, pamphlet at Schlesinger Library, Cambridge, Mass., p. 11).

92. Cott, *Grounding of Modern Feminism*, pp. 121–22, 124–25.

93. Nancy Cott and Eugene Tobin both make and document this important observation (Cott, *Grounding of Modern Feminism*, p. 252; Eugene M. Tobin, *Organize or Perish: America's Independent Progressives, 1913–1933* [Westport, Conn.: Greenwood, 1986], p. 155). Stanley Lemons stresses larger political tensions between progres-

sive and conservative women over La Follette's candidacy (*The Woman Citizen: Social Feminism in the 1920s* [Urbana: University of Illinois Press, 1973], p. 122).

94. Mabel Leslie to Maud Swartz, July 19, 1924, reel 12, NYWTUL.

95. Rose Schneiderman to Alice Henry, July 23, 1924, reel 12, NYWTUL.

96. Smith to Mabel Leslie, August 9, 1924, reel 12, NYWTUL.

97. "Woman Political Leaders Speak," *Washington Evening Star*, October 3, 1924, n.p., scrapbook, People's Legislative Service Records.

98. "Women Organizing for La Follette," *New York Times*, August 12, 1924, p. 6.

99. For letterhead, see Mabel Costigan to Robert La Follette, September 15, 1924, La Follette Family Collection, Manuscript Division, Library of Congress; for Catt's refusal, see Carrie Chapman Catt to Blatch, August 16, 1924, CCC-LC.

100. "Mrs. La Follette Champions Husband," *New York Times*, October 1, 1924, p. 1.

101. Both Cott (*Grounding of Modern Feminism*, p. 152) and Tobin (*Organize or Perish*, p. 155) think women did not have any more power in the La Follette camp; here they rely heavily on Anne Martin's acid assessment of the campaign after the fact (Martin, "Feminists and Future Political Action," *Nation*, February 18, 1925, p. 185). As evidence to the contrary, consider the report in the *New York Sun* of September 24, 1924, that the AFL Political Action Committee had instructed all state and local federations to add women to the membership of their executive committees, as "a step to enlist women's support in the AFL campaign" for La Follette (clipping in scrapbook, People's Legislative Service Records).

102. For a list of members of the National Committee see box 2, People's Legislative Service Records.

103. "Women Leaders of Both Old Parties Unite in Appeal to Women to Register and Vote," *New York Times*, October 6, 1924, p. 2.

104. Kristi Andersen, *After Suffrage: Women in Partisan and Electoral Politics before the New Deal* (Chicago: University of Chicago Press, 1996), pp. 80–84.

105. "Answers Mrs. Kelley," *New York Times*, October 5, 1924, p. 7.

106. "Women Will Strive for a Congressional Bloc," *New York Times*, August 17, 1924, p. 1; "Moves to Elect Women to Congress," ibid., September 29, 1924, p. 2; Ernestine Parsons, "Why We Should Campaign for Women," *Equal Rights*, August 16, 1924, p. 215.

107. Blatch, "Speech at the Hippodrome Theatre, Baltimore, on Sunday Afternoon, November 2, 1924," HSB-NY.

108. Ibid.

109. Ibid.

110. Ibid.

111. On the political scientists' blaming women for decline in voter participation, see Cott, *Grounding of Modern Feminism*, pp. 102–5.

112. Blatch, "Speech at the Hippodrome Theatre." Political scientist Paul Kleppner comes to the same conclusion: "If female participation initially lagged well beyond male turnout that may have been as much a response to contemporary political stimuli as a product of prior cultural conditioning" (Kleppner, "Were Women to Blame? Female Suffrage and Voter Turnout," *Journal of Interdisciplinary History*, spring 1982, p. 622).

113. Blatch to Fola La Follette, January 8, 1925, La Follette Family Collection.

114. Blatch to Eugene Debs, February 9, 1925, Debs Papers.

115. My understanding of the National League of Progressive Women comes from material in the Alice Park Collection at the Hoover Institute, which was shared with me by Nancy Cott; the quotation is from "The Need for a League of Progressive Women," January 1925, Park Collection.

116. Cott, *Grounding of Modern Feminism*, pp. 249–50.

117. Interestingly, in 1934, when self-identified socialists and communists had again become the target of anticommunists, Blatch was listed in *The Red Network*, self-published by Elizabeth Dillenger in 1934 (copy at the Huntington Library, San Marino, Calif.). Ironically this book helped me to trace Harriot's activities in her last years.

118. Evidences of her political activity in these years are too numerous to cite comprehensively. See, for example, Blatch's name on Emergency Committee for Strikers Relief, established by the League for Industrial Democracy and the American Civil Liberties Union (list of committee members in box 36, NAWSA-LC).

119. Letter to the editor (advocating the planting of trees as a memorial for the war dead), *New York Times*, November 23, 1925, p. 20; "Mrs. Blatch Protests Census Is Haphazard," ibid., December 30, 1925, p. 25.

120. Cott, *Grounding of Modern Feminism*, p. 262.

121. Letter to the editor, *New York Times*, March 27, 1928, p. 26; also see the reply of the New York Hoover Committee, ibid., March 29, 1928, p. 26.

122. Harriot Stanton Blatch and Alma Lutz, *Challenging Years: The Memoirs of Harriot Stanton Blatch* (New York: G. P. Putnam's Sons, 1940), p. 39; Blatch to Lucy Maynard Salmon, January 22, 1925, Salmon Papers, Vassar College, Poughkeepsie, N.Y.

123. Press release for Blatch's eightieth birthday, January 1936, BH-Mass.

124. Harriot to Nora, June 30, 1927, HSB-NY.

125. "Intense Enthusiasm Aroused by Initial Trip in Airplane," *New York Times*, August 28, 1927, sect. 7, p. 12.

126. Harriot to Nora, May 26, 1929, HSB-NY; Rhoda Barney Jenkins to author, September 2, 1992. There is no indication that she ever published the article she planned on the trip.

127. Interview with Harriet de Forest, July 14, 1985, Londonderry, Vt.

128. Harriot and Harriet may have developed their joint love of flying during the war. While in Europe to attend the Paris Peace Conference, Harriot Blatch took time to write a detailed letter to her granddaughter describing a giant German airfield in defeated Koblentz. "How I wished you were there to tell me about [the airplanes] for the Captain who was my escort did not know," she wrote to her granddaughter (Harriot to "Perriwinkle" [Harriet], April 16, 1919, HSB-NY). Harriet began with a commercial pilot's license, which she says she got at her grandmother's request, so that she could "fly her around." During World War II, she got a flight instructor's license, with which she taught young male pilots.

129. Clipping from *Rockland County Journal News*, January 15, 1936, n.p., BH-Mass.

Chapter Nine: History

1. Rhoda Barney Jenkins to author, September 2, 1992.

2. Harriet de Forest interview, July 14, 1985, Londonderry, Vt.

3. Rhoda Barney, Harriot's other granddaughter, is of the same opinion (interview with Rhoda Barney Jenkins, June 24–25, 1988, Buffalo, N.Y.).

4. De Forest interview; Blatch to Alma Lutz, October 26, 1932, AL-NY.

5. Mona Rivers, "Morgan Barney: Naval Architect," *Log of Mystic Seaport*, autumn 1994, pp. 50–53.

6. Blatch to Grace Ellery Channing Stetson, August 27, n.y., Stetson Papers, Schlesinger Library, Cambridge, Mass.

7. Rhoda Barney Jenkins to author, September 7, 1995.

8. Interview with Rhoda Barney Jenkins, June 24–25, 1988.

9. Blatch to Grace Ellery Channing Stetson, January 24, 1937, Stetson Papers.

10. Nora to Grace Ellery Channing Stetson, January 12, 1928, Stetson Papers.

11. Rhoda Barney Jenkins to author, October 5, 1985.

12. De Forest interview.

13. Interview with Rhoda Barney Jenkins, June 16, 1982, Greenwich, Conn.

14. Blatch to Villard, March 19, 1925, Villard Papers, Houghton Library, Harvard University, Cambridge, Mass.

15. Obituary, *New York Times*, November 26, 1930, p. 23.

16. Interview with Caroline (Kiki) Babcock Furlow, March 1983, Nyack, N.Y.

17. Blatch to Grace Ellery Channing Stetson, January 24, 1937, Stetson Papers. There are numerous letters between Harriot and Grace in this collection.

18. Milinowski to Blatch, May 5, 1936, HSB-NY. Obituary for Harriot Ransom Milinowski, April 1, 1946, unnamed paper, Biographical Files, Buffalo and Erie Public Library, Buffalo, N.Y.

19. Anna Howard Shaw, *The Story of a Pioneer* (New York: Harper & Brothers, 1915), pp. 230–32.

20. "The Cause of States and Nations," *Woman Citizen*, February 16, 1918, pp. 230–31.

21. Adelaide Johnson, "Susan B. Anthony, Militant Revolutionist," *Suffragist*, v. 8, September 1920, p. 215.

22. "Miss Anthony's Vindication," *Suffragist*, v. 7, January 19, 1918, p. 8.

23. Paul to Blatch, August 15, 1920, reel 4, NWP-ERA. Antisuffrage congressmen opposed plans by the National Woman's Party to place the statue in the Capitol Rotunda ("Suffrage Memorial Halted at Capital," *New York Times*, February 9, 1921, p. 28). In 1995 the placement of the statue in the Rotunda once again became a cause célèbre for feminists.

24. Paul to Blatch, August 15, 1920, reel 4, NWP-ERA; typed copy, Blatch to Emma Wold, September 17, 1920, AL-NY. She wanted to include a socialist and a spokesperson for African Americans, and she suggested Bertha Mailly for the former and W. E. B. Du Bois for the latter. Veteran suffragists on her list for the committee included: Florence Kelley, Jane Addams, Julia Lathrop, Alva Belmont, Louisine Havemeyer, Lillian Wald, Margaret Dreier Robins, Inez Irwin, Mary Anderson, Rheta

Dorr, and Ida Harper. Several of these women were WTUL activists and supporters of the special welfare laws she had fought the year before in New York.

25. There is extensive correspondence surrounding this incident, which includes: Paul to Blatch, November 5, 1920, Blatch to Paul, November 6, 1920, Blatch to Paul, November 7, 1920, Blatch to Paul, November 13, 1920, all reel 4, NWP-ERA. Also Blatch to Dora Lewis, November 16, 1920, AL-NY; Blatch to Dora Lewis, November 11, 1920, reel 4, NWP-ERA.

26. Blatch to Paul, November 3, 1920, reel 5, NWP-ERA.

27. Marjory Nelson, "Ladies in the Streets: A Sociological Analysis of the National Woman's Party, 1910–1930," Ph.D. dissertation, SUNY–Buffalo, 1976, pp. 170–71.

28. Searching for the origins of Anthony's sanctification and her mother's decline, Harriot concentrated on this period. "In 1895 my mother set forth all her heresies in *Eighty Years and More*, in important magazine articles on divorce, in the *Woman's Bible* and the then leaders began to bury her alive and began to revivify Miss Anthony" (Blatch to Lutz, n.d. [c. September 1993], AL-NY).

29. "Seneca Falls Then—and NOW," *Equal Rights*, May 19, 1923, p. 110.

30. *Equal Rights*, June 30, 1923, p. 156.

31. Carol Rehfisch, "Historical Background of the Equal Rights Campaign," *Equal Rights*, September 15, 1923, p. 245.

32. See for example "1848–1921–1927," *Equal Rights*, July 9, 1927, p. 172, in which Stanton is nowhere mentioned. Sue Shelton White (ibid., October 1, 1927, p. 269) places Anthony at Seneca Falls along with Mott and Stanton. In general, despite its location in Seneca Falls, the National Woman's Party convention in 1923 paid much more homage to Anthony than to Stanton; its climax was to be a "giant pilgrimage" to Anthony's grave sixty miles away in Rochester. Alva Belmont took a special interest in this event and announced her intention to establish an international equal rights "shrine" at the Rochester site.

33. Blatch, letter to the editor, *New York Times*, June 27, 1923, p. 14. "TS," letter to the editor, ibid., July 19, 1923, p. 14.

34. Harriot and Theodore made certain to include a document in their 1922 collection of their mother's letters substantiating this claim of authorship (Stanton to Anthony, January 14, 1878, in Stanton and Blatch, eds., *Elizabeth Cady Stanton as Revealed in Her Letters, Diary and Reminiscences*, v. 2 [New York: Harper & Brothers, 1922], p. 153). Also see Stanton's magisterial constitutional argument, "National Protection for National Citizens," delivered to the joint Congressional Committee on Privileges and Elections, simultaneous with Senator Aaron Sargent's introduction of the wording of the proposed amendment in 1878 (Anthony, Stanton, and Harper, eds., *History of Woman Suffrage*, v. 3, [Rochester: Susan B. Anthony, 1886], pp. 80–93).

35. See, for example, Blatch's underlinings on her copy of an article in *Equal Rights*, February 4, 1928, pp. 5–6, in which Anthony is credited with introducing the amendment in 1878 (HSB-NY). This misattribution can be found in the *Suffragist* as early as May 20, 1916, p. 6.

36. See for example articles in *Equal Rights*, January 7, 1928 (coinciding with the anniversary of Mott's death): "Carry on Lucretia Mott's Work," "Lucretia Mott, Feminist" (p. 379).

37. Blatch to Catt, May 15, 1923, HSB-NY; Blatch to Catt, October 24, 1923, NAWSA-LC.

38. "Elizabeth Cady Stanton," *New York Times*, December 24, 1924, p. 12; press release, n.d. [December 1924], HSB-NY. Like so many of their historical correctives in these years, their intervention at the Smithsonian on their mother's behalf failed. In 1940, suffrage historians who were cataloging the Smithsonian exhibit made no mention of Elizabeth Stanton and credited a table in the exhibit on which the 1848 Declaration of Sentiments had been written to Susan B. Anthony, who once again was incorrectly placed at the site (v. 1, p. 1, SBA-CA).

39. Published in 1922 as the two-volume *Elizabeth Cady Stanton as Revealed in Her Letters, Diary and Reminiscences*.

40. Susan B. Anthony to Robert L. Stanton, April 15, 1904, ECS-NY.

41. Blatch to Alice Paul, December 20, 1916, AL-NY.

42. Harriot and Theodore's editorial alterations are traced in Amy Dykeman, "To Pour Forth My Own Experience: Two Versions of Elizabeth Cady Stanton," *Journal of Rutgers University Library*, v. 44, June 1982, p. 9; Ann D. Gordon also traced these alterations extensively in her work as editor of the *Papers of Elizabeth Cady Stanton and Susan B. Anthony* (Wilmington, Del.: Scholarly Resources, 1990).

43. Blatch, essay on Elizabeth Cady Stanton, and Beard, essay on Susan B. Anthony, both in HSB-NY. Beard's sketch of Anthony is much bolder politically; she links Anthony to Hicksite Quakers, whom she characterizes as "left wing," and emphasizes her broad reform interests including trade unionism; Blatch's piece on Stanton focuses instead on her many contributions to and high standing within the nineteenth-century woman suffrage movement.

44. The editor omitted the following: "She had a way of being first, usually one jump ahead of the game" and "no one was more responsive to federal domination than Elizabeth Cady Stanton." The original manuscript is in the Blatch Papers, Vassar College, Poughkeepsie, N.Y.; the edited version was published in the *Woman's Journal*, v. 14 (new series), December 1929, pp. 22–23.

45. For a fuller discussion of this development, see Ellen Carol DuBois, "Making Women's History: Historian-Activists of Women's Rights, 1880–1940," *Radical History Review*, no. 49, 1991, pp. 61–84.

46. Emanie Sachs, *"The Terrible Siren": Victoria Woodhull, 1838–1927* (New York: Harper & Brothers, 1928).

47. William L. O'Neill, *Everyone Was Brave: The Rise and Fall of Feminism in America* (Chicago: Quadrangle Books, 1969), p. 32.

48. Query for information on Woodhull from Sachs, *Equal Rights*, July 23, 1927, p. 192.

49. Kirchwey, "To the Terrible Siren," *Nation*, v. 128, January 16, 1929, p. 83.

50. Book reviews, *Woman's Journal*, February 1929, v. 14 (new series), pp. 34–35.

51. Paxton Hibben, *Henry Ward Beecher: An American Portrait* (New York: George H. Doran, 1927).

52. Sachs, *"Terrible Siren,"* pp. 84, 112.

53. Ibid., p. 423.

54. As reported in Catt to Alice Stone Blackwell, September 18, 1930, reel 2, NAWSA-LC.

55. Ida Husted Harper to Mary Grey Peck, July 13, 1920, reel 4, CCC-LC.

56. Rheta Childe Dorr, *Susan B. Anthony: The Woman Who Changed the Mind of a Nation* (New York: Frederick A. Stokes, 1928).

57. The split had begun over the Fourteenth Amendment, which the Stone group endorsed and the Stanton-Anthony group criticized. Dorr's account of this conflict is racist. She regarded as accurate Stanton's and Anthony's incendiary charge that votes for black men unleavened by the enfranchisement of white women would "culminate in fearful outrages on womanhood, especially in the Southern States." ibid., p. 214.

58. Ibid., p. 220.

59. Ibid., pp. 241, 279.

60. Catt to Stone Blackwell, September 19, 1930, reel 2, CCC-LC.

61. Dorr, *Susan B. Anthony*, p. viii.

62. Ibid., p. 80.

63. Ibid., p. 76.

64. Alma Lutz, *Emma Willard: Daughter of Democracy* (Boston: Houghton Mifflin, 1929).

65. Lutz to Blatch, April 28, 1930, AL-NY.

66. Lutz, notes on meeting Harriot Blatch, May 10, 1930, and Blatch to Lutz, May 27, 1930, AL-NY.

67. Blatch to Lutz, May 5, 1931, and July 15, 1931, AL-NY.

68. Blatch to Lutz, May 16, 1930, AL-NY.

69. Blatch to Lutz, June 27, 1937, AL-NY.

70. Catt to Alice Stone Blackwell, September 8, 1930, reel 4, CCC-LC.

71. Blatch, "Pioneering in the Fight for Women's Rights: A Daughter's Eulogy," n.d. [November 1930], n.p., clipping, AL-NY. I have been unable to identify the periodical in which this review appeared.

72. Blatch to Lutz, May 27, 1930, AL-NY.

73. Blatch to Lutz, n.d., AL-NY.

74. Blatch to Lutz, n.d., comments on manuscript of *Created Equal*, AL-NY.

75. Blatch to Lutz, September 2, 1934, AL-NY.

76. Blatch, "Pioneering in the Fight for Women's Rights."

77. Marguerite Wells, "The Anniversary and Memorial Plan," *Woman's Journal*, v. 14 (new series), December 1929, p. 28.

78. Blatch, To the Editor of the *New York Times* (unpublished), HSB-NY.

79. Mildred Adams, "Carrie Chapman Catt—Leader of Women—Pioneer for Peace" *Pictorial Review*, v. 32, January 1931, pp. 14–15.

80. Interview with Harriet de Forest.

81. Blatch, probably to Lena M. Phillips, July 26, 1933, AL-NY

82. Blatch to Dora Albert, July 30, 1930, HSB-NY.

83. Albert to Blatch, n.d. [August 1930], HSB-NY. I have been unable to locate whether and where this article was ever published.

84. Blatch to Lutz, n.d. [probably October 1933], AL-NY.

85. Adelma Burd to Blatch, January 27, 1931, HSB-NY.

86. Christabel Pankhurst to Blatch, October 29, 1930, HSB-NY.

87. Blatch, draft autobiography, p. 134a, HSB-NY.

88. Paul refers to and dismisses this suggestion in a letter to Blatch, September 30, 1920, AL-NY.

89. Nancy Cott, ed., *A Woman Making History: Mary Ritter Beard through Her Letters* (New Haven: Yale University Press, 1991), p. 110.

90. Mary Beard, *On Understanding Women* (New York: Longmans, Green, 1931); and *America through Women's Eyes* (New York: Macmillan, 1933).

91. Beard to Blatch, December 5, 1934, HSB-NY. Similarly, see her critique of the "military emphasis" in the second inaugural (Beard to Blatch, January 2, 1937, AL-NY).

92. "The Most Vital of All Human Rights," *Equal Rights: An Independent Feminist Weekly*, June 29, 1935, pp. 133–134. This speech was delivered to a National Woman's Party splinter group, led by Edith Houghton Hooker of Maryland, that had split away from Paul's leadership over economic issues. Harriot testified before the House Labor Committee on May 5, 1933, in favor of regulating child labor and not regulating women's labor (speech, HSB-NY).

93. Beard to Blatch, June 15, 1933, HSB-NY.

94. Beard to Blatch, n.d. [dated by Cott as January 1934], HSB-NY.

95. Beard to Blatch, July 16, 1934, HSB-NY. Harriot was worried that Beard might disagree with her over the dangers of sex-based labor legislation.

96. Mary Beard to Maud Wood Park, March 13, 1933, cited in Cott, *Woman Making History*, p. 106.

97. Draft manifesto, June 2, 1933, HSB-NY.

98. Ibid. For the final version of the manifesto, which was different, see *Our Common Cause: Civilization*, Report of the International Congress of Women, July 16–22, 1933, Chicago (New York: National Council of Women, 1933), pp. 252–53.

99. Blatch to Lutz, July 19, 1933, AL-NY.

100. Ibid.; also see "Suffrage Myths: Making Up History," draft article, Blatch to Lena M. Phillips, July 26, 1933, and Blatch to Anita Pollitzer, July 20, 1933, all HSB-NY.

101. Beard to Blatch, June 14, 1936, HSB-NY. The story of the archives project and why it failed can be found in Cott, *Woman Making History*, pp. 47–48, and Maryann Turner, *Biblioteca Femina: A Herstory of Book Collections Concerning Women* (New York: Tower Press, 1978), pp. 35–40. Harriot was assembling her personal papers when she died, and planned for them to go to Vassar College, where they are now located. The Gilman Papers were not secured for many decades, but can now be found in the Schlesinger Library, Cambridge, Mass.

102. Their interactions on these issue are complicated. Harriot accuses Mary of being "obsessed with women" (Blatch to Beard, May 1935, HSB-NY), and yet Mary characterizes Harriot as an "intransigent feminist" (Beard to Stevens, November 14, 1935), cited in Cott, *Woman Making History*, p. 354.

103. Blatch to Lutz, September 25, 1933, AL-NY.

104. Beard to Blatch, September 7, 1934, HSB-NY.

105. Beard to Blatch, January 24, n.y. [c. 1934], HSB-NY.

106. Beard to Blatch, October 29, 1930, HSB-NY.

107. Cott suggests that this intervention "presages" Beard's own mammoth archival project, the World's Women's Archives (Cott, *Woman Making History*, p. 119).

108. Beard to Blatch, October 29, 1930, January 1934, and July 16, 1934, HSB-NY.

109. Beard to Blatch, October 10, 1934, HBS-NY.

110. Beard to Blatch, October 7, 1935, and June 14, 1936, HSB-NY.

111. Beard to Blatch, September 22, 1936, HSB-NY.

112. Blatch to Lexow Babcock, September 3, 1933, BH-Mass.

113. Blatch to Lexow Babcock, April 28, 1936, BH-Mass.

114. Annotation by Caroline Lexow Babcock, much later, on letter from Blatch to her, July 27, 1936, BH-Mass.

115. Beard to Lutz, November 19, 1939, HSB-NY.

116. Stanton, "Solitude of Self," first published in 1892, republished in Ellen Carol DuBois, ed., *The Elizabeth Cady Stanton—Susan B. Anthony Reader*, 2d ed. (Boston: Northeastern University Press, 1992), pp. 247–54.

117. Ann Gordon, "Afterword," in Elizabeth Cady Stanton, *Eighty Years and More: Reminiscences, 1815–1897* (Boston: Northeastern University Press, 1992), pp. 469–83.

118. Blatch to Lutz, July 12, 1939, AL-NY.

119. These papers were located in 1988 by Rhoda Barney Jenkins; I am indebted to the family for allowing me unlimited access to them.

120. Lutz to Helen Davis, Publications Committee, Vassar College, April 25, 1939, AL-NY. The book industry was in dire financial straits; moreover, there was almost no public interest in woman suffrage. At this point, the biography was titled *Take Down Every Barrier*; later, the publisher, the John Day Company, changed the title to *Created Equal*.

121. Lutz to Davis, June 13, 1939, AL-NY.

122. Blatch to Lutz, July 12, 1939, AL-NY.

123. Lutz to Blatch, August 22, 1939, AL-NY.

124. Lutz to Nora Stanton Barney, September 8, 1939, HSB-NY.

125. Lutz to Helen Sasse, June 13, 1939, AL-NY.

126. Lutz to Blatch, July 9 and 16, 1939, AL-NY.

127. Lutz to Blatch, August 1, 1939, AL-NY. Later Lutz wrote to Helen Sasse of Vassar that the book would be particularly important for its account of the WPU. "The story has never been told before and Mrs. Blatch feared that it . . . would slip into oblivion, while [those] who came after and made use of the methods which she had introduced would come down in history as the originators" (Lutz to Sasse, September 11, 1939, AL-NY).

128. Blatch to Lutz, August 12, 1939, AL-NY.

129. Blatch to Lutz, August 20, 1939, AL-NY.

130. Lutz to Blatch, August 22, 1939, AL-NY.

131. "Woman's Party Honors Two Famous Mothers," June 1919, p. 77, and "She Believed in Women," *Equal Rights*, v. 25, November 1919, p. 98.

132. She may have returned to the Woman's University Club and fallen there, because Mary Beard reported that she was at first taken to a New York City hospital (Beard to Lola Maverick Lloyd, February 7, 1940, Schwimmer-Lloyd Papers, New

York Public Library; thanks to Nancy Cott for this letter).

133. Lutz to Babcock, September 20, 1939, BH-Mass.

134. The dedication was Lutz's idea; other possibilities, which she rejected, were to dedicate the book to Nora or to Caroline. Blatch to Lutz, February 28, 1940, AL-NY.

135. Lutz to Babcock, September 20, 1939, AL-NY.

136. Babcock to Lutz, October 21, 1939, BH-Mass; Lutz to Davis, October 26, 1939, AL-NY.

137. Alma Lutz to Helen Davis, January 5, 1940, AL-NY.

138. Beard to Lutz, April 15, 1940, AL-NY. Babcock to Lutz, n.d., AL-NY.

139. Beard to Lola Maverick Lloyd, February 7, 1940, Schwimmer-Lloyd Papers.

140. Ibid. The "great vision" phrase comes from Roger Baldwin's letter of condolence to Nora, November 22, 1940, HSB-NY.

141. Harriot Ransom Milinowski to Sigfried Milinowski, May 17, 1940, in the possession of Arthur and Alice Milinowski, Fort Erie, Ontario.

142. "Mrs. Blatch Dead: Famed Suffragist," *New York Times*, November 21, 1940, p. 29.

Conclusion: Significance

1. Beard to Rosika Schwimmer, September 3, 1935, Schwimmer-Lloyd Papers, New York Public Library. Thanks to Nancy Cott.

2. David McDonald, "Organizing Womanhood: Women's Culture and the Politics of Woman Suffrage in New York State 1865–1917," Ph.D. dissertation, SUNY–Stony Brook, 1987.

3. Blatch to Anne Martin, May 14, 1918, Anne Martin Papers, Bancroft Library, University of California, Berkeley.

4. Nancy Cott, *The Grounding of Modern Feminism* (New Haven: Yale University Press, 1987), p. 66.

5. Beard to Blatch, September 22, [1934], published in Nancy Cott, ed., *A Woman Making History: Mary Ritter Beard through Her Letters* (New Haven: Yale University Press, 1991), p. 119.

6. Beard to Blatch, January 24, 1935, HSB-NY.

7. Ellen DuBois, "Eleanor Flexner's *Century of Struggle*: Reviewing and Previewing a Women's History Classic," *Gender and History*, v. 3, 1991, pp. 81–90; Eleanor Flexner, *Century of Struggle: The Women's Rights Movement in the United States* (Cambridge, Mass.: Belknap Press of Harvard University Press, 1959). Also see a related discussion in my "Woman Suffrage and the Left: An International Socialist-Feminist Perspective," *New Left Review*, no. 186, March-April 1991, pp. 20–45.

Index